SUPERCLASS

ALSO BY DAVID ROTHKOPF

Running the World:
The Inside Story of the National Security Council and the
Architects of American Power

•

Cuba:
The Contours of Change *(coauthor and coeditor
with Susan Kaufman Purcell)*

•

The Price of Peace:
Emergency Economic Intervention and U.S. Foreign Policy

•

The Big Emerging Markets *(editor and principal author)*

•

The Common Market *(coauthor with Carol Zeman Rothkopf)*

SUPERCLASS

THE GLOBAL POWER ELITE AND THE WORLD THEY ARE MAKING

DAVID ROTHKOPF

Little, Brown

LITTLE, BROWN

First published in the United States of America in 2008 by
Farrar, Straus and Giroux
First published in Great Britain in 2008 by Little, Brown

A CIP catalogue record for this book
is available from the British Library.

ISBN HB 978-1-4087-0109-6
ISBN CF 978-0-316-02730-4

Printed and bound in Great Britain by
Clays Ltd, St Ives plc

Little, Brown
An imprint of
Little, Brown Book Group
100 Victoria Embankment
London EC4Y 0DY

An Hachette Livre UK Company
www.hachettelivre.co.uk

www.littlebrown.co.uk

For my mom and dad,

from whom I learned

that the greatest family legacies

are not wealth and power

but are love and a good sense of humor.

Or at least that's what they keep telling me.

Nearly all men can stand adversity,

but if you want to test a man's character,

give him power.

—ABRAHAM LINCOLN

CONTENTS

CHAPTER 6

THE AGE OF ASYMMETRY: DECLINE OF THE TITANS
AND THE RISE OF SHADOW WARRIORS
190

The Terrorist Threat in Perspective • The Roots of Global Networks •
Green Is Not Just the Color of the Uniforms • Consolidation and
Concentration of Military Power • Networks Among Defense Firms •
They're All in a Tiny Room • The Privatization of the Military: A
Two-Way Street • Permanent War's Bottom Line: A Country and an
Alliance Beyond All Others • The Fly and the Lion

CHAPTER 7

THE INFORMATION SUPERCLASS: THE POWER OF IDEAS
221

Fresh and Yet Strangely Familiar • An Ascendant Voice of Change in
the Middle East • New Media Monkey-Gland Injections: A Quick Shot
of Sizzle • Pro Bono • Saving the World One Idea at a Time •
The Reenchantment of the World • Pastor of Partying •
The Telemuslim • Dissident Spirituality or Subversive Cult? •
The Pragmatic Fanatic

CHAPTER 8

HOW TO BECOME A MEMBER OF THE SUPERCLASS:
MYTH, REALITY, AND THE PSYCHOPATHOLOGY
OF SUCCESS
254

A Very Short History of Things That Didn't Really Happen—And Their Very
Real Consequences • When Is a Trowel Just a Trowel? • Can It Be
Considered an Academic Elite Society If George W. Bush Was a Member?
• The "Ex-Presidents' Club" • The Big Events: Less Than Meets the Eye?
• The Clinton Global Initiative and the Power of Global Philanthropy •
California's Superclass Summer Camp • Asian and Latin American
"Wannabes" or Harbingers of the Supermeetings of Tomorrow? • How to
Become a Member of the Superclass • The Psychopathology of Success

CHAPTER 9
The Future of the Superclass—And What It May Mean for the Rest of Us
296

In Praise of Our Elites vs. Their Elites • Disproportionate Concentration of Power • Agenda-Setting • Informal Mechanisms of Governance • Elites vs. the Disenfranchised • Elites vs. Women • Elites and Mobility • Institutions vs. Individuals • The Emerging Superclass: A Coming Culture Shock? • Global Governance vs. Global Government • Is a Crisis Inevitable? • On Balance

PREFACE

God is on everyone's side . . . and in the last
analysis, he is on the side with plenty of money
and large armies.

—JEAN ANOUILH

This is a book about power. It is about the fact that power is concentrated in the hands of a remarkably small number of people around the world. It is about who they are, how they compare to the elites of the past, and how they differ from the rest of us. Most of all, it is about the profound impact this group has on our lives and how it is shaping our times.

Power is, of course, hard to quantify. Wealth is often a source of power. Position regularly translates into power. Perhaps the most ancient source of power is the ability to project violent force. But sometimes power is grounded in subtler things, like access or ideas. There is no single or universally accepted metric for power, so a certain amount of subjective judgment is inevitable. Determining who has it and who does not is made more difficult because some of the most influential among us commonly mask their power or use it infrequently. What is more, only a very few people have the sort of international power that is the subject of this book. Many of those we are accustomed to thinking of as powerful actually have very limited impact in a global sense. Formidable as they may be, they are figures of only local or national importance.

A global elite has emerged over the past several decades that has vastly more power than any other group on the planet. Each of the members of this superclass has the ability to regularly influence the lives of millions of people in multiple countries worldwide. Each actively exercises this power, and they often amplify it through the development of relationships with others in this class. The age of inherited lifelong power is largely behind us, and for most members of the group influence is transitory; to truly be a member of this superclass one has to hold on to power for at least long enough to make an impact—to enter or affect the world of other members of this superclass—a period of a couple of years or more.

That such a group exists is indisputable. Heads of state, CEOs of the world's largest companies, media barons, billionaires who are actively involved in their investments, technology entrepreneurs, oil potentates, hedge fund managers, private equity investors, top military commanders, a select few religious leaders, a handful of renowned writers, scientists, and artists, even terrorist leaders and master criminals, meet the above criteria for membership.

By posing the idea of the existence of a superclass, some key questions emerge. The most obvious is: how big is it? Using the above parameters and combing systematically through publicly available resources, my researchers and I identified just over 6,000 people who qualify. As will become clear, it is a choice based on natural cutoff points, providing us with a group that is both small enough to analyze in some rational way and large enough to encompass all the core international communities from politics, business, the military, and the world of ideas needed for it to be representative of the most important sources of power worldwide.

The most common question I have been asked since undertaking this book is: Is there a list? As it happens, there is. Many people have suggested I publish it—partly because people love lists, but mostly because many of those who are members of the superclass or who aspire to be are interested in seeing who is "in" and who is not. But publishing such a list would be an exercise in futility. The day after it was published, it would be obsolete. As I noted earlier, power is transient: Many members of the superclass qualify because of jobs they hold, but people come and go from such jobs. Some retire, some die. Others suffer financial or professional calamities. Some members of the group are each year deposed. Others are incarcerated. For these reasons, I have attempted to include a few sublists to illustrate the overall nature of the group, but I have done so with the clear recognition that I am painting a picture of a moving object.

Some—mostly Americans—have suggested that by using the word

"class" I am at risk of entering the intellectually disreputable territory of Marxism and class warfare. If acknowledging what is obvious to any sentient being—that social and economic classes remain in the world even as mobility between those classes has improved for a few subsets of humankind—is intellectually disreputable, well, then I'm all for it. In fact, I embrace it. This book is, by its nature, very much about the gross inequality in the distribution of power and wealth in the world. My position is that these are issues we ignore at our peril—in practical terms, in political terms, and perhaps most of all, in moral terms.

The reality is that the combined net worth of the world's richest thousand or so people—the planet's billionaires—is almost twice that of the poorest 2.5 billion. The human race may have made great progress over the centuries, but such disparities are an indictment of our civilization. And, I believe, they are a threat to its stability.

Having said that, this is not an "eat-the-rich" book. I'll admit I am disgusted by the behavior of some of the world's richest—those who pathologically acquire and give back, on average, something like 1 percent of what they make to society (a far cry from the almost 90 percent Andrew Carnegie gave back during his lifetime). And certainly one cannot help but be disturbed and often horrified by those who abuse political or military power, often to the detriment of the most helpless. But there are many deservedly respected and accomplished members of the superclass, individuals who have offered a great deal to the world. In every pursuit there are the best and the brightest, the people who rise to the top by virtue of their merits, and immense good often comes from their leadership. So, in the end, every era has its elites . . . and has a complex relationship with them.

This is also not a volume for conspiracy theorists. I do believe that some of the networks that exist among the most powerful people in the world have enabled a remarkable few to shape the global system and often to set the terms of our discussions about that system. But I have seen enough of the world of backroom conversations and discreet meetings of the powerful to know that conspiracies are hard to come by. These elites are in fact riven with differences and challenged by the practical impossibility of most conspiracies; old fantasies about world domination just don't add up.

In the course of writing this book, I have looked pretty long and hard at a number of theories regarding who runs the world and at the rumors that swirl around high-level conclaves of the superclass such as Davos and Bilderberg, the Trilateral Commission and the Bohemian Grove. I'll admit, I certainly would not want to miss out on such global conspiracies were they to exist and offer me a spot. As John Lehman, former U.S Secretary of the Navy, once said, "Power corrupts. Absolute power is kind of neat." I had lunch with Eduard Shevardnadze shortly after he had stepped down as foreign minister of the former Soviet Union, and he had unabashedly expressed a similar thought. The collapse of the USSR had already taken place and he was, it seemed, relieved by it. He was relaxed and chatty, enjoying a good meal at Windows on the World, the restaurant that used to be on the top floor of the World Trade Center in Manhattan. A discussion broke out about power and the abuse of power, and after a while Shevardnadze, no longer obligated to couch his words in diplomatic terms, said, "You know, I know something about totalitarianism. I have been a totalitarian ruler. And I have to admit, it was a great job while it lasted." Everyone laughed, and soon after Shevardnadze took the democratic route to becoming the president of the Republic of Georgia, where he ruled again for many years.

As a Jew, I have always had a particularly soft place in my heart for the old notion of a world Jewish conspiracy. I figured there were not so many Jews and so if we were in control, the odds were pretty good I could secure a respectable position in the inner workings of the world-domination machinery. (I had a friend who used to assert that such a conspiracy really did exist, and that he was responsible for global zinc prices.) As far as I can tell, however, either there is no such conspiracy or I have been the victim of some kind of special discrimination against Jews from New Jersey—or Jews who would be unable to keep the conspiracy a secret if we were let in on it. To this day, I am always astonished when people attempt to assert that somehow Jews are running the show, when the headlines of the past several millennia of Jewish history include exile, the Inquisition, the Holocaust, the acquisition of a tiny desert nation surrounded by enemies, and more or less relentless hatred and abuse. Had we really been in charge, surely we could have done better on all counts.

Setting aside both the fanciful and the insidious theories of puppet masters and cabals, we must recognize that there is something new afoot, a huge imbalance in the global distribution of power that concentrates great influence among informal clusters of elites. These elites often transcend or supplant the institutions of the past: national governments, systems of law that could not keep pace with global realities, and even the earnest but incomplete efforts of the past half century at creating effective multinational organizations. At the heart of this new reality are the members of the superclass, individuals whose daily decisions redirect massive assets among markets; create, dislocate, or eliminate jobs around the globe; determine the viability of government programs and sometimes of governments; and also play a vital role in shaping the global era, because so many of the institutions on which we have depended to play such a leadership role in the past have not or cannot because they have grown too weak or obsolete, and are ill-suited to the task. Furthermore, these individuals as a group, because of their influence, play a big part in defining the tenor of our times, determining which views are accepted and which are not, and what our priorities are. The influence of this transnational superclass is often amplified as the members act in clusters knit together by business deals, corporate boards, investment flows, old school ties, club memberships, and countless other strands that transform them if not into the conspiring committees of legend then at least into groups that are proven masters at advancing their aligned self-interests.

To move beyond the abstractions of political theory and the over-simplifications and absurdities associated with fantasies of secret conspiracies requires that I tell this story as one about people. In order to understand the impact of the superclass, we have to understand who its members actually are. This entailed interviews with more than a hundred international leaders in government, business, the military, the media, and religion, as well as extensive digging into the histories of hundreds of others. A census was undertaken (the list I mentioned earlier), surveying various characteristics of the roughly 6,000 selected for the group: their gender, their national backgrounds, where they went to school, their various affiliations, and their personal wealth. Through the interviews I have done and the background information I have collected, a picture begins to emerge—both of the group as it is today and as it is likely to be in the future.

Of course no such analysis takes place only in the limited context of the time it takes to write a book. This book is as much the consequence of my experiences in life as it is of the past two years of specific research. Throughout my career I have encountered members of this superclass and those who aspired to it. My first two jobs, in fact, included working for a prominent Wall Street financier and later for a member of Congress from Brooklyn, New York. Both were superclass aspirants, but because the financier was content with merely being very rich and the congressman was a better policy maker than he was a politician, neither ascended to the first tiers of global influence, although they exposed me to many who did. Subsequently, I worked for a while in television and then at a series of publications: *Financial World,*

Institutional Investor, CEO Magazine, and *Emerging Markets* news-papers (which were published by a company of which I was a co-founder, International Media Partners [IMP]). We were in the midst of a financial boom, and I had the opportunity to get to know many of the top leaders of the financial community, the group that has been at the vanguard of globalization. From behind the scenes, it was clear that these individuals influenced everything from the way currencies were priced worldwide to which political candidates would have sufficient funding for their presidential campaigns. The people I met from that era included financing titans who were destined for greatness, like future Blackstone CEO Steve Schwarzman and future New York City mayor Mike Bloomberg; a few who later ran afoul of the law, like Michael Milken and Ivan Boesky; godfathers of globalization, like Citibank CEO Walter Wriston and Chase Manhattan Bank chairman David Rockefeller; and countless others in London, Tokyo, Frankfurt, Paris, and other financial capitals.

At IMP, we published newspapers covering the big annual meet-ings of the financial community like the Joint Annual Meeting of the International Monetary Fund (IMF) and World Bank, and meetings of the regional development banks. At such events we watched as a few hundred bankers and finance ministers worked together on global financial issues: bailing out failing countries at breakfast, forming alliances over canapés, funding deals at cocktail hour. Of course, occasionally we were also reminded just where we fit in the picture at that time. I vividly recall crossing 59th Street one cold rainy night to at-tend a reception at the Plaza Hotel for the king of Morocco, Hassan II. The lighting in the lobby was a soothing golden color, flattering to guests, muting the bustle of the hotel. As I entered the small ballroom in which the reception was being held, there was a receiving line, and im-mediately before the king was a protocol officer who discreetly leaned forward to ask me my name. I said, "David Rothkopf." Mishearing me, his eyes lit up and he stood up quite a bit more erect and repeated with great reverence, "David Rockefeller?" He drew out the last four syllables so each was a complete word. "Rock-e-fell-er?" I hated to disappoint him. (Heck, given the response, I hated to disappoint me.) But I said no, just David Rothkopf. He let out a long sigh that trailed off in a whimper. "Ohhhhh," he said. "Your majesty, may I present, Mr. Rothberg."

While at IMP we also created the CEO Institutes, which ran events on global themes for the chief executives of big companies. Some of these business leaders were chillingly deal-oriented, as I saw at dinner one night when I was seated between the CEO of a leading aircraft manufacturer and Representative Pat Schroeder, then the ranking Democrat on the Armed Services Committee. The CEO leaned across me to speak to Representative Schroeder. "Here's the deal," he said. "I want to sell a plane to Muammar Qaddafi and he wants to buy one. But we have sanctions in place that won't let me sell to him. The U.S. wants this guy dead. So, what I'm thinking is, if you help me get the okay to sell him the plane, I'll build it with explosive bolts connecting the wings to the fuselage. Then, one day he's up flying over the Med and we push a button. He's gone. I make my sale. Everyone's happy." It was so bald-faced that even the experienced Representative Schroeder seemed nonplussed.

This CEO had built a fortune by outright asking for what he wanted. Nonetheless, some of the other individuals I got to know at our events were more subtle. Once, at a reception we were holding for former secretary of state Henry Kissinger, I noticed the wife of a prominent diplomat slip out of the room. When I got to the ballroom for dinner, I observed that she had rearranged all the place cards at the head table, shifting me and two other guests (Hank Greenberg, the CEO of AIG; and Fred Smith, the CEO of FedEx) away from Kissinger so she and her husband could sit next to him.

Naturally, I restored the arrangement of the tent cards—so that I would sit next to Kissinger, whom I had always found a fascinating character. During dinner he ignored me altogether. He chatted with the few people at the table he wanted to speak with: Greenberg, Smith, and the diplomat among them. This was enormously frustrating. I had been through an entire dinner with one of the world's great raconteurs and I did not have a single story to show for it. Finally, as he got up to give the after-dinner address, he turned to me and in his famous Teutonic rumble said, "Mr. Rothkopf?" I eagerly answered, "Yes?" This was my moment to glean a gem.

"Let me give you some advice," he offered, "When you are having an after-dinner speaker, it is best if you eliminate the salad course." And with that he stood up and gave his remarks, knowing from experience that our overly long dinner had exhausted his audience and that his lone comment had thoroughly deflated his thirty-two-year-old host.

A couple of years later, I joined the Clinton administration as U.S. deputy undersecretary of commerce for international trade. Once again, I found myself in a job that brought me into regular contact with high-level executives, senior U.S. officials, and other world leaders. Working to remove trade barriers and ensure the enforcement of trade laws, we were unabashed cheerleaders for business-led globalization, involved in everything from helping Raytheon capture a big technology project in Brazil, to helping Exxon develop oil and gas fields off the coast of Indonesia, to helping Boeing secure big aircraft contracts in Saudi Arabia.

Immediately following my time in government, I was invited to become a managing director of Kissinger Associates, the international consultancy founded and run by Kissinger himself. It was a small firm: just Kissinger, myself, a former investment banker named Alan Batkin, and a fellow named L. Paul Bremer—Jerry to his friends—who later would go on to fame and not a little controversy as the U.S. administrator in Iraq. Kissinger's office, and indeed his life, was like a revolving door for the superclass. Kissinger was an extraordinary education, brilliant and charming and a magnet for fascinating people and discussions. Whether he was relaxing at the vacation home of the CEO of Asea Brown Boveri, or hosting a private dinner for the CEO of Gazprom, Kissinger was the master of every occasion. (And always knew just how many courses to serve at each meal.)

I eventually moved on from Kissinger Associates to start a company with Anthony Lake, who was, like Kissinger, a former U.S. national security adviser. Together we launched a firm called Intellibridge that used open-source Web technology to support the intelligence efforts of companies and government agencies. Although the plan was initially to support businesses, we soon found ourselves working primarily within the U.S. national security community. In this capacity, we spent seven years dealing regularly with the most senior officers of the U.S. military: three- and four-star generals and admirals who rival the best in any other part of the government for intelligence, creativity, and character. The venture gave us an inside view of the military-industrial establishment in the United States and around the world.

After Intellibridge was sold, I wrote a book called *Running the World: The Inside Story of the National Security Council and the Architects of American Power*. I drew on relationships from my time in Washington and ended up interviewing more than 150 leaders of the U.S. foreign policy establishment since the Eisenhower administration. It is a remarkably closed world, as I pointed out in the book. Every U.S. national security adviser since Henry Kissinger has either worked with or for Kissinger—or he or she has worked with or for someone who worked with or for Kissinger: two degrees of separation. Many went to the same schools. Many had fathers and brothers in the same line of work. Mostly old white guys. Not too many women. A classic elite.

So I came to this book with not an insignificant amount of relevant personal experience—experience that has given me useful perspectives into the connective tissue of the global superclass and introduced me to representatives of the group from every sector and from every region of the world.

To have reached the top of the pyramid, it stands to reason that many of the members of the superclass are exceptional. They are often brilliant, full of energy, and creative. They are also lucky and most of them know it. Many are rather happy. Money, which nearly all these elites have in abundance, doesn't make you happy. But, as Woody Allen once said, "Money is better than poverty, if only for financial reasons." It is hard not to prefer the vision and energy of the best among them to the hidebound narrowness of many of the national political opportunists who sometimes seek to score points by attacking them. But many among the superclass are also deeply self-interested and far removed from the world of most of the people of the planet. One billionaire CEO with whom I spoke responded to the idea of a superclass by saying, only half jokingly, "That's the way it should be. The only thing I'd change is that we should have . . . I should have . . . more power." In his joke was a more serious suggestion that things were actually working better than ever despite huge global inequalities in the distribution of wealth and power. He did not for a moment question whether his business success should have given him not just more money than other people but more power than them as well. He felt he had earned the power, too.

There have been many books written about the inequitable distribution of wealth on the planet, but few on the inequitable distribution of power. There have been books written about the most salacious and grotesquely appealing theories about the influence of the few, but few that tackle the realities of today's rapidly evolving global elites. Understanding this group is vital to understanding the nature of the global era and the future we are presenting to our children. Further, by examining this group, we may come to question some of our own assumptions not only about how the world does work but also how it should work. With some luck, even members of the superclass may see this and recognize that the imbalances that exist are not only unjust, they are the deepest and most deadly threat to their long-term interests.

What is more, of course, these are really interesting people. Their stories are often more intriguing than the tabloids and other fiction they inspire. Seeing them up close reveals, in microcosm, much about the world. It is a small enough group that we can focus in on them, see into their eyes a little, and get a glimpse of their perspective. For a moment or two anyway, we can ride along with people like the former prime minister of a Latin American country, who once settled into the first-class compartment of a long flight only to discover that he was seated next to a woman who had attended kindergarten with one of his best friends. "Small world," he said. "Yes," she agreed, "at the top."

David Rothkopf
Bethesda, Maryland
December 2007

SUPERCLASS

Introduction

THE POWER ELITE ON THE PROMENADE

> Any city, however small, is in fact divided into
> two; one the city of the poor, the other of the
> rich; these are at war with one another.
> —PLATO, *REPUBLIC*

Gentiana is a small restaurant that would scarcely warrant a second glance in any other village in Europe. It is rather traditional, only slightly more charming than the bland shops and modest hotels around it. One nearby storefront offers a remarkable array of Swiss Army knives, another boxes of chocolates, another fur hats and mountain gear. The restaurant has a cozy, neighborhood feel to it. Beside the door there is a blackboard highlighting a few specials, and on the ground floor there may be seating for twenty if they are both thin enough and friendly enough. Upstairs there are a few small rooms for private parties, the biggest of which seats ten people squeezed in on either side of a long narrow table. Most of its character comes from a feel of woody intimacy, the dark wood façade, dark wood floors, dark wood tables. In fact, for all its charm, it is definitely not a place for claustrophobes—or people with an extreme fear of splinters.

The reason to go to Gentiana is the fondue, especially the cheese fondue, which is offered in robust portions that recall an era before cardiologists. My wife, Adrean, has a special weakness for fondue, and every year that we have gone to the annual meeting of the World Economic Forum in Davos we have gone to Gentiana for her birthday. We make reservations long in advance because during the week of the January meetings, which are attended each year by more than 2,000 business and government leaders from around the world, getting a table at Gentiana is not much easier than getting one at renowned eateries like Aragawa in Tokyo, Gordon Ramsay in London, or Le Bernardin in New York. Perhaps more surprisingly, for that one week the clientele at this humble Swiss bistro looks pretty much the same as what you might find at those world-class restaurants.

Of course, even during that week, there are still a few tables at Gentiana occupied by locals. One regular is a particularly garrulous drunk who loves to hobnob with the CEOs, heads of state, and rock stars who are wedged in, elbow to elbow, spinning hunks of bread on long forks in the pots of bubbling Gruyère. The local speaks only Swiss-German to the polyglot crowds around him, and few understand him, although judging by his demeanor the casual observer is not sure whether that has to do with the language he speaks or the local beer that he favors. No matter. He smiles and they smile, and the general effect is cheerful and relaxed.

One afternoon during a recent Davos, my wife and I were hurrying along the sidewalk on our way to Gentiana. This can be dangerous, as the locals do not shovel away the snow and ice lurks just about everywhere. In fact, attendees at Davos can see with some regularity central bank governors and senior executives of the IMF and other distinguished middle-aged men and women swaddled in cashmere, calfskin, and politically incorrect pelts of many origins launched skyward, only to land on their broader, softer regions. We walked gingerly, therefore, but with purpose, knowing we were meeting our friends in just a few minutes.

The weather was typical. A light snow was falling. It was very cold. But the Alpine air was crisp and dry and invigorating. We chatted about the meetings, who we had seen and who we hoped to run into. As we walked, we reflexively did what most of the visitors to this small mountain town do: We glanced at the people passing us in the street, trying to determine who they were. (Given the nature of Davos, they were likely to have been somebody.) It's a ritual made easier by the fact that everyone at the meeting has to wear a badge around his or her neck at all times. The badge is used to get through the many security checkpoints—there are at least two Swiss soldiers and policemen in Davos for every delegate who attends the meetings—to register for sessions, and to let everyone know who you are. Your name is on the badge, along with the organization you represent. So too is your picture. People tend to walk with their badges dangling in plain sight so they don't have to fumble with them getting in and out of buildings or past police. That's how it was for everyone except for the universally recognizable—people like Bill Clinton, Bill Gates, Tony Blair, Bono, or Angelina Jolie. The badge-scanning move is so ubiquitous you might call it the Davos dip: Bend the knee slightly, cast a subtle glance downward, assess and move on.

Leaving the Congress Centre and walking along Davos's main street, the Promenade, we passed Thierry Desmarest, the CEO of Total; a small cluster of Harvard professors; a senior executive of Saudi Aramco; and a woman pulling her two small children on a sled. (She was local and the sled seemed to hint at the reason they don't shovel the sidewalks.) We stopped briefly to chat with Tom Donohue, the CEO of the U.S. Chamber of Commerce, who happens to be my wife's boss, then paused a few steps later to chat with an Indian-born U.S. venture capitalist with whom I had some business. It was a typical sample. Five minutes along the Davos Promenade in January offered a cavalcade of freeze-dried economic leaders from three continents.

About two blocks from Gentiana, I was grousing about how one of the conversations that I had most wanted to have had resulted in a frustrating series of near misses. The objective was a long-delayed chat with Paulo Coelho, the Brazilian author of *The Alchemist*. Coelho has sold more than one hundred million copies of his books worldwide and is, after the *Harry Potter* author, J. K. Rowling, the second-best-selling author on the planet. He is also one of the few cultural regulars at Davos, one of a handful of people who might offer a different perspective on the Davos zeitgeist. We had intended to meet almost a year earlier but, due to a series of scheduling mishaps, had repeatedly failed to do so. Finally, we aimed for Davos, but I had yet to lay eyes on him. What did I expect from a man who lived on the other side of the world and was constantly in motion—a Brazilian who lived much of the time in Europe and sold many of his books in Russia? There was a little bit of hubris in thinking we might ever be able to end up in the same place at the same time. And then: "Oh, my God," said a voice I did not recognize, "it's you."

A smallish man in a fur hat was staring at my name badge. He had a graying goatee, and he greeted me like a long-lost cousin. It was Coelho, appearing almost miraculously out of the Alpine mist as if conjured by our conversation.

Passing along the sidewalk from the Congress Centre where we had just heard an address by the German chancellor, Angela Merkel, and comments from the Indian steel magnate Lakshmi Mittal, through the stream of big name boulevardiers, and then walking directly into this icon of the global literary scene—it was made clear again that Davos was truly the incarnation of Marshall McLuhan's global village. It was like small-town Planet Earth, or the once-a-year Brigadoon of globalization: a community connected to everywhere and, in one way or another, to everyone. Indeed, during the course of this meeting, top trade ministers would caucus to try unsuccessfully to rescue global trade talks, Africa activists would meet with corporate chiefs and political leaders to seek funding for medical aid programs, global warming would "go mainstream" as mostly American skeptics were persuaded by session after session of expert views, and proponents of different solutions for dealing with everything from anxiety about immigrants to anxiety about terrorism would present their views directly to those in a position to implement them. If, as Hillary Clinton has asserted, it takes a village to raise a child, this seemed to be the village it took to run the world.

Coelho and I had never met, but thanks to the wonders of the information age we had enough e-mail history that our conversation was familiar and fairly ebullient. He offered to have lunch, but we gestured toward Gentiana, explaining that we had a prior engagement. I eagerly made an appointment to sit down with him later that afternoon at the Kongress Hotel.

Over the three and a half decades of its existence, this mountain-top gathering clearly had done more than merely transform Davos from sleepy ski town to cosmopolitan hub. More than a meeting place for international business, government, media, and cultural leaders, it now was a symbol for the knitting together of the world, literally and figuratively a summit of summits. The concept of what the political scientist Samuel Huntington called "Davos man"—the global citizen, the leader for whom borders were increasingly irrelevant—described a new leadership class for our era.

When founded in 1971 by Klaus Schwab, the organization that would become known as the World Economic Forum had a narrower mission. It was focused on convening European business leaders for a discussion of that continent's rather uncertain economic fortunes.

To put the moment in context, it is worth recalling that in 1971, Europe was still living in the aftermath of World War II and was on the front line of the cold war, still more the self-anointed seat of civilization than the "modern" Europe of more modest, less imperial, more multilateralist inclinations. In fact, it was not until three years later that the first of Europe's great colonial powers, Portugal, granted independence to Guinea-Bissau, Angola, and Mozambique. The United Kingdom, Ireland, and Denmark did not join the European Union until 1973. Though the Treaty of Rome had initiated the creation of Europe's Common Market in 1957, it would be more than two decades before the Maastricht Treaty institutionalized the idea of a true single market among the nations of the continent. Europe was clearly in transition at the moment of the forum's birth.

I was in high school at the time, and in college when the World Economic Forum was really gaining its sea legs in the late 1970s. I'll admit, international conferences didn't really capture my imagination when I was a teenager, but my education was absolutely colored with the Western worldview of those times, with classical education built on the presumed superiority of European ideas and the history and cultural contributions of other regions seen as exotic and secondary. At Columbia University, we were required to take the "core curriculum," which was built around two major courses. One, Humanities, was a survey course of the defining works in literature. The second, Contemporary Civilization, was a survey of the great works in political philosophy and related disciplines, beginning with the Greeks and continuing through the modern era. The two courses, in retrospect, were undoubtedly the highlight of my education and have benefited me probably every day of my life since I took them. (Of course, I did not recognize this at the time.) In Contemporary Civilization, we read—at the pace of one significant, sometimes mind-blowing, occasionally mind-numbing book a week—the writings of everyone (male and white) from Plato to Descartes to Darwin. Somewhere around Max Weber and other analysts and critics of modernity, the curriculum got more varied, with different professors assigning different texts, as it was harder to agree on what qualified as essential reading. One of the more popular assignments at that point in the course was *The Power Elite* by C. Wright Mills, a 1956 book that explored the national power structure in the United States.

Mills, a former Columbia professor of sociology, wrote the book as a study of how America really worked. His central claim was that at the top tier of the business, government, and military communities, there was a remarkably small and overlapping echelon of "deciders." This national "power elite" was

> composed of men whose positions enable them to transcend the ordinary environments of ordinary men and women; they are in positions to make decisions having major consequences . . . They are in command of the major hierarchies and organizations of modern society. They rule the big corporations. They run the machinery of the state and claim its prerogatives. They direct the

military establishment. They occupy the strategic command posts of the social structure, in which are now centered the effective means of the power and the wealth and the celebrity which they enjoy.

Mills asserted that these elites took similar paths to positions of privilege, ensuring that many among their homogeneous numbers knew one another. In addition, they often crossed sectors: from top roles in government to top roles in business, from the the White House cabinet to the boardroom, from military commands to politics, from one position of great responsibility to another. Thus, Mills claimed, they created a kind of interlocking directorate for the United States of America.

Mills's book was as much a critique as it was a description of this group and America's midcentury leadership. It explored, in meticulous detail, the concentration of power among a comparatively few corporations and individuals, and the manifold links of American leaders to key institutions. The book then veered into polemic, lamenting the disproportionate influence of this group. One of the men who no doubt inspired many of Mills's points, President Eisenhower, also best illustrated them. A former supreme allied commander in Europe as well as a former president of Columbia University, Eisenhower captured much of Mills's spirit in his farewell address as president in 1961:

> [The] conjunction of an immense military establishment and a large arms industry is new in the American experience. The total influence—economic, political, even spiritual—is felt in every city, every State house, every office of the Federal government. We recognize the imperative need for this development. Yet we must not fail to comprehend its grave implications. Our toil, resources and livelihood are all involved; so is the very structure of our society.
>
> In the councils of government, we must guard against the acquisition of unwarranted influence, whether sought or unsought, by the military-industrial complex. The potential for the disastrous rise of misplaced power exists and will persist.

One little-remembered aspect of Eisenhower's speech is that it contained not one but two central warnings. While the first, concerning the military-industrial complex, is more often cited, he also expressed equivalent concerns about the emergence of what he called the "scientific-technological elite." His concerns, like Mills's, reflect the zeitgeist of the

1950s, in which the predominant historical memory was of World War II and the subjugation of all U.S. political, financial, and industrial efforts to the goal of military victory. The predominant fear of the moment was of technology run amok as manifested in the growing threat of global thermonuclear war.

Since Eisenhower spoke in 1961, technological innovation has not only fueled America's unprecedented growth but it has empowered people in new ways; it perhaps even helped to bring down the United States' cold war adversary, as the rise of the information age made it impossible for a closed society to compete. Yet, despite the resilient strength of America's military-industrial establishment, defense spending and manpower have receded from their highs during World War II and the cold war years. In his speech, Eisenhower speaks of a 3.5-million-person military; today the U.S. military is only 1.5 million men and women strong (with nearly 1 million more in the reserves). He also notes that at the time of his speech the U.S. military budget exceeded the total net income of all U.S. companies. Today, while the defense budget exceeds $425 billion, the earnings of only the fifty most profitable U.S. companies top that number and, indeed, the combined revenues of just the top two, ExxonMobil and Wal-Mart, dwarf it, beating it by more than 50 percent. Without a doubt, corporate economic clout has grown dramatically.

Mills's book is still read and is now considered a classic critique of America's power structure, but it is also clear that the world has changed profoundly in the fifty years since its publication.

Crunching through the snow on the Davos Promenade after a long cholesterol-rich lunch, observing the remarkable assortment of world leaders, I found it striking just how much had changed since Mills's day. The distribution of power has clearly shifted, not just away from the United States and Europe, but away from nations. Even the casual observer in Davos would have to conclude that had Mills been writing today, he would have turned his attention from the national elite in America to a new and more important phenomenon: the rise of a global power elite, a superclass that plays a similar role in the hierarchy of the global era to the role that the U.S. power elite played in that country's first decade as a superpower.

Evidence of that new reality was observable in the hotels and cafés and on the frigid sidewalks along Davos's main street. Fortunately, the Congress Centre was soon in sight. It was right next door to the hotel Coelho had suggested for our meeting and, more important, it was warm. The temperature was hovering somewhere between 15 degrees below zero Celsius and holy-crap-I-have-lost-all-feeling-in-my-extremities. Two Swiss soldiers at the door, both in black uniforms and carrying automatic sidearms, both smiling and saying "Good afternoon" to everyone who entered, checked my badge for the second time in fifty yards and let me into the building.

There is a small anteroom in which people typically stomp the snow off their shoes—the mudroom of the global elite—followed by a very long hallway along which were scores of coatracks and attendants busily hanging hats and scarves. In the middle of the hallway were metal detectors and guards letting people into the main lobby of the Congress Centre. Judging from the badges, there must have been people from at least twenty countries in the hall as I passed through. Virtually all spoke English. Virtually all dressed in a similar uniform: a dark coat, a well-tailored suit or blazer, and slacks (even the Russians, who just three or four years earlier were famous for their shiny sharkskin suits). Women were mostly present in their role as spouses, with a still small though gradually growing number among the actual delegates.

Regularly you could see people, CEOs or government leaders, academics or media people, embrace, warmly shake hands, and greet each other like long-lost buddies. Over the years of Davos and similar meetings around the world, many connections were made and friendships formed within this elite peer group. Listening to the observations of people at Davos and afterward, a similar theme was reiterated about how closely knit this global elite had become, how it had become a community unto itself. Mark Malloch Brown, former deputy secretary-general of the UN and now a foreign ministry official in the British government, recalled a Davos reception held in New York City, shortly after 9/11. "As my wife and I were walking through that room, greeting friends all the way through, we turned to each other and shook our heads and said, 'What happened to us, that we walk through the Davos party and know more people than when we were walking across the village green in the town we live in?'"

Witnessing the reunions of the superclass in the coatroom, one had the impression that while yes, Davos itself was a small, isolated village high atop a mountain, the same was true for the tiny, insular community that flocked to it every year: Despite differences in their places of origin, the Davos crowd now had more in common with one another than with those who did not live at such a rarefied altitude. A former senior U.S. official confirmed this observation. "I think what is happening is in their own self-identification," he told me. "They have more allegiance to Davos and their ilk than they do to the people at home."

Something powerful is happening among the powerful. There have always been national elites, like Mills's "power elite" in the United States. There have always been connections between the elites of different countries, but they were typically "foreign relations"—connections between distant power centers, discrete alliances between sovereigns. For several decades now, though, a new community has been forming, at the same time that economies are spilling across borders, global entities are proliferating, and the world is, well, flattening.

One of the first to observe this phenomenon was the former Citibank chief executive Walter Wriston, a true visionary of both globalization and the information age. Wriston's prescient and seminal work *The Twilight of Sovereignty* was published within a year of the launch of the World Wide Web in 1991. In it, he wrote that "those who fully participate in the information economy benefit most from it . . . They will feel more affinity to their fellow global conversationalists than to those of their countrymen who are not yet part of the global conversation."

A couple of years after Wriston, Christopher Lasch observed similarly in *The Revolt of the Elites* that

> The market in which the new elites operate is now international in scope. Their fortunes are tied to enterprises that operate across national boundaries. They are more concerned with the smooth functioning of the system as a whole than with any of its parts. Their loyalties—if the term is not itself anachronistic in this context—are international rather than regional, national or local. They have more in common with their counterparts in Brussels or Hong Kong than with the masses of Americans not yet plugged into the network of global communications.

In fact, over the past several years, this particular observation has slipped into fairly common usage. While Wriston accepted the idea from the perspective of a protoglobalist, similar theories have come from critics of globalization who feel threatened by the emergence of this new class without a country. They perceive this international group as a threat to various national communities, from local power elites to the disenfranchised they see buffeted by the choices of the global decision makers. An example comes from the American free-trade skeptic Jeff Faux, who describes in his book *The Global Class War* an illuminating moment: After hearing a U.S. official advocate the passage of the North American Free Trade Agreement because Mexico's Harvard-educated president of the time was, by virtue of his U.S. education, "one of us,"

Faux writes, "I realized that globalization was producing not just a borderless market, but a borderless class system to go with it." He goes on to conclude, "Markets within nations inevitably produce groups of people who have more money and power than others. So, it would be odd if global markets did not create an international upper class of people whose economic interests had more in common with each other than with the majority of people who share their nationality."

Although I disagree with some of Faux's more extreme antiglobal, antitrade impulses, his concerns about the dislocations caused by globalization are as legitimate as his desire to pin them on the new global leaders is inevitable. (He calls the political actors who advance the views of this international elite "the party of Davos.") Where Faux and others who have identified this coalescing at the top find common ground is recognizing that something new is happening. As Prince Turki Al-Faisal, the American-educated former Saudi Arabian ambassador to the United States, observed, "I believe the issue of elites is a historic issue. It is not particular to these times. I think ever since the creation of mankind, whether you believe in Darwin or in the revealed religion, there has always been an elite that seemed to be in charge of things in one way or another. But now," he said, pausing thoughtfully, "now this is very different . . . a different kind of relationship. And something very important but not well understood."

The emergence of a different, global power elite went unforeseen by Mills fifty years ago. He was still reeling from the breakdown of small-town America and preoccupied with the fact that modest businesses and family farms had been transcended in importance by big corporations and political figures with national influence. If he worried that such concentrated power would not be healthy for American democracy, one could only imagine how he might react to an emerging elite without a country—an elite occupying a global playing field that is for the most part unregulated by governments or law.

Certainly, others are worried about the rise of this group. Populists and nationalists like Hugo Chávez and Evo Morales in Latin America, Vladimir Putin in Russia, Mahmoud Ahmadinejad in Iran, or Austria's Jörg Haider, France's Jean-Marie Le Pen, or American TV talking heads Lou Dobbs and Pat Buchanan—all regularly conjure the threat posed by a global cabal of the rich and powerful who have lost touch with their homelands and who act only in the name of their self-interests and greed. Because this global cabal lacks national ties, it is by default unpatriotic in the eyes of the most extreme critics. It poses a threat to culture and tradition and national sovereignty. For these people, Davos is much more than a business conference; it is an enemy camp: the place where the generals of globalization plot their conquests. Because each culture has so diligently knit together the concepts of country and of God, over thousands of years, those who look beyond country or see a community of interests that transcend those of their nation are suspected of being very nearly blasphemous, or are associated with dark forces. For many, globalization was and is westernization. Worse, it is Americanization, which in turn links it to Zionism and ancient threats of Jewish conspiracy. It is the collapse of borders and cultural barriers, and thus it conjures for some, somewhat ironically, the spread of Islam. For others, like Dobbs and Buchanan, it is about the Latinization of the United States and the loss of America's "Anglo-Saxon" identity. In this view, national identities are under siege. For still others in the developing world, the pronouncements of the IMF or WTO seem designed to protect the interests of the rich and and conjure the specter of Imperialism 2.0, a neocolonialism overseen by corporate viceroys in which the Internet homogenizes the young and turns everyone into a materialistic capitalist cog in the global clockwork.

In Mills's era, at the height of a global struggle between capitalism and communism, when Socialist views were considered intellectually fashionable in American academia because they represented the most direct way to assault the establishment, the study of elites was not just an imperative of social science, essential to understanding how societies functioned. It was also an examination of the relevance of a core idea of Marxism, that of class. After all, Marx had said at the beginning of *The Communist Manifesto,*

> The history of all hitherto existing society is the history of class struggles.
>
> Freeman and slave, patrician and plebeian, lord and serf, guild-master and journeyman, in a word, oppressor and oppressed, stood in constant opposition to one another, carried on an uninterrupted, now hidden, now open fight, a fight that each time ended, either in a revolutionary reconstitution of society at large, or in the common ruin of the contending classes.
>
> In the earlier epochs of history, we find almost everywhere a complicated arrangement of society into various orders, a manifold gradation of social rank. In ancient Rome we have patricians, knights, plebeians, slaves; in the Middle Ages, feudal lords, vassals, guild-masters, journeymen, apprentices, serfs; in almost all of these classes, again, subordinate gradations.

Mills was living in a society that distinguished itself from that of its Soviet adversary by its rejection of this notion of class struggle, in particular by its assertion that it had found a solution: a path to a classless society via capitalism, markets, and specifically through the idea of equal treatment of all citizens under the law. When Mills looked around, of course, he did not see anything like a classless society. Without saying it explicitly, his study of American elites resonated with classical Marxist critique: A handful of families controlled the wealth, a handful of companies controlled the means of production, a handful of political and military leaders controlled the levers of power, and they were all linked, sometimes informally, sometimes quite closely, but often with the effect of amplifying their power and securing their station—and implicitly with the consequence of heightening inequity within society.

In short, Mills's study of elites in America at midcentury was tacitly an exploration of the dynamics that lay at the heart of the world's great dilemma of the moment: the choice between capitalism and communism—between a system that subordinated everything to the will of the state, which was asserted to be a steward for the greater good, and one that identified the will of the individual as the central driver for good within a society.

Now, the elites of Davos seem to embody the emergence of a new tension, or, more properly, an additional one. Fifty years after Mills, it seems that these global elites have crystallized a tension between the almost-400-year-old idea of the nation-state as the defining unit of global governance, and the emerging reality of a world in which nations are not only diminishing in influence but also are being transcended both by transnational needs beyond their reach and transnational power centers advancing internationalist or supranationalist agendas.

Internationalist vs. nationalist. Globalist vs. regionalist. A battle not over the redistribution of wealth but over the redistribution of sovereignty and power. Mills had in fact seen evidence of the first phases of this dynamic even within the context of cold war reality when he noted that "on each side of the world-split running through central Europe and around the Asiatic rimlands, there is an ever-increasing interlocking of economic, military, and political structures." Indeed, perhaps through this observation he hinted at how cold war exigencies had helped drive globalizing forces—alliances, trade, infrastructural links, institutional ties—among the parties on either side of the East-West struggle.

Yet, even acknowledging that the elites of today are different from those studied by Mills, several of the central questions that he raised and that bedeviled his times remain. Despite assertions to the contrary that emerged in the wake of the end of the cold war, we have not resolved the central debates about how to order our societies. We have not reached, as Francis Fukuyama put it, "the End of History"—an ideological consensus that the liberal Western view of government and economic life is the best way to order society. Nowhere is this clearer than with the issue that provoked the split between mainstream capitalism and Marxism—that of the just distribution of wealth. Contentious sessions at Davos in 2007 turned on issues like executive pay and whether it is fair that the average American CEO makes 350 to 400 times what his or her average employee makes. Others touched with the best of intentions but also an ironic subtext on the plight of the world's poor as roomfuls of the planet's most privileged pondered the fate of the three billion people who live on less than two dollars a day. The divide is growing, and some see globalization as being two-speed—offering accelerating benefits to some while others are told to wait, wait for the process to benefit their children or their children's children.

Of course conflicts between the elites of the world and everyone else are not the only reason such groups are interesting. Understanding who sits atop the social order is essential if one is to understand power, gain it, or oppose it. It is also irresistibly interesting merely to discover who among us are the most successful and powerful, and how their lives are different from our own. It wasn't only the despair of Shakespeare's beset Richard II that led him to say, "For God's sake let us sit upon the ground and tell sad stories of the death of kings." We have always had a particular fondness for stories of kings. History itself is the story of those with the most—the most to lose, the most to gain, the most power, and the most glamour.

Elites are masters of their eras, but they are also metaphors for them. They illustrate what is valued, how success is earned, and how power is garnered and wielded. They also reflect what flaws we tolerate in those at the top and what flaws we find unacceptable. Indeed, elites reveal how we see our own societies, and throughout history we have created elaborate mythologies to justify and preserve the systems they built or ran. For millennia, power was seen to flow on the one hand from heaven and on the other from the ownership of land. These beliefs gave way to the embrace of meritocracy—of Weber's Protestant ethic and the rags-to-riches appeal of Horatio Alger. What do the crowds at Davos say about our time? About how it is different from previous eras? About what changes may be yet to come? What is their current mythology? And what does it say about the rest of us?

After a time schmoozing and restoring my body temperature at the meeting center, I pressed on to my late afternoon appointment. The Kongress Hotel, where I was now headed to meet Coelho, is one of the better places to stay while attending the World Economic Forum's annual meeting. It is certainly unassuming. That is not surprising in Davos where, other than the traditional "grand hotel" style of the Belvedere, where most of the topmost government and business leaders stay, virtually every hotel looks like the kind of modest place you might expect in a midlevel European ski resort. As a consequence, Davos imposes a certain kind of situational humility on the exalted of the world, or, in the case of the worst hotels, even humiliation. One senior Latin American official complained of being boarded atop a mountain in a ski lodge that required a cable car and a bus ride to transport him, forty-five minutes later, to the Congress Centre. One very distinguished American NGO head was placed in a one-and-a-half-star hotel that was practically in Klosters, the next town down the road. Some people rebel and commute in to Davos from Zurich, three hours away, or, as one Persian Gulf sheikh did, they helicopter in from better digs elsewhere. My wife and I, in view of our own less than lavish accommodations, tried to imagine that we were in touch with Davos's roots as a destination for a spa cure—literally the place about which Thomas Mann wrote *The Magic Mountain*.

Mann, of course, had no idea quite how magic the mountain would become. Walking through the metal detector into the welter of activity in the Kongress Hotel's lobby, it was once again clear. A small pride of women swaddled in mink and all manner of tasteful bling glided past looking vaguely predatory and, frankly, frightening. Behind them came their husbands, a group of U.S. senators including John McCain of Arizona. In the tiny lounge area, a group of Brazilian officials had cordoned off the conference space for the imminent arrival of Brazil's President Luiz Inácio "Lula" da Silva, almost certainly the only Davos attendee that year with only a fourth-grade education. Next to where I settled in the lounge, a lively discussion was taking place about a major charitable initiative to raise money for a health-care NGO doing work in Africa. (Africa had been the theme of Davos for the past couple of years thanks to high-profile activists like Bono, the earnest "improving the world" commitment of Klaus Schwab, and the presence of the likes of Angelina Jolie—though there were not very many African govern-ment or business leaders attending.)

I ordered a Diet Coke and eavesdropped while waiting for Coelho to arrive. Two people from an NGO were speaking to, apparently, a potential donor, trying to shake loose some funding. One mentioned a donation that the benefactor's group had made during the most recent meeting of the Clinton Global Initiative (CGI), a similarly high-level fo-rum organized in New York by the former president to mobilize sup-port for important international causes. CGI had clearly tapped into what many perceived as a "hot" trend of the moment: philanthropy. Some $7 billion had been committed at the Clinton event, dedicated to specific projects addressing mainly global health, poverty alleviation, and education.

Indeed, in the era of record gifts to philanthropy (such as Warren Buffett's $31 billion provided to the Gates Foundation), one senses that a major issue global elites seek to discuss—or like to be seen dis-cussing?—is their own generosity. The charity craze is a good thing. But why is it happening now? It could be related to the business cycle: Aging Internet and hedge fund millionaires and billionaires, for example, seek to be more generous in hopes of leaving a legacy. It could also be associated with the cyclical rise and fall of elites: Elites of an age known for breathtaking growth in inequity might seek to do damage control before the inevitable backlash comes.

The late-nineteenth-century American social critic Thorstein Veblen would have recognized the development. The man who coined the term "conspicuous consumption" to explain what the rich spend their money on—ostentations—would probably simply see at least an ele-ment of this as a piece of the same cloth. He would probably observe that for all the very considerable good that is done by CGI and at Davos, the spirit of the times or at least of the events also leads at least some of the world's elites to wear "conspicuous conscience" as they might a new Rolex.

Coelho appeared on time and settled in at our small table. He would not have been mistaken for the CEOs or senators in the room, having adopted a deliberately bohemian quality, with a bright orange scarf draped around his neck, his gray hair cropped close except for a small rectangle of slightly longer hair at the nape of his neck that seemed to offer a kind of back-of-head counterpoint to his goatee. A former lyricist for leading Brazilian composers and a former hippie, he is of another time and place in many respects. He was so relaxed and seemingly guileless that the New Yorker in me started out by assuming that his openness was a kind of affectation, but after only a few minutes' talking I developed the sense that he was very much who he seemed to be. In this respect, he did have something in common with the chief executives and government leaders in the room, whose success gave them less to prove. So it was with Coelho, one of the most popular authors in history: When you have one hundred million books in print and national governments and leading organizations are offering you medals and plaques and other knickknacks of professional status, you certainly don't have to defend yourself to the world as you once might have.

So how does the hippie who has attended the past ten Davos meetings see the inner workings of the system? Does he identify with other members because of his success and influence? Or does he feel like an outsider, an anthropologist visiting the village of the ultrapowerful? How does the allegorist view this group that defines the emerging power structure of our time?

In a way that would be not much of a surprise to anyone who has read any of Coelho's works, he began to describe Davos in terms of its mythology. He said, "The classical myth about Davos is that they're here to divide up the cake, to get their piece. But that's not my vision.

"I think there are two levels in Davos, today more than ever, because I have been coming here for ten years. The one is the business level. I don't fully understand it. But they have real money. They have power. It is part of their reason for coming. But there is another level, a second level, that is the human level. And it is a bigger and bigger part of the meeting. It creates a kind of constructive self-consciousness. Who are you? What about your identity? Are you your company? Are you your country? Are you something else? Are you yourself? And how do you integrate being yourself and being what you do? It enables us, at the end of the day, to get past the political discussions, the business discussions to what we really believe as human beings. It lets people get acquainted more and more with the human side. So we have an elite meeting, yes. But not to regulate the world but to see each other."

Sociologists like Mills and Weber would observe that it is precisely such human interaction that more deeply integrates the group, turning it from a random gathering of peers into something more. Human interaction allows for a community of interests that is capable, through shared knowledge and relationships, of managing itself and coordinating subsets of the group to advance desired goals. When pressed on this, Coelho is a little uncomfortable. Perhaps he hesitates because he is on several boards and committees associated with the forum and wants to defuse the critiques of the antiglobalists and the conspiracy theorists. As a true Davos insider, he wants to suggest that there really is no system but merely individuals connecting with one another.

Coelho argues that as a humanist he sees beyond the façade of systems and into a world of typical relationships much like any others. He offers as an example the story of meeting Bill Clinton during the last year of his presidency. Coelho was invited as one among twenty to meet the president, and he arrived at the designated time to a conference room where he stood alone on the periphery of a crowd of seemingly important people. The people were, in fact, so important that the system should have kept him, just a writer from Brazil, out of such a gathering altogether. He felt humiliated at being so ignored and out of place.

But when Clinton entered the room, he asked, "Which of you is Paulo Coelho?" As Coelho describes it, he said, "'It's me, Mr. President.' And then everybody looked at me and they looked and I smiled and I suddenly became a friend of all of them, you know? And Clinton came to me and said, 'Hello, how are you? I really wanted to meet you because I read your book, my daughter forced me to read it . . .' And then we started talking about the most surrealistic things, about jet lag and things like that, and people all around us are just waiting to talk about the system and how they were going to control it and 'what is the next step, Mr. President' and ba ba ba. But they end up standing there listening to me and Clinton talking about jet lag and afterwards they treated me completely differently. I was in with them."

He offers the story to illustrate the looseness of the system, and certainly it is a revealing snippet about how this elite differs from past aristocratic elites. Here was a Brazilian and former hippie songwriter who had failed in an attempt to join the priesthood meeting the son of a broken, lower-middle-class Arkansas home: two individuals thrown together by their accomplishments at the pinnacle of the world, with a bond and a common language, with influence over one another and over countless millions beyond them. But in fact the story also illustrates the compounding impact of elite interaction, recalling the famous story of the young man who comes in the nineteenth century to the floor of the New York Stock Exchange to meet with J. P. Morgan to ask him for a loan. Morgan ponders the request and then says, "Let me offer you something equally valuable," and he puts his arm around the fellow and walks him around the exchange floor chatting with him, thereby sending the message that the young man was well connected. The point being that the very fact of the existence of status creates a system whereby those who have status can transfer it to those around them and determine who is elevated and who is not. Power can be meted out by choice.

Coelho's conversation moved a bit like wind across a bay, shifting with the passing clouds and the time of day. He sipped his coffee and then offered another story. He enjoys archery, he said, and often practices in a hilly area not too far from his house in the French countryside. One day, while practicing, he was approached by a soldier who was passing through from a nearby military base. The soldier smiled when he learned who Coelho was and proceeded to tell the famously inspirational author about a recent experience he had speaking at a local school. "I went to talk to a group of students," he said, "and I decided to ask them what they wanted to learn about. So they made a list of questions, and to be honest, I don't know how to answer those questions and that is why I am so glad I have run into you up here on this hill. Perhaps you can help me." Coelho, curious, offered to help and asked what the questions were. The officer replied, "Is there a God? What happens after we die? Is there life outside the planet earth? Why do people hate each other? Things like this. Philosophical questions that you have as children and that we still have as adults."

Coelho's point, he explained, was this: We want to believe in a system. We want to believe in higher powers. Chaos and randomness make life too threatening, too hard to understand, too easy to see as meaningless. So as human beings, we seek order in the universe. As he spoke, I heard more resonances with what Mills wrote as he pondered why people viewed the question of the existence of elites in different ways:

> The view that all is blind drift is largely a fatalist projection of one's own feeling of impotence and perhaps, if one has ever been active politically in a principled way, a salve of one's guilt.
>
> The view that all of history is due to the conspiracy of an easily located set of villains, or of heroes, is also a hurried projection from the difficult effort to understand how shifts in the structure of society open opportunities to various elites and how various elites take advantage or fail to take advantage of them.
>
> To accept either view—of all history as conspiracy or of all history as drift—is to relax the effort to understand the facts of power and the ways of the powerful.

For many, like Coelho, order comes from a belief in God and a divine plan. Others, because they are uncertain about supernatural higher powers or because they seek to supplement them, find some comfort in the idea that someone is in charge here on this earth. Indeed, we accept power in others because it brings order with it, suggests that we are not random clouds of subatomic particles appearing and bouncing off of one another and disappearing without rhyme or reason. In times of great change and uncertainty, such as the epochal transformation we are now experiencing as we enter the global era, there is an even greater need to seek out such order. This fundamental need has benefited ambitious individuals throughout human history, as they have translated it into acceptance of their power in the name of providing order and leadership.

•   •   •

As the meeting with Coelho ended, the president of Brazil walked by and warmly greeted his country's most famous writer. We all chatted briefly, and in the context of that room, and of Davos at large, the conversation attracted little attention because so many so similar to it were happening everywhere.

As I stood there, in our little corner of this very modest hotel in this otherwise very ordinary corner of Switzerland, it was difficult not to feel that this community of leaders truly was part of something exceptionally important and different in the history of the world. Its emergence represented a watershed in how power was distributed among individuals and among nations, and it was vital to understand because it was directly connected to the fate of every man and woman on the planet. Villified by some, feared by others, only vaguely comprehended even by its members, around me were members of a new elite that surpassed in power, resources, and especially global influence all those other elites, all the kings and emperors and titans of industry who had come before them.

They are the superclass, the global power elite that is reshaping the planet. The purpose of this book is to attempt to better understand them, their influence, the trends that are shaping them, and the consequences of their existence for us all.

1

EACH ONE IS ONE IN A MILLION:

MEET THE SUPERCLASS

We are all worms, but I do believe that I am a
glowworm.
> —WINSTON CHURCHILL

They call them "green" planes. They get the name not because they are
more environmentally friendly or because they are new and untested.
They actually are green, a pale lemon-lime color, yet to be painted or
fitted out to the final specifications of their future owners. On any given
day there are four or five of them positioned in two rows, nose to tail,
in the main assembly facility at Gulfstream Aerospace's headquarters in
Savannah, Georgia.

As I walk through the cavernous hangar with Bryan Moss, at the time
Gulfstream's president, there is no mistaking the pride of the workers.
Gulfstream employs five thousand people in Georgia, most of them in
its main facilities near Savannah's international airport. As we pass
by, workers pause from riveting or installing the miles of wiring that
run through Gulfstream aircraft to joke with Moss or smile and wave.
Some are especially enthusiastic as they mistake me for the owner of a
NASCAR racing team, Rick Hendrick of Hendrick Motorsports, who is
due to visit later the same afternoon.

Gulfstream, a division of U.S. defense contractor General Dynamics, specializes in private jet aircraft. It offers a line of planes ranging
from the midsized G150 and G200 to the gold standard of corporate
jets, the G500 and G550. The G550 can travel almost seven thousand
nautical miles—the distance from New York to Tokyo—transporting

eight passengers in the lap of luxury: reclining leather lounge chairs, polished wood paneling, a well-equipped galley and bar, high-tech entertainment and communications systems, and one or more convertible beds. The price tag for such opulence? Typically over $45 million.

But the eighty or so individuals and organizations that purchase Gulfstream aircraft this year will not simply be buying the Rolls-Royce of general aviation. (As it happens, one of the G5s I walk through during my visit is destined for use by the senior management of the Rolls-Royce Company.) These clients are increasingly looking for something more—more security, more privacy, more flexibility in their travel schedules, and a more efficient return on their investment of the time every trip takes. Perhaps they are lured by the advanced avionics that give Gulfstream pilots more tools, more information, more technology at their disposal than the pilots of the most advanced commercial aircraft. For example, the new aircraft typically come equipped with the Gulfstream Enhanced Vision System, which provides pilots with the ability to "see" in low-visibility and night conditions by superimposing symbols and infrared imagery on top of the images the pilots see optically. Soon these will be supplanted by systems that actually offer "synthetic" vision, essentially a system that fills in what you can't see with what a computer "knows" to be there—mountains, for example, or radio towers, or runways.

That's not the kind of luxury that the general public imagines when they think of CEOs and celebrities racing from one corner of the globe to another at 41,000 feet, being served scones with clotted cream or freshly prepared sushi platters. But in a world where commercial aviation is fraught with stress and delays and a host of security risks, more and more of those who can afford the private aircraft option are seeing it not as a self-indulgent luxury but as a risk-management tool—a necessity of the global era.

As Moss says, "We serve a very, very narrow portion of the people on this planet. They have very specific needs, they require certain capabilities, and for them to do the things they believe they need to do, to go the places they need to go, to see the people they need to see, to make those decisions that influence how investments are made at the time and in the place they need to—that group of people focuses more and more on productivity and global mobility, and that's what we're all about."

As he speaks, one of the senior workers on the production line, a tall older man in a white shirt and goggles, emerges from the tail section of an aircraft and comes over to shake Moss's hand and discuss the production schedule. Others join in, and the chat is focused and friendly. There is no question that the blue-collar workers of Savannah, Georgia, don't resent the success of Gulfstream. They build aircraft that roll out of the factory and literally ascend to a level of society that they will never enjoy, but they do it with evident pride and perhaps a sense that they are the beneficiaries of globalization, proving the quality of American workers and enabling them to enjoy the considerable down-home benefits of middle class life in the American South.

Another worker, a short woman with an unmistakable Georgia accent, comes over to tell Moss how thrilled she was to have won two tickets to a NASCAR race from the company. As NASCAR has become America's biggest spectator sport and as many of its drivers and their corporate sponsors have become Gulfstream owners, the aircraft manufacturer has devoted more and more time to becoming part of that world, a world that has long been a part of the lives of the workers who make the planes themselves.

The woman from the assembly line and Moss joke about the race car event and then she and the other workers who had gathered around us return to their duties. Moss and I head to a large hangar space where two G450s and two G550s are being completed—now recognizable as finished aircraft, with long, graceful lines, large oval windows, and upswept winglets.

There is no symbol in the world of today's global elite that surpasses the Gulfstream jet. Only 1,500 are in service. Only the most privileged can possess them or enjoy the benefits they offer. Eighty percent of those sold go to leading corporations that can afford what Moss estimates as the $1.25 to $1.5 million that it costs to maintain an aircraft for 500 hours a year of service. Only 5 percent are sold to individuals, with the rest going to government leaders and "special missions," such as providing planes for military transport or medical evacuation purposes. Internally, Gulfstream considers the threshold for real sales prospects to be a company with annual revenues in excess of $1 billion or an individual with financial assets in excess of $25 million. But most owners easily surpass those projected barriers to ownership.

When the "standard" private jet isn't enough, there is a modest but growing number of superjets in service—larger passenger aircraft like the Boeing 737 and Airbus 320 that have been converted from commercial transport to private use. Even bigger models are entering the market, like the used 767 that Google's bargain-hunting Larry Page and Sergey Brin bought for only $15 million. Now Boeing has begun booking orders for private versions of its new wide-body 787—the "Dream-liner"—and for the next iteration of the 747, the 8 series. Airbus too has done a small amount of business in super-high-end private aircraft, no-tably the custom versions of the double-decker Airbus 380, purchased by mostly Middle Eastern clients for "personal use." Each of these mam-moth aircraft costs $300 million as its base price, plus another $100 mil-lion or more for the customizations.

These megajets are anomalies in the private jet world, however, con-jured up by some seeming glandular malfunction in the part of the brain that calibrates ambition to fantasy. Certainly, some of these jets are for heads of state who require secure transport wherever and whenever diplomatic duty calls. But many are also home to game rooms, multiple dining areas, and even whirlpool bathtubs.

When it comes to the most over-the-top jets, of course, it's not about need. Or perhaps, more accurately, it is about a different kind of need, one born not of necessity but of compulsion. Perfectly rational individuals, successful beyond imagination, grow very animated when they discuss the rationale for having their G5 fitted out not in Savannah (better for purely corporate needs) but rather in Long Beach, California (reputedly better for the special needs of rich individuals); they speak knowingly of where to find a particular cappuccino maker, advanced entertainment system, or special upholstery for the jet's interior. For some, these planes are the metrics of a lifetime. While most of us may measure our lives, like J. Alfred Prufrock, in coffee spoons, there are a few who measure them in high-performance aircraft that can fly them from Hong Kong to Cape Town in twelve hours.

The most extreme forms of private aviation excess, however, are the exception to the rule at Gulfstream, which typically views the task of customization much as does a Savile Row tailor. The majority of these aircraft are bespoke, but subtly—typically so subtly that even their dis-tinctive liveries, the patterns in which their exteriors are painted, vary only slightly. Perhaps the difference, say, between the gray pinstripe suit in a banker's wardrobe and the navy blue. As Moss says, "Some-times an individual will bring in an outside designer to work with them and they'll end up with a particular piece of art or a lamp or something like that in the airplane; but for us, there really isn't any squirrelly stuff anymore." CEOs, wary of what shareholders may think of their pur-chases, try to downplay the aircraft and treat them like they are simply necessary pieces of office equipment—like very large BlackBerrys that happen also to fly and offer filet mignon. Besides, for most of the world's top executives and richest people, there are practical and security reasons not to draw too much attention to themselves. The flamboyant American real estate mogul Donald Trump's plane has his name painted on the side of it, but he is an anomaly, and perhaps not a very surprising one at that.

Moss notes that the Gulfstream's reputation as the ne plus ultra of global leadership accessories is increasingly an international one. Whereas traditionally only about a quarter of the planes were sold overseas, today the number is approaching 40 percent and rising fast. At a recent Davos meeting, Moss said he happened to "crash" a dinner hosted by Nigerian President Olusegun Obasanjo. He introduced himself, and when he explained that he was with Gulfstream, Obasanjo "grabbed my hand like this [he clutches my hand]—he's a big man— and the next thing you know I'm not on my knees but I'm bent over and for twenty minutes hearing him talk about what a great airplane it was and how much he loved it. The whole dinner just stops. He was so enthusiastic."

Davos is the one gathering of potential prospects and clients that take place around the world each year that Moss says he "will not miss." It's not surprising when you consider that Davos is, according to Gulfstream's own records, the one annual event that brings together the largest percentage of its client base. In a typical year, almost 10 percent of all Gulfstream clients—between 140 and 150 jets and their owners— will fly into Zurich's international airport, deposit their guests at the general aviation terminal, and then wait for them as they are limoed up the mountain to the meeting and back.

Gulfstream jets also gather at major international sporting events. One hundred and twenty aircraft descended on Germany for the 2006 World Cup soccer championship, for example. You would have found almost the same number at the airport in Monaco at the time of the Grand Prix. The Geneva Auto Show and the Super Bowl are similarly big destinations, as are the Winter Olympics and the Ryder Cup golf championship. You'll also find large concentrations of such aircraft at the small airport in Sun Valley, Idaho, where Allen & Company holds its annual retreat for leaders of the media industry, or at the airport on Hainan Island where China's Boao Forum takes place.

Airport logs offer a clear indicator of a convergence of the powerful: Satellite shots of clusters of G5s and Falcons on the tarmac serve as a sign of economic activity that seldom shows up in newspapers but one that speaks volumes about markets and power in a rapidly changing world—and about the airborne caravan routes that link the global trade in influence that is at the core of those markets and is the source of much of that power.

For private jet travelers, globalization is not an abstract concept but a day-to-day reality. Travel across oceans or continents is little more than a phone call away. It is commonplace to the point of routine, and it is typically a pleasure instead of a hassle. When these select few— those who consider first class a downgrade—arrive at the airport termi- nal, they do not wait in lines. They are not buffeted by rude airline personnel or security staff, or delayed by an unending stream of cir- cumstances beyond their control. Bags are whisked to aircraft. Arrival arrangements are made by concierges. And in moments, without pass- ing through security, with less fuss than it takes to enter a typical office building today, they are airborne on flights whose routes they deter- mine, whose menus are catered to their needs and wants. If they don't like turbulence, they direct the pilots to fly around it. If they need to conduct business, most of these aircraft have high-speed Internet connections and satellite phone service. They need never leave the "office"—or their comfort zones—as they circle the globe.

This is worth noting not simply because it is so alien to most of us or so appealing; it is also significant because for the CEOs and heads of state and billionaires and financial executives for whom private jet travel has become a way of life, it changes their worldview. "Distance in just an attitude," was how one veteran media executive described it. Barriers are removed. From such a vantage point, the world shrinks. Acquaintances on opposite sides of the globe are easily accessible to one another, and circles of friends and colleagues grow more geo- graphically diversified.

There are six billion people in the world. For half of them—the three billion living on less than two dollars a day—travel much beyond one's own village in a lifetime is unlikely, or in any case a rarity. But for a tiny handful, perhaps just ten thousand, anywhere, anytime is the reality. For them, the greeting card platitudes of globalization are truths proved by their daily existence: Borders have disappeared and the world is truly one global community.

Within this tiny community you will find many members of the world's superclass. This emerging group both shapes globalization more than any other group and is shaped by it more than any other group. As such, it offers a test case for the impact of the evolving "world without borders" while also offering a glimpse into how it is likely to develop. We ought to look closely at the members of this community, their ambitions and their weaknesses and the reactions of others with agendas different from their own. We should look closely because we are likely to see hints of the fissures and the tectonic shifts that will remake the world in major ways during our lifetimes and those of our children and grandchildren.

Each One Is One in a Million

As uncommon as—by definition—they are, we are all familiar with the extraordinary among us.

In almost every human pursuit, levels of talent and accomplishment seldom ascend in smooth, small increments. In sports, for example, the levels of proficiency are more like the quantum levels of an atom, representing substantial, geometrical leaps in capability. The gap between the average amateur and the top amateurs—between the weekend tennis hacker and the ranked college player, for example—is enormous. The gap between top amateurs and average professionals is typically very great as well. The gap between average professionals and those who can play at the top level of their sport year in and year out is yet again exponentially greater. And finally, most strikingly, there is the chasm that separates the top ten or twenty in any sport, and the once-in-a-generation best of the best who appear in ones and twos sprinkled through history. Among millions of dedicated, talented, and enthusiastic athletes, an amazingly gifted few set themselves apart: the Michael Jordans and Pelés of the world. The pattern persists from sport to other human pursuits, from art to literature to politics to business: Tolstoy and Dickens, Rothschild and Rockefeller, Mao and Mandela. These are the few who define the direction for their professions and their eras. They are emulated, become beacons, and very often serve as drivers or catalysts for change. In every era, in every pursuit, there are clusters of such individuals atop their fields—some well-known, some invisible—who dominate the worlds around them.

Markets reflect and reinforce this quantum structure in society in the way they compensate individuals. Of the hundreds of millions of people in the world who play a sport, for example, only a few thousand can earn a living doing so. Analyzing the salaries of professional baseball, football, and basketball players in the United States, two professors at the University of Chicago, Steven Kaplan and Joshua Rauh, found a striking disparity: In 1995, there were 1,259 athletes who earned more than $500,000 a year and only 37 who earned more than $5 million annually (perhaps a surprisingly small number given the headlines those salaries generate). Even accounting for the wage inflation that has affected the top tier of almost every human pursuit during the past decade, the gap remains remarkable and has persisted to the present day. By 2004, the number at the half-million-dollar level had climbed to just over 2,000, and the number making more than $5 million was still only 369—a tiny fraction when you consider that these athletes are drawn from a pool of talent encompassing hundreds of millions. Each one of this top cadre is literally one in a million, perhaps even more elite than that. Of course, some top athletes are compensated for other qualities—popular appeal, for example, or how they look in a tennis skirt. But it is hard to dispute that the likes of Roger Federer or Tiger Woods—the once-in-a-lifetime greats with truly exceptional skills— deserve to be compensated at a different level if they so dominate a sport and drive public attention to it more than any other athletes.

This intensive concentration of recognition and rewards is typical at the top of other fields as well, most often illustrated by compensation levels. This is not true in every area, of course; in fact, modern society exhibits profound defects in the degree to which the best teachers, doctors, and other contributors to human knowledge are not offered the same incentives as those in other fields.

Nonetheless, in those areas where compensation is more directly tied to perceived value, the pattern of a few exceeding the many—and even of the very few exceeding the very top performers—repeats. In 1981, University of Chicago professor Sherwin Rosen wrote a landmark paper on the subject titled "The Economics of Superstars," in which he noted that "certain economic activities admit extreme concentration of both personal reward and market size among a handful of partici- pants." The trend has since been exacerbated by advances in technol- ogy that enhance the visibility of superstars and their ability to better leverage their advantages.

Former treasury secretary and former president of Harvard Univer- sity Lawrence Summers explained it this way: "Once, say seventy-five years ago, if you were the best concert pianist in the world and I was also a good concert pianist, we might make roughly the same thing each year because the way we were compensated was playing at the leading concert halls. There was a circuit and there was room for and demand for a bunch of us to be playing in any given city at any given time. Today, however, the big money is made through recordings, and if I am a record company, who am I going to invest in signing, produc- ing, and marketing? The number one pianist or the number fifteen pianist? And if you are a consumer, why not buy the best recording by the best pianist? So at the top, technology has helped the superstars perform even better than in the past. The same is true with money managers and others who have a unique skill or quality associated with their reputations." For example, one economist observed, Citibank paid Summers's predecessor, treasury secretary Bob Rubin, roughly $20 million a year to join them, because he could easily repay the investment through just a couple of deals brought in or by a small uptick in stock price due to investor enthusiasm about his hiring.

Issues of fairness and burgeoning inequality aside—I will come to those later—it is clear that in field after field, the same pattern follows, with a tiny percentage of superachievers standing apart from the crowd in terms of their compensation.

For the purpose of this book, however, I am focused on the group that illustrates this paradigm as it applies to international *influence*, rather than simply to wealth or achievements in a particular field of endeavor. Roman Abramovich—Russian oligarch, Siberian governor, and owner of the UK's Chelsea Football Club—is one of these elite. Eighty-three-year-old Birgit Rausing, worth $11 billion thanks to her husband's Swedish packaging company Tetra Laval but living quietly in Switzerland, probably is not. Colombian rock star Shakira is one. All but a tiny handful of the world's most famous movie stars are not. Mukesh Ambani—chief executive of India's Reliance Industries and one of the world's richest men—is certainly one, as is his billionaire brother Anil. Margaret Thatcher, Mikhail Gorbachev, Carlos Menem, and Mahathir bin Mohammad were members of the group but aren't any longer. But former leaders like Lee Kuan Yew, Bill Clinton, and Henry Kissinger, who have maintained their international influence, certainly are. Osama bin Laden is one. Cherie Blair, Tony Blair's accomplished wife, probably was but now, with Blair no longer the British prime minister, no longer is. Hundreds of Chinese who are not superclass members today almost certainly will be soon. Only a tiny handful of people living in all of sub-Saharan Africa currently make the list.

Each one is one in a million. Of six billion people on the planet, there are approximately six thousand of them. You can name them in every field of human endeavor. Some are easy to spot: top government leaders from countries that are internationally active, the ones with the kind of political, economic, or resource leverage to influence others. Military leaders from those few dozens of countries with the ability to effectively project force across their borders. The key executives and active shareholders of the world's two thousand leading corporations.

Most of the planet's roughly one thousand billionaires. Dot-com whiz kids. Chinese cowboy capitalists. Arab sheikhs. The giants of Wall Street, London, and other financial capitals. Extraordinarily influential artists, scientists, academics, and writers. Leaders of the world's religions.

The defining, distinguishing feature of these individuals is power, power that on an ongoing basis touches millions or billions of people, not just in one nation but across borders. They employ people or move markets or launch invasions or inflame passions or alter deeply held beliefs. You know them when you see them, not just by their ranking on some magazine's Top 100 list but because they so often take on iconic status within their fields.

They are the few who have accrued immense influence by virtue of talent, work, fortune, or some combination of the three. Sometimes their power is associated with their own personal financial resources. Sometimes it is associated with a political or a religious following they have built up over a lifetime. More often than not it is associated with an institutional role they play, such as being a chief executive, a chief investment officer, or a military chief of staff. Frequently power flows from being in the right place in the right time. Sometimes it flows not from character but from character flaws: ruthlessness, monomaniacal commitment to a single idea, or greed.

It is not difficult to accept that given his or her ability to launch a war without congressional approval, the president of the United States has sufficient power to change millions or billions of lives across borders. So, too, do the heads of state whose decisions might directly impact other nations in terms of trade or alliances or conflict or even indirectly by causing refugee flows or environmental changes. Senior cabinet ministers in foreign and defense affairs, who have the ability to shape diplomacy or command military movements worldwide, have a similar kind of power. At one time many central bank governors were important members of this group, but as the number of viable international currencies has shrunk, the number of these individuals on the list has dwindled. Similarly, leading an NGO that can alter political debates in scores of countries constitutes international influence. The pope is the spiritual leader of a billion Catholics. It is not hard to see how he qualifies.

In addition to its most visible members, this elite includes some who are less easy to identify. Some of these seek out the shadows. Others are slowly emerging from them. These include leaders of terrorist organizations and the masters of organized crime families, from

Hong Kong triads to Russian mobsters. The faceless criminals who direct the world's illegal trade in drugs, arms, counterfeit goods, and human beings are also among the members of the shadow elite.

The Corporate Side of the Superclass

Of all the different types of individuals who make up the global superclass, the single largest group is leaders in business and finance.

There are several reasons for this. For one thing, their power is not circumscribed by national borders, and, increasingly, extends far beyond them. The rise of transnational corporations and financial institutions has driven globalization, and such businesses are now the largest and most significant transnational actors. There are, according to conservative estimates, more than fifteen hundred with annual sales or assets in excess of $5 billion. The individuals in charge of these corporate giants have truly global reach. In contrast, the power of national political leaders originates within the borders of their country, and only those countries with meaningful economic ties beyond those borders, or countries that have sufficient resources to project force or mobilize the opinion of other nations, have leaders who can be counted among members of the global superclass.

In fact, one of the most important phenomena of the global era is the rise of corporations to economic and social roles that are sometimes equal to or larger than those of states—and that are often divorced from the interests of states.

How can you compare the power of companies to the power of countries? In 2007, for example, global GDP was estimated to be $47 trillion. That same year, the top 250 companies in the world had combined sales in excess of $14.87 trillion, equivalent to nearly a third of global GDP and an amount exceeding the GDP of the United States or the European Union ($13.20 trillion and $13.74 trillion, respectively). Just the top one hundred companies had sales worth over $9.72 trillion, and the combined sales of the top five (Wal-Mart, ExxonMobil, Royal Dutch Shell, BP, and General Motors) was nearly $1.5 trillion—larger than the GDP of all but seven countries. Although imperfect, direct corporation-to-country comparisons of sales vs. GDP provide some striking illustrations in terms of economic clout: ExxonMobil is bigger than Saudi Arabia (the world's twenty-fifth largest economy), Wal-Mart ranks between Indonesia and Poland, and General Motors tops Thailand.

Indeed, given the scope of influence wielded by these companies—their potential effect on other industries and companies, their global networks of employees and shareholders—you might argue that they are even more powerful than countries of comparable size. After all, companies determine compensation and work schedules, where employees work and what their benefits are. While government laws guide these decisions, today companies have the option of relocating their operations, and thereby redirecting investment and activity to locations where such obligations are less burdensome. Furthermore, large companies represent large blocs of people, people with political power interested in the preservation of opportunities within their organizations. They also direct resources toward lobbying, supporting politicians, presenting media campaigns to advance their views, and shaping the public debate nationally and internationally. And companies often work together on issues where their interests align, magnifying their power and extending their reach.

For purely illustrative purposes, take all entities with sales or GDP in excess of $50 billion. One would be hard-pressed to argue that these are not among the most powerful economic units in the world. Remarkably, of this group—166 in total at the time of writing this—only 60 are countries, and 106, a substantial majority, are companies. Of course, it is an imperfect comparison. Corporate and national governance structures and reasons for existence are entirely different. GDP is also a measure of value added, whereas sales are not. Also, national government budgets, the money states can spend, are only a fraction of GDP. And one set is linked to national interests while the other is driven by the interests of the major shareholders and the chief executives and the board members who work for them. What is clear, however, is that the individuals running big corporations have extraordinary power and resources. Who they are, where they come from, and what issues are important to them thereby become important issues. It is significant, for example, that of the 106 megacompanies cited above, 91 are based on one side of the Atlantic or the other—53 are based in Europe, and 38 are in the United States. (Eight are in Japan.) Surely this has an effect on how large business groups—and political entities that depend on those large business groups for support—set their priorities. Look at the campaign contribution figures of major political candidates in the United States and you will see that the most successful candidates depend on the ability of networks within companies and industries to raise the mega-amounts they need. In Tokyo, in Brussels, in New York and elsewhere, businesses not only bear the weight of responsibility for funding lobbying efforts but they also create the environment into which government officials go to work before or after public service; they remain the path to wealth, another source of influence. It is also worth noting how this geographic distribution will likely shift in the future with the rise of China, India, and other emerging powers—and contemplating what it may mean when more and more of the companies exerting this influence are transpacific rather than transatlantic in origin.

Although no measure perfectly conveys the scope of the influence of the world's largest corporations, viewed from any perspective it is considerable. The world's two thousand largest corporations at the time of this writing collectively account for $27 trillion in annual sales and $103 trillion in assets. (For a comparison, the total market value of the assets traded in global capital markets is estimated by McKinsey at $140 trillion.) In terms of manpower, these companies employ more than seventy million workers worldwide. If each of these employees has just four dependents, that would mean these companies directly sustain 350 million lives. But, in fact, they sustain several times that by virtue of the jobs that they create through trade with other companies. Thus the decisions of a few thousand individuals, board members, and top management of these companies directly impact the lives of perhaps a billion or more people in the world. Their actions determine job creation or cuts, work conditions and environmental standards, which local politicians are supported and which are undermined. Furthermore, with three to four billion people struggling to make ends meet in the world, the community of those dependent on the decisions of that handful of senior decision makers represents perhaps half (and almost certainly more) of the well-employed on the planet.

The rise of companies to a position of such relative power—and the consequent rise in importance of their leadership—is a fairly new phenomenon. Major companies have been important since the days of the British East India Company and the Hudson's Bay Company, engines of the mercantile greatness of imperial Britain, but nowhere near the presence in the global economy that they are today. Even a quarter century ago their share was significantly smaller: In 1983, the top five hundred companies had revenues equal to 15 percent of global GDP; today that has more than doubled to over 40 percent. Or, as another metric of growing influence and global scope, consider the increase in the number of international subsidiaries of global corporations: In 1962, the one hundred largest corporations in the world had 1,288 foreign subsidiaries. By 1998, the top one hundred had more than 10,000 such subsidiaries. Siemens, a German engineering conglomerate and the world's twenty-second-largest company in terms of sales, has operations in more than 190 countries worldwide; Hewlett-Packard, ranked twenty-fourth, operates in 170.

The power within the global financial community is extraordinarily concentrated. Not only do markets like the United States (which has $50 trillion in assets) and Europe (nearly $30 trillion) dominate the $140 trillion pool of global capital markets, but individual institutions dominate within those markets. According to *Forbes*, there were twenty-one banks and other financial institutions managing assets of at least $1 trillion in 2007. The top fifty financial institutions combined account for $48.5 trillion in assets—more than a third of the global total. The top one hundred account for more than two-fifths: $60.4 trillion.

To give you a further sense of how similar concentrations of control carry over into the realm of individual investors, the richest 10 percent of Americans owned nearly 85 percent of all stock in 2001, with the richest 1 percent of Americans controlling one-third of America's total wealth. It should be unnecessary to note that those who control the greatest concentrations of wealth and those whose wealth takes the form of shareholder equity also therefore have great clout within the corporations whose influence is so great. Shareholder votes determine the fate of boards and managers whose decisions impact, in the case of the largest companies, millions of workers, families, customers, and suppliers worldwide.

Nowhere is the concentration of wealth more astounding than in the case of hedge funds. In just a few years, hedge funds have grown almost exponentially in economic significance, from controlling $221 billion in 1999 to more than $2 trillion by mid-2007. But more important, given their active trading strategies—for example, making money from small movements in the daily prices of securities—these ten thousand funds are, according to some estimates, responsible for between 30 and 50 percent of the trading on most major equity and debt markets in which they participate. That means that the individuals controlling these funds' trading activities, along with a handful of other major institutional and professional investors, play the central role in determining the share price of the world's largest companies. Since share price is what chief executives are charged with maximizing, being embraced or rejected by this group determines the fate of the chief executives of most large global enterprises referred to earlier. Some hedge fund managers are even more hands-on than others when it comes to turning their money into influence. For example, hedge fund billionaire Eddie Lampert has

been at the vanguard of "activist" investment approaches that turn ownership into a transformational tool, as when he bought Kmart, merged it
with Sears, fired Sears management, and rolled up his sleeves and started
making key marketing and merchandising decisions for the merged re-
tailer. Jobs were cut and Sears stock initially rose almost tenfold.

What is more, the three hundred largest hedge funds control 85
percent of all hedge fund assets and the one hundred largest control 60
percent of such assets. Thus, it is only a small fraction, a handful really,
of investors, driving investment decisions that in turn are a referendum
on the future of an also comparatively small group of top corporate
leaders who exert such influence in the world today.

So a picture begins to emerge that suggests that power on the planet
is not only concentrated, it is extraordinarily concentrated. There are
people who are on top and people who are not—and, among those
who are on top, the few at the very top have hugely disproportionate
influence.

VILFREDO PARETO'S ENDURING INSIGHT:
THE 80/20 RULE AND THE SUPERCLASS

Another way to think about the allocation of power and resources in
the world is to explore the stratification of global society along the lines
of the Pareto principle of distribution (also known as the "80/20" rule).
Inspired by an observation made by French-Italian economist and sociologist Vilfredo Pareto with reference to unequal income distribution
in Italy, what later became known as the Pareto principle more or less
observes that for many phenomena, 20 percent of the causes are responsible for 80 percent of the consequences. The corollary for income
allocation would state that 20 percent of a population makes 80 percent
of all income. Pareto may understate matters when it comes to global
wealth distribution, but it's close: A 2006 study by United Nations University (UNU-WIDER) reports that the top 10 percent of adults worldwide own 85 percent of global wealth, while the bottom half of the
world's population owns barely 1 percent of the total.

Though within that top 10 percent, a group that requires $61,000 in
assets to qualify for entry, a similarly stark stratification occurs. While
this particular "elite" controls 85 percent of global wealth, the top 2 percent in this group owns half the planet's wealth, and the top 1 percent
possesses around 40 percent. (Each of those in the top 1 percent owns
a minimum of $500,000 in assets.)

This top 1 percent of global adults, this group of quasi-millionaires, represents about 40 million people. Within this group, however, according to a 2007 report by Merrill Lynch and Capgemini, there are 9.5 million individuals whose financial assets exceed $1 million. And that group, which a Merrill Lynch study has termed High-Net-Worth Individuals (HNWIs), controls over $37 trillion in global assets—double what it controlled just ten years earlier. (Interestingly, growth among this group was most rapid in Latin America, Eastern Europe, the Asia Pacific Region, Africa, and the Middle East, due in part to rapidly appreciating emerging markets asset values.) However, within this group of exceptionally fortunate individuals is another group cited earlier—the 1 percent of them, or roughly 95,000, who each own financial assets in excess of $30 million (these are the UHNWIs, or Ultra-High-Net-Worth Individuals), for a total of $13 trillion. And we know that within this group there is another approximately 1 percent elite, the world's thousand or so billionaires.

While making direct comparisons among multiple studies poses some difficulties, a pattern clearly emerges. Within most elites there are higher tiers of elites; within most concentrations of wealth or power, there are those who represent an even greater concentration. Or to put it another way: When seeking to understand elites, always look for the elite within the elite. Within almost every application of the 80/20 rule there's another one waiting to be discovered. And oftentimes it turns out that an 80/20 rule understates the case. The reality is that when it comes to the unequal distribution of power, we will often find that within the broader application of the 80/20 rule lies a 90/10, or even sometimes a 99/1 rule waiting to be revealed. Of course, this often stops with a single individual or a small group, but the pattern reappears within almost any community we examine.

Or, setting aside the business sector for a moment, consider the power stratification in another arena: the military. Among the world's roughly two hundred armies, there are only between thirty and forty with weapons of mass destruction. There are fewer than twenty with any kind of missile capability, only nine with nuclear weapons capability, only six armies with roughly five hundred thousand or more troops, only three air forces with more than one thousand planes, and arguably, among these, only one that—thanks to its unequaled technology, presence in space, and financial and material resources—is truly capable today of waging modern global warfare. Despite its recent tactical debacle in Iraq, the U.S. military remains a quantum level above all others.

Or consider religion: In the same vein, there are perhaps forty-three hundred religions in the world today, but fewer than twenty have more than one million adherents each, fewer than eight have more than one hundred million, and only two have more than one billion each (not counting the amalgamation of "secular, nonreligious, agnostic, atheist" individuals, of which there are more than one billion). So just two identifiable religious groups—Christianity and Islam writ large—have over one billion adherents each. Naturally, leaders within these groups have disproportionate power. Yes, individual leaders' power is fragmented given the decentralized structures within subgroups (Catholics, Protestants, Sunnis, Shiites), yet it is still substantial.

A SNAPSHOT OF THE SUPERCLASS

Taking into account these concentrations and recognizing those among the wealthy and powerful whose influence extends in a significant way beyond national borders, it is possible to sketch a picture of the global superclass. Take the top officials of the 120 or so governments that have the ability or any proven inclination to meaningfully impact through design or through calamity on major populations beyond their borders. (By this calculus, the nation ranking 157th in GDP, Eritrea, which has periodically waged war with neighboring Ethiopia for years, makes the list, whereas Malta, 129th, under most circumstances probably does not.) Add the leaders of the world's most powerful militaries; the key executives from the two thousand biggest corporations, from the one hundred richest financial institutions, and from the five hundred or so largest global investment firms; the heads of the biggest NGOs and the leading international institutions; and the spiritual leaders from the religious groups that are largest or whose actions may impact others the most. Be sure to include the most important members of the shadow elites—terrorist leaders and criminal masterminds, the most widely read few from the blogosphere. Then throw in leading thinkers, scientists, academics, and artists who also influence millions across borders. Take them all together and you arrive at a rough membership in the superclass of around six thousand, perhaps a few hundred more. Could you define a group of exceptionally influential individuals that is two or three times that? Yes. Are there even smaller circles of ultra-elites within the superclass? Certainly. Are the lower tiers of elites—the ninety-five thousand Ultra-High-Net-Worth Individuals, for example, or additional senior business executives—important? Of course. But this core group of approximately six thousand remains as good a definition of the world's most influential international actors as one might want for the purpose of understanding the nascent power structures they comprise and how they shape the lives of each and every one of us. It is a sample large enough to be representative of groups that altered definitions might make several times larger, yet small enough to be manageable for analysis. It is important to remember also that we are not simply describing the inhabitants of what one recent book characterized as "Richistan"; we are going a step further and limiting our interest only to those who translate their wealth, position, and abilities into the regular application of international power in ways that affect millions of lives. Thus this is just a small subset of the rich lists, the CEO lists, and the lists of the biggest or best known.

WHAT DOES DISPROPORTIONATE POWER LOOK LIKE?

In searching for the elite within the elite, there are many illustrations of global power that simply can't be disputed or denied. There are awesome, even a little frightening cases of truly disproportionate power or influence. To give a sense of what such concentrated power looks like, here are a few examples.

Carlos Slim Helú, one of the richest men in the world with over $67 billion, controls 94 percent of Mexico's telephone landlines and 70 percent of the country's broadband Internet market through the companies he owns. Between 2006 and 2007, his fortune grew by $19 billion, or about $2.2 million an hour, and in 2007 was equivalent to nearly 8 percent of Mexico's GDP. Through his companies, he has used effective monopoly power and huge political influence to push prices up, such that the average monthly phone bill for a small business in Mexico is 120 percent higher than that of a similar business in the United States. According to *The New York Times*, Slim has "used his influence over the government to fight off attempts by competitors—including MCI and AT&T—to get a piece of the Mexican market." Now he extends that control regionally and worldwide by hosting an annual meeting of the richest family groups in the Americas (the Fathers and Sons Forum), and through global business holdings including CompUSA, the Texas-based electronics retailer.

Rupert Murdoch controls media outlets that reach hundreds of millions of people around the world. As of 2007, his News Corporation owned Fox Broadcasting Company, 20th Century Fox, HarperCollins, the *New York Post*, *The Weekly Standard*, *The Wall Street Journal*, MySpace, DirecTV, five British newspapers, 110 newspapers in Australia, and satellite-TV providers throughout Europe and Asia. Because its holdings include Internet sites and services, News Corp. can reach the vast majority of people in the world with a computer. AOL, Yahoo, MSN, and MySpace, for example, together reach approximately 96 percent of all Internet users in the United States.

The president of the United States has ultimate command and control of the U.S. military, the most technically advanced and powerful force in the world. The U.S. military possesses more than 10,000 nuclear warheads, comprises over 2.5 million active and reserve military personnel, and has an active presence in more than 130 countries around the globe. The United States spent more than $630 billion on defense in 2007, more than the rest of the world's defense budgets combined.

Edward C. "Ned" Johnson is, as of this writing, the CEO of Fidelity Investments, the world's largest mutual fund, which accounts for 24 percent of the global 401(k) market and over 12 percent of the world's equity market. It manages more than $3 trillion in financial assets. In terms of influence, consider that Fidelity holds at least 10 percent of the shares of more than one hundred of the United States' largest corporations.

The pope speaks for more than one billion Catholics in the world, or about one-sixth of the human population. His edicts have the effect of law on their daily lives, whether pertaining to the so-called Ten Commandments for Drivers, promulgated in 2007 by Pope Benedict's Vatican, or in his reassertion that the Catholic church is the "one true Church of Christ" and that other Christian denominations lack the "means of salvation."

Wu Xiaoling governs the foreign reserves of the People's Bank of China, which amount to more than $1.4 trillion. The bank controls more financial assets than any other single public financial institution in the history of the world, with the total expected to pass $2 trillion by 2010. It has already extended its reach overseas with a $3 billion investment in the New York–based Blackstone Group. Wu also ranked eighteenth on *Forbes*'s list of the world's most powerful women in 2007—probably an understatement of her global influence.

Rex Tillerson oversees ExxonMobil's energy reserves, which span six continents and produce nearly twice as much oil and gas every day as all of Kuwait. In 2007, his company earned nearly $40 billion in profits, more than the combined GDP of Yemen and Bahrain, and more than any other company in history.

H. Lee Scott, CEO of Wal-Mart, manages a corporate behemoth with annual revenues in 2007 exceeding $350 billion, more than the GDP of all but twenty-two countries. Its annual sales are five times greater than those of Microsoft, and more than those of Ford and General Motors combined. The company is three times the size of the entire U.S. domestic airlines industry.

Lakshmi Mittal's steel company, Arcelor Mittal, is by far the largest in the world, with more than 330,000 employees in sixty countries and factories on five continents. It is responsible for more than one-tenth of global steel production, more than three times the output of its closest competitor. Mr. Mittal is as of 2007 the world's fifth-richest man, with a net worth of more than $32 billion.

WHAT THE PEOPLE WHO HAVE EVERYTHING REALLY WANT

For the members of the superclass, there is a commodity more precious than gold, silver, gems, or oil. It is access. The importance of access flows from the fact that the one thing neither money nor power can buy is time. With limited time and great influence or broad interests, every decision about the allocation of time gathers weight. In speaking to hundreds of CEOs, government leaders, generals, and admirals over the years, the one common complaint I have heard most frequently is frustration with the shackles of time.

Given those frustrations, it is only natural that schedules are meted out carefully and that time is shared only with those who can offer the greatest returns. Sometimes such returns are business or financial deals or political inside information. Other times, they are status or prestige. In any event, it very often means choosing meetings with others who are highly empowered, who can make decisions directly for themselves, who can mobilize significant resources—and whose status is a validator, a demonstration in itself that the meeting is worth having. There is a broad perception that meetings among elite peers are more useful also because few others can understand the position the leaders are in. Aides close to Bill Clinton reported that over time he became very close to other leaders like Britain's Tony Blair and Russia's Boris Yeltsin because they were the only people who truly understood the issues he was facing. Unlike his staff and those around him, who for the most part depended on his approval for their jobs, these few men and women emerged as valued peers and sometimes, as in Blair's case, confidants.

Access and exclusivity go hand in hand, and many aspects of the superclass lifestyle speak to both. Flying in private aircraft, for example, saves precious time and enables small, private meetings to take place in an exclusive setting. It limits access and offers an assurance of exclusivity among those present. Look elsewhere in the lives of the superclass and you will see similar use of the twin tools of access and exclusivity. Visit the office of Indra Nooyi, the CEO of Pepsi, at the company's sprawling offices in Purchase, New York. Although the design of the headquarters is open and light, with sculpture gardens decorating the many acres of manicured grounds, Nooyi's wood-paneled office is located on the executive floor, the farthest from the entrance to the suite, accessible only through the office of a secretary. Everyone is polite and hospitable, but the message to visitors is clear. Surrounded by great windows and views of the parkland setting, Nooyi's office feels like an inner sanctum.

Some offices are much more imperial in nature and isolate their elite occupants even more. Often one must travel down long halls and pass through multiple checkpoints—secretarial or security or both—as was the case for the chairman of Daewoo Industries in Seoul, Korea (before he fled the country to avoid prosecution). The chairman's penthouse surroundings were accessible only via private elevator, perched high atop a hotel he owned, and comprised dozens of rooms full of ancient Asian art. Political leaders often have even more ceremonial offices—settings that emphasize power as well as exclusivity, whether it is in the cavernous ceremonial meeting chambers in the Great Hall of the People on Tiananmen Square in China or the Casa Civil, the presidential palace in Brasília where uniformed guards stand at either side of an entry hall that is the entire, open-air, first floor of the building.

Similarly, participation in high-level meetings or eating in the "best" restaurants or staying in prohibitively high-end hotels or resorts is not simply a luxury or a manifestation of snobbery; it is also an effort to maximize the likelihood of interacting with the people to whom you would wish to grant access and to exclude those to whom you might not wish to grant such access. The same is true about choosing to live or vacation in exclusive settings. A concentration of others with power and wealth increases the likelihood that not only will you interact with such neighbors but also that the environment in which you live will be able to support the special needs of such people and have the tax base to provide essential services (such as security) that might not be available elsewhere, and so on.

For this reason it is not so surprising to find a single street in London such as Kensington Palace Gardens, which has become one of the showcase addresses of the global superclass. There you will find Lakshmi Mittal living in a house for which he paid £57 million in 2004. (The house was once owned by Baron de Reuter, a representative of the superclass of an earlier era.) Nearby you will find not only embassies of ten countries but also homes belonging to the Saudi royal family, the sultan of Brunei, UK real estate mogul Jonathan Hunt, and another poster boy for the global superclass, Len Blavatnik, who made his billions in Russian oil and aluminum. Few cities in the world are so attractive to members of the global superclass as London, given its cosmopolitan nature, its links to every corner of the world, its tax laws, the concentration of others of similar profile and needs, and the infrastructure to meet those needs. As an enclave of the super-rich, its Asian doppelgänger might be Hong Kong, with its lavish Peak neighborhood that is home to three of the four most expensive houses on the continent. Paris, Dubai, Shanghai, Moscow, Mumbai, Tokyo—all have their special neighborhoods for the super-rich. Others can be found in resort communities along the Côte d'Azur in France, in the Hamptons on Long Island, or in West Palm Beach in Florida.

New York, like London, is in a class of its own, but even more so. Its most exclusive addresses play second fiddle to none on the planet, from the Dakota on the Upper West Side (where John Lennon was a resident) to 740 Park Avenue, profiled in Michael Gross's *740 Park: The Story of the World's Richest Apartment Building.*

Once home to the Rockefellers and the family of Jacqueline Kennedy, 740 Park is now the residence of a number of New York's most famous billionaires. Leveraged buyout pioneer Henry Kravis, private equity titan Stephen Schwarzman, and Revlon owner Ron Perelman all have homes at the famed address. The lobby to the building is subdued and the security is discreet, which isn't to say that once you enter the apartments such subtlety is the norm. I once had dinner at the Kravises' apartment, which occupies three floors of the building, and while the evening could not have been more pleasant or convivial, I certainly had the sense that I had entered an alternative universe. A maid greeted my guest and me and led us from the elevator through a gorgeous antique-laden hall into a drawing room in which the gilded paneling, eighteenth-century French furniture, and resplendent paintings by some of Europe's greatest artists were awe-inspiring. Dinner was a more subdued affair, in which the other guests included literary agent Mort Janklow, former deputy treasury secretary Roger Altman, and, to my immediate left, Canadian publishing magnate (and later convicted felon) Conrad Black. Black flirted vigorously with my date, despite the presence of his own wife, as the others debated the relative promise of the world's emerging markets—all the while eating off of china, each piece of which would literally have supported one family in some of those markets for a year. It was breathtaking and, for one visitor, confirmed the building's reputation.

Stephen Schwarzman, during lunch in the Grill Room of the Four Seasons Restaurant on Park Avenue, brought more of the carefully circumscribed world of the elite into focus. Our conversation was friendly and relaxed, over chopped salads and Diet Cokes. The table at which we sat side by side looked out over the rest of a room filled with the likes of David Rockefeller, Washington power broker Vernon Jordan, CEOs from the financial world, the media, the fashion industry—it was as though we were in the cafeteria of the superclass. This was where those who spend their days running giant enterprises come to casually mingle with one another as they hop from table to table, working the room, planning formal meetings, advancing ideas, spreading gossip.

Schwarzman, chief executive of the Blackstone Group, is now acknowledged to be one of the financial world's most powerful men, but he has been prominent on Wall Street for two decades. Today he has assumed roles of prominence across some of the core institutions of American society: He is chairman of the Kennedy Center for the Performing Arts and a board member of the New York Public Library, the New York City Ballet, the Film Society of Lincoln Center, and the New York City Partnership. Much like a good address or the right table at the Four Seasons, such roles enable him to build his networks and advance his interests, tying him in ever more ways to the other members of the leadership communities he seeks to interact with, to do business with, or to influence.

"The world is pretty small," Schwarzman told me during our lunch. "In almost every one of the areas in which I am dealing or in which we at Blackstone are looking at deals, you find it is just twenty, thirty, or fifty people worldwide who ultimately drive the industry or the sector." He noted that his business networks are augmented by the networks he makes serving on the boards of artistic institutions. They afford many opportunities to meet with other similarly inclined members of the elite and to open new relationships, because, just as in business, the world of top artists is interconnected.

"The arts," he observed, "are its own subgroup, and the heads of the major companies in the arts know each other. They develop repertory and other productions that they want to sell to their audiences, not just in their home countries but on a more global basis. Companies travel now. We constantly have different groups at the Kennedy Center, whether it is from Russia or England or Denmark or China or Japan. And so there is almost a seamless subworld in the performing arts— much like the ones you'll find in banking or in politics or business. And people would be just as comfortable dealing with somebody in England or in St. Petersburg . . . in fact, more so than maybe somebody from their own country who is located two states over doing a completely different line of work. It is a very transparent, porous world."

Schwarzman is one of a special breed within the superclass, the crossover elites who are as dominant in finance and business as they are in the arts. He points out that Blackstone today controls companies with over 350,000 employees. "That would make us one of the *Fortune* 20 if we were an industrial company," he commented. That also, by extension, translates into significant influence for Blackstone's major investors—such as China, whose $3 billion stake must be seen as a two-way street, as the people of China become increasingly dependent on the success of the capital system to preserve and expand their national patrimony, and as Blackstone gains access within the PRC.

Schwarzman is not unique in his role as a connector, linking several domains of power. The power elite contains interlocking directorships, not only of companies but of society as a whole. Leadership communities connect across all the important power clusters: business and finance, politics, the military-industrial complex, and the arts and the world of ideas. In fact, such linkages are as distinguishing a characteristic of members of the superclass as wealth or individual position. Trace them and you will find a daisy chain of connections linking remarkably diverse groups. Such connections reduce the degrees of separation between individuals, enabling them to get to the people they need directly, when they need them, to operate at the highest level as efficiently as possible, and in so doing to maintain their status— because access to that level is so jealously guarded by those who have it.

A quick glimpse of a few superclass members drawn from my list reveals the multiple ways such connections may emerge—and parallels in the approach to power and its maintenance and uses that is emblematic of the group as a whole.

Schwarzman can, for the purposes of illustration, be the first in a chain of interconnected superclass members. A quick look at his background offers a number of affiliations that carry with them important networks. One, of course, is that he is chairman of the Blackstone Group. Consider the following language about its variety of holdings from its website:

> Blackstone has invested in over 100 companies in a variety of industries, geographies and economic environments. Blackstone's current holdings include such diverse companies as Celanese, CineWorld, Extended Stay America, FGIC, Freedom Communications, Graham Packaging, HealthMarkets, Houghton Mifflin, Nalco, Orangina, Southern Cross/NHP, SunGard, Travelport, TRW Automotive, TDC, Universal Orlando, Vanguard Health Systems, and VNU. The total enterprise value of all transactions effected up to December 31, 2006, is over $191 billion.
>
> In many of its investments Blackstone has partnered with leading corporations around the world, including Time Warner (Six Flags transaction), AT&T (Bresnan transaction), Northrop Grumman, Sony, Union Carbide, Union Pacific (CNW transaction), USX, and Vivendi.

Schwarzman graduated from an elite university, Yale, where he was, like both Presidents Bush, a member of the secret society Skull and Bones. He also, like the younger Bush, has an MBA from Harvard. He worked at Lehman Brothers before teaming up with former commerce secretary Pete Peterson to found Blackstone. Today, in addition to the cultural board memberships cited earlier and those board relationships associated with his work at Blackstone, he is a member of the Business Council, the British-American Business Council International Advisory Board, the JP Morgan National Advisory Board, the World Economic Forum, the Council on Foreign Relations, and the Committee to Encourage Corporate Philanthropy.

Such boards and memberships offer direct connections to a wide variety of other leaders, and so the daisy chain begins. For example, other members of the JP Morgan advisory network include, from Japan, former chairman and president of Mitsubishi Corporation, Minoru Makihara; one of India's richest men, Ratan Tata of Tata Industries; and former Mexican president Ernesto Zedillo. Makihara attended Harvard, albeit a decade and a half before Schwarzman. Zedillo got his MA and PhD at Yale. Tata is also a member of the British-American Business

Council International Advisory Board. There, he and Schwarzman are joined by current BP chairman and former director-general of the World Trade Organization Peter Sutherland, recently retired BP CEO Lord Browne of Madingley, and Jeffrey Immelt, chairman and CEO of GE. Immelt attended Dartmouth and got his MBA at Harvard. GE has partnered with the Tata Group and done deals with Blackstone. Sutherland, Zedillo, and Makihara are all members of the Trilateral Commission, a nongovernmental policy group—where they are joined by Pepsi CEO Indra Nooyi and by Banesto executive chairman and one of Europe's most powerful female executives, Ana Botín. Nooyi got her MA from the Yale School of Management and serves on the board of Lincoln Center with Schwarzman. Botín is a former vice president of JP Morgan. Nooyi is a trustee of the Asia Society and Tata is a member, as is Tata's rival as India's most important business leader, Mukesh Ambani. Ambani, Schwarzman, Sutherland, and Zedillo are all members of the Council on Foreign Relations. Sutherland, Zedillo, and Ambani's former partner Akhil Gupta are on the board of the World Economic Forum. Botín and Ambani cochaired a panel at Davos in 2006. Schwarzman, Sutherland, Zedillo, and Ambani's brother Anil are all recent Davos participants. Ambani's graduate business degree is from Stanford, as is Browne's. Ambani, Browne, and Immelt served together on the board of Catalyst, a corporate advisory organization. Makihara and Zedillo are on the Coca-Cola International Advisory Board. Browne, Immelt, and Schwarzman are members of the Business Council, an association of business leaders.

Overwhelming and perhaps confusing as this list may be, it reveals the complex nature of connections among members of the superclass. It is, by necessity, a partial list for a small cross section of people, but already it illustrates how tangled the web of relationships between individuals is. For all its twists and turns and intricate linkages, it explains in the clearest way possible how Schwarzman and others in the superclass have come to see their group as such a "small world," with everyone just a connection or two away from everyone else.

So among the roughly six thousand members of the superclass there are countless threads linking members to one another. Business associations. Investments. Board memberships. Old school ties. Exclusive neighborhoods. Aviation terminals. Meetings. Restaurants. Hotels.

In fact, spread around the world though they are, rare as they may be among the teeming billions on the planet, it is easy to see them as a community and to see the geography of that community take shape at least in the mind's eye—a geography that stretches from South Kensington to the Upper East Side of Manhattan; from St. Tropez to Dubai; from the breeding grounds at Harvard, Yale, Cambridge, and Tokyo University to meeting places on the boards of cultural institutions, banks, and political bodies. Linked together by common interests, a common culture, and private aircraft, these islands become a glittering, superpowered archipelago amid oceans of aspirants and of the disenfranchised—oceans of people who work for them, are buffeted by their market decisions, are swept along by their political impulses, are profoundly influenced by their views.

It is not a geography visible on any map, yet it touches lives in the global era more surely than do the fading borders and old distance scales found on any common globe. Over the course of the next several chapters, I try to put that geography into context—in terms of issues, history, and a more detailed look at the membership of this emerging superclass.

SIX CENTRAL ISSUES ASSOCIATED WITH THE SUPERCLASS

In studying this extraordinary landscape, several central themes regularly arise: power, global inequality, governance, global vs. national tension, alternatives, the future. These themes lead to a number of important questions:

What is the nature of the power of the superclass? What are its origins and its scope, and how is it likely to evolve?

Has the superclass used its power in a self-serving way that has exacerbated global inequality? Is there a link between the growing global inequality of wealth and global inequality in the distribution of power? What are the roots of the inequality?

Does the nature of the distribution of power in the global era call into question the relevance of our global legal and governmental institutions? In our effort to preserve national sovereignty in an era demanding transnational governance, are we hampering our ability to address global challenges?

Will the divide in interests between the global superclass and national elites be one of the central conflicts of our era, potentially rivaling and in some ways echoing the divide between capitalist and socialist doctrines in the last century?

Is this the superclass we would choose if we could choose one? How does the superclass fail to reflect in its composition the public at large, and what are the implications of underrepresenting a number of prominent populations?

How is the superclass evolving and what will that mean for us? If the rise and fall of elites is part of the story of every era, what does the nature of this group and its likely fate suggest about our own?

In the remainder of the book I will deal with each of these, sometimes in discrete chapters, sometimes over several chapters returning to the points from multiple perspectives. As with any such complex world-scape, cartographers or census takers can tell only part of the story. Parts of it are best viewed from forty-one thousand feet where, paradoxically, we can see not only the world to the horizon but also the superclass up close, speeding through the rarefied air that is regularly home to so many of them.

CETERIS NON PARIBUS:

INEQUALITY, BACKLASH, AND THE NEW ORDER

An imbalance between rich and poor is the
oldest and most fatal ailment of all republics.
— PLUTARCH

On a rainy night, the El Golf neighborhood of Santiago, Chile, could be an elegant corner of any world capital. The cordillera of the Andes that enfolds the city is shrouded in mist, and despite the mountains' awesome size, they simply disappear into the darkness. All signs of the Mapuche Indians and other indigenous peoples for whom the country has been home for thousands of years have been scrubbed away, pushed back, paved over, built over, towered over by neon signs.

A friend who lived in Chile once told me of a conversation she had with a group of bright, liberal, enlightened Chileans, in which one—a Chilean diplomat—asserted that the country had no indigenous people to speak of. He was right, of course. Because while the Mapuche and other native groups make up more than 5 percent of Chile's population, this guy and his friends simply didn't want to speak of them. When challenged by my friend, they explained that they meant native peoples weren't visible everywhere as they are in neighboring countries like Bolivia and Peru. (In those countries, indigenous groups are not only visible but in recent years, after an absence of half a millennium, have resumed top positions in their national political lives.) But what my friend's Chilean acquaintances revealed was a desire to separate themselves from those native roots, to cast themselves as something different—residents of a piece of Europe that had somehow drifted westward, perhaps, or young globalites representing a culture without a country.

Economically, Chile has no peer in Latin America. It is truly sui generis—a model of development and reminder of what other countries might be if they got their acts together. In a way, Chile has taken a page out of the marketing handbook of 7UP, the American soft drink. As 7UP is the uncola, Chile sells itself to investors as the un–Latin America. When the current foreign minister, Alejandro Foxley, crafted an initiative to link Chile to "like-minded countries," for example, his list included Ireland, New Zealand, and Norway—and no countries from South America.

El Golf has all the obvious trappings of global capitalism: tall towers and Starbucks; malls and Mercedeses; T.G.I. Friday's and BMWs—all mark it as both the most privileged and the most global part of town. Indeed, it is perhaps the most sophisticated such urban neighborhood in all of Latin America. (Residents of Recoleta in Buenos Aires or the Jardins district of São Paulo might argue otherwise, but El Golf can certainly hold its own with any of them.) Some of Chile's richest reside in gated enclaves on the nearby edges of Santiago, while others among the country's upper crust have their vineyards or houses by the sea in Zapallar or Viña del Mar. But El Golf, for all its corporatized, globalized, name-branded sterility, is perhaps the ultimate expression of the Chilean miracle: Chile is the first country in Latin America to escape the cycles of boom and bust, eschewing empty populism and finding both sustained growth and stability.

How did this happen? Chile's geography, location, and size shaped an independent-minded country, fairly isolated from its neighbors and possessing a natural impulse to look outward. Its back is literally against the wall of Latin America: the towering Andes mountains form most of Chile's six-thousand-kilometer border with the continent, almost all with Argentina. The historical relations between the two countries may be illustrated best by the fact that, despite the existence of thirteen major mountain passes connecting them, only one features a paved road, even today. The prospects for a more benign relationship with Chile's other closest neighbors, Bolivia and Peru, declined after the 1879 War of the Pacific. At the time, Chile claimed an important section of the Atacama Desert that included Bolivia's only seaport, Antofagasta, and seized the Tacna and Arica provinces from Peru. They are wounds that still fester.

So Chile had no choice but to look to the sea and beyond. The country's natural resources (copper, timber, agriculture, and fisheries, among others) gave it goods that the world wanted, and despite its location at the far end of the earth—so far off that it is the favored jumping-off point for trips to Antarctica—it immediately had the makings of an attractive trading partner. It was helped in this respect by its early and committed adoption of the market-oriented economic prescriptions of the "Chicago boys," top economists from the University of Chicago and disciples of Nobel Prize winner Milton Friedman. The policies introduced by this group, which called for fiscally disciplined growth and openness to trade and investment, helped fuel Chilean growth for what will soon be two full decades.

In effect, Chile chose to be a trailblazer of the new era that is transforming international markets and today has become something of a poster child for globalization. It has trade agreements with forty-seven countries and is negotiating with several more, making it one of the most open trading countries in the world. Successive administrations have remained true to the principles introduced in the early 1980s, at the forefront of which is a desire to connect with other nations and let markets work their restorative magic without too much interference from the government—even an avowedly Socialist government. As an illustration, I traveled to Chile with then Commerce Secretary Ron Brown. Our mission was to advocate for American business, and one large American company was eyeing a particularly large Chilean contract that was up for grabs. Brown pleaded our case, only to be interrupted halfway through by the minister with whom we were meeting, saying, "These are good points, Mr. Secretary, but here in Chile the government tries not to get too involved in these matters. We believe if we leave it to the market the best company will win and the best projects will get done." Brown couldn't help but chuckle. After traveling around the world promoting market doctrine, he had been out-free-marketed.

The lessons of the Chicago boys were so well learned, in fact, that they became practically a religion. Although Chile is a mostly Catholic nation, it could also be said to be one that worships at the altar of the "Washington Consensus," the prescription of market-oriented reforms that became the primary intellectual product offered by the IMF, the World Bank, and other mainstream international financial institutions during the 1990s. The term was coined by John Williamson of Washington's Institute for International Economics in a 1989 paper in which he described how old and generally discredited development ideas that had resulted in, among other things, the regional debt crisis of the '80s, had been overtaken by what he described as a list of "ten policies that I thought more or less everyone in Washington would agree were needed more or less everywhere in Latin America." As Williamson himself has acknowledged, the list of policy ideas—ranging from privatization to fiscal discipline to broad economic liberalization—has been somewhat lost in the outcry that the term implied the ideas were imposed by Washington, when they really represented an emerging post–cold war consensus about the role of markets and the state. Controversy aside, Chile was so successful in applying the formula—with average growth of around 8 percent a year in the 1990s—that it has often been held up as an example of how to make development work in the global era, not just in Latin America but around the world. Just ask the Russians, who, when communism tottered, were advised to consider "the Chilean model."

NOT ALL BOATS ARE LIFTED

The neighborhood through which we were driving stands as a monument to that history of success. It is a corner of an ancient and beautiful city that is in some ways more connected to New York and Singapore by ideology, temperament, and even culture than it is to poorer neighborhoods a few blocks away. Office towers and gated apartment blocks rise up like graphics on a bar chart, tracking an irrefutable and remarkable rise.

Yet off in the darkness—somewhere off the chart—as invisible as the mountains at night, there is the remaining conundrum with which the country's leaders still struggle: Today Chile's poorest are farther away in economic terms from Chile's richest than at any time in its modern history. The top 20 percent of Chileans earn almost 67 percent of the country's income while the bottom 20 percent earn just over 3 percent. Indeed, not only is the gap between rich and poor in Chile worse than it was during the decidedly unsentimental Pinochet years, it is among the worst in the world on a continent sadly marked by the distinction of producing the worst inequality indicators on the planet.

As the taxi driver sent us skittering down the wet side streets—with completely unjustified assertiveness, given that he clearly had no idea where he was going—I couldn't help but wonder why the famous rising tide wasn't lifting all boats as it should. Some of my development economist friends would point out that the bottom is in fact rising modestly in many places around the world, and that is a positive trend to be sure. But is it tolerable or even sustainable that the gaps that do exist are so egregious, that the economic prescriptions of our age have helped the richest not just more but almost inconceivably much more? Yes, the incentives given to business and investment leaders to motivate them to work harder and trigger growth benefit all. But are the incentives really market incentives, predicated on unfettered economic interaction, or has the system been fine-tuned to disproportionately benefit those who lead organizations, make investment decisions, and run boardrooms? It is true that governments have been unable to do much of what they should to improve the welfare of their people, and in a vast number of cases markets have done much more. But is creating a false choice between governments and markets, as so many politicians have done, productive or practical when neither can do the job of creating a thriving or just society alone?

Perhaps to distract myself from the insane maneuvering of my cab-driver—who, like cabdrivers the world over, was more focused on his cell phone conversation than the well-being of his passengers—I thought back to the conversation with Lawrence Summers at the Charles Hotel in Cambridge, Massachusetts. Summers had suggested that the reason the most economically successful members of society are getting so much more might be that the world is actually becoming more efficient: The system is rewarding the more skilled at proportionally higher rates, giving those with access to technology greater rewards for their heightened productivity, and giving those leading enterprises of growing scale greater returns for their companies' incremental growth. Unfettered markets are doing their job. Isn't it possible, he was positing, that overachievers are now finally able to capture their fair share of returns given their relative talents, productivity, and contribution of value to economic outcomes?

Not a Country But a Country Club

Summers's point haunted me as we drove through the streets of Chile, on our way to a dinner party with one of his former Harvard colleagues, Andrés Velasco, the country's finance minister. In Chile one cannot help but be struck by the very stratified nature of society. There are the poor and the working class, and there are the fairly well-to-do and educated who are making the Chilean "miracle" work. And then there are the few at the very top of the business world who reap hugely disproportionate rewards from that miracle. In fact, for all its progress, Chile is much like a number of other countries in the developing world, in that it has a handful of elite families and individuals who dominate. It is true of the oligarchs of Russia, the men and women who run Korea's *chaebol*, the leading family-owned companies of the Philippines and elsewhere in Southeast Asia, and here in successful Chile. A close Chilean friend who rose up from a privileged corner of that small society once described Chile to me as being "not so much a country as a country club." The club includes a few key families: Angelini, Matte, Piñera, Luksic, Saieh, Claro, Edwards, and a handful of others. According to my friend, "That's the inner circle, and to get anything meaningful done you need some of them on your side."

While this statement is something of an oversimplification, there is much truth in it. Each of these families controls a few key enterprises—timber or airlines or banking or shipping or media—and related groups that produce a wide range of products and services. A few have billionaires among their ranks, such as Anacleto Angelini, Eliodoro Matte, and Sebastián Piñera. Nearly all have significant political clout. Piñera, owner of the country's leading airline, LAN Chile, for example, was the right's candidate for president of Chile in the last election cycle. He is handsome, articulate, self-confident to a fault, and a good and impassioned speaker whose only oratorical weakness is a fondness for hearing his own voice. He did well in the elections and, as one of the country's richest men and one of the leading voices of the opposition to the Socialist government, is a major force in the political, economic, and social life of Chile. Listening to Piñera, one cannot help but believe he is sincere in his desire to help Chile grow and in his belief that the approaches he advocates are the right ones.

This is also an increasingly cosmopolitan group. Talk to any of them and you see very sophisticated, well-educated, often comparatively enlightened global business leaders. Earlier in 2007, I spoke with Andrónico Luksic in his office at the Banco de Chile, Chile's leading privately owned bank, about his active involvement in the markets of Asia. His bank had just opened offices in Vietnam and completed a major investment in Pakistan, and Luksic himself had in fact just purchased an apartment in Beijing so that he could "get a sense of the people and of the place." His perspective was clear: "This is the fastest-growing market in the world in the middle of a large number of other fast-growing markets," he told me, "and I want to get a part of that business. Also, I don't think Chile can compete unless we have close ties and active trade with China and the rest of Asia. That's the future." Luksic understands as well as anyone in the country what it will take to help Chile grow. He is forward-looking and creative, and regularly consults with

President Michelle Bachelet and her government about issues of policy and priorities, often advocating policies that he and others like him in the business community feel will make the country more globally competitive, from improving education to reducing red tape that is seen as an obstacle to investment. He takes part in global conferences like the World Economic Forum's Latin American business summit, which he cochaired in 2007. He, like the others, is as comfortable on Wall Street or in global markets as any business leader you would meet anywhere in the world. There is nothing the least bit provincial or disconnected about this group, as there might have been about most Latin business giants, say, twenty or thirty years ago.

Soon after visiting with Luksic, I spent an afternoon with Alvaro Saieh, a leader of the Chilean business community who also made his money in banking. We met in his mansion, which sits atop a long and twisting road in the foothills of the Andes overlooking Santiago. Turning through the gate into the driveway, one finds a modern triumph of design—evocative of a Roman courtyard, yet full of clean lines that are exceptionally sophisticated and aesthetically pleasing. Saieh too is a thoughtful man, deeply concerned about Chile's future and particularly passionate on the issue of education. He would like to help endow and build a new university for the country, one that will help educate new generations of leaders to be more competitive in the world. "We cannot be complacent," he said. "To continue to grow, to lead, to solve our problems, we have to push ourselves forward." Despite his lavish residence, far removed from the dirty streets of the city, Saieh recognizes his country's shortcomings and wants to use his fortune to find a solution. Like Luksic, he uses international organizations of business leaders as a way to better understand current thinking worldwide and to expand his network of connections. For example, he is an active member of the Group of Fifty, an organization of some of the hemisphere's most important business leaders who meet once a year, typically in Washington but recently in locations as far-flung as China and Santiago.

Yes, Chile's elites are promoting growth and progress and—in some cases—concrete measures to address the country's persistent inequality. But conversations with these elites often contain subthemes that offer a more complex picture. Speaking with a top executive of one of the country's leading timber companies, I could detect something like an unhealthy comfort with and support for the status quo. His company dominates the market, and when asked whether Chile needs to do more to stimulate foreign investment, the CEO became hesitant. Yes, investment is good, he observed slowly, but his words and the pauses he took as he chose those words implied otherwise. Competition from major multinationals is viewed, understandably, with much wariness. Thus far in each of Chile's major sectors only a couple of companies dominate, typically either locally owned companies or companies with-ties to significant local interests. Entrepreneurial activity is noticeably constrained, with few big success stories emerging from small and medium-size enterprises. Chile has grown and modernized, but the social and structural status quo has remained remarkably unchanged—a truth not wholly disagreeable to members of the elite like the timber executive. In many ways the distribution of wealth and power can be traced to historical inequities dating back to the colonial era, not just in Chile but throughout Latin America. Those inequities in turn have been perpetuated by the fact that key assets that could have pro-moted greater equality were available primarily to elites—such as edu-cation, which, when available mostly to the few, actually worsens disparities.

When the issue of addressing such historical imbalances arose in discussion among the handful of Chile's dominant business leaders, however, most framed their answers in the language of the Chicago boys. Ricardo Claro, the head of shipping giant CSAV and owner of one of Chile's most famous vineyards, Santa Rita, supported orthodox eco-nomic reforms during the Pinochet years. Intellectually curious and ex-ceptionally intelligent, he is also worldly, active in elite international circles and well-known outside Chile. But the message that he and many others in the Chilean business establishment offer in conversa-tion, directly or by implication, is a particularly distilled version of the economic prescriptions from the 1980s: "Leave it to the markets. Be patient. Keep taxes low for those who create the jobs." They adhere to the axiom of trickle-down, twenty-five years after the term was coined, even as compelling evidence has built up that, as Cornell University economist Robert H. Frank has written, trickle-down theory is "sup-ported neither by economic theory nor by empirical evidence."

NOT JUST A CHILEAN PARADOX

Our taxi finally arrived at our destination, a modern white stone apart-ment building. From the front door, a maid ushered us across a pristine marble lobby and into a tiny elevator, which took us up to the apart-ment of the chairman of Chilectra (one of two major electric utilities in Chile). As we proceeded, the seeming paradox of Chilean progress remained heavy on my mind. How could the country be so advanced, with a cadre of leaders who are so well educated and cosmopolitan, and yet be home to such intractable problems of income and social inequality?

Entering the apartment, the first person I saw was Andrés Velasco (whose finance ministry, for the record, has been a sometime client of my consulting firm). He was seated in one of those living room chairs of Scandinavian design that are virtually impossible to get comfortable in—yet somehow he appeared comfortable and even serene. Beside him sat our host, Jorge Rosenblut, who was a senior official in a previous Chilean administration and one of the top fund-raisers for current President Bachelet. We were soon joined by the minister of the presidency, Ricardo Lagos Weber; the undersecretary of finance, María Olivia Recart; and the head of the finance ministry's international division, Raúl Sáez. It was a casual discussion among friends, with no business transacted and plenty of very good Chilean wine consumed.

Chile's numerous successes were easy enough to understand. Velasco, who had a brilliant career as an economist leading to his tenured appointment to Harvard's economics department, is a truly blue-chip finance minister, the latest in a long line that has included current foreign minister Alejandro Foxley and former deputy IMF managing director Eduardo Aninat. He had recently convinced the country to save, instead of spend, nearly $20 billion in profits from high copper prices— the kind of move that has led global financial markets to have growing confidence in Chile. When the issue of inequality first came up, early in the evening, Velasco was very thoughtful about it. It obviously troubled him. "Clearly, this is a central problem for us, and a vitally important one for our future," he said. "There is much work that remains to be done on this front just in terms of framing the problem, even before we begin to tackle it. What are the causes? What are our real options? What are the cures that will not make the disease worse? We need to come to grips with problems within our education system, with infrastructure, with job creation, with really opening our economy."

But when it was suggested that meaningful changes would require broad political support, Lagos Weber and the others shook their heads and suppressed smiles. There are opponents of change in the establishment on both the right and the left. They see social spending as potentially inflationary. They view educational reform as overly complicated. And most important, with reference to the key leaders of the business community, Rosenblut noted that "the group that has the most power within the Chilean business community is just too comfortable in this twenty-first century, and the ones who are uncomfortable, the small and medium-size enterprises, don't have that much influence." Many of the charter members of the "country club" see no need to change the membership rules.

The dinner party guests were too polite or too politic to say it, but the reality is that while many of the most powerful people in the country embrace "progress," they use their energy and political capital primarily on behalf of the changes that benefit them most directly. Elites in Chile have implicitly or explicitly resisted the changes that might create more competition, more entrepreneurship, more access to capital for the poor and middle classes. The doctrine of the Chicago boys says that's okay, because it is the doctrine of the rising tide and trickle down—a Reagan-era vintage that, as noted, has not aged as well as the Chilean reds and whites that were highlights of our meal. The mainstream suggestion has always been that patience would be enough; promoting competition and opening to investment would someday translate into creating real opportunity for everyone and making capital much more broadly available.

You can call the ideas underlying that vintage Reagan-Thatcherism. Or you can, in a nod to the intellectual leaders who have driven the phenomenon, call them Volcker-Greenspanism after the high priests at the U.S. central bank. I once heard someone, seeking to frame them in terms of free markets and globalization, call them Friedman-Friedmanism, after the Chicago Boys' mentor Milton and Thomas, author of *The World Is Flat*. But perhaps the best way to characterize this family of ideas is market-marketism, the notion that central planning and big government have proved such a bust that the best way to solve any of society's problems is by leaving it to the markets.

But more than a generation after this doctrine began to be embraced by the world's most influential people—by the evolving new global elite—it is now clear that it leaves many questions unanswered. Markets are marvels in many respects, and the growth produced by free-market policies has benefited billions. But markets don't have consciences and would sooner leave behind the sick, the untrained, and the aging. Markets seek efficiency, and this often means consolidation of resources and power, economies of scale, and considerable human costs. Market-marketism does not deal sufficiently with the inefficiencies, weakness, and failings of markets at producing the kind of just society that is at least as important a goal as fostering prosperity. The genius of the approach is that it suggests good will ultimately come to all in society if we just follow the simple formulas. To me, this sounds a little bit too much like the promise of heavenly rewards that enabled clerical elites to collaborate with political elites throughout history as a way of promoting stability in the face of widespread suffering among the poor. There has to be a better way. There has to be a way that we can harness the power of markets, recognize the limitations of government, and still address the growing, glaring, unjust, and corrupting inequities in our world.

Velasco seemed to sense the need for change and new ideas. He clearly doesn't trust most interventionist, big-government solutions, but he knows that leaving it to the markets is inadequate. "Perhaps," he acknowledged, "we may be at the beginning of a new period of thinking. Perhaps we need to find a new balance." He recognized that for the past quarter century the thinking on which he and other mainstream economists were raised—that of constraining the role of government, promoting fiscal austerity, combating inflation, deregulating, and letting market dynamism drive growth—has not had precisely the results expected. Many have gained hugely and others have lagged far behind, and that, he noted, "certainly calls for some reflection and likely for some new approaches." But he, like many, doubts that this will or should usher in a new era of greater government activism. Yes, government must take the lead in providing the educational and infrastructural resources necessary to be competitive. Yes, it must play a part in regulating the industries that will likely drive growth tomorrow. "I can see there is a role for government there," Velasco said, "but how to balance that with the fundamentals, the things we know work—and what we know doesn't work. That is difficult. That's our challenge."

AND AFTER THE EASY PART . . .

The following day, I met with Chile's former minister of the economy, Jorge Marshall, in his roomy but dimly lit office. At the time the number two man at Chile's central bank, Marshall tackled the issue another way. "We have come a long way, here in Chile," he said. "We stabilized the economy. Controlled inflation. And we then opened up. We embraced privatization and trade liberalization. But the secret is that we did those things because they were, comparatively speaking, the easy things for us to do politically. Fixing the core problems within our society—like the inequality issue and finding new ways to stimulate growth—those are much harder." The necessary reforms, in other words, may not be politically possible, let alone popular.

Chile has achieved a level of economic stability and growth far and above that of many other countries in which inequality remains a huge issue. But, as in Chile, the reforms embraced across Latin America and the emerging world over the past two decades were the ones that suited those who were already in positions of power: the small clusters of families that controlled the largest business groups and the small group of political and military leaders with whom they had established relationships. These elites had run things for years, making money regardless of the conditions in their countries. When, after the debt crisis of the 1980s, banks that lent money to these nations sought reforms as a way of ensuring that their rescheduled debts would actually be repaid, the deals these national elites cut were deals they could live with, crafted in negotiations with the bankers for whom they were the only real customers in each country. Paradoxically, while the banks were unhappy with the bad debt that mismanagement had brought to their clients, ultimately they wanted the clients to survive to borrow again another day. That gave great leverage to governments and to the business leaders and local bankers who consulted and cajoled during the negotiations. The elites embraced privatization because they had the assets that allowed them to borrow and to invest and to own the newly privatized entities. They promoted deregulation because it gave more latitude to the business leadership and diminished the role of government leaders. They welcomed market opening because, as owners of large entities, they were the most likely to benefit from new capital flows and the increased trade opportunities.

But when it came time to address ownership structures that favored—sometimes grotesquely favored—majority shareholders and diminished the rights of minority shareholders, or that produced more competition, those in power dragged their feet. And as trade liberalization connected them to the world, they began to recognize that keeping labor costs down in their countries would help them attract investment capital. Their interests actually grew less and less aligned with those of their workers and more tied to those of the investment bankers and others who could offer them big paydays or accelerated growth (read: wealth creation) for their companies.

This was possible largely because the term "free market"—a bumper sticker description of the complex ideas described among those of Williamson's Washington consensus—is typically a misnomer. There are always rules: those set by governments, like tax structures and incentives, often tuned to promote the development interests successfully promoted by segments of the business community; and those inherent to markets, like the fact that cost efficiency favors the creation of entities of scale, and compensation structures for bankers favor doing fewer big deals for big companies (which also typically have better credit profiles) rather than many for smaller companies or for individuals. Even today, while microlending and other programs target poor individuals, the vast majority of investment capital goes to the biggest firms. In Chile, leaders have cited this as a particular concern linked to underdevelopment of small- to medium-size enterprises in that country.

Amid all this, other factors—factors not traditionally or effectively studied by economists—loomed large and remained largely unaddressed. Among these were issues of a culture that maintained many elements of class structure even in the face of reform. It is an awkward subject to raise because culture is tied up in national identity and religion and even race, and thus is kind of a radioactive subject in development circles, seldom spoken of in polite wonk society. But it is a fact.

Just as we are coming to the painful realization that introducing the institutions of democracy without promoting the true culture of democracy and freedom produces what *Newsweek* editor Fareed Zakaria has described as "illiberal democracy"—Venezuela and Russia are excellent illustrations of the point—we should also be able to see that the same holds true for the institutions and culture of markets. Introducing market structures and approaches without fostering a culture of entrepreneurship, or one that promotes genuine equality of opportunity and rights, will produce "illiberal markets"—systems that will appear to be free markets but will be rife with inefficiencies and injustices. The result will most likely foster destabilizing forces, political and otherwise, and will in any case constrain societies from achieving their full potential. Any such system requires effective legal frameworks that are actively and fairly enforced and, to date, often missing. In the global sphere, in the transnational or supranational realm, oftentimes they have never existed. As Harvard's Dani Rodrik has written, "Globalisation's soft underbelly is the imbalance between the national scope of governments and the global nature of markets. A healthy economic system necessitates a delicate compromise between these two. Go too much in one direction and you have protectionism and autarky. Go too much in the other and you have an unstable world economy, with little social and political support for those it is supposed to help."

Observers like the Nobel Prize–winning economist and Columbia University professor Joseph Stiglitz have argued that elites in Chile and elsewhere in the world have accepted the reforms that suited them, but they have stopped short of accepting the ones that would do the most for society at large. One of Stiglitz's former colleagues and President Clinton's chief of staff, Mack McLarty, suggested that the issue of resistance to change has a generational component. "Generational wealth—and I am generalizing here—but . . . the big families that have been dominant in their economies for a long time, many of them have been disengaged from social issues or concerns," he told me. "They just kind of put the blinders on and run their particular enterprises. Especially in cases where even the patriarchs today are third or fourth generations of wealth and have been insulated their whole lives, they simply don't get it or don't want to get it." As a former *Fortune* 500 CEO, McLarty has known plenty in this moneyed class and seen firsthand the obstinacy that makes reform so difficult.

Moisés Naím, a former Venezuelan trade and industry minister and the current editor of *Foreign Policy* magazine, believes that the problem goes beyond passive resistance. "In many respects, the elites are responsible for the problems of these regions," he told me recently. "How can the Saudi elite not be responsible for what is happening in Saudi Arabia? How can the Venezuelan elite not be responsible for having brought the country to the point where a person like Chávez has ascended to power?" Naím carefully delineates his use of the word "elites," seeking to avoid some of the old traps of class warfare. He is careful not to overstate their influence, but he agrees that, particularly in the developing world, they have been a significant part of the problem for a long time.

My conversations with the leaders of Chile and with experts like McLarty and Naím set off a flood of new questions. If national elites are playing a role in the evolution of inequality at home, do international elites play a similar role on a global scale? How do the aligned interests of global elites influence political, policy, and market developments in these early years of the global era in ways that are affecting inequality? How positively? How negatively? What is the real rather than the imagined role of members of the global elite who exert special influence?

CETERIS NON PARIBUS: INEQUALITY OF POWER, INEQUALITY OF WEALTH

If you toss the term "inequality" into a room full of international economists or policy wonks, it can have the same effect as tossing a rattlesnake into a room full of normal people. All sorts of mayhem ensue.

Fierce arguments break out along fine academic divisions. Inadequacies of statistics are cited. Accusations about motives fly. High horses are mounted. Epithets are thrown.

But the question is central to any study of the existence of the superclass because not only are they at the most extreme high end of the inequality continuum but they are perceived to be the rule setters—and self-interested ones, at that. For this reason, we ought to dig a little deeper into the issue of inequality before proceeding on to other dimensions of the superclass, such as its history, its component parts, its impact, and its future.

As far as I can tell, there are schools of very distinguished, prize-winning economists who assert via extremely well-substantiated academic papers that global inequality is (1) increasing, (2) decreasing, (3) stabilizing, after increasing for some two hundred years, (4) the inevitable result of well-functioning markets distributing rewards to the deserving, and/or (5) a threat to society that will undermine stability and invalidate our assertions about the progress of civilization.

Recently, a long line of books and articles have taken up the cause of inequality, extending the debate beyond academic argument into the field of punditry. Many of these implicitly endorse the theory that inequality is on the rise and blame it on the ultrarich and their fellow travelers, the ultrapowerful. These accusations are often aimed even more specifically at the elite advocates and beneficiaries of globalization, who are seen as a force that may be exacerbating inequality. On the other hand, a number of columnists and business magazine editors defend elites for their role in globalization, believing that by globalizing they will ultimately help create a more equitable system.

To some, therefore, the members of the superclass are the heroes of the process of globalization that will, someday, help the poorest out of poverty. To others they are the "new robber barons," standing astride what observers from the *Financial Times*'s Martin Wolf to *The New York Times*'s Paul Krugman have called a new "gilded age"—or circling it in their G5. They are either pioneers who earn the benefits they reap, or they are exploiters who should beware the impending backlash or global revolution. But they are, in either case, important to the story of inequality.

Now, I'm not one for frittering away time on contorted academic debates while people are starving to death. You can't eat a Gini coefficient (the economic measure of inequality). But I do know a couple of things that are hard to argue with. First, there is economic inequality. Second, it is getting worse in some places. Third, those with the most power are undoubtedly in the best position to fix it—and often also happen to be those who are on the "have lots" end of the have/have-not continuum. Consequently, it is important to lay out a few of the basics of the economic inequality picture.

Nancy Birdsall, the founding president of the Center for Global Development, explained clearly the link between inequalities of wealth and inequalities of power. In a lecture called "The World Is Not Flat: Inequality and Injustice in Our Global Economy," which she delivered at the United Nations University, Birdsall asserted that as a result of globalization, "existing rules tend to benefit most those countries and individuals who already have economic power; it is natural that the richer and more powerful manage to influence the design and implementation of global rules—even those rules meant to constrain them—to their own advantage."

Agree with the point or not—and I will return to this—if we acknowledge that some people are more powerful than others, then we must attribute to them disproportionate responsibility for the nature of the society over which they have influence. According to the United Nations, despite economic gains in many regions, the world is less equal than it was even a decade ago. Gaps exist within countries and between them. For example, the richest countries in the world, such as the United States, the EU, and Japan, are now on average more than one hundred times richer than the poorest, such as Ethiopia, Haiti, and Nepal. A hundred years ago, the ratio was closer to 9 to 1. In fact, the ratio between the GDP of today's richest country in per capita GDP terms, Luxembourg, and today's poorest, Guinea-Bissau, is 267 to 1, when thirty years ago the same ratio between the richest, the United States, and the poorest, Bangladesh, was 88 to 1. The world's billionaires, those roughly one thousand individuals, have combined wealth greater than that of the poorest 2.5 billion. In some places, the concentration of poverty is not unlike the concentration of wealth you find in the United States, Europe, and Japan. In sub-Saharan Africa, almost half of the population lives on less than a dollar a day, while only 3.5 percent of Europeans live with such agonizing, life-crushing deprivation. Even in China, which has shown such remarkable growth over the past two decades, inequality is increasing; in the period between 1984 and 2004, China's Gini coefficient almost doubled, from 29 to 47.

Disputes arise over the interpretation of these figures. One often-cited distinction is the difference between measuring inequality among the peoples of a country and inequality among all peoples. The World Bank's Branko Milanovic has argued that measuring intracountry income gaps is a useful metric when testing the effectiveness of policies. By this measure, inequality has been on the rise for almost seven decades, with a period of "steady and sharp" increase between 1982 and 1994. Some of the lower-income countries, like those in sub-Saharan Africa, have struggled with negative per capita GDP growth for a quarter century, while the developed, free-trading countries of the Organisation for Economic Cooperation and Development have seen their fortunes rise over the same period. However, as Milanovic notes, if you look at this metric and weight the increases by population size, global inequality can be seen to have declined. This is due primarily to the performance of the two most heavily weighted nations, China and India, which have seen some income growth. When one excludes China and India from the list, in fact, weighted inequality is shown to have been on the rise since the mid-'80s, the same as the unweighted results.

However, when seeking to assess inequality not just between countries but among all people, the debate gets a little trickier. Milanovic, in his excellent book *Worlds Apart*, asserts that a global survey of household incomes shows "true inequality"—inequality across all individuals—to be high, with the Gini for all adults in the world nearly sixty-five. He notes that the "hollowing out" of the middle classes in places like Eastern Europe and Latin America caused global inequality to rise between 1988 and 1993, but this trend reversed from 1993 to 1998 as a result of rising rural incomes in India and China.

Professor James Galbraith of the University of Texas takes a similar line on the issue of cross-country inequality. When World Bank economists David Dollar and Aart Kraay offered an argument that global inequality had been declining since 1975 and that "globalizing" countries were outperforming nonglobalizers, Galbraith shot back. "Missing from Dollar and Kraay's list of successes are the true globalizers of recent times," he argues, "including Argentina, until just a few months ago the leading neoliberal poster child, or Russia, now attempting to recover from the collapse that followed shock globalization. So too are the erstwhile 'Asian tigers,' who liberalized in the early 1990s and failed before the end of the decade. Nor are these examples isolated. World growth rates were systematically higher under the structured international financial regime of Bretton Woods from 1945 to 1971 than they became in the era of deregulation after 1980." Asserting that he works from a bigger, more accurate data set (UN vs. World Bank data), Galbraith claims that "rising inequality after 1980 is the rule in this data, with limited exceptions mainly in Scandinavia and Southeast Asia before 1997. The patterns strongly suggest that the forces of globalization including high global interest rates, debt crises, and shock liberalizations are associated with rising inequality in pay structures. Pay is, of course, the major component of income, and if pay inequalities are rising, it is a good bet that broader income and social inequalities are rising too."

Examining inequality within countries presents a more mixed picture. In the last two decades, income inequality has risen in China, India, and most of Eastern Europe and the former Soviet Union, as well as in a number of Latin American countries. In the cases of China and India, extraordinary growth has been heavily concentrated in urban areas, widening the income gap with rural regions. In many countries, inequality has remained relatively stagnant, however, and it appears actually to have declined in a number of both industrialized and developing countries, including Italy, Japan, Bangladesh, Ghana, and the Philippines. Recent studies based on tax data, for example, have found that in the past quarter century the top income shares increased substantially in many English-speaking countries but remained unchanged in Japan and much of continental Europe.

Emmanuel Saez of the University of California at Berkeley and Thomas Piketty of the Paris School of Economics argue that "the rise in top income shares is not due to the revival of top capital incomes, but rather to the very large increases in top wages especially top executive compensation beginning in the 1970s and accelerating in the 1990s." In other words, the guys running the big companies started to make a lot more money. There are multiple explanations for this phenomenon. Some cite the growth of the companies in question. Some cite the advent of compensation packages laden with options. Others cite the market benefits of hiring "brand-name" CEOs and the consequent earning power of high-profile executives. Finally, still others saw it as part of a cycle of self-congratulatory self-dealing among a small community of business leaders who ran companies and served on the boards that approved compensation packages. Whatever the real reasons, the upward spiral of executive pay has in turn triggered another even more high-profile debate.

WAR OF THE RICH AND THE SUPERRICH?

The prominence of this second debate derives from the fact that while global income inequality and the plight of the world's poorest are the stuff of lively debate among economists, NGOs, and the philanthropically inclined, it suffers from lack of broader awareness. The people most directly involved are far away and poor—not exactly the type of audience that attracts advertisers in rich countries. This is especially the case in the United States, where stories about the poorest are left to MTV telethons, *American Idol Gives Back*, and *People* magazine interviews with Angelina Jolie and Brad Pitt.

Shift the focus of the story to inequality in the United States, however, and then it starts to get some attention. Better yet, make it a story about the growing gap between the rich and the superrich—then you get to combine moral outrage with glamour and famous names. Then you've got a story people can care about. In the recent past we have seen stories titled "Revolt of the Fairly Rich: Today's Lower Upper Class Is Seething About the UltraWealthy" (*Fortune*); "The New Rich-Rich Gap" (*Newsweek*); "A New Class War: The Haves vs. the Have Mores," "In Web World, Rich Now Envy the Superrich," and "Richest Are Leaving Even the Rich Far Behind" (all from *The New York Times*). We have also seen a long list of books on the subject, including Robert Frank's aforementioned *Richistan: A Journey Through the American Wealth Boom and the Lives of the New Rich*.

These stories tug at our heartstrings with the plight of the top 1 percent of American earners, who make over $350,000 a year and who watch in despair as most of the spoils go to the top one-tenth of 1 percent (who average $2.3 million) and the top hundredth of 1 percent (who average $14 million). As *The New York Times* explains in its series "Class War," "While the percentage change in average real household income between 1990 and 2004 was an increase of 2 percent for the bottom 90 percent of American households, it increased 57 percent for the top 1 percent and shot up to 85 percent for the top .1 percent and up to 112 percent for the top .01 percent. That is, the richest are getting richer almost twice as fast as the rich." And, as is noted but not underscored, while the rich are getting much richer, most everyone else—well, they are just treading water.

The trend extends beyond American borders. Similar phenomena can be found in Britain, where the superrich have seen their wealth rise by between 500 and 600 percent while average retail prices increased only 60 percent over the same seventeen-year period. Today the top one-tenth of 1 percent in Britain are taking a bigger slice of the pie than at any time in modern history. Rather than wallowing in rich vs. very-rich envy that preoccupies the U.S. press, however, surveys suggest that the British people are more comfortable with the disparity. While almost 90 percent of UK citizens surveyed thought income differences were too large in that country in 1995, the number fell to 73 percent by

2004. *The Economist* explains that the meritocratic aspect of today's nouveau riche has helped their reputation:

> Even compared with ten years ago, more of these fortunes have been earned. Philip Beresford, a professional compiler of rich lists (including a yearly one for the *Sunday Times*), says that when he started counting in 1989, about three-quarters of the fortunes he unearthed had been inherited. Since then his list has expanded from the 200 wealthiest to the top 1,000, which makes direct comparison hard. But he reckons that work overtook inheritance as a source of fortunes in the mid-1990s. His most recent list shows that over 70% of the 1,000 biggest have been made by their owners.

Such magnaminity apparently is not found in the United States. In one of the more influential of the plethora of rich vs. rich articles, Matt Miller wrote in *Fortune*:

> Here's my outlandish theory: that economic resentment at the bottom of the top 1 percent of American's income distribution is the new wild card in public life. Ordinary workers won't rise up against ultras because they take it as given that "the rich get richer."
>
> But the hopes and dreams of today's educated class are based on the idea that market capitalism is a meritocracy. The unreachable success of the superrich shreds those dreams.

As dot-com millionaires stew over the $1.65 billion won by the kids who created and sold YouTube, theories swirl about the underlying reasons for this new phenomenon. Some blame Bush tax cuts that reduced the tax burden on the wealthiest. Others cite new forms of compensation like options grants. Still others cite "the economics of superstars" or other market factors. But Miller gets closer to one essential truth when he talks about how the current phenomenon undercuts the idea of meritocracy. For example, he follows two individuals who both went to Harvard—equally smart, with equivalent skills and advantages, both hard workers—and finds that one ends up a member of the billionaires' club while the other is an attorney "struggling" along on $1 million a year. This creates unsettling questions. Capitalism has been sweetened (made to go down easier) by Horatio Alger–ism: Work hard and the sky's the limit. The assumption is that the playing field is level. Economists imply this when they qualify their analyses with the phrase "ceteris paribus," meaning "all things being equal." But, of course, all things aren't equal. Sometimes one hardworking Harvard graduate has something else on his side: serendipitous timing, a roommate who has good connections, or an interest in some obscure field that suddenly becomes hot.

THE INEQUITABLE DISTRIBUTION OF LUCK

Well, I'm not an economist, but I call it "luck." And one of the key things that leaps out when you study the inequitable distributions of wealth and of power today is that inextricably linked with both is the inequitable distribution of luck.

That sounds like a small thing. Or something light and amusing. But it's not. It is hard to lament the plight of the millionaire whose dumber but luckier classmate becomes a billionaire—or president of the United States. But luck takes all forms. If you happen to be born in the wrong place, like sub-Saharan Africa, for example, that's bad luck. You can be just as smart and as hardworking as the next guy or woman and almost certainly you will struggle more, reap fewer benefits, and die younger. Or you can be born without access to good education. Or you can be born stupid. Imbedded in the Horatio Alger notion is the profoundly inequitable idea that somehow the smart are entitled to better lives than the less intelligent.

Whom you are born *to* is also a matter of luck—and a key factor in determining your earning potential. As far as the American dream goes (or the dream of many other countries), the best measure of whether the system works is social mobility. But Tom Hertz of American University has revealed that in the United States there is "less than a 2 percent chance that an American born to parents whose income is in the bottom 60 percent of all incomes will end up in the top 5 percent. Americans born to parents in the bottom 20 percent, meanwhile, have a 40 percent chance of staying at the bottom." Of the nine high-income countries in Hertz's study, only Britain had a lower rate of mobility. It is hard to maintain the façade of a meritocracy in the face of figures like those.

Of course there are countervailing factors, such as the greater good, and we certainly want a system that gives incentives to the best and the brightest to work their hardest, because that brings more benefits to more people. But such a system can be fine-tuned by those people, once they reach positions of power, so that they get and maintain more.

Nancy Birdsall calls the distinction between these two approaches the distinction between "constructive inequality" (that which is necessary to help fuel growth and provide benefits to society) and "destructive inequality" (that which goes too far is economically inefficient and thus constrains growth or threatens stability as inequity produces unrest).

The question is: When is the line crossed and why do we cross it? Perhaps even more important, how does one transform a destructive system into a constructive one?

For example, of all the cities in the world, New York has the highest concentration of billionaires. A full 5 percent of the *Forbes* billionaires list lives there. That is good and speaks of prosperity, right? But of the more than three thousand counties in the United States, New York County has the highest income disparity. In the late 1970s, the ratio of wealth held by the richest one-fifth to that of the poorest fifth in Manhattan was about twenty to one; today it is fifty-two to one. Is that constructive inequality or destructive inequality? Is it encouraging hard work and promoting growth? Or is it a harbinger of unrest to come?

PREMIUM PAY IN THE EXECUTIVE SUITE

Nowhere does the debate about inequality and fairness get colored by rhetoric and self-interest as much as in the debate about executive pay. Lately this issue, perhaps more than any other, has cast a bright light on the superclass and the system that they have shaped. And effectively no changes have resulted from the choruses of criticism—suggesting that whoever makes the rules isn't listening and is not unsympathetic to the situation of those being criticized.

CEO compensation in the United States has skyrocketed in recent years. Executive pay has more than quadrupled since 1993, and today the average CEO of a large company takes home 364 times the income of his or her average employee (a ratio that is ten times higher than when I started in the working world, in the late 1970s). The numbers are astounding. In 2006, the average take-home for the chief of a *Forbes* 500 company was $15.2 million, but a number of individuals made vastly more than that. Accounting for exercised stock options, Terry Semel, then chief of Yahoo!, netted $174 million in 2006. That same year, Barry Diller of IAC/InterActive took in $295 million, and Ray Irani of Occidental Petroleum made more than $321 million. The compensation king, Apple's Steve Jobs, took home an astronomical $646 million.

The money doesn't stop flowing when the chief steps down, either, as more and more companies have taken to handing out so-called golden parachutes: Home Depot's Robert Nardelli, for instance, reportedly received a $210 million severance package for his six years as CEO (during which the company's value dropped 7.9 percent). Outgoing Pfizer CEO Hank McKinnell left with more than $200 million as well. The board of Exxon (and its shareholders) gave CEO Lee Raymond a going-away gift of $357 million. AT&T bid farewell to CEO Ed Whitacre to the tune of $158 million—in addition to a $1-million-a-year consulting contract, $24,000 annual "automobile benefits," more than $6,000 a year for private home security, $25,000 for country club fees, and free use of AT&T corporate jets. Parting ways was never sweeter.

Juicy pay packages are catching on internationally—an example of U.S. cultural influence that those at the top of the business community, at least, are not so vocal about decrying. The median pay for CEOs of Britain's top one hundred companies in the FTSE (Financial Times Stock Exchange) index was $4.3 million in 2005, almost four times the level of a decade earlier. (The average for CEOs of the top 350 American companies was $6.8 million.) That same year, the head of Dutch baby-food producer Royal Numico took home more than $13 million, then chairman of BP John Browne made $18.5 million, and a French construction company boss, Antoine Zacharias, won a golden parachute worth $22 million when he left the company.

Critics often see astronomical executive salaries as the failure of corporate governance and regulation. On a practical level, a number of factors play into the determination of CEO compensation. One is the boom in stock options, which have grown from $11 billion issued in 1992 to $119 billion awarded at their recent peak in 2000. More salient to assertions about the links between economics and power is the role of boards, which are often appointed by CEOs and which in many important ways depend on CEOs for their positions (even though it is supposed to be the other way around). A 2006 study by finance professors Amir Barnea and Ilan Guedj at the University of Texas found that firms whose boards were "more connected"—with members sitting on boards of multiple companies—granted higher compensation to their CEOs. This suggests that the most popular directors, the ones who had met with the approval of multiple CEOs, were also the most "generous." (A nice term for knowing which side of the bread the butter goes on.) Among firms in the S&P 1500, for example, a chief executive whose firm was in the top fifth of well-connected companies received a 10 percent higher salary and a 13 percent larger pay package than a CEO whose firm was in the bottom fifth.

Another important aspect of CEO compensation is the increasingly influential role of compensation consultants, who advise the contract negotiation process. Since they benefit according to the size of the contracts, they have a vested interest in driving companies to raise CEO pay. Despite having profited enormously from the system in which they thrive, Barry Diller opined in 2006 that "the whole consultant group should be flushed into the East River and no loss would ever be seen by man." Warren Buffett once ridiculed compensation panels for following consultants' recommendations like "tail-wagging puppy dogs." To oppose their advice, he went on, "would be like belching at the dinner table."

Economists cite a host of other reasons for the pay gap between executives and their employees. Steven Kaplan and Joshua Rauh argue that three factors have driven the phenomenon: Technology has helped skilled workers worldwide outproduce unskilled workers. Increasing scale has meant that the stakes are higher for ever-larger companies, and it is therefore more important to find and properly compensate top people. And globalization has borne out Sherwin Rosen's theory of superstar economics, by bestowing the greatest rewards on the superstars or specially talented individuals among us.

An opposing cadre has of course emerged who argue that CEOs simply deserve to earn vastly more than the average worker, and that their salaries are the result of market demand. "There is an incredible shortage of qualified people to manage and lead big companies today," Kenneth Langone, former director of the New York Stock Exchange and cofounder of Home Depot, told *The Wall Street Journal* in 2006. Or, according to *The Economist*, "The lion's share of the executive's bonanza was deserved—in the sense that shareholders got value for the money they handed over. Those sums on the whole bought and motivated the talent that managed businesses during the recent golden age of productivity growth and profits. Many managers have done extremely well over the past few years, but so too have most shareholders."

In fact, recent research and anecdotal evidence show that the link between executive pay and executive performance is tenuous at best. In June 2006, the Corporate Library, a U.S. corporate-governance consultancy, published a report focusing on eleven of the largest companies in the United States, all of which "combined high levels of CEO compensation and poor performance over the past five years." Another study demonstrated that the relative performance between well-known

CEOs (those who supposedly warrant high pay because of their market impact) and lesser-known ones was similar, and that in fact the lower-profile players often performed better. One striking example of overpayment is the former CEO and chairman of packaged foods giant ConAgra, Bruce Rohde, who earned more than $45 million in his eight years at the company and who took home $20 million when he retired in 2005. Under his leadership, ConAgra's share price fell 28 percent, nine thousand workers were laid off, and the company closed thirty-one plants. The company also regularly missed earnings targets and underperformed its competitors. As Harvard's eminent economist John Kenneth Galbraith once wrote, "The salary of the chief of a large corporation is not a market award for achievement. It is frequently in the nature of a warm personal gesture by the individual to himself."

INEQUALITY REVISITED

The distinguished journalist Bill Moyers framed the executive pay debate another way, one that resonates with our overall discussion of inequality: "Aristotle thought injustice resulted from pleonexia, literally, 'having more.' A class of people having more than their share of the common wealth was the characteristic feature of an unjust society. Plato thought that the common good required a ratio of only 5 to 1 between the richest and poorest members of a society. Even J. P. Morgan thought bosses should only get 20 times more than their workers, at most. How quaint," Moyers goes on, when in the United States today that ratio has surpassed 350, and CEOs are taking home annual paychecks in the multimillions or, in a few cases on Wall Street, billions. As so many in the world barely scrape by on a dollar or two a day, one would be hard-pressed to argue that our modern, global society is a just one.

At a development level, economists and others often cite lack of education, little or no access to capital, and social barriers to mobility as reasons for this astounding inequity. David Dollar, Aart Kraay, and others make the case that globalization is helping to close the gap, at least a little, at least in a few places. But for most countries—from Chile to the United States and Britain to the nations that fall far behind in what they are able to offer their people—the problems continue to loom and will do so for the foreseeable future. Inequality fosters tension, undercuts good policy processes, and reveals gross injustices in a world that regularly seeks to congratulate itself on the progress of human civilization. Who is responsible? Who sets the rules for this system?

It is clear that the influence of the few at the top far exceeds that of the many below, and it is hard to ignore the many ways they are the primary beneficiaries of the global order that they shape. To understand them and how we arrived at such a circumstance, not only must we look to the contrasts we find worldwide between the lives of the globalized elites such as those of Davos or Santiago and those of the poorest living not too far away, but we must also go even further, back into the pages of history. There we will find both patterns and lessons that seem strikingly familiar, and important distinctions that set the elites of our era apart from any who have come before them.

3

Lessons of History:

The Rise and Fall of Elites

> History doesn't repeat itself. At best, it rhymes.
> —Mark Twain

Besides the six thousand or so members of the superclass, there are the numerous elites who surround them, work with them, work for them, affect their actions and decisions. Indeed, many of them are important and influential actors in their own right: business leaders, political leaders, academics, former officials, those who shape public opinion and discourse. But these are not the globally superempowered individuals who interest us. They don't have the clout of those at that very highest level of the power pyramid, the members of our one-in-a-million club, the ones whose hands are on the levers of power and influence.

It is important, then, to explore just what I mean when I speak of power in this context. Where does the power of the superclass come from and what does it look like? Those few individuals who are the world's most influential exist in the realms of wealth and business, politics and government, militaries and militias, media and the arts, academia and religion. Within these various groups, they derive, maintain, and consequently often express their power in a few recognizable and repeated ways.

THE POWER OF HISTORY

Throughout history, the best path to becoming a member of any era's dominant elites was to be the offspring of a member of the preceding generation's dominant elites. One of the central reasons for this stems from the two most important allies of the elites of every era: ambition (or as it is referred to in some pursuits, greed) and inertia. The drive that brings people to the top is typically matched by a desire to hold on to the position, power, and possessions that they have acquired, and to pass them on to chosen successors—typically family members. With this in mind, elites have most often tried to accumulate the tools of maintaining power that they feel will be most valuable. These could be armies, titles, or laws to secure their position and keep others from seizing it—everything from rules of inheritance and concepts like primogeniture (passing assets to the oldest male child, perceived as the offspring with the best chance of defending the inheritance) to rules limiting the rights of minority shareholders.

Children raised in an atmosphere of power are educated in its uses in ways that those who are distant from it cannot be. They are taught tricks and given catchphrases to use to help maintain the public's goodwill or cooperation ("noblesse oblige" comes to mind), and they inherit networks of contacts and often a support system of staff and/or institutional affiliates who can assist them and who, as part of the existing establishment, share their desire to maintain the status quo. It is a natural system and one that has helped produce and maintain the class structures that have dominated social hierarchies since the dawn of time. Today, even as some elements of these class structures have faded (such as the relevance of aristocracies), evidence in politics, industry, finance, the military, and elsewhere reveals that those who come from power acquire important advantages in maintaining or gaining it. The access that comes with being a family member provides a range of benefits, whether within an organization run by the family or through the network of other elites established by the family over time. Such benefits might include receiving legacy admissions to the best schools, having financial resources that enable rising generations to pursue their own ambitions, or simply having a name that opens doors. In every field, in every corner of the world, certain family names keep recurring—from the Murdochs and the Bushes, to the Lis and the Tatas, to the Coppolas and the Wallenbergs.

It's true, historical factors were much more important in past eras when elites endured for longer periods of time and movement between classes was more difficult. While such class distinctions clearly remain today (whether we acknowledge them or not), one of the most striking dimensions of our era is the enhanced mobility afforded to many. This does not mean we don't have elites or even that some among them are not entrenched dynasties. Rather, it means that the membership list of the superclass is more volatile than that of most comparable groups at different stages in history.

In fact, as we shall see, the structure of the global superclass is much less stable, much less formal, and much less formalized than that of national or other elites with deeper historical roots. This is as much a result of enhanced mobility and democratization of societies as it is due to the fact that this new elite has had less time to set up mechanisms to ensure its status. In part, the rise of this group and its coalescence in the supranational—and thus often supralegal—void above the structures of traditional governance is a result of an inevitable effort among leaders to find "open spaces" in which to work and assert themselves relatively unfettered. Suggesting that there is more turnover at the top does not deny the existence of the top. There are a number of trends afoot to indicate otherwise, such as the remarkable concentration of recent economic gains among comparatively tiny subsets of society, and movements toward legislation and established networks that might help the current structure grow more stable.

One consequence of the top fractions of a percentile of a society reaping more benefits is that more of those benefits are retained by those closest to them; greater concentrations for this generation give a greater leg up to those who inherit it in the next. Some organizations promote these links, like the annual private gatherings of one of the world's richest men, Carlos Slim Helú, the Fathers and Sons forum that connects the biggest family businesses of the Americas. What is more, showing favor to the offspring of someone powerful is a classic method of gaining the goodwill of both—building relationships with today's elites and helping to create tomorrow's.

THE POWER OF INSTITUTIONS

Among the mechanisms by which people have attempted to make permanent their acquisition of power and property is the development of institutions that can outlive individuals. It is unlikely that those who helped develop the idea of the first corporations could imagine a time when they would be somehow uprooted from the geographical stakes that connected them not only to countries but also to the laws of those countries. Even just a few decades ago, the vast majority of companies primarily did business in one nation because establishing and maintaining connections to more distant locations was so costly and complex. The transportation and communications revolutions at the heart of globalization have changed all that, to the point that today the vast majority of the world's largest companies are international in scope.

Corporations now enjoy transnational status which, while still subjecting them to national laws everywhere, often allows them to exert significant power on the governments whose laws define them. Halliburton derives important revenue from the U.S. government and its U.S. operations, for instance, but when public opinion turned against the company, it moved its headquarters to the Persian Gulf. It happens every day, as companies seek government financing or dispensation to conduct certain activities: When one government won't oblige, they move to another. If American regulations and disclosure laws like the Sarbanes-Oxley Act are too tough or expensive for companies deciding where to list their stocks, they do as a disproportionate number of international new listings have done and choose to list in London instead. If the U.S. Export-Import Bank or the Overseas Private Investment Corporation won't help finance a project, companies that once waved the American flag vigorously in their efforts to win Washington's support lower that banner and instead raise flags in other countries where their subsidiaries make them eligible for those countries' support. I saw this time and time again when in government. And of course, with these moves go jobs and tax revenues and investment dollars and the other benefits associated with a company's location. Countries around the world offer special economic zones, tax breaks, and other inducements, seeking to lure international direct investors who now shop for investment locations in the way people shop for cars, haggling over the deal and playing one national "dealer" against another.

It has been said that an institution is just the lengthened shadow of a single individual. This may certainly be true in cases where institutions are new and the product of one individual's special efforts or in which governance processes place a substantial portion of decision-making authority in the hands of a single individual. But one of the great strengths of modern institutions is that often they represent a core network that extends out beyond the legal limits of the institution's formal structure to include other organizations and individuals with which it deals, buys, sells, collaborates, and otherwise interacts.

This has led some to suggest that the great power of institutions is impersonal and that individuals who run such institutions do not have special power in their own right. There is some merit to this. Certainly one thing that strikes any student of elites throughout history is that more today are associated with great institutions (rather than, say, status derived from family ties or purely from individual accomplishments) than at any time in the past. Nonetheless, in most organizations, one or two—at most just a tiny handful—of senior executives have the preponderance of power to make critical decisions. Perhaps the most important of these have to do with asset allocation, the central decision-making responsibility of any leader, and agenda-setting, the often underestimated tool that as we will see is perhaps the single greatest unifying perquisite of the superclass.

THE POWER OF MONEY

Historically, the definition of being rich was having the resources that enabled one not to have to work for a living. Certainly, in a practical, day-to-day sense, that definition still passes muster. But there is rich and then there is oh-my-God-there-are-countries-with-smaller-bank-accounts rich. I'm not exaggerating for dramatic effect. According to *Institutional Investor*'s *Alpha* magazine list, three hedge fund managers made more than $1 billion in 2006: former math professor James Simons, known for his $6 billion Medallion fund; Kenneth C. Griffin of Chicago's Citadel Investment Group; and Eddie Lampert, discussed earlier, whose largest investment is an $11 billion stake in Sears. That means these three guys—whose companies did not produce anything as tangible as a single paper clip—each raked in annual income that dwarfed the GDP of more than thirty different countries. Given that none of them has to bother with actually running a national government, their disposable resources are presumably available for exerting their influence in other powerful ways, whether by backing political candidates, giving to prominent charitable causes, or investing in other deals that extend their business holdings even more broadly.

When justifying the benefits to society of allowing giant paydays for the wealthy, one of the first rationales given is that such people are best able to reinvest the money and thus create jobs and fuel growth. The merits of the argument aside, it is certainly true that having substantial financial resources translates into that asset allocation power mentioned earlier, enabling those who have it to decide which projects get resources, which ideas are supported, and who will have a chance at big returns in the future. Today, for example, many of the business leaders who grew rich on the information technology boom—Sun Microsystems cofounder Vinod Khosla, Google founders Sergey Brin and Larry Page, AOL founder Steve Case, eBay founder Pierre Omidyar, and Microsoft founders Bill Gates and Paul Allen, to name a few—are all invested in one way or another in alternative energy companies, another "paradigm-shifting" set of technologies. Big companies and national governments have the ability to exert this kind of influence as well: BP has directed hundreds of millions to American universities to help develop next-generation biofuels, while political officials in China have committed more than $180 billion to "clean energy" projects. In a similar way, Gates and Warren Buffett use their foundation money to direct resources to NGOs and academic institutions, and thus, in the words of former Johns Hopkins Bloomberg School of Public Health dean Dr. Al Sommer, "have a profound impact on the direction of public health research and program development worldwide."

But of course money translates into power in many other ways. Take politics in a place like the United States. To run for president in 2008 will require that candidates raise in excess of $100 million each in order to be truly competitive. That means that before there was one primary election among voters, there was a "money primary" in 2007 that selected which candidates voters would see. Although donation amounts to individual candidates are limited by campaign finance law ($2,300 per individual for the primary season and $2,300 for the general election), there are still ways to raise piles of money quickly. You could have powerful people hold large, lucrative fund-raisers, like billionaire David Geffen, the Hollywood music producer and head of Geffen Records, did for Senator Barack Obama. Or you could win generous donations from individuals who circumvent the campaign finance law by giving big to both parties (as opposed to making donations to individuals), as have people like Israeli-American billionaire media mogul Haim Saban, who individually has contributed more than $13 million to various party initiatives as well as campaigns in just the past five years. Or get the leadership in major companies or Wall Street firms to encourage donations from employees. Those firms then become the top sources of funding, increasing the leverage of their leadership among candidates and eventual officeholders. For example, during the first quarter of 2007, the number one donor with over

$500,000 in contributions to presidential campaigns was Goldman Sachs. The next nine companies on the list: Citigroup, UBS-Americas, Credit Suisse, Merrill Lynch, Morgan Stanley, Lehman Brothers, Bear Stearns, and two hedge funds, Fortress Investment Group and SAC Capital.

Similarly, American politics is flush with those who have used their personal fortunes to win political office, from billionaires like New York mayor Michael Bloomberg to the profusion of millionaires who still dominate the American political scene, including names like Kennedy, Corzine, Kerry, Kohl, Schwarzenegger, and many, many others. In fact, 40 out of 100 members of the Senate and 123 out of the 435 members of the House of Representatives are millionaires, which raises all sorts of questions about terms like "representative democracy."

Of course, this is not just an American phenomenon. The list of recent international political leaders who were also extremely wealthy and who used that wealth to help gain political power is a long one, including—to name but a few—Israeli Prime Minister Ehud Olmert; Thailand's Prime Minister Thaksin Shinawatra; Indian actor and member of parliament Amitabh Bachchan; Nigeria's late president-elect Moshood Abiola; Ukraine's on-again, off-again prime minister Yuliya Tymoshenko; French right-wing xenophobe Jean-Marie Le Pen; and Brazilian soybean magnate and governor Blairo Maggi. Silvio Berlusconi of Italy offers a striking example, having used his media empire to dominate the Italian political scene and served five years as prime minister. Lebanon's former prime minister, the late Rafik Hariri, made billions in real estate helping to rebuild Lebanon after the wars of the early 1980s before assuming national office. There are literally hundreds of other examples.

Money plays into political power in other ways, such as the funds doled out to lobbyists. According to the Center for Public Integrity, the top twenty pharmaceutical companies alone spent over $600 million on lobbying between January 2005 and June 2006. According to the Center for Responsive Politics, the top five oil companies alone spent almost $200 million lobbying between 1998 and 2005. Businesses and individuals alike can direct money under the table to political decision makers themselves, or use it toward media coverage to influence public opinion on key issues. Through such an approach, individual companies and industry groups undertake global campaigns to advance special interests, such as pharmaceutical companies' desire to promote the creation and enforcement of intellectual property laws protecting their patents.

Business and financial interests have regularly been at the heart of decisions about war and peace, whether it is the cozy relationship of big oil with U.S. administrations that has resulted in wars to protect their vital supply lines in the Middle East, or the wars to preserve mercantilist business interests during the colonial era, or the resistance of big businesses in the United States to confronting the Nazis prior to World War II. Today there is the pressure of multinational corporations to reduce political and trade tensions between the United States and China. Sure, in many instances there is a direct connection between the interests of these businesses and the national interest, but that is not the case often enough to suggest that this historical power of money to do more than just purchase a luxurious lifestyle has been sufficiently constrained. Indeed, one of the surest signs of the potency of political money is that for all the outcries against its influence, it has managed to forestall real reform. In fact, in the political bloodstream of the United States, money often serves the role of both the red cells, carrying ideas to the heart and brain of the system, and the role of white cells, killing ideas that special interests find threatening.

Outside of politics, money offers additional forms of influence, as the recent boom in high-profile philanthropy illustrates. If Bill Gates's foundation can dole out more money to health care–related NGOs more quickly than the World Health Organization or the World Bank, who then has more influence? Bill Gates and Eli Broad, the billionaire founder of SunAmerica and KB Home, decided they wanted to help improve public schools and have together contributed $2 billion so far. That's good for American society, no doubt. But it also gives these two men considerable influence over the people who seek and later depend on their funding. The same is true across the spectrum of vital institutions of global society that depend on such donations, whether they are NGOs, cultural groups, religious groups, political groups, or other special interest advocates.

The same forces are at play worldwide, of course. Money works its influence publicly, through lobbying and advertising to shape public opinion, for example. Its public influence through political donations and other forms of support, as in the coordinated efforts of groups such as tobacco manufacturers, who are estimated to spend tens of billions of dollars annually worldwide to stem the backlash against cigarette smoking and to promote the sale of their products. In addition, money works behind the scenes in multiple ways. Some of it is benign, such as the coalition of international businesses involved in the fight against AIDS, and other coalitions fighting poverty—all of which seek to promote good government policies and changed behavior through donations, activism, and endowing NGOs to manage these processes. Sometimes the power is behind the scenes—and below the table—as in the case of corruption. For example, when I was in the Department of Commerce, we began efforts to identify corruption by major international corporations where payoffs were made to influence the outcome of deals. Even with very limited resources, we were able to identify instances of corruption affecting nearly three hundred commercial contracts worth more than $140 billion over five years.

THE POWER OF POLITICS

Clearly, the richest would not be drawn to politics if politics did not offer them additional power above and beyond that which they had already acquired through financial or other professional success. Winning (or seizing) political office, or having the ability to influence political decisions, or having a base of political support directly empowers individuals. The source of the power is multifold. It is the power of the institutions that one has leadership within. It is the power of allocating the resources and setting the agenda for those institutions. It is the power to influence the creation of new laws and regulations, which offer the ability actually to institutionalize key ideas. It is the power of the history and national identity associated with those institutions. It is the power that comes from having quantifiable support among the people of a country or region. Government service is seen as legitimizing, as service to the community, with high posts also seen as the capstone of a career (although they often provide additional access and networks that can offer further opportunities for profit postgovernment). This leads directly to many top business leaders taking massive pay cuts to work in government.

The complication in the era of the superclass is that political institutions, for the most part, are linked to nation-states. Those seeking to win or use political power on a transnational basis must choose between working with comparatively weak international institutions and contending with a vast array of uncoordinated, often competitive or conflict-divided national political systems. One of the considerable strengths of the superclass is its ability to build political potency on a cross-border basis, and to do so with both those internationalized elites that also operate within the global economy, and national elites that are important within individual countries. In the absence of global political institutions, the best path to influencing global outcomes is building networks of individuals and organizations that have influence in key countries. This is the special strength of the superclass given its positions, resources, and global orientation, and it is part of the reason that gatherings of these elites are so important—they become hubs at which ideas can be advanced globally. Thus unable to lobby or serve in a global government, the superclass effectively employs a global political strategy the only way possible, via influencing the influencers.

THE POWER OF FORCE

The most primal of all sources of power, the power of force, has fallen on comparatively hard times. To some extent it is a victim of its own success—or excess. The twentieth century saw the marriage of science and warcraft produce devastation on an unimaginable scale. Indeed, one of the great ironies of the cold war is that the United States emerged victorious with an undeniable and unique capability to wage and "win" a global thermonuclear war. But fighting such a war is unthinkable and thus the huge investment in this capability is mooted; the United States finds itself in the difficult position of being militarily paramount but unable to win in asymmetric conflict with a foe or foes such as those found in Iraq or Afghanistan.

From this it can be concluded that having the ability to use force, while a source of some leverage, is nothing like having the will to use that force. Will is the greatest of all force multipliers, as suicide terrorists regularly demonstrate. In today's world, the threat of force remains a potent source of power, but only when the threat is credible. Given that this is rarely the case among the world's most empowered nations, where the economic disruptions caused by war are often too great and where the toll of modern warfare is too high (the lesson of the last world war, one many generations of technology ago, when casualties exceeded one hundred million), those who are most likely to use force become those who have the least to lose. (American intervention in Iraq is a tragic anomaly here, but it is worth remembering that in the prewar "selling" of the invasion, the core ideas from "shock and awe" to the very structuring of the invasion force all sent a message of quick-in, quick-out, of a modern war in which U.S. technology would make it possible for the country to avoid the kinds of costs cited above. As it turned out, of course, a different set of lessons emerged that only validate the preceding point. The United States discovered both that "low-cost" war is elusive and that enemies who feel they have little to lose but who have the will to lose everything can be deadly and difficult to subdue.) Paradoxically, in most circumstances in today's world, force is reverted to more often than not by the weakest (although this does not preclude a return to great power confrontation at some point in the future).

THE POWER OF NETWORKS

During the late 1990s, at the height of the dot-com boom, I helped run a company called Intellibridge that provided open-source intelligence and access to a global network of national security analysts. It wasn't a giant company; in fact, it was a small one, but it did manage to putter along for half a dozen years, serving a modest but fascinating array of military commands, companies, and other national-security-related organizations. The experience illustrated to me in myriad ways the power of networks. Our team, some with policy backgrounds, some with military backgrounds, literally built the company through the networks of people we knew. In fact, our "product" was to a great degree providing access to the special insights of a global network of former and current senior government, military, and business leaders—the ability, thanks to the Internet, to connect the best minds on the ground with planners and policy makers. We built and marketed a network.

During the years I spent working at the company, I witnessed many raw illustrations of the power of networks, but one stands out as particularly vivid. It occurred not in the office but during a birthday celebration for my business partner, former national security adviser Tony Lake. His friends had decided to celebrate with a boat trip on the Potomac. Twenty or thirty people gathered for a dinner cruise up and down the river. It was the waning years of the Clinton administration, to which both Tony and I had belonged, and many current and former officials including CIA director George Tenet came aboard for the ride. At one point that evening I found myself standing along the rail with Leon Fuerth, then the deputy national security adviser.

Fuerth, like a good many others at the party, was deeply involved in managing the war in the former Yugoslavia, and he spoke about the frustrations of the seventy-plus-day bombing campaign the United States was waging against Milosevic. He then began to describe a shift in tactics that he and others had been recommending. Apparently the bombing of "strategic targets" like bridges, roads, and military installations was not producing the desired movement in the Milosevic regime (the idea was to bomb them into submission so a costly ground war did not have to be fought). At the time there was much skepticism that such an air-power-only approach would work, but Fuerth and the others recognized that Milosevic was hardly a leader who worried about the plight of his people. Rather, he ruled the country with and for the benefit of a small cadre of his closest associates—his network. Instead of bombing the standard targets, therefore, Fuerth and the group advocating a new approach recommended destroying the factories and assets of those closest to the ruler so that they would feel the pain and transmit their dissatisfaction to the barbarous head of state the United States was trying to depose.

Soon after the policy was implemented, it began to bear fruit. Shortly thereafter the campaign ended and Milosevic was on his way out. The Serbian leader, like all of us, was perhaps a man of his country, but mostly he was a man of his circle of friends.

Connections with others who are willing to collaborate to advance common interests, to extend influence across groups or around the world, are vital, as they have always been. They are also, thanks to new technologies that make the formation and maintenance of such networks possible across international boundaries, increasingly significant.

These networks were once limited to the hierarchies within organizations one was physically part of, such as families, communities, and institutions. But one of the greatest changes that are a consequence of the twin revolutions in transportation and communications is the ease with which people can form, reconfigure, extend, and draw upon networks in which geography is no longer a factor, or is only a minor one. This is made easier by the evolution of a common culture of global elites: a growing and widespread use of English, common reference to certain information resources, standardization of business practices, metrics, and standards, etc. Consequently, as important as networks have always been, they are even more important today, growing to rival static institutional relationships in many cases.

The connective tissue in such networks can take many forms. The superclass is knit together by its mechanisms of access and exclusion, including family ties, old school ties, membership in exclusive organizations, membership on company boards, relationships forged through working together, relationships forged through deals done together. Indeed, it is rare to find a member of the superclass who does not have comparatively vast networks. When networks are composed of the powerful, each node of the network is by default that much more powerful and the ability to leverage influence that much greater. One can only wonder just how much broader the networks will be for the rising generation of practiced social networkers—the MySpace and Facebook crowd who, if they are anything like my teenage daughters, already have networks numbering in the hundreds before they enter college.

FROM THE WANAXES TO THE ROBBER BARONS: THE RISE AND FALL OF ELITES

Every era has its own elites, and in the history of their rise and fall there are at least three major themes that recur in addition to the consistent aggregation of political, military, and economic power in the hands of a relative few.

Major historical upheaval, including both war and technological or social revolutions, spurs change in the ruling structure and values of societies. "War," Herodotus said, "is the father of all things." And no single phenomenon throughout history does as much to produce change in elite structures as does war, although major technological and social transitions, themselves sometimes accompanied by war, do likewise. This is not simply because wars are fought to change the ruling order. More often than not the changes produced by such upheavals are wholly unexpected and unintended. For example, in ancient Greece, military innovations unexpectedly empowered a new class of farmer warriors (known as *hoplites*), who began to demand greater powers and, when their agitations failed, backed tyrants who upended the old order. In China, the failure of the late Ming emperors to protect their citizens from peasant unrest or raids from the north led directly to the end of the dynasty and the rise of a new elite structure under the Manchu Qing family. Similarly, the United States Civil War, itself a consequence of the country's internal struggle between its agricultural past and its industrial future, altered the economic and social landscapes both with the end of slavery and the flowering of the industrial era that enriched the class of business leaders who were able to take advantage of the birth of a new, continental economy that supplanted the once fairly separate state economies.

Limited or weak institutional constraints invite the changes associated with political and economic "creative destruction." One of the conundrums posed by history is that the same conditions that promote creativity and entrepreneurship also can invite abuse, inequality, injustice, and eventually social upheaval. Yet societies that impose too many rules to preserve order often stifle creativity. For example, Sparta, the most powerful Greek city-state, militarized its society to such a degree that both dissent and creativity were suppressed. Its struggle to contain the population of those it had enslaved, called *helots*, resulted in conditions that made it difficult for it to adapt to changing political and economic conditions at the eastern end of the Mediterranean prior to the unification of Greece under Philip of Macedon. China, which had achieved world-leading feats of exploration and development by the early 1400s, invited its own downward spiral when nationalism and a belief that China had little to gain from the world led to a curtailment of maritime travel and foreign trade. Meanwhile, rival powers, not similarly constrained, gained strength and positioned themselves for their ultimately successful onslaught against the Ming regime. In the post–Civil War United States, Washington did little to regulate most emerging industries even as a tangle of state regulations often produced confusion. Some, like the Vanderbilts and the Carnegies, saw this as an opportunity rather than as an impediment and seized the moment in much the same way as do the statesmen that Henry Kissinger once admired as having "the strength to contemplate chaos, there to find material for fresh creation."

Elites tend to overreach and to thereby trigger a backlash from other segments of the population, typically other elites acting "on behalf" of the people at large. As elites continue to aggregate power, they often go too far, galvanizing efforts by rival elites to challenge their authority or to foment discontent among the public at large. Elites must then either make some concessions to regain their legitimacy and restore the balance of power that allows them to prosper or risk sudden and irreversible change. The oligarchs of ancient Greece competed bitterly with one another, sparking clan conflicts that alienated commoners. As a consequence, the majority of people often sided with tyrants who offered peace in exchange for power. Alternatively, Athenian leaders, fearing the rise of a dictator, adopted political reforms and established democratic institutions that preempted social conflict. As the Ming rulers grew more arrogant and less attentive to the needs of the people, they opened the door—literally, as we shall see—to the Qing rulers, who despite being foreigners were seen to be more responsive. In the United States in the late nineteenth century, the story is the same: The megarich robber barons of industry emerged, their displays of opulence and indifference to the needs of common workers outraged the public, and populist reformers were able to pass a series of antitrust and interstate commerce laws that checked the growth of the industrialists. In each of these cases, it was common for those who championed reform to be members of elite groups themselves. From Solon, Cleisthenes, and Pericles in Greece to the Emperor Kangxi in Qing China, to Teddy Roosevelt in early twentieth-century America, it was the privileged few who stepped in and were accepted by peoples who seemed content to be led and sought a change of leaders only when those at the top proved to be incompetent, ineffective, or insensitive to their obligations to broader society.

Each of these themes is relevant today. Both war and technological upheaval mark our era. Whether you characterize the conflicts as between civilizations or haves and have-nots, a symptom of post–cold war reordering, or the emergence of the global era, it seems clear that we are entering a new landscape while holding on to the vestigial power structures of the past. In an era of networks, most established institutions are still hierarchic. State power is declining and major multinational actors from corporations to terrorist organizations increasingly operate across borders or in the infosphere. While history, money, and local political power and force are still salient, global elites are navigating a world that neither laws nor customs nor traditional governments have caught up to. Like the robber barons who recognized and capitalized on the opportunities of interstate commerce before lawmakers and regulators knew what was happening and had a chance to react, networks of globalizers are defining the times by working around the edges of the old world. And like the robber barons, they are reaping amazing rewards for which they are resented by many. And so the question is posed: If our times are like those past in important respects, what are the implications for tomorrow? And if there is something new happening today, it is important to have the basis to understand just how our elites are different from those of the past. A closer look at my three historical case studies—Ancient Greece, seventeenth-century China, and Gilded Age America—might provide a few clues.

STIRRINGS OF DEMOCRACY: GREECE FROM 2000 TO 323 BCE

Although Greece is known as the cradle of democracy, in its prehistory it was a pretty rough-and-tumble place, ruled, like most of the world then, by force. In the Mycenaean age, for example, each community was organized around a ruling *wanax*, or lord. These lords helped farmers who were having an unlucky patch, thus winning loyalty and reducing the likelihood of rebellion in periodic bad times. The *wanax* was assisted in his duties by a secondary set of elites, called *pasireu*, who were his eyes and ears as well as his agents. Beneath these elites were free citizens who worked in the fields or as craftsmen and who would serve in the military as required. As in many societies, the *wanax* gained power by virtue of his control over sanctuaries and priests and the fact that he presided over religious ceremonies as the people's representative before the gods. The *wanaxes* had title to the lands, controlled the economy, were the interlocutors with the gods, levied taxes, redistributed wealth. They were the highest local powers. But sometime around 1200 BCE, their world was undone by a combination of events including foreign incursions that precipitated mass migrations, bad weather, village-to-village competition, and other factors enabling mercenary bands to fill the power void. Dorians from northwest Hellas invaded southern Greece and the old ways and the Mycenaean age came to an end. Writing, art, great architecture, and detailed craftsmanship largely disappeared for hundreds of years. Populations dropped 60 to 90 percent, depending on the area.

But as is often the case, such downturns contained the seeds of the next rebirth. The *pasireu*, now known as *basileis*, became smaller-scale chieftans, ubiquitous and eager. There were many of them and each had to prove his own worth. They had lost their special status in religious matters and though they officiated at sacrifices, they were not seen as the representative of the people before the gods. By the late ninth or early eighth century BCE, the *basileis* would meet in an assembly to formulate policy under the titular leadership of a paramount *basileus* whose control was itself limited. The council's focus was on generating a consensus because these were leaders who had to persuade their people to follow. The decrease in population meant that more land was available for all who survived. A resurgence began: Gradually a few of the landowning families were able to gain control over more and more of the land, and this new elite emerged as a kind of aristocracy.

The historian A. M. Martin argues that the emergent aristocracy was distinguished not only by their landholdings but, as education once again began to be highly valued, also by the code of ethics they developed. This code called on them "to develop an exceptional excellence (*kleos*) to set themselves apart from others of more ordinary character." *Kleos* could be won not only in battle but also in sport (as in the Olympics, begun during this era) and in social exchange with one another. Significantly, most people lacked the wealth or leisure time to let them participate in the games, rituals, and feasts at which the elites could distinguish themselves. Class differences developed and were even cultivated. Elites were able to justify their leadership roles based on these differences, despite rules that were clearly rigged in their favor.

Greek elites built on this differentiation by intermarrying and shaping cultural distinctions through language and other tools. For example *hoi agathoi* ("the good") came to mean only those born into eminent families, while the poor were derided as *hoi polloi* (literally: "the many"). Growing numbers of poor became dependent on aristocrats for survival as sharecroppers or as *thetes*—hired hands who worked for room and board. It is estimated that 12 to 20 percent of Greek families had enough land to be classified as elites, 20 to 30 percent couldn't support themselves, and 50 percent fell in the middle. The elites altered the political structure to suit their needs, putting more emphasis on the council (which they dominated) and less on any one leader. Nonnobles were kept out of office. An oligarchy was created.

Soon again, however, the middle class grew frustrated, as evidenced by the poet Hesiod, who wrote, "work is no disgrace, idleness is the disgrace." At the same time, families among the elites wanted more and more for themselves and often fought one another. In response to this disorder, J. B. Bury and Russell Meiggs note, "Discontented nobles came forward to be leaders of the discontented masses." Some of these "tyrants" were benign, as in the case of Cypselus of Corinth, described as "courageous, prudent and helpful to the people, unlike the oligarchs in power, who were insolent and violent." However, as Aristotle wrote, "History shows that almost all tyrants have been demagogues who gained the favor of the people by their accusation of the notables."

By the seventh century, Athenian leadership positions were divided among nine archons (leaders) who were elected for one-year terms by an assembly of all freeborn male citizens, called the *ecclesia*. Members of a small circle of wealthy families, called the *eupatrids* ("people with good fathers"), dominated the archonships. After a *eupatrid* named Cylon launched an abortive attempt at establishing a tyranny, the noblemen appointed an aristocrat named Draco in 621 BCE to restore stability and equity. Draco was thus given the opportunity to offer his name to posterity via the term "draconian." When asked why he required the death penalty for most crimes, even nonviolent offenses, Draco replied, "Small ones deserve that and I have no higher [punishment] for the greater crimes."

The public response, in 590, ultimately resulted in the elevation of another leader. An aristocrat named Solon was asked to draw up laws that would ease the plight of the poor without undercutting the elites too much. Solon abolished debt slavery, liberated debtors who were jailed, and canceled the debts of sharecroppers. He also introduced a new political system in which influence was allotted in accordance with wealth: The greater a man's wealth, the higher the office he could hold. For example, the richest could stand for state treasurer, the second tier could become archons, and so forth. Solon also created a Council of Four Hundred to balance the aristocratic Council of Elders (a precursor of bicameral systems such as those employed in many democracies today). Solon was not an egalitarian, but he did provide more balance and mobility within society and was popular as a result.

A subsequent attempt to reestablish a tyranny by an aristocrat named Pisistratus did not undercut Solon's system, and when Pisistratus's son alienated the people of Athens, a power void was created out of which emerged another aristocrat, Cleisthenes. Cleisthenes introduced a series of democratic changes that are still felt in most parts of the world today. He created a constitution that organized the government around villages and neighborhoods (*demes*), each of which was assigned to thirty different larger groupings, and these in turn were assigned to a tribe (*phylai*). This approach undercut the influence of elites on individual regions. He also expanded the Council of Four Hundred to Five Hundred and made representation proportional to population. Cleisthenes' system worked, but more important from his perspective, it was designed to preserve the base of power of his family and other allied noble families. In other words, this architect of many of the basic elements of democracy was acting in his own self-interest. Social cohesion and stability legitimized and reinforced his own power.

The reign of Cleisthenes and the system he introduced helped usher in the classical era in Athens. In this period, before the outbreak of the Peloponnesian War (431–404 BCE), Athens rose to its zenith as it led the formation of the Delian League of city-states and witnessed an explosion in art and culture. However, the war, a twenty-seven-year struggle with Sparta, marked the beginning of the end. When Athens finally fell, Sparta installed a regime of Athenian collaborators whose reign of terror earned them the name the Thirty Tyrants. They were then overthrown by a more democratic regime that reintroduced a greatly watered-down form of democracy. With both Athens and Sparta weakened and unity among the city-states shattered, a vacuum was created into which came Philip of Macedon, who seized control following the Battle of Chaeronea in 338 BCE.

With Philip came the end of the Greek city-states and their experiments in democracy. Their legacy echoes through history, as do the lessons of the consequences of overreaching by aristocrats and the difficulties of fine-tuning a system to balance the power of elites with the rights and expectations of the masses.

THE FORBIDDEN CITY OPENED FROM WITHIN: CHINA IN THE SEVENTEENTH CENTURY

At the dawn of the seventeenth century, Europe was at the height of the Renaissance: Shakespeare was writing plays for the Globe Theatre in London, Rembrandt was about to be born, and Galileo and Kepler were entering their prime. All this and yet no kingdom in Europe or anywhere else could compare with China, home to 130 million people, the world's largest economy, and what historian Jonathan Spence called "the most sophisticated of all the unified realms on earth."

At the center of a carefully nurtured and balanced bureaucracy, within the walls of the Forbidden City, sat the emperor. His political power had for generations been anchored in the economic clout of upper-class landowners, many of whose offspring served in the emperor's bureaucracy. This may sound like a typical aristocratic system, but China was different from Europe in that there were few inherited titles and society lacked the heightened sense of class cohesion found in the West. In a system where land ownership was uncertain, necessity called for groups from one level to work for others but in a relationship that was typically seen to be without exploitation and consequent dissatisfaction.

Nonetheless, by the middle of the century, the centuries-old Ming dynasty found itself sitting atop a powder keg of social instability. Two centuries earlier, before Europe's self-defined "Age of Exploration," Ming rulers had sent their fleets around the world, reaching India, Indonesia, Arabia, Africa, and, according to some theories, the Americas. The great admiral who oversaw this exploration was Zheng He. Europe had nothing like Zheng's massive ships—they reached 440 feet in length and could carry up to five hundred men—and nothing like Zheng, a Muslim eunuch. Yet soon after his remarkable voyages ended in 1433, the emperor issued an edict banning the construction of oceangoing vessels. Once again, China was bedeviled by Mongol invasions in the north, and to the south a military foray into Vietnam was not going well. Buoyed by the general belief that China was superior to the rest of the world, elite opinion turned against trade and foreign contact altogether.

The conservatism and general complacency of Chinese elites had a chilling effect. The ossified and centralized structure of society discouraged entrepreneurship and independent thinking, and the country grew gradually weaker as a result. By the time of Ming Emperor Wanli (1572–1620), China's politics had grown increasingly factional, while the weakened economy made it difficult for the central government to distribute aid or support to the countryside, adding to discontent in rural areas. Wanli was in the midst of a decline of his own. Once a conscientious monarch, by the 1580s he had become frustrated over spats with his bureaucrats about which of his sons should be named heir, over where and when he should be allowed to travel, and by debates among his court over ideological issues. He disconnected. He would go for years without holding audiences or addressing crucial issues. "Considering the emperor's required role as kingpin of the state," writes the historian John King Fairbank, "this personal rebellion against the bureaucracy was not only bankruptcy but treason."

As a result of Wanli's burnout, his coterie of eunuch advisers and the bureaucrats who had access to him gained power. (This is a common phenomenon. When a leader withdraws, is ill, or even just whispers, those around him gain his power. For more on this see Ryszard Kapuściński's *The Emperor*, in which he describes how during court audiences, Ethiopia's Haile Selassie would listen to entreaties and then whisper instructions to an aide, who wrote them down. This individual, known as the minister of the pen, was seen to be hugely powerful as he was the only one who heard the emperor and had his full authority.) The eunuchs took advantage of the situation, charging fees for taking messages to Wanli, assuming the right to collect taxes, and even using military guards to impose their will. Disgrace and damage to the emperor were inevitable.

Foreign raiders from the north and from Japan noticed and exploited Beijing's weakness. Resources became further diverted to pay off the Mongols so they would cease their attacks. Famines spread. And in Manchuria a chieftain named Nurhaci, leader of a group of Jurchen tribesman, saw a moment of great opportunity. Creator of the "banner system," which divided his people into different banners and served as a useful organizing principle, Nurhaci cultivated both his economy and his knowledge of Mings. He and his people were very organized and could manage both complex military campaigns and the well-being of society when it was not at war. Seeking legitimacy, Nurhaci declared the foundation of his Qing ("pure") dynasty in 1616. Around the same time, he identified seven key grievances with the Ming leadership, effectively formalizing his conflict with the power in the Forbidden City. Within the next decade, before his death in 1626, he had captured more than seventy cities in northern China and his heirs were waging successful campaigns in Korea and Mongolia, enticing Ming generals to join their ranks and steadily gaining power at the expense of Beijing.

The Ming response was bumbling. In an effort to divert resources to pay for troops, they cut back their bureaucracy in the northwest, a region that seemed safe. As a result they were unable to collect taxes, and their fiscal crisis worsened. Laid-off bureaucrats were also angered and some took mutinous action, such as Li Zicheng, who in 1630 led thousands of young men in a violent spree across central and northern China. At the same time, plague was decimating villages throughout the country.

As emperor, Wanli's grandson Chongzhen attempted to reverse the problems and reassert control over the bureaucracy, but years of factional fighting and financial problems made it impossible. In 1644, Li Zicheng mounted a massive assault on Beijing and enjoyed considerable success, largely because he exploited anger at the Ming regime. In fact, when he entered Beijing in April, he did so through gates that were opened from the inside. Abandoned by his ministers and his people, Chongzhen hanged himself from a tree in the imperial garden, thus ending a dynasty that had ruled China since 1368.

Soon after Chongzhen's suicide, Nurhaci and the Manchus seized Beijing and spent the next generation cementing control of the country. Once they had done so, they ruled for almost three centuries, in large part because they were able to appeal to both the disaffected masses and the equally alienated elites within the sprawling but respected Chinese bureaucracy. Jonathan Spence writes in *The Search for Modern China* that while Nurhaci was alive, he "would take over the charitable functions of the ideal ruler that had so obviously been neglected by Wanli in his waning years, saying that he would never let the rich 'accumulate their grain and have it rot away,' but would 'nourish the begging poor.'" Nurhaci also gave important posts to former members of the elite, recognizing that the power of the institution of emperor depended on his ability to operate the networks within it. His son, Huang Taiji, and grandson, Shunzhi, continued the tradition, helping consolidate the empire under the Qings.

The six-decade-long rule of Emperor Kangxi, the great-grandson of Nurhaci, oversaw a return to stability in a largely united China. According to the historian Immanuel Hsu, Kangxi "approached the ideal. He was intelligent, understanding, lenient, diligent, conscientious and attentive to state affairs . . . It was under K'ang-shi [Kangxi] that the insecure Manchu rule was turned into a stable and prosperous state." Other accounts concur.

In many respects, Kangxi became the first Chinese emperor since the era of Zheng He to constructively reengage with the world. He led the conquest of three southern regions that had been ruled by Chinese defectors, captured Taiwan, and, in the face of the threat of conflict in the north, negotiated China's first treaty with a foreign power, the Treaty of Nerchinsk, which set the boundaries with Russia in much the same position they are found today. At home he traveled widely, cut taxes, and patronized both the arts and education. To build support with his Manchu base he respected Manchu religious practices and replaced eunuchs with Manchu leaders. To foster allegiance among the Han, he invoked Confucian values as a foundation of his rule and the kingdom. With typical shrewdness, he created a new system of exams to give the fifty wisest applicants a special degree and then assigned them to write a history of the Ming dynasy, thus demonstrating deference to those his family had conquered. In short, Kangxi finished the work that Nurhaci had begun one hundred years earlier and achieved what Spence calls "a depth and extent of power matched by only a few rulers in times of China's earlier greatness."

Again the lessons resonate. Complacency is fatal for elites. Neglect of power is as corrosive as abuse of power. By even the fifteenth century, disconnecting from the world at large carried a high price. And again and again popular unrest has paved the way for one elite to unseat another. Nothing succeeds like good governance.

ROBBER BARONS OR INVENTORS OF MODERNITY: AMERICA AFTER THE CIVIL WAR

"Had they been Tyrian traders of the year B.C. 1000, landing from a galley fresh from Gibraltar, they could hardly have been stranger on the shore of a world so changed from what it had been ten years before," wrote Henry Adams on his family's homecoming to the United States in 1868 after ten years overseas. As Adams observed, the Civil War had transformed America. The economy burgeoned, growing from a real GDP of $72 billion in 1860 to almost $170 billion twenty years later. Two decades after that, America's GDP was flirting with $400 billion. (It would be over a century before such growth would be approached again, with the rapid rise of China and Asia's tigers in the late twentieth century.)

The war effort had produced an industrial bonanza in the North that resulted in a remaking of the rosters of the country's richest. The term "millionaire"—although in use since the late eighteenth century—was popularized in the United States in the 1840s, when the richest Americans boasted fortunes in the range of $10 million to $20 million. By the 1880s and '90s, the wealthiest had built fortunes in the hundreds of millions, and by 1892 there were more than four thousand millionaires identified in the United States. While the middle 60 percent of the population enjoyed unprecedented social mobility, the poorest quintile remained fairly stagnant, and the richest simply got much, much richer. Commenting on the opportunities offered by the war economy, railroad and banking mogul Daniel Drew observed, "It's good fishing in troubled waters."

Theirs was a time of great upheaval: the first total war, the world-changing inventions of the Industrial Revolution, and the integration of the American economy. The tycoons of the Gilded Age were also unfettered by institutions that might have regulated the rough-and-tumble business that brought so much wealth to the fortunate few. The emergence of a class with such extreme wealth produced political backlash and led to the rise of reform groups like Grangers, Greenbacks, and Populists. Drawing on the century's most radical "big idea," it also produced the notion of social Darwinism, which suggested that growing inequality was inevitable; it implied that successful businesspeople were somehow more highly evolved than the less successful. While the theory is now seen as antiquated and more than a little ugly in its implications, many historians hold that the business titans of that era were, while perhaps not more advanced in their evolution, at least more complex than simplistic descriptions and denigrating titles like "robber baron" would suggest. To some, students of economic history in particular, these individuals were reformers and innovators, ushering in a period of great growth through applied creativity. The business historian Maury Klein writes, "Although no group of people has done more to shape and change every aspect of American life since 1850 than the great entrepreneurs, no group is less understood or more defined by clichés."

Sketches of two of the era's most prominent business leaders will almost certainly do more than broad overviews to illustrate the period's contradictory elements and the degree to which many are so relevant today. Andrew Carnegie and John D. Rockefeller are real forebears of today's superclass in ways that are considerably more direct and easier to see than, say, Pericles or Kangxi (though I would argue both are somewhere in the DNA of the current group).

Andrew Carnegie: Conflicted King of Steel

The father of the steel industry, Andrew Carnegie worked hard to ensure that he was remembered well. He was the model of the conscientious industrialist, preaching as he gave away much of his fortune in his lifetime, "The man who dies thus rich, dies disgraced." Yet Carnegie was not precisely what he seemed to be to the public. While a champion of a just society and unfettered individual initiative and a noted philanthropist, he also embraced a social Darwinist view that justified his wealth and the struggles of those who worked for him. He fancied himself a hero of the working man but tacitly approved one of the most violent attacks on strikers in American history, in which more than one hundred were injured and thirteen killed. He gave away hundreds of millions but slashed workers' salaries, offering to many just the barest necessities of life. In the parts of Pittsburgh he built, there was little plumbing and no paved roads. On his watch, according to one biographer, "one fifth of all Pittsburgh men, most in the prime of their life, died due to accidents—a large majority were in the iron, steel, railroad and construction industries—and the rate was probably even higher as many accidents went unreported." Thousands died of typhoid from drinking water from polluted rivers. Homestead, the site of his most advanced ironworks, was described as "hell with the hatches on."

Arriving in America from Scotland at the age of fourteen, Carnegie got his start as a telegrapher, an entry-level participant in the communications revolution of his age. Soon after, he was hired as the personal telegrapher of Thomas Scott, the Pennsylvania Railroad's general superintendent, who recognized considerable qualities of intelligence and industry in Carnegie and, soon after getting to know him, invited him to be a partner in an investment in the Woodruff Sleeping Car Company. Admittedly, the company supplied sleeping cars to the Pennsylvania Railroad and thus a considerable conflict of interest was involved, but this also ensured success, and Carnegie's initial fortune was made. "Blessed be the man who invented sleep," Carnegie later said.

When Scott was promoted to vice president of the railroad, young Carnegie, only twenty-four years old, was promoted to superintendent of the railroad's Western division. From there, Carnegie reinvested his sleeping car proceeds in a new industry built up around the discovery of "rock oil" in western Pennsylvania. He did so well that he soon resigned the railroad job and focused on his own enterprises, which included paying $500 to hire someone to fight in his place in the Civil War, a common practice among the wealthy. Thereafter he moved into a series of investments in railroad bridge construction, iron production, and the telegraph business before finally settling on steel. He later wrote in his autobiography that he had decided to "put all good eggs in one basket and then watch that basket," adding, "I believe the true road to pre-eminent success in any line is to make yourself master in that line . . . The men who have succeeded are men who have chosen one line and stuck to it."

Carnegie embraced the most modern steel-production techniques, focusing on scientific innovation and readying the industry for the kind of mass production that could meet the demands of a rapidly growing U.S. economy. He began to integrate his company vertically along the entire supply chain, buying coke, coal, ore producers, railroads, shipping lines, and a variety of mills. Through such a strategy he was able to manage costs much more effectively and compete in ways that less integrated competitors could not. He sought to dominate and crush competitors. He was brutally demanding of his workers and seldom gave them much beyond further encouragement to work harder. By 1899, Carnegie Steel was the largest steel company in the world, with total production equal to half that of Great Britain and supplying one quarter of America's steel.

Recognizing the value of friends in high political places, Carnegie supported politicians such as James Blaine, who ran unsuccessfully for president and later became secretary of state, and Benjamin Harrison, who was elected president in 1889 and rewarded Carnegie by appointing his lawyer to the Supreme Court. The lawyer, George Shiras, was confirmed in a week even though he had neither judicial nor political experience—the only Supreme Court justice to be so unqualified. Lack of qualifications did not stop Shiras from being a friend of industry, however. In *U.S. v. E. C. Knight*, he voted that the American Sugar Refining Company had not violated the Sherman Antitrust Act even though it controlled 90 percent of its industry. Later he cast the deciding vote declaring the income tax unconstitutional, and soon after upheld an injunction sought by the government to break a strike at the Pullman Company. Carnegie became a confidant of Harrison, and it may or may not be a coincidence that even though the president signed the Sherman Antitrust Act into law, his administration prosecuted only one case during his tenure.

In March 1901, Carnegie retired, selling his company to J. P. Morgan for $480 million. With this asset and several others, Morgan created U.S. Steel, the first company with a capitalization over $1 billion. Its capital—then amounting to 7 percent of America's GDP—was twice that of the capital stock for all the national banks in the country. Through its subsidiaries, U.S. Steel employed more people than lived in the entire state of Maryland and controlled two-thirds of the steel market. Meanwhile, Carnegie's attention turned to philanthropy, where he set a standard for generosity that exceeded the ruthlessness he had shown in business. He gave away $350 million in his lifetime and his major trusts and foundations remain active today, including the Carnegie Trust for the Universities of Scotland, the Carnegie Dunfermline Trust, the Carnegie Institute, the Carnegie Endowment for International Peace (where I am a visiting scholar and where I did the work on this book), the Carnegie Hero Fund Commission, the Carnegie Institution of Washington, and the Carnegie Corporation. He is also responsible for building more than twenty-five hundred libraries throughout the English-speaking world.

Carnegie's record of philanthropic generosity is remarkable and stands in stark contrast to his unwillingness to share any of his gains with his employees. Though he wrote passionately about the right to form unions, he forced workers at one of his plants to renounce unionization in writing. While families in Pittsburgh had to earn $600 a year to stay out of debt, he paid many of his employees less than $400 annually. The lowest workers made $300, almost ten thousand times less than Carnegie. "It is a waste of time to criticize the inevitable [gap between the classes]," he wrote in an essay titled "Wealth" in 1889. According to his social Darwinist views, the concentration of riches among the few resulted from the unequal distribution of talent. In that same essay he went on to write that "wealth, passing through the hands of the few, can be made a much more potent force for the elevation of our race than if distributed in small sums (through wages) to the people themselves." He suggested that higher salaries "would have been wasted in the indulgence of appetite, some of it in excess, and it may be doubted whether even the part put to the best use, that of adding to the comforts of the home, would have yielded the results for the race as a race." In his autobiography, written after his retirement, he exhibited an about-face: "If I returned to business tomorrow, fear of labor troubles would not enter my mind, but tenderness for poor and sometimes misguided though well-meaning laborers would fill my heart and soften it." Is it a contradiction that the brutally competitive—like Carnegie or Bill Gates, who crushed competitors like bugs—might then become so intently and productively philanthropic? Or is their embrace of charity just another way of exercising power and ensuring their legacy with a clear conscience?

Carnegie's success as a donor certainly helped offset the reputation he might have had as a result of his tough business tactics. He approached giving systematically, identifying a hierarchy of worthy investments and ranking them from highest to lowest priority: universities, libraries, hospitals and laboratories, parks, music halls, public baths, and finally churches. Not only did others appreciate this commitment, so, apparently, did he. At the opening of the Carnegie Library in Allegheny, Pennsylvania, attended by Carnegie's friend Benjamin Harrison, Carnegie offered a moving tribute—to himself: "The poorest citizen, the poorest man, the poorest woman that toils from morn till night for a livelihood (as, thank heaven, I had to do in my early days), as he walks this hall, as he reads the books from the alcoves, as he listens to the organ and admires works of art in this gallery equally with the millionaires and the foremost citizen, I want him to exclaim in his heart: 'Behold all this is mine.'"

Others were less impressed. "We'd rather they hadn't cut our wages and let us spend the money for ourselves," steelworkers told a Pittsburgh newspaper. "What use has a man who works twelve hours a day for a library, anyway?"

John D. Rockefeller: "The True Embodiment of His Age"

Thin, aloof, pious, John D. Rockefeller looked like a parody of the bloodless businessman. But in many respects he was the singular author of the modern era. No other American has created a greater fortune; in constant dollar terms his was the greatest of all time. His business was oil. In *The Prize: The Epic Quest for Oil, Money & Power*, Daniel Yergin explains that Rockefeller's Standard Oil "operated according to the merciless methods and unbridled lust of late-nineteenth-century capitalism; yet it also opened a new era, for it developed into one of the world's first and biggest multinational corporations." Simply put, Rockefeller was "the single most important figure in shaping the oil industry." Ron Chernow, the author of a magnificent biography of Rockefeller, notes, "By creating new industrial forms, Rockefeller left his stamp on an age that lauded inventors, not administrators." His multinational corporation became a model that literally would transform the world.

Sensing a void in Gilded Age America, Rockefeller helped create a new economic order. Where the government failed to regulate industries effectively, he grew so large that he regulated them himself. Before federal incorporation laws, Standard Oil—a national company from the start—had to contend with a mishmash of state laws that hampered business and invited corruption. But Rockefeller was inspired to find a way ahead that created a new kind of company. And when that company grew so large that the Supreme Court mandated its breakup, in 1911, he was hardly defeated. The component parts of the Standard Oil empire grew independently to be even more valuable, increasing his wealth to $900 million. Chernow writes: "More than anyone else, Rockefeller incarnated the capitalist revolution that followed the Civil War and transformed American life. He embodied all its virtues of thrift, self-reliance, hard work, and unflagging enterprise. Yet, as someone who flouted government and rode roughshod over competitors, he also personified many of its most egregious vices. As a result, his career became the focal point for a debate about the proper role of government in the economy that has lasted until the present day."

Rockefeller and a group of partners started an oil-refining enterprise when he was only twenty-four. From the beginning he wanted to expand the company, but his partners were more cautious, and in order to pursue his vision Rockefeller bought them out. The early days of the oil business were full of start-ups and small operations, the costs of entry were low, and Rockefeller saw an opportunity to step in and dominate. Within four years, with his like-minded partner Henry Flagler, he began to build a company that could subdue any competition. In 1870, the two established Standard Oil, a joint-stock company that would enable them to raise the kind of capital they needed to expand, increase efficiency, and thus enhance profits. The company got its name from the commitment that Rockefeller made to produce a standardized and consistent product, an important development in a day and age when inconsistent production of kerosene resulted in five to six thousand fatal accidents a year.

Flagler used Standard's increasing size to negotiate preferential freight rates with the railroads. This was the kind of not-quite-legal advantage that larger companies enjoyed before such practices were eliminated with the Interstate Commerce Act and the 1903 Elkins Act. One year after starting Standard, the company launched the South Improvement Company (SIC), a cartel of the region's largest refineries. Not only did this group enjoy freight rebates, but railroads also agreed to pay Standard a fee every time they transported crude from nonmember refineries. As a consequence, the more competitors produced, the more SIC would make. The historian John T. Flynn dubbed this "drawback" scheme "an instrument of competitive cruelty unparalleled in history." But given the competition among railways, the Rockefeller approach had the advantage of ensuring traffic to all. He promised to become the industry's "official umpire," thus solving major challenges for both the oil and the rail industries in one stroke. When the plan was discovered, it produced a chorus of protest and had to be abandoned, but while it worked, Standard and the railroads benefited greatly.

In the wake of the SIC setback, Rockefeller embarked on an acquisition initiative. From 1872 to 1879, Standard bought refineries in a pattern that involved making reasonable offers for available properties and, if the offers were not accepted, undercutting the prices of the resistant producers and driving them out of business or back into Standard's arms. Rockefeller's careful attention to detail and efficiency enabled him to shrewdly undercut competitors. When he discovered that it took forty drops of solder to seal a can of kerosene, for example, he suggested that they try thirty-eight drops. When a fraction of these cans leaked, he suggested trying thirty-nine. This worked and became the new, infinitesimally cheaper standard. The approach—focusing both on massive scale and on the smallest detail—produced extraordinary results. By 1879, nine years after Standard was organized, the company controlled 90 percent of America's refining capacity.

With the wisdom of the Qing emperors, Rockefeller invited the best managers of companies he acquired to join him at Standard's headquarters at 26 Broadway in Manhattan. Unlike Carnegie, Rockefeller was regarded as an excellent manager. He was comfortable with delegating and committed to building consensus among his directors. His one special quirk was an insistence on secrecy that later would lead the world to wild speculation about what was actually going on behind the plain stone façade of the lower Manhattan office building.

Rockefeller's company did not face the same kind of labor problems that had beset Carnegie. Because Standard became a virtual monopoly so quickly, it ultimately did not face the pressures of competition that often caused price cutting and might negatively affect the ability to pay workers a decent wage. Rockefeller resisted unions but paid above market and introduced the idea of employee stock ownership, declaring, "I would have every man a capitalist, every man, woman and child.

I would have everyone save his earnings, not squander it; own the industries, own the railroads, own the telegraph lines."

Despite this view, Standard's dominance and its practices went too far for some. Investigations and even an indictment for criminal conspiracy were levied against the firm and Rockefeller in 1879. Nonetheless, he continued to work to build efficiencies. When the law prevented Standard from owning companies outside the state of Ohio, Rockefeller named three employees to serve as trustees of out-of-state assets. This maintained appearances even as dividend checks for the trustee-owned companies were passed on to thirty-seven shareholders of Standard (of which Rockefeller was by far the largest). But this was an awkward arrangement and Rockefeller devised the idea of creating a holding company: It would consist of nine trustees that would hold shares in each of the state companies owned by Standard. The trust, according to Yergin, "made possible the establishment of a central office to coordinate and rationalize the activities of the various operating entities—a task made more urgent by the growing scale of the business. And the trust gave Rockefeller and his associates the shield of legality and the administrative flexibility they needed to operate effectively what had become virtually global properties." The approach was soon copied by companies in a host of other industries, notably many in the agribusiness sector.

In response, a movement began among members of the public and political elites to rein in what they saw as overly powerful companies. Indeed, according to the historian Richard Hofstadter, for many Americans trust-busting became "a way of life and a creed." The first major legislative initiative to contain the trusts was the Interstate Commerce Act of 1887, which specifically sought to end the discriminatory multitier pricing of the railroads. The act was full of loopholes, however, and the railroad industry took full advantage of them. Three years later came the Sherman Antitrust Act, which prohibited "trusts and combinations in restraint of trade" and threatened serious punishment for violators. The act itself was more a triumph of intention than execution, given its many ambiguities, and companies like Standard hardly paid it any heed. Rockefeller even supported Senator John Sherman's reelection efforts in 1891.

The public mood took its toll elsewhere. Ohio successfully sued Standard for violating its state charter as a consequence of transferring control to out-of-state trustees. While this led to the dissolution of the trust in 1892, Rockefeller took advantage of New Jersey laws that now allowed companies to own shares in other firms and created Standard Oil of New Jersey to supplant what had been the Standard Oil Trust.

The company's capital increased 1,000 percent. It quickly acquired holdings in forty-one other companies, which in turn controlled numerous others. And so the company had changed its legal clothes but underneath it was the same giant: John D. Rockefeller remained firmly in control and raked in the profits. Between 1893 and 1901, Rockefeller's share of Standard dividends was approximately $65 million.

By 1897, he had shifted some of the management responsibilities to top directors, but he remained the face of the company and was the target of repeated and high-profile investigations and journalistic critiques. For all the fervor of his critics, changes were relatively few and unthreatening to the company until the assassination of the recently reelected President William McKinley, which opened the door to the presidency of Theodore Roosevelt.

Like Pericles, the reformer of this era came from the aristocracy, a rich New York State family that could hardly have been expected to become the bane of the moneyed class. Roosevelt was a former crusading New York police commissioner and governor, and a complex character. Hofstadter writes: "He despised the rich, but he feared the poor. While bigness in business frightened the typical middle-class citizen for economic reasons, it frightened Roosevelt for political reasons." Roosevelt was afraid that the growing clout of the trusts and other large corporations might overwhelm that of the elected government. He did not want to do away with large companies, which he saw as inevitable by-products of national growth. Rather, he felt the government should play a more effective regulatory role. In his first inaugural address he said, "Great corporations exist only because they are created and safeguarded by our institutions; and it is therefore our right and duty to see that they work in harmony with these institutions." And while he was more talk than action for much of his presidency, he not only fueled the progressive fervor in America but took a number of important steps to address the situation. He established the Department of Commerce, the Department of Labor, and a Bureau of Corporations empowered to investigate companies. He also signed the Pure Food and Drug Act and the Hepburn Act, which strengthened earlier regulations directed at the railroads. Among other moves that resonate today, he sought to prohibit corporations from providing political funds. Many of the initiatives Roosevelt championed were not adopted until the next administration, that of Woodrow Wilson, but the foundational steps he took were indispensable.

As for Rockefeller, Roosevelt's government brought suit against Standard Oil in federal court under the Sherman Antitrust Act in November 1906. It was one of forty-five antitrust cases prosecuted by his administration. The decision came in 1911, with a majority opinion that read, "We think no disinterested mind can survey the period in question [after Standard's incorporation in 1870] without being irresistibly driven to the conclusion that the very genius for commercial development and organization . . . soon begat an intent and purpose to exclude others." The government gave Standard six months to dissolve itself. The pieces became Exxon, Mobil, Chevron, Sohio (which later became the U.S. subsidiary of BP), Amoco, Conoco, Arco, and Sun. In 2006, the collective sales of these successor organizations was $963 billion. If they were still a single corporation, they would equal three times the next largest, and their combined sales would exceed the GDP of Russia.

Rockefeller lived to be ninety-seven. His wealth of $900 million exceeded the U.S. federal budget by $185 million and at its zenith was equal to 2 percent of U.S. GDP (three times Bill Gates's share today). But, like Carnegie, he gave most of it away, establishing among other institutions the University of Chicago, the Rockefeller Institute for Medical Research, and the Rockefeller Foundation. One grandson, David, became chairman of the Chase Manhattan bank. Another, Nelson, became vice president of the United States. Another, Winthrop, became governor of Arkansas. A great-grandson, Jay, at the time of this writing serves as senator from West Virginia.

Rockefeller's most influential progeny, however, are the companies that succeeded the one he built, and perhaps even more so the ideas that shaped those companies. Thanks to his unparalleled success, his guiding principles and practices have not only influenced the shape of every multinational corporation on earth today but have led to a profound shift in world power structure. His legacies in this regard have included a wide range of contributions, from his collaborative style of management to his centralized ownership but decentralized decision structure, from his focus on consolidation which he described as "cooperation" and his ideas about the vertical integration of enterprises, to his political strategies and views on charitable giving. The actions of the successor companies to Standard Oil in reshaping much of the modern world, leading the exploration for oil in the Middle East, Latin America, the former Soviet Union, and now Africa, have changed the international order, giving once small and secondary nations great influence even as those companies exerted great influence within and on behalf of those nations. Today the energy industry is the world's largest and most influential, and the mark of John D. Rockefeller is still squarely on it. More broadly speaking, multinational corporations themselves have risen up to rival nations in economic and political clout while exceeding countries in their ability to maneuver across borders—much as Standard Oil initially did across state lines in the United States. In a way, these companies have followed the lead of Rockefeller in seeking to stay a step beyond the controls of the regulatory environment while all the while trying to influence it. The breakup of Standard Oil in fact produced a new generation of multinationals that continued to grow out and across borders and dominate the competition even if they never achieved the complete mastery of a single market that the initial company did when it controlled 90 percent of the U.S. oil market. At the same time, Rockefeller, like Carnegie, remains a model of the corporate titan who is both an innovator and a symbol of the great disparities of his era. Like the modern CEOs and investors who are his heirs in this regard, he was an example and a lightning rod.

In much the same way as we still feel the effect of the democratic innovations of Cleisthenes and Pericles, much as we feel the consequences of the leadership of Nurhaci and Kangxi and their role in laying the key foundations of today's Chinese ascendancy, we are still grappling with the implications of the changes these giants of the Gilded Age ushered in, and wondering whether in fact Theodore Roosevelt's concerns about the relationship between them, their companies, and government were well founded. Yet his concern takes on a different resonance and greater urgency when companies are multinational and operate in a realm in which government influence is diminished by everything from lack of jurisdiction to the mobility of business organizations. At the same time, as companies grow globally, they also grow in resources and potential influence. So does a concern from an era of trust-busting echo even more troublingly today.

As we have seen, every era of elites has been marked by overreach on their part and a consequent backlash. The question many are now starting to ask is whether our own time will see the same, whether current efforts to rein in CEO salaries and trim tax advantages for private equity companies are the extent of that backlash, or whether, given the global scope of the activities of current elites, it will take a different form, perhaps a further institutionalization of the reaction against globalization or perhaps something new, unexpected, more sweeping, and even more disruptive in its implications.

To understand the answer to this question, we need to study our own superclass more systematically. Mills's model is useful here, and so in the next four chapters I will do as he did and consider our current elites in clusters—business and financial, political, military, and those who influence through the power of ideas (religious, media, and cultural leaders). Not only does such an approach reveal the differences among these groups but it also allows us to explore how the global nature of the superclass sets it apart from past generations of elites. It also lets us see how these groups are evolving and consider the implications of that evolution.

Nowhere are the changes coming more rapidly than in business and finance, and no group is better adapted to the global nature of the current era. In many ways these elites have come to dominate and define the superclass—and the successes and challenges associated with it—much as their predecessors, Rockefeller and Carnegie, did their own gilded and divided age. And so, I will begin my examination of the clusters that comprise modern elites by following the money.

4

THE MULTINATIONAL MOMENT:

WHEN FINANCE AND BUSINESS BECAME THE CENTER OF IT ALL

> To turn $100 into $110 is work. To turn $100
> million into $110 million is inevitable.
> —EDGAR BRONFMAN

When I first met Mikhail Khodorkovsky, he was not an oligarch, not the modern Russian equivalent of a nineteenth-century American robber baron—nor was he a prisoner. In fact, there were no Russian oligarchs back then. The Soviet era had just ended, and Moscow was captivated by a moment of potent and infectious hope, riding a transformational tide that elevated the aspirations of everyone to levels that had been unimaginable only a couple of years earlier. Many of the Russians I met were still somewhat ill at ease with newfound freedoms, however. It was difficult to completely set aside their suspicions, their intuitions about invisible conspiracies, and their enduring certitudes about the value of the right connections. In that sense it was a perfectly Russian moment, both deeply romantic and laced with something darker. Depending on your taste, Gogol, Dostoevsky, Tolstoy, or Pasternak could have captured the mood perfectly—and indeed, each had done so in his own way in different eras.

We met for supper in a small, rustic Georgian restaurant in downtown Moscow. The host was Russian journalist Artyom Borovik, who had made his name testing the limits of glasnost as a front-line reporter during the Soviet debacle in Afghanistan. At the time of our meeting, Borovik was the founder and head of a fledgling publishing company called Top Secret. (Within a few years, he would be dead, a victim in the crash of a private jet. He had alienated many powerful people, and Russia had become more than a little bit like the Wild West. Laws were followed and enforced only selectively. When crusading journalists died in plane crashes, not only was the immediate assumption that foul play was involved, but no one thought such an assumption was the least bit paranoid.)

Borovik was excited to introduce me to this quiet young man. Khodorkovsky was a rising star who had become wealthy leading a new post-Soviet banking venture called Menatep. The money for the bank, it was hinted to me, had come from Soviet sources—perhaps KGB sources—but whatever the origins, Khodorkovsky, in his late twenties, was turning the bank into something remarkable.

In retrospect, I half think that Borovik had set up the meeting not just because he was trying to help me develop a network in the new Russia, but because Khodorkovsky was also Jewish. Borovik always seemed acutely aware of my Jewishness and eager to point out and denounce anti-Semitism wherever he saw it. Given Russia's inglorious history in that respect and the presence of looming nationalist figures like the bombastic Vladimir Zhirinovsky, still touted as a possible president of Russia, and the more subtle but also, according to Borovik, somewhat bigoted General Aleksandr Lebed, another erstwhile presidential hopeful, such examples were not hard to find. While this sort of hamfisted pandering was somewhat hard to take, it was well intentioned, I think. It was also not unusual in my travels. It was a kind of treatment I would also find sometimes in Japan, where business partners would try to bond by catering to my perceived "Jewish interests."

Borovik and I had arrived to find Khodorkovsky waiting. He was reserved, very young looking, and for the first ten or fifteen minutes of our meeting he hardly spoke. But eventually, prodded by our garrulous host, he began to open up about the transformation of Russia and the business opportunities that were being created. What he really wanted to know, though, was whether this American visitor was in a position to help him expand his company, to connect with American bankers and corporate leaders. He felt it was important for new Russian businesses to become part of the global economic system and suggested that the failure to do so had helped bring down the old Russian economy.

Khodorkovsky had that look that I have seen before in the eyes of the intensely ambitious, a look that marks them long before they have achieved the high visibility associated with their greatest triumphs. It is a look of special intensity, discipline, and obsessive attention to detail associated with the monomaniacal focus often required to achieve great success. But Khodorkovsky had something else. He was a little spooky, wanly mysterious. He didn't display much of a sense of humor. He was very guarded about the origins of his business. I sensed he felt that openness was dangerous, that there were enemies out there and that all serious business had to be conducted in whispers. In this, you could see he was a child of Soviet communism (and maybe a little prescient). For all that, though, it was easy to see in Khodorkovsky and the other Russian business leaders who emerged in the wake of communism's fall traits that are familiar from our brief look at the history of elites—particularly business elites like Rockefeller and Carnegie. At a moment when the new rules weren't clear, Khodorkovsky was taking advantage of the chaos. He had studied at the Mendeleev Institute of Chemical Technology and served as the deputy chief of the Komsomol at the university. There, he was given special opportunity to experiment with creating small business ventures, "self-financing," in the vernacular of bureaucrats uncomfortable with the language of capitalism. His first effort was a café that did not succeed. His next venture was the Foundation of Youth Initiative.

Khodorkovsky originally conceived the Foundation of Youth Initiative as a shell under which students of the university could offer their services to enterprises of the state, such as scientific and technological institutes. But Khodorkovsky saw an opportunity within the opportunity. Post-Soviet enterprises dealt in two kinds of money: cash (*nalichnye*) and a kind of internal currency that could be used only between state-sponsored enterprises (*beznalichnye*). Despite having the same face value as cash, because of its limited utility, the "noncash" was really worth only about a tenth of the currency that could actually be used outside of government channels. Khodorkovsky saw that there was an arbitrage here that could be leveraged to his advantage. In exchange for providing services to state enterprises, the state would transfer noncash to his account, which he could then convert into cash to be used for the salaries of his young consultants. Of course, he was also able to hold on to significant amounts of it. It was the ultimate moneymaking scheme, a kind of post-Communist philosopher's stone process by which something of little value was turned into gold.

Of course, while Khodorkovsky had an important insight—a business innovation well suited to the transformational moment at which Russia found itself—he couldn't have done it alone. Part of his genius, at least at the time, was his cultivation of friends in high places. In his wonderful book *The Oligarchs*, David Hoffman offers this insight from Olga Kryshtanovskaya, a sociologist who studies Russian elites: "The industrial directors who cooperated with Khodorkovsky knew 'that they were working with the authorities, that it wasn't con artists.' In this case, the transaction was a breeze, a simple bank transfer which would have been difficult or impossible if not for Khodorkovsky's good connections."

Building on his networks and the easy access to cash, Khodorkovsky made the meteoric rise from capitalist guinea pig to legitimate fat cat in just a few years. After creating Menatep bank, he served a brief stint as a government adviser and then, with Menatep and the help of his friends in the government, he engineered the purchase of a vertically integrated oil giant, the second largest in Russia, called Yukos.

Yukos proved to be both Khodorkovsky's triumph and his downfall. Rumors swirled that he was able to purchase Yukos only through favoritism, and it was hard to deny the self-dealing involved in the 1995 Russian privatization process. (Banks that were awarded oversight of the auction of state assets typically ending up owning those assets themselves, for example.) Furthermore, one of his alleged financing innovations with Yukos was his ability to pay for the acquisition of the company through borrowing against its future earnings. But for a man who sought legitimacy and also for one who had seen the centrality of political control to creating wealth in the new Russia, the siren song of politics was irresistible. Yukos made Khodorkovsky one of Russia's richest men, a billionaire many times over, but once he began to contemplate a future in Russia's political life, he faltered. Or rather, he was brought down. He became a threat to the government leadership that he once recognized as central to his success. He overreached, and the questions about his finances provided the pretext for Russia's president, Vladimir Putin, to throw him in jail, which is where he sits today.

This cycle—innovation, followed by exceptional expansion and accumulation of power, followed by difficulties with the state—was as common among Russia's oligarchs as it was among America's robber barons. Oligarch after oligarch followed it, each taking advantage of the opportunities created by a great moment of historical upheaval. Oligarchs were then co-opted or constrained or intimidated into exile or a reduced role by another elite seeking to establish itself in the name of the masses.

A few of Russia's oligarchs have learned to avoid some of the pitfalls that plagued their predecessors. Roman Abramovich, an associate of Boris Berezovsky, another oligarch forced into exile, assumed the reins of much of Berezovsky's empire and built upon them. He quietly acquired large chunks of Russian industrial enterprises, ultimately controlling 80 percent of Russian oil company Sibneft; 50 percent of Rusal, the Russian aluminum monopoly; and 26 percent of Russian national airline Aeroflot. Abramovich, unlike Berezovsky, carefully maintained a low profile for as long as he could and then, when he could do so no longer, he hired world-class press agents to manage his image in an attempt to avoid the fate of his onetime mentor. He maintained a close relationship with Putin and even serves as governor of a Chukotka territory in Siberia. But, perhaps mindful of the lessons of Russia's recent past, he also diversified his assets to include the London-based Chelsea Football Club and vast homes and luxury yachts in the West, and arranged to be able to relocate at a moment's notice should the weather change for him in the volatile environment of Putin's Russia.

Like Rockefeller, the Russian oligarchs seized a moment, made the most of it, and then retrenched as government stepped in to constrain them. While Putin seems ascendant today, it is unclear whether his brand of authoritarianism will ultimately triumph or whether it will quash Russia's entrepreneurial spirit and scare away the global investors on whom it depends to tap its enormous resources. What is clear is that in the tug-of-war between state and business there has been an ebb and flow. Even with Putin's recidivist impulses, Russia's future depends on its connections with the global economy and the ability of its elites, its growing membership roster among the numbers of the superclass, to maintain a place as an influential force within the country.

In some respects, the Russian story of cowboy capitalism, the rise of the oligarchs and the reaction against them, is not just reminiscent of the history of elites past. It is also consistent with similar present-day struggles among business elites and government elites worldwide. The distribution of power has shifted. Business leaders are benefiting from the vitality and opportunities created by globalization: easy access to capital, to new markets, to the leverage that comes from multiple power sources and bases of operation worldwide. Government leaders are more constrained by the geographically bound nature of their roles, and in some cases are taking draconian steps to try and tip the balance back in their favor through renationalization, tougher regulations, and selective enforcement or creative interpretation of the law. All are seeking new models, new approaches to the relationship between business and government in the global era.

THE CORPORATE CLUSTER
WITHIN THE SUPERCLASS

When C. Wright Mills's *The Power Elite* was published in 1956, he focused on different clusters of elites. Some had to do with social status or with origins of wealth. The chapters carried names like "The Celebrities" and "The Very Rich." Others focused on the nature of the power elites wielded: "The Chief Executives," "The Corporate Rich," "The Warlords," "The Military Ascendancy," and "The Political Directorate." He emphasized the crossover among these groups and the changes affecting them, changes from what had been historical norms in the United States and earlier in Europe.

Writing of the "corporate rich," Mills noted a change in which "now the corporate seats of the rich contain all the powers and privileges inherent in the institutions of private property." In other words, he acknowledged that the world of midcentury America had moved to a business-centered system not only of wealth but also of class. The consequences of the Industrial Revolution were becoming clear. Mills marveled at how the chief executives of companies had assumed much of the power that once belonged to the owners. "Are not," he asked, his Marx-influenced views showing more than a little, "the old expropriators now expropriated by their salaried managers?" Like much of America in the post–World War II era, Mills was struck by a changed order in which corporations were assuming an even greater role than in the past, when the real center of gravity of the country was with smaller business, the middle class, and, earlier still, with those who owned and worked the land.

Mills concluded his look at each elite cluster with a discussion of how power is balanced within society and how past theories of this balance were in need of revision.

> Americans cling to the idea that the government is a sort of an automatic machine, regulated by the balancing of competing interests. This image of politics is simply a carry over from the official image of the economy: in both, an equilibrium is achieved by the pulling and hauling of many interests, each restrained only by legalistic and amoral interpretations of what the traffic will bear.
>
> The ideal of the automatic balance reached its most compelling elaboration in eighteenth century economic terms: the

market is sovereign and in the magic economy of the small entrepreneur there is no authoritarian center. And in the political sphere as well: the division, the equilibrium, of powers prevails, and hence there is no chance for despotism. "The nation which will not adopt an equilibrium of power," John Adams wrote, "must adopt a despotism. There is no other alternative."

Mills, it is clear, believed that the balance was gone, that the small actors had been succeeded by big actors who often moved in concert, who collaborated to eliminate balance altogether. He lamented that big decisions were taken without public debate (a sentiment easy to understand in the wake of America's decision to enter a war in Iraq without benefit of a congressional declaration of war or any real national deliberation). And when he argued that the middle class, the country's "pivot and stabilizer," was becoming increasingly weak, we of the current era—an era in which middle classes have shrunk everywhere in the world but China and India for over a quarter century—again hear unsettling echoes.

Such echoes are among the reasons his book retains its relevance today, but what is most striking about Mills's observations is that while they raise important questions about how societies function, they are also anachronistic. He was writing not only about just one country but also about the results of the epochal transition triggered by one event—World War II—and the economic, social, technological, and political trends leading up to it. Indeed, he was measuring the aftermath of the kind of great upheaval that we have seen causes fundamental changes in elite structures.

Now, fifty years later, another such epochal transformation is taking place with the advent of the global era. Global capital and information flows are already instantaneous and transportation times and costs have declined markedly. The result makes global enterprises possible but it also carries their message to diverse audiences, knitting them together. Global branding is an important element of the formation of global culture with companies like Coca-Cola, Microsoft, IBM, GE, Nokia, Toyota, and Intel all deriving more than $30 billion in estimated value from the international awareness they have built over the years. Furthermore, for most large companies, the greatest growth markets are overseas, in China or India for developed country companies or in the United States or Europe for the emerging blue chips of China and India. With such developments also comes a need for the big corporates to seek harmonized regulations and standards so that they don't incur the great costs of customizing products to the needs of individual countries. Thus the globalization of business produces changes in governments, and the mobility of businesses, their ability to project influence anywhere rapidly and effectively, and their growing resources give them even greater leverage than Mills could ever have imagined when considering the big companies of his era, many of which were rooted in a single nation and had to play by a single set of rules. In addition, not only has the onset of the new era shifted the central story of importance away from the power elite of the world's richest and most powerful single country to that associated with the borderless realm of the global economy, but it also raises many questions about just what clusters of power are important and how their relationships may have changed since Mills's day.

One perspective on the nature of that transition was recently offered in what might be considered an unlikely setting, one of Washington's many black-tie galas, events that typically serve up little more than gossip and rubbery chicken. It was the annual dinner of the Atlantic Council, a think tank supporting the transatlantic relationships that have been a mainstay of U.S. foreign policy since, well, always. This dinner featured five hundred business, government, and military leaders, and was held in honor of three current or former superclass members. Steve Schwarzman, who thanks to the ascendancy of private equity had become the flavor of the month on Wall Street, was receiving an award for business leadership. General Jim Jones, former supreme allied commander in Europe and former commandant of the U.S. Marine Corps, was receiving an award for military achievement. And for government service, the award went to a man who has sat near the apex of the pyramid, a member of the superclass within the superclass, Alan Greenspan, who for roughly two decades served as the inscrutable Yoda of global financial markets in his role as chairman of the U.S. Federal Reserve. Even after his retirement, Greenspan has proved he can move markets with a well-turned phrase.

Introduced by former secretary of state Colin Powell, who received an adoring reception from the tuxedoed audience, each of the award recipients settled into a chair to participate in a question-and-answer session with a past award winner, former two-time U.S. national security adviser, General Brent Scowcroft. Scowcroft, who was typically wry and wise while questioning the recipients, turned to Greenspan first. The question probed into the impact of the Atlantic alliance on Greenspan's work at the Fed, but Greenspan dove deeper, exploring the end of the cold war as a pivotal moment not only in a geopolitical sense but also in terms of the global economy. When the Berlin Wall came down to reveal the economic disaster and utter failure of central planning, he said, it was a moment of awakening not only for those directly engaged in the cold war. Greenspan saw the fall of the USSR and communism not only in terms of the opportunities it opened up within those countries directly affected, as in the case of the rise of the oligarchs, but also as a signal to the emerging world that there was now only one path: to accept the results of the seventy-five-year experiment in comparative political-economic philosophy and engage in global markets. The profound potential of this moment was a billion new workers and consumers in the global economy embracing our views. Greenspan spoke of this promise with deep conviction as demonstrating, even in our complex world, the surpassing "power of ideas."

His comments stood in stark contrast to the much more narrowly focused and practical observations of Schwarzman. The Blackstone CEO spoke of how America was losing its competitiveness because of regulations like the Sarbanes-Oxley provisions that required more detailed disclosure and oversight of corporate finance. He observed that some corporate boards were now spending a third of their time on compliance issues and that as a consequence U.S. business leaders were not able to focus on the right issues, the ones associated with building value for shareholders. He also noted that such regulations had resulted in a 90 percent drop in U.S. initial public offerings because companies that wanted to go public were listing overseas in markets where regulations were looser. He urged the American government officials in the audience to adopt a less intrusive role or the market would simply go elsewhere. And he characterized the rise of private equity companies as a "capitalist response" to the problems created by a Washington that did not realize the damage their laws were doing to the competitiveness of U.S.-based firms.

While not speaking with the kind of historical insight of Greenspan, Schwarzman illustrated another major consequence of the epochal awakening of our age that was comparable to the end of World War II for Mills, or the end of the Civil War for the robber barons, or the decision to disconnect from the world for the Mings. In a global economy in which multinational corporations are no longer bound to any single country, they have gained a new kind of power over national governments, which by their nature are confined by borders. Companies have created a new kind of marketplace in which governments compete with one another for investment, essentially undercutting in a fundamental way some of the most familiar, potent, and until recently enduring foundations of sovereignty. *New York Times* columnist Thomas

Friedman related a pertinent conversation he had had with Intel CEO Craig Barrett: "There was a shocking quote. He said, 'Intel can thrive today and never hire another American. It is not our desire, it is not our intention, but we can do that.' So what it means is that global companies are now hovering over countries. They get disconnected from their moorings. Intel hovers over Southern California, over the U.S., over wherever it may operate in the world. It is not really headquartered."

Take the world's ten biggest corporations: Wal-Mart, ExxonMobil, Shell, BP, General Motors, Chevron, DaimlerChrysler, Toyota, Ford, ConocoPhillips. Besides the fact that four are offspring of the Seven Sisters spun off from Standard Oil over a hundred years ago, in 2006 roughly six out of every ten dollars of revenue came from operations outside their country of origin, and roughly the same portion, 59 percent, of their employees were employed outside that country. This internationalization carries over to their boards as well, with an average of one out of five board members coming from outside the country of origin. In fact, for the S&P 500, the biggest publicly listed companies on U.S. stock exchanges, 2007 was a watershed year: For the first time, the five hundred companies earned more than half of their revenues internationally rather than from their "home" market. That's up from 35 percent overseas revenues just five years earlier, in 2002. The trend has become so pronounced that investment banks are offering U.S. investors seeking a "safe" way to invest internationally baskets of U.S. companies that earn most of their revenues abroad. Goldman Sachs introduced one in 2007 that includes thirty-four major U.S. companies that derive almost two-thirds of their sales internationally. In stock appreciation terms, this group during the first half of 2007 outperformed the market as a whole by more than two to one.

In terms of company size, we have clearly come a long way from Mills's day, when the thirty or so companies with revenues in excess of $1 billion a year were the obvious titans of industry. In 2007 the smallest company on the *Fortune* Global 500, a Canadian aerospace firm called Bombardier, had revenues of $14.9 billion and assets of over $18 billion. The *Forbes* Global 2,000 companies hail from fifty-seven countries and the smallest has revenues of $40 million. (The total assets of these companies are estimated to exceed $100 trillion.) In fact, my own company has estimated that there are well over one thousand companies that we call emerging multinationals that have sales in excess of $1 billion and are located in the world's emerging markets. Our cutoff for superclass membership at being one of the world's two thousand largest companies means that literally thousands of billion-dollar-plus companies don't make the list. Another way to put how little $1 billion in annual income means today is that among the world's billionaire individuals, the top sixty-two—twice Mills's number of billion-dollar U.S. *companies* in the late 1950s—would earn over $1 billion a year in income if they made only 10 percent returns on their assets. (Most earn much more.) Is this all inflation? No. Inflation would take 1956's $1 billion and make it worth roughly $7 billion today. But that $7 billion puts a company at only number 333 on the 2007 *Fortune* 500. Clearly the driving factors are economic growth and corporate consolidation.

In fact, the numbers associated with today's power elite would likely make Mills's head explode. After all, American GDP in 1956 was $438 billion, not too much more than the current annual revenues of WalMart or ExxonMobil. The federal government spent around $70 billion, which today could be personally funded by one or two of the richest people in the world. Today we measure power in trillions. The more than $100 trillion in assets owned by the world's two thousand largest corporations. The $10 trillion controlled by just the ten thousand U.S. mutual funds (which means an average size of $1 billion each). The $2 trillion controlled by the world's ten thousand hedge funds. The $2 trillion in buying power ($400 billion in assets plus available leverage) currently controlled by the world's few hundred private equity firms. The more than $1 trillion in reserves controlled by SAFE (State Administration of Foreign Exchange), China's monetary authority. Each of these trillion-dollar-plus pools of capital, all controlled by fairly small groups of individuals, represents an unprecedented concentration of power. There is a group of a few thousand people among the corporate elite who effectively control perhaps $100 trillion, two-thirds of the world's total assets.

THE INTERLINKED CORPORATE ELITE

Mills observed how associations and interlocking directorates increased individuals' influence. But in the global era and the Internet age, such associations are burgeoning and the opportunities for linkages and collaboration have grown dramatically. Giant companies like Procter & Gamble and Boeing carefully coordinate and nurture relationships among the tens of thousands of supplier, distributor, and collaborator companies with which they work. Events like Davos, the Boao Forum for Asia, the Allen & Company event in Sun Valley, the IMF/World Bank annual meetings, and thousands and thousands of such programs (in 2006 there were over a million conferences held in the United States alone) knit elites together. Industry associations do the same, and many such groups have grown to great size and wield great power. For example, the U.S. Chamber of Commerce has an annual budget of $150 million and more than three million members, and is a powerful voice, particularly for the largest members of the business community. In 2004, they deployed over two hundred political operatives to more than thirty states to seek to influence election outcomes on behalf of probusiness candidates. *The Washington Post* cited the chamber and five other organizations, collectively known as "the Gang of Six," as being a source the Bush administration has looked to for vital support of its economic initiatives. The other five were the Business Roundtable, the National Association of Manufacturers, the National Restaurant Association, the National Federation of Independent Businesses, and the National Association of Wholesaler-Distributors. Such associations, of which there are thousands today, often have extensive international reach as well, as they include highly influential global corporations.

With regard to the concentration of power among individuals, perhaps a more telling demonstration is how boards and management of the biggest companies overlap, linking the superclass in an extended network. For example, if you were to take just the top three corporate executives (in most cases the chairman, CEO, and executive director) of the top five biggest companies as well as the members of their boards— approximately seventy people—you would find that they have active connections fanning out to more than 145 other major companies either through board memberships, advisory positions, or former positions in senior management. Of these 145, thirty-six are among the one hundred largest in the world and fifty-two are in the top 250. Sixteen of these companies have more than one representative from the top five companies on their boards. These sixteen are Akzo Nobel, ABB, Astra-Zeneca, British Airways, Deutsche Bank, Ernst & Young, Ford, GE, Goldman Sachs, Lehman Brothers, Lloyds TSB, Pfizer, Royal Bank of Scotland, Sara Lee, Unilever, and Vodafone—all major, major players in their own right. Of these, which one has the most crossover to the top five companies? Goldman Sachs, with four links.

Positions of prominence within the corporate superclass bring with them crosscutting influence in other areas as well, especially given the enormous wealth that now accumulates in the hands of the corporate elite. I was particularly struck by this fact one day while driving to my office at the Carnegie Endowment for International Peace. Carnegie is on a stretch of Massachusetts Avenue in Washington, D.C., that is known for its think tank community, a row of institutions that are central hubs for generating the policy ideas that ultimately guide the U.S. government.

Think tanks and the stories of their endowments illustrate well how business elites can influence the process of agenda-setting. The Carnegie Endowment, for example, was one of the long list of philanthropies endowed by Carnegie but one that gave him special access to the top opinion leaders in the United States and worldwide. Immediately next door is the much larger Brookings Institution, today headed by former deputy secretary of state and *Time* magazine reporter Strobe Talbott and home to many former senior U.S. government officials. The institution was originally funded with a donation from a St. Louis businessman named Robert Somers Brookings, who made his fortune in the late nineteenth century in the household goods firm of Cupples and Marston and devoted his later life to philanthropy, becoming the patron of not only what was to become perhaps Washington's most enduring and influential think tank but also Washington University in St. Louis. In a not entirely surprising sequence of events, in 1916 Brookings endowed something called the Institute for Government Research in the U.S. capital, and one year later he was appointed by President Wilson to the War Industries Board, where he became chair of its price-fixing committee. Two other Brookings-founded entities merged about a decade later to become the institution that now sits next to Carnegie.

Across the street, that morning, I noticed the new sign in front of the influential Institute for International Economics, a firm that had been founded by former Treasury official Fred Bergsten and that was actually the building in which the term "Washington consensus" was coined. The sign read: The Peter G. Peterson Institute for International Economics. Peterson, Stephen Schwarzman's partner in founding Blackstone and a former commerce secretary, was an original patron of Bergsten's think tank and now it bore his name. Also bearing his name are the Peter G. Peterson Chair for the editor of *Foreign Affairs* magazine at the Council on Foreign Relations, where Peterson is himself the longtime chairman of the board. He also established the Peter G. Peterson Chair in Corporate Ethics at the Kellogg School of Management at Northwestern University.

And so it went up and down the street, examples of corporate patrons donating their money to the pursuit of big ideas and, not surprisingly, exerting some influence on what those ideas would be. This is especially the case in the politically motivated think tanks like the right-leaning American Enterprise Institute, funded initially in large part by several family foundations, notably the Howard Pew Freedom Trust. Its founding chairman William Baroody was forced to resign when his more centrist policies ran afoul of two other major donors, the Smith Richardson and Olin foundations. Similarly, on the left, the Center for American Progress was heavily funded both by George Soros, as a result of his concerns about the administration of George W. Bush, and by a group of rich Democrats called the Democracy Alliance. Soros and billionaire Peter Lewis were the dominant voices in the alliance because of the extent of their wealth. (Disclaimer: I did some work for the Democracy Alliance during its formative years as an adviser to the founder, Rob Stein, an attorney and former chief of staff at the Commerce Department.)

Donations can be used to buy global influence, in what is now a part of the standard operating procedure of the superclass. Endowments of many kinds, from public buildings to academic titles, add to an individual's prominence and prestige and expand his or her networks of connections. They also help set the agenda and often can be used to motivate think tanks and other not-for-profit organizations to provide "independent" validation of ideas that are important to the donor or his or her business or political interests. Just a few examples of such endowments—and there are more such examples than there are members of the superclass, however you might define it—include (and even the following are only partial lists for each individual cited):

Mukesh Ambani, Ambani Family
Chairman and Managing Director, Reliance Industries, Ltd.
Dhirubhai Ambani International School, Mumbai, India
Dhirubhai Ambani Institute of Information and Communication Technology, Gujarat, India
Dhirubhai Ambani Knowledge City, Navi Mumbai, India

Michael Bloomberg
Mayor of New York City; founder, Bloomberg LP
Bloomberg Tower, New York City
Bloomberg School of Public Health, Johns Hopkins University
Bloomberg Hall, School of Natural Sciences, Institute for Advanced Study, Princeton University
Emma B. Bloomberg Hall, Princeton University
Bloomberg Chair in Journalism, Columbia University
Charlotte Bloomberg Chair in Art History, Johns Hopkins University
William Henry Bloomberg Professorship, Harvard University

Maurice R. "Hank" Greenberg
Chairman and CEO, C. V. Starr & Co.; former CEO, AIG
Maurice R. Greenberg Center for Geoeconomic Studies, Council on Foreign Relations
Maurice R. Greenberg International Conference Center, Yale University
Weill Greenberg Center, Weill Cornell Medical College, New York City
Maurice Greenberg Center for Judaic Studies, University of Hartford
Maurice R. and Corinne P. Greenberg Building, Asia Society, New York City
Maurice R. and Corinne P. Greenberg Pavilion, New York–Presbyterian Hospital

Ratan Tata, Tata Family
Chairman, Tata Group
Tata Institute of Fundamental Research, Mumbai, India
Tata Institute, Bangalore, India
Tata Institute of Social Sciences, Mumbai
Tata Management Training Centre, Pune, India
Jamsetji Tata Centre for Disaster Management, Mumbai
Tata Memorial Hospital, Mumbai
JRD Tata Ecotechnology Centre, Chennai, India
Tata-Dhan Academy, Madurai, India
Tata Centre, Calcutta, India
Sir Ratan Tata Chair Professor, Indian Institute of Management, Bangalore

Donations to charities are a form of influence not only because they support given causes; they also underscore one's social position. For example, the Robin Hood Foundation annual benefit in New York brings together financial big shots to participate in displays of generosity laced with an element of that "conspicuous conscience" I mentioned earlier. According to *The New York Times*, "the event raised $71 million, up 32 percent from a year ago, in what was a display of gilded age excess." Larry Robbins, a hedge fund manager, started the evening with a donation of $10 million to the charity, which raises money for teacher training and other efforts to assist poor children. Twenty-two people followed with commitments of $1 million each. Dinner for ten with the famous chef Mario Batali went for $1.3 million. A trip to the Olympics and a chance to spend time with a television personality brought in almost twice that. Two people paid $400,000 each to sing with the aging heavy metal band Aerosmith. The affair, peppered with stars like Gwyneth Paltrow, Ben Affleck, Martha Stewart, and Michael Douglas—as well as the ubiquitous Steve Schwarzman—was the culmination to date of a program that has raised almost $1 billion for its favorite charities.

Networking among the corporate elite can thus take a variety of forms. Working together, doing deals together, sitting on boards together, even attending gala events together—all these things help forge the networks that empower and define the superclass. And these networks begin early. For example, take the Harvard Business School class of 1979. This class alone graduated Meg Whitman, the CEO of eBay; Jeffrey Skilling, the former president of Enron; John Thain, former president of Goldman Sachs and currently head of the New York Stock Exchange; Ron Sargent, the CEO of Staples; George McMillan, the CEO of Palladium Group; Elaine Chao, the secretary of labor (who also happens to be married to Republican Senator Mitch McConnell of Kentucky); and Dan Bricklin, who developed the first electronic spreadsheet. And because schools like Oxford, Cambridge, France's École Polytechnique, the Indian Institute of Technology, and the University of Tokyo all perform a similar function, cadres of leaders emerge into the world with important linkages even before other layers of ties begin to form.

WHAT GLOBAL POWER CAN DO

More important even than these ties, however, is how those who benefit from them actually exercise their influence in a global way. According to Schwarzman, he and Pete Peterson spent a number of years shifting Blackstone's focus from America to the rest of the world. "There are a number of reasons for why it took us a while to become the global firm we are today," he told me. "First, our home country, the United States, comprises about 30 percent of global GDP and typically has the friendliest regulatory environment for transactional activities. Also, it offers the ability to transact business with like-minded people who are problem solvers. And so a lot of the financial innovation that gets done in the world has historically been done in the United States.

"Being in this primary market discourages you initially from going anywhere else because it's always harder to do business," he went on. The development of video conferencing, which was sufficiently perfected around the year 2000, led to some considerable expansion. "This enabled us to open our European operations, which have been extremely successful for us. We then turned to Asia." Describing with enthusiasm what they found in India, he explained, "Starting with private equity, we now have gone into money management. We operate the second-biggest mutual fund in India and we are going to be soon starting real estate activity there. In large part, because we believe in doing things sequentially, we want to start with one country and then we will move to others . . . but what we like about India is they speak English, our native language. It is a huge competitive advantage to be able to communicate. They also have laws and they have a court system, and even though it is cumbersome, they do have a democracy, so that becomes familiar. Now we are moving into China and Japan, which will become very important markets for us." Schwarzman has seen firsthand the trends that have made global expansion possible for firms like Blackstone and that have given rise to the leverage that big financial players now have over the governments of the world.

A *New York Times* op-ed I once wrote called "Whistle Stops on Wall Street" commented on an increasingly common phenomenon: Candidates for high political office and current occupants of those offices frequently stop to meet with senior financial officials whenever they are in New York or other financial capitals. The rationale is straightforward. Political leaders recognize that they now report to two constituencies— the voters who elected them and the financial markets that daily conduct a referendum on their policies. This is the market at work. The system offers a check to political power. It results in major infusions of needed capital and it helps produce transparency, fuel job creation, and enforce rules that are proven to lead to economic growth.

For example, daily trading in the government bonds market is influenced by traders' views on whether or not government programs are likely to succeed at promoting growth or stability, as well as other factors they feel impact the ability of governments to repay their debts. In the same way, investors reflect their perspectives on political leaders in the prices they set for currencies, stocks, and key commodities that are affected by the decisions of national governments. In just one afternoon in late July 2007, for instance, the Argentine peso fell to its lowest exchange rate level in four years; investors, concerned about the country's upcoming elections and the antimarket leanings of likely victor Cristina Fernández de Kirchner, had grown skittish, reducing positions in the peso or betting on it to fall. At the same time, Russian debt

markets were pushed down as investors worried that the Putin administration's pressure for more mortgage lending as a stimulus for growth
would expose the country's banks to unacceptable risks if the economy
soured.

While these decisions are not made by a single individual in a
room, the community of the largest traders in Russian debt or Argentine pesos is small; they know each other, they know how they will react, and together just a few shape market sentiment. Sometimes, said
one experienced trader, "It is a dozen guys who set the price. Sometimes, when people worry about a big investor, like a George Soros, it
can be about what one man thinks . . . or what investors think he
thinks." In this way big market players keep political leaders and other
policy makers on a short leash: If a minister or president or central bank
governor makes a pronouncement that markets find unpalatable one
day, the country may find it difficult to borrow the next. This in turn will
restrict economic growth, which means fewer jobs or less money for
consumers. The rise of the markets as a counterweight to political leaders (coming as more countries are linked to global markets) is primarily
a healthy trend. But if the system favors shorter-term returns, large-
scale operations, and partners who have influence on the markets, it is
also a trend that undercuts longer-term growth needs, hurts smaller
countries and economies, and exacerbates the inequitable distribution
of money and power in many of those countries worldwide.

Joe Stiglitz argued in the same vein, only more starkly, during a
conversation one evening at his paper-filled office at Columbia University, "Capital market liberalization—free and unfettered movement of
capital across borders—can, in some sense, undermine democracy.
Some developing countries have experienced this very strongly: When
a Wall Street–oriented party loses the election, the markets become unhappy and start pulling their capital out. And because voters know this,
they worry about Wall Street's reactions. Wall Street votes as much as
the people of the country. The interesting thing is that some markets,
like Korea, do not need the money from Wall Street because their
people have saved enough on their own. They've linked their market
to the global system, so that the people in the country with money can
move their money to Wall Street and the people from Wall Street can
move the money into and out of the country freely. Liberalizing capital
markets—making it easier for those on Wall Street to move their money
in and out of the country—gives more voting power to Wall Street."

Schwarzman saw the consequences: "We have become more central to each economy we are in. We realize we have to be responsible players . . . We would expect not to have people react adversely because what we are doing is trying to develop companies and make them better, and usually we can make that sale almost everywhere in the world." Then he explained another dimension of influence that such firms have: "Every once in a while, though, something goes off the rails and you need help from people you don't know personally. That is one of the wonderful things about finance. You can get to anybody in the world with one phone call.

"We do not try and do these things," he said, "but sometimes it is necessary. As private equity, this marching around the globe occasionally hits a speed bump. We hit such a speed bump with a series of accidents in Germany with the 'locust debate.' For those of us who were in business, even private equity, this was shocking. At that point in history, in other countries where we bought companies, it appeared that there was no major opposition to what we did. In Germany all of a sudden we were becoming objects of criticism and hostility. And so we looked at that and found that there are a number of studies that have been done in Europe and in Germany in terms of job creation in relation to private equity investments, and I wanted to get the message through. So I asked someone I know to set up a meeting for me with Mrs. Merkel, the chancellor of Germany. I spent an hour with her and went over the studies and what our objectives were. Mrs. Merkel by training is a physicist, so she is very datacentric and very logical. She listened to all that and said, 'If you can get your companies to grow much better and hire more people, we should want to do more of that in Germany, not less, because ultimately that is good for us. Our companies will be more competitive because they are facing threats from the East. So I can support you in what you do because it is very logical.' And about eight weeks later, we bought a big stake in Deutsche Telekom from the government and are helping to improve that company, and that's how we have now really gained the chance to turn around the attitude in Germany toward private equity, although others still think negatively about our industry."

Schwarzman describes such working of global connections as "just the nature of finance. Every country has its large financial institutions that are central to the development of that country, and everyone else in finance knows somebody who will know the head of one of those companies. That person knows a senior person in their government that could be useful in a situation. That does not mean that you will always get your point of view adopted, but all you want is an open hearing to put forward what is on your mind. If people choose not to respond to it, then you cannot do anything about it. But the key is the network. In the end, the world is pretty small. In almost every one of these areas I am looking at, it is twenty, thirty, fifty people worldwide who ultimately drive the decisions. It amazed me when I was younger. When I was more junior, it was two degrees or three degrees of separation. As you get older and a little more senior, that number of degrees of separation sort of goes down. It is part of what makes business life so interesting and exciting. You fundamentally can transport yourself with the same alphabet to different geographic places and be able to understand an enormous amount of what is going on because they are using the same language."

Speak to private equity executive after private equity executive and it is clear that this is a business that depends on having the right people in charge. Many of the management teams at the large private equity firms have a revolving-door relationship with the most important corporate executive suites or top government offices. While most of the firms are actually run by hard-core Wall Street types, they dress up their executive suites, buy entrée and also buy real management savvy through such associations. For example, in addition to Pete Peterson, who was formerly secretary of commerce, Blackstone has former treasury secretary and Alcoa CEO Paul O'Neill as a senior adviser. Cerberus's chairman is former treasury secretary and CSX Corporation CEO John Snow; its global chairman is former vice president Dan Quayle, and according to *Fortune* magazine, whatever problems Quayle may have had with spelling in a previous life, he has had no problem putting two and two together. Quayle was also on the board of Japan's Nippon Credit Bank and used his connections there to help prepare the way for Cerberus's takeover of that institution. The chairman of the Carlyle Group, famed for its labyrinthine connections to former top government officials including George H. W. Bush, is now former IBM and American Express CEO Louis Gerstner. From his office in Carlyle's duplex suite in New York City, Gerstner explained, "I cannot argue that a class of global elites does not exist. If you are running a multinational corporation, or are a scientist, or a serious clinician in a research-oriented organization or are a journalist, you do not think about ideas and opportunities coming with a tariff or through a border. What I'm trying to say is that such elite networks are not about snobbery. They're just there, they evolve. So why not take advantage of it? Why not become part of it? It is so natural today to be a part of a broader community if your purpose is to get better information, sell more products, access more customers."

Bill McDonough, vice chairman of Merrill Lynch and former president of the New York Federal Reserve Bank, agreed that a few hundred people are the real "movers and shakers" in global finance: "Each of them does everything possible for the success of his or her firm, but they are fully aware of the need to safeguard the system by not having their elbows too sharp in times of market difficulties. In my experience both at the Fed and in my various positions in the private sector, the leaders of the world financial community are quite endowed with realism about how much power they have and when and how to use it."

Private equity firms, like most financial institutions and big corporations, have the ability to buy high-profile, well-connected individuals who can help expand their networks and influence. So it is in their interest to do so. They also, of course, have another advantage: the ability to buy the best and the brightest when they are still young. One top hedge fund executive said to me, "There are only every year a few hundred people coming out of the best schools in the U.S.—maybe a few thousand worldwide—who are the cream of the crop. Where do they start? Once it might have been the foreign service or law or some other field. But today, we have such a huge advantage in terms of the compensation we can offer that we get first crack. Of course, all that ebbs and flows too with market cycles. A couple years ago, we hedge funds were the pinnacle because we were paying starting MBAs base salaries of a couple hundred thousand and bonuses that could double that. Now private equity firms are offering bases of $300,000, $400,000, and total first-year packages of like $1.2 million. This is to Harvard MBAs or whatever, twenty-five-year-olds. So what would you do if you were that MBA? Where would you work?"

Trends in the financial community aside, for the past several decades one of the surest answers to that question has been Goldman Sachs. Since its founding in 1889, Goldman has grown to be the most respected name on Wall Street. The firm's annual revenues are now heading toward the $70 billion level, primarily as a result of its incredibly profitable proprietary trading business and its leadership in investment banking. The firm earned almost $10 billion in 2006. Its office tower at 85 Broad Street in New York City and satellites worldwide house a remarkably privileged group of approximately thirty thousand employees. How privileged? The average employee makes $622,000 a year. (Next highest paid on Wall Street: Lehman Brothers at $334,000 a year per employee.) The top twenty-five executives in the firm in 2006 were estimated to make $25 million each, with CEO Lloyd Blankfein the top earner on Wall Street with $54 million.

Blankfein's office in Goldman's tower is on the top floor. Entering through a large, serene lobby, visitors are escorted into a curved suite, the office of the chairman. Blond paneling, glass, tasteful art, and a bank of assistants constantly in motion create much of the ambience, but most affecting is the sense that this is truly the center of the business universe. When Henry Paulson was Goldman's chairman before becoming U.S. treasury secretary, he created a formidable figure that seemed suited to the setting. Paulson is tall, forceful, and imposing—even in the context of an office at Goldman that featured environmental photographs and books reflecting his deep and abiding passion for birds.

Lloyd Blankfein cuts a different image. Smaller, balding, born in the Bronx, he is a master of self-effacing humor although he is one of those best-and-brightest types lured to Goldman from Harvard Law School in 1981. He started as a gold salesman at the commodity trading arm of Goldman because he was not considered slick enough to appeal to the investment-banking side of the operation. Thirteen years later he headed that commodity division, and within four more years he was cohead of Goldman's fixed income, currency, and commodities operations. In 2003 he became president, beating out the very buttoned-down, central-casting investment banker John Thain. Cautious and brilliant, Blankfein does enjoy the benefits of his success. During the week, while working around the clock, he lives in a $27 million apartment on the Upper West Side. And for weekends he *almost* had a 10.6-acre estate in Southampton, on the eastern end of Long Island. The $41 million estate, named Old Trees, features a tennis court, a pool with a view of the ocean (connected to the main house by a heated walkway), and a guest cottage with a pool of its own. But when news of the planned purchase leaked, Blankfein was reportedly furious and canceled the deal, committed as he was to maintaining his low-profile lifestyle. To this day, according to observers in the Hamptons, the low-key Goldman CEO can still slip in and out of the local shops unnoticed, even as sightings of B-list movie stars send waves of gossip through the small downtown.

Goldman's influence extends beyond the ability of its analysts and traders to drive stock or bond prices up and down, as they do daily with the reports they write and the decisions they make to buy or sell securities. The firm shapes new views of the world, as it did in 2003, for example, with its suggestion that Brazil, Russia, India, and China were a special class of emerging markets they called BRICs that would become especially important in the decades ahead. It creates new financial instruments that shape the global marketplace, it can make or break the CEOs and government ministers who regularly pass through its doors looking for capital and for "buy" recommendations linked to their decisions, and it serves as the hub of an international network of deal makers.

Goldman has a long history of involvement in the public sector. Of Blankfein's four predecessors as CEO, two were secretary of the treasury (Hank Paulson and Bob Rubin), two were the head of the National Economic Council (Rubin and Steve Friedman), and one is the current governor of New Jersey and a former senator (Jon Corzine). White House chief of staff Josh Bolten is a Goldman alum; former deputy treasury secretary Robert Zoellick served a stint at Goldman before returning to public service as head of the World Bank; and Zoellick's former post at the Treasury Department is now held by former Goldman CEO John Whitehead. During the Clinton years, Treasury Secretary Rubin was joined by former Goldman banker Ken Brody, who ran the U.S. Export-Import Bank. The list extends to scores of senior-level and midlevel officials over the past several administrations who worked at Goldman before and after their government service. It caused business commentator Kyle Pope, writing in the *Los Angeles Times*, to suggest that no firm has held such economic influence since Standard Oil.

Why do rich men undertake low-paying government jobs that are accompanied by press scrutiny and the annoyance of dealing with bureaucracies? It is much the same as it was for Khodorkovsky: There is legitimacy and prestige associated with those jobs, and there is also a chance to go from indirect influence of policies to hands-on management. When I visited the office of a noted Wall Street gray eminence the day after Paulson accepted the job as treasury secretary, my host said to me, "There's been a lot of talk about why he did it, and the best explanation I have heard is that he and a lot of the guys he is close to worry about potential market disruptions that could be big problems if the right guy is not in there with his hand on the tiller. I think he feels like he can really add some value and that he may really be needed." (The mortgage crisis later suggested there may have been some merit to this thesis.)

It is remarkable that there has been a relatively low level of outcry about the steady flow of executives from 85 Broad Street to offices inside the Washington beltway. Vice chairman of Goldman Sachs International Bob Hormats, himself a former senior official, said, "It is fairly unusual . . . I think it is because it has been demonstrated that when Goldman Sachs people get into these jobs, they give no preference to Goldman Sachs. There is no shred of evidence that they use any of their influence on behalf of Goldman Sachs. If there were, just once, given the remarkable activity of Goldman Sachs in the private sector, it would be over. There would be an incredible hue and cry."

Hormats's observation resonates with McDonough's comment about senior financial executives knowing enough not to play too rough with one another. The good of all depends on the successful functioning of the system. Within the system, rules do not have to be broken (although they often are) to do well and exert enormous influence. One of the primary achievements of the leaders of the global financial community over the past several decades has been its ability to globalize markets while promoting the concept of self-regulation, or very light supervision. Having senior representatives of that community in the government helps ensure that this remains the case and that any regulatory initiatives that are put forth are crafted with them at the table in influential roles. Especially since these individuals ultimately usually return to the financial sector after their time in government, there are often more than just ideological rewards in store for keeping the system strong.

ENERGY ELITES:
A UNIQUE PUBLIC-PRIVATE NETWORK

Blurring the line between business influence and government influence is exceptionally common regardless of sector. We see the same kind of revolving door in defense contracting, in media, and especially in the energy sector. This is due in large part to the fact that most of the world's largest energy companies are state-owned; more than three-quarters of the world's oil and gas is found in countries whose production is government-controlled, according to estimates by PFC Energy consultants. It is also due to the fact that energy flows are crucial to the functioning of states, and many oil- and gas-rich regions are racked by instability; thus military force, primarily in the hands of governments, is key to the functioning of the industry.

The government–private sector tug-of-war has affected elites in many nations, especially, as we have seen, major oil-producing countries like Russia. Indeed, the private sector leadership of the energy community has formed one of the most important global power networks, intensely concentrated in the hands of a few key players, and one that—like finance—globalized early on, well ahead of many other industries. (Much of this process was driven by the Seven Sisters offspring of

Standard Oil.) It is also a network in turmoil today, thanks both to geopolitical upheaval and to the recognition that the global energy paradigm is changing as a consequence of global warming, innovations in alternative technologies, and persistent national security concerns about the current system—notably its pricing mechanisms and the unintended consequences of whom it empowers.

One set of the principal actors in this hybrid power network are the senior executives of the world's leading nationally owned energy companies (national oil companies/NOCs), or the government officials to whom they ultimately report. On the other side are independent oil companies (IOCs) working with them, often possessing more advanced technology and key resources. The two exist in a careful symbiosis, mutually dependent on one another, influencing one another, interacting with one another.

Within the realm of the NOCs, Abdallah Jum'ah, CEO and president of state-owned Saudi Aramco, is arguably the most important executive. He took the position in 1995, following the appointment of Ali I. Al-Naimi, then head of the company, as Saudi minister of petroleum and mineral resources. Jum'ah effectively commands the behemoth of the fuel industry. Aramco stands above all other IOCs and NOCs, holding one-quarter of the world's oil reserves in addition to the fourth-largest natural gas reserves in the world. Jum'ah himself has embarked on a mission to both stabilize the price of oil and expand the reach of the corporation into new markets. He undertakes this mission with the ease of a global diplomat, frequenting meetings like Davos and big-energy symposia, and although respectful and a good listener, dominating the rooms he is in due to his position.

Aramco has made special efforts to form partnerships with non-OPEC members under Jum'ah's leadership. For years, Aramco has formed the backbone of strong Saudi-American relations and remains a major supplier of oil to Europe. Jum'ah has sought to diversify Aramco's distribution with a notable focus on the emerging economies in Asia. He recently cited Saudi Arabia and China as "one of the most important energy relationships on the planet" and said "we plan to stand with you [China] for the next century to come." The company has also made considerable efforts to enter into the Indian market, despite a failed attempt to buy Hindustan Petroleum. In 2005, Aramco exported 450,000 barrels of crude oil each day to India and another 500,000 barrels a day to China. These numbers are likely to increase as the Indian and Chinese economies continue to mature and grow in coming decades. Aramco has also made efforts to enter the South Korean energy market and holds a 35 percent stake in South Korea's third-largest refiner, S-Oil.

Due to its importance to Saudi Arabia and the rest of the world, Aramco has inevitably become a lightning rod for criticism. Some religious conservatives have seen the company as too "Western" and distant from Saudi Arabia itself. Indeed, the company employs two thousand Americans in Saudi Arabia alone, and English remains its official language. To counteract the criticism, the company has embarked on a mission of "Saudi-ization" and, as of 2006, claims that 85 percent of the workforce is made up of Saudi nationals. The trend toward global integration is not consistent throughout Jum'ah's management of Saudi Aramco; he has been able to direct and in some cases mitigate the forces of globalization so as to maximize profit margins and minimize disruptions.

Jum'ah's predecessor at Aramco, Ali I. Al-Naimi, has been called the "Greenspan of oil," after former U.S. Federal Reserve Bank chairman Alan Greenspan. As Saudi Arabia's oil minister, he is one of the industry's most long-standing and influential players, and when Dan Yergin, Pulitzer Prize–winning author of *The Prize* and chairman and CEO of Cambridge Energy Research Associates, is asked which individuals comprise the energy cluster of the superclass, Naimi is one of the first names he mentions. Naimi's position atop the Saudi ocean of oil makes him, in the eyes of some observers, the de facto leader of the OPEC cartel, which in turn empowers him to effect change throughout the international energy industry.

Naimi's climb to the top of Saudi Aramco and later his appointment as oil minister place him among the technocratic members of the superclass. Educated at Lehigh University in Pennsylvania before studying geology at Stanford, Naimi represents the links between the NOC and the IOC worlds as he attempts to create a supply of fuel that will benefit both the Saudi kingdom and the global economy. This global perspective has helped him iron out numerous problems, from lagging oil prices in the late 1990s to potential oil crises in the face of international instability. He was the man who taught OPEC that ballooning oil prices were not as beneficial as stable prices. Naimi is such an important figure that he has become a weather vane of sorts for the sector. Journalists literally tag along on his morning jogs for a chance revelation about the future of the oil industry.

Yergin provided additional insights into this class and how it has evolved. He pointed to the Iranians and an interesting phenomenon in the energy world in which what might otherwise be considered bad behavior produces positive business results. "One of the things I've been struck by," he noted, "is how many times over the past couple of years when the Iranians say something about their nuclear program or regional politics, that they can drive up the price of their oil . . . and everyone else's. They make a statement or two and the price climbs $5 a barrel and, like that, they've made an extra $85 million that week."

According to top Middle Eastern oil executives and industry experts like Yergin, another one of the industry's most important players is Fu Chengyu, chairman and CEO of China National Offshore Oil Corporation (CNOOC). Fu was little known outside of China until his company's failed $18.5 billion takeover of American oil and gas company Unocal in 2005. This move was another example of the expanding power of the Chinese economy, which will increasingly flex its muscle in the coming decades. In Fu's words, the bid represented "the changing nature of corporate China." As a native Chinese, Fu's nationality is one of the few characteristics that set him apart from traditional energy superclass. Otherwise, he fits the mold: He is highly educated, first at China's Northeast Petroleum Institute and then at the University of Southern California. As the chairman of numerous joint ventures, he was able to form extensive links with established oil companies including BP, Amoco, Texaco, Chevron, and Phillips early in his career. He joined CNOOC when it was started by the Chinese government in 1982 and worked his way up to become president in 2000 and CEO and chairman in 2002. Like Naimi in Saudi Arabia, Fu was not assisted by political connections in the Communist Party but rather succeeded by being "a non-smoking, non-drinking workaholic with an international outlook." During his time at the head of CNOOC, he has gained the trust of the party and will likely remain as long as it is appeased.

Fu's international experience is evident in his management style and aims. He did not see the bid for Unocal as different from any other transaction: It simply made good business sense. He understands the importance of stock markets and believes that "transparency makes shareholders love you." The presence of four internationally respected board members, including former Shell CEO Evert Henkes, gives CNOOC an added air of business independence. Nonetheless, the company is controlled by the state, which founded CNOOC to explore China's offshore oil and gas reserves and retains a majority holding in the company. This is a double-edged sword. It gives Fu a strong base of support in an economy that the state sector still dominates (although it is no longer responsible for the majority of Chinese GDP). But it was the government ties that made U.S. lawmakers wary of CNOOC's takeover of Unocal. Since then, Fu has sought to expand CNOOC's international portfolio with investments in Nigeria and Malaysia, among other countries. These deals bring in both traditional oil and liquefied natural gas to China and will ensure that its economy can continue to grow in the future.

FROM THE "SUN KING" TO THE "GOD POD"

On the more purely private side of the energy industry (if such a thing can be said to exist, given the dependency of energy majors on government concessions, regulation, and protection), there is evidence of the kinds of interlocking relationships I have spoken of repeatedly as linking those at the top of the business and government worlds.

Few instances illustrate this as well as the case of John Browne's mostly glittering although slightly truncated career as chief executive of British Petroleum. To begin with, of course, BP's American assets are the offspring of Rockefeller's monolithic enterprise, Standard Oil. And, as in the daisy chain described in Chapter 1, Browne himself was one of those individual connective nodes of the superclass, active in key associations and a member of key corporate boards. Notably, he served on the international advisory board of Goldman Sachs even as then BP chairman Peter Sutherland, a man who would later become Browne's nemesis in bitter corporate infighting, was chairman of Goldman Sachs International.

The son of a former BP manager, Browne was educated at Cambridge before going to Stanford Business School. He joined BP in 1966 as an apprentice and worked his way up to become the company's chief executive in 1995. In the following years, before his resignation in 2007, the "Sun King" became the darling of the energy superclass through his adept risk taking and business savvy, which transformed BP into the second largest IOC behind ExxonMobil. Browne's multibillion-dollar acquisitions of Amoco, Arco, and Castrol ushered in an epoch of mergers that led to the emergence of "supermajors" in the energy sector. The reason? "It's to do with economies of scale," he told *The Guardian* in 2005. "It's to do with a company like BP getting access to the kind of things that only a big company like BP can do, such as take risks, big risks, and go to places where we can find the great hydrocarbon provinces." With its massive size, BP is now able to reach into new markets all around the world, forming partnerships in countries that had formerly been off limits to Western IOCs. One such market is China, where BP is now expanding its efforts to supply the booming economy with fuel resources. In recent years, the company has dedicated around $1 billion to this end. "China, as one of the most rapidly expanding economies, offers significant opportunities for [BP]," Browne explained in 2004, "particularly its customer-facing businesses . . . [We] look forward to expanding this through new projects in the future."

One of Browne's unique contributions was to turn BP toward more environmentally friendly "green" policies. This initiative was the result of his growing concerns about the effect of fossil fuels on the environment and, consequently, on the world economy. Beginning by reframing the company's mission as taking it "Beyond Petroleum," Browne put in place measures that led to the reduction of BP's emissions to "10 percent below its 1990 levels, without cost. Indeed, the company added around $650 million of shareholder value, because the bulk of the reductions came from the elimination of leaks and waste." Even so, some critics said he did not do enough, with one environmental organization castigating him with an ironic award for "Best Impression of an Environmentalist." Nonetheless, through his emphasis and his words if more so than the company's actions, Browne acknowledged the effect of a globalized economy and set a precedent in the business community by pressing world leaders to recognize the threat of global warming.

In addition to his position at BP, Browne has served as a nonexecutive director of both Intel and Goldman Sachs. Through these boards, Browne had regular contact with the current treasury secretary, Henry Paulson, and Intel founder Andy Grove. As he himself once put it, "I serve on these boards because I believe I can contribute but also because I can learn from great people." His other commitments included the emeritus chairmanship of the advisory board of the Stanford Graduate School of Business and chairmanship of the International Advisory Board at the School of Economics and Management at Tsinghua University in Beijing. Browne was listed as one of *Time* magazine's most influential people in 2004. He has also been a regular attendee at the annual Bilderberg conference. With his innovative leadership and extensive connections, John Browne propelled himself to the top of the energy superclass and transformed the global energy market in the process. Even though he ultimately was forced into early retirement due to a series of management misfires and the threat of a personal legal scandal, his influence as a modernizer is still felt. BP continues to advance his "Beyond Petroleum" message and strategy (even as it also seeks to tighten the management controls that led to the problems precipitating his departure), and still seeks to adapt to a changing global energy paradigm. As a further sign of his influence, despite the problems he faced in his last days with the company, his replacement, Tony Hayward, was known throughout the company as a close associate and protégé of Browne.

One of the critiques of Browne's tenure at BP during his last tumultuous days was that he was more focused on managing perception of the firm, especially with government and opinion leaders worldwide, than on actually managing the firm's operations, which led to a series of embarrassing and tragic refinery and pipeline accidents. But cultivating high-level ties is hardly unique to BP. In the United States, the close ties of the energy superclass to the government have been the subject of countless books, movies, media exposés, and public debate. From Michael Moore's *Fahrenheit 9/11* documentary to Craig Unger's *House of Bush, House of Saud*, ties between big oil and American political leadership have prompted much study and speculation. The facts suggest that the links are extensive: The Bush family, Vice President Dick Cheney, and former secretary of state James Baker have been or continue to be directly involved with America's energy leadership, for example. A former secretary of commerce ran an energy company. Condoleezza Rice was a director of Chevron for ten years. Donald Rumsfeld and former Environmental Protection Agency administrator Christine Todd Whitman held considerable holdings in energy-related companies. In 2004 and 2006, major energy companies gave between $20 million and $25 million per election cycle to candidates who supported their agenda— on average about 80 percent to Republicans and 20 percent to Democrats. Key agenda items for these lobbyists were domestic policies that would curb or forestall costly environmental regulation and, more notoriously, foreign policies—such as intervention in the Middle East or intense pressure on countries like Venezuela, Bolivia, and Ecuador when they threatened to nationalize U.S. energy company assets—that protected their interests. If it does not produce the direct and sinister collaboration that marks movie depictions like *Syriana*, it is also indisputable that time and again, the United States has chosen policies that satisfy the industry agenda, whether wars or tax breaks, resistance to tougher environmental regulations, or looking the other way when oil producers misbehave. (See Chapter 9 for the story of Teodoro Obiang, kleptocrat in chief of Equatorial Guinea.)

Energy industry ties to the U.S. government were particularly controversial during the early years of the Bush administration, in the months prior to 9/11. At that time, Vice President Cheney was given responsibility for a reassessment of U.S. energy policy that resulted in a series of more than three hundred meetings between the vice president and his energy task force—the vast majority of which, according to *The Washington Post*, were with top energy industry executives. Although most of the meetings have remained secret, reports confirm that they included representatives of ExxonMobil, Duke Energy, Constellation Energy, BP, and more than three dozen top industry groups, as well as major Bush supporter and Enron chairman Ken Lay.

I remember the mood at the time. My company helped organize a conference on the future of the American energy industry, and Enron was one of its sponsors. The meeting took place at the Ritz-Carlton in Pentagon City, just days after the 9/11 attacks. Enron was still riding high, ranked number seven on the *Fortune* 500 list, and one after another, congressmen, senators, and regulators came by to greet Lay, treating him with the kind of deference usually offered to visiting heads of state. It was clear to all that given the prominence of his company, his leadership as a Bush fund-raiser, and his special closeness to Cheney, this Houston resident had become a major Washington power broker. He was busy advancing to responsive ears his proposals for less regulation and more market freedom for his traders who, within a few months, would be revealed to have abused the freedoms they had and many they did not have. One regulator in particular, Federal Energy Regulatory Commission chairman Patrick Wood, surprised several observers by not simply delivering his speech and leaving, as did many top officials, but by devoting himself to the event for almost its entire duration and spending a significant amount of his downtime with Lay.

The eight-hundred-pound gorilla in the U.S. energy superclass today, with the decline and fall of Lay and his associates, is clearly Rex W. Tillerson, who further illustrates the propensity for coziness between big oil and political elites, as well as the cluster's increasingly global reach. Tillerson took the reins at the world's largest public corporation, ExxonMobil, on January 1, 2006. As *The Wall Street Journal* eloquently describes him, with "a Texas twang, rugged visage and real-life skills on horseback, Mr. Tillerson personifies Hollywood's image of the swashbuckling American oilman." He is one of the few big oil CEOs who never received an MBA or master's degree, but that has not stopped him from reaching a position of extraordinary power and influence.

Any inhabitant of the aptly named "God Pod" (Exxon's executive suite) is by default a major player in the energy cluster of the superclass. ExxonMobil provides 83,700 jobs in ninety-five countries around the world. In 2006, the company pumped twice as much oil and gas as Kuwait and hauled in $370 billion in revenue with record profits of

$39.5 billion. In the United States, the power of the position has provided Tillerson close relations with the White House and a number of high-ranking Republicans, including the former speaker of the House, Illinois representative Dennis Hastert. These ties seem to get results when it comes to influencing the political agenda. Immediately after a "private meeting" with Tillerson in 2006, for example, Hastert took to the floor of the House and called on Congress to allow drilling in the Arctic National Wildlife Refuge, a position for which he had not previously taken such a vocal stand. Tillerson's de facto clout with political elites also comes as a result of his company's generous budget for lobbyists. ExxonMobil spent more than $7.5 million on lobbying in 2004, and nearly the same amount in 2005. (In comparison, its big oil cousins BP and Shell spent just $2.8 and $1.4 million, respectively.) Political connections extend abroad as well, especially in Russia, where according to CNN Tillerson is "well-connected to officialdom, all the way up to President Vladimir Putin."

As Tillerson said in 2006, "We live in a global community, our economies are interdependent and since energy is such a post of the economic growth, it's only natural that some of the energy supply demand is going to be interdependent as well." As a result, he planned to spend as much as $20 billion in 2007 on oil exploration and production efforts. Adding to the company's existing refinery operations in twenty-six countries and oil and gas exploration in thirty-seven, Tillerson has launched a number of initiatives in the unforgiving tundra of Siberia, where natural gas fields have already provided windfall profits. There, the company controls the U.S. portion of the Sakhalin projects, a consortium of American, Russian, Japanese, and Indian oil companies worth more than $12 billion.

Tillerson has another challenge to confront: public opinion. The company and its iconic former CEO, Lee Raymond, whom Tillerson served directly under for thirteen years, presented a brash persona that was often characterized as arrogant. Raymond became the bane of environmentalists in particular with his persistent skepticism about the role of fossil fuels in causing global warming. Tillerson has made clear he shares his predecessor's doubts. As *Fortune* wrote in 2007, in reference to BP's eco-friendly trademark, "Beyond petroleum? At Exxon it's all petroleum."

Despite his defiant stance, Tillerson has attempted to soften the company's image. He argued that "despite gaps in the scientific evidence, the 'risk to society posed by greenhouse gas emissions may prove significant [enough] . . . [that] action is justified now.'" The importance of one man's view on this issue, given his seat atop the world's largest company, further underscores the centrality of the opinion-leading role of the superclass. But it is also important to remember that these top industry executives touch the lives of millions in other ways, too—like through the price of gasoline at the pump. While industry defenders argue that all such prices are simply a result of the market's supply-and-demand tug-of-war, that is only part of the story. Companies make decisions about the profit margins they seek and those decisions take money directly out of the pocket of consumers just as price increases associated with supply shortages do. And of course, oil producers make other decisions, such as whether or not to invest in new production or even to increase output, which also impact supply and prices. Consequently, the men at the top of the energy industry influence billions of lives in the most direct ways possible, making decisions impacting key components of the price of a vital commodity.

GLOBAL INDUSTRY, GLOBAL LEADERSHIP

Today, companies dominate the superclass and Americans dominate the leaders of those companies. Of the top twenty-two companies in the world, half are currently led by Americans—a concentration of power in the hands of representatives of a country that is home to only 5 percent of the earth's population. But the situation is rapidly changing. The trend lines clearly suggest that more chief executives and top bankers will come from the rest of the world, as more of the largest companies increasingly come from places other than the transatlantic region.

In the late eighteenth century, the Rothschild family built one of the world's great international business networks the old-fashioned way: They had children. The clan's patriarch, Mayer Amschel Rothschild, fathered nineteen offspring, ten of whom lived to adulthood and launched businesses throughout Europe, from Germany to England to Austria to Italy. Today, of course, mergers and acquisitions and new technologies make giving birth to networks considerably easier. This in turn opens new opportunities for business leaders from the emerging world to tap into capital and to grow: the Mittals and the Abramoviches, for example, and people like Yan Cheung of Nine Dragons Paper Company, one of China's richest women.

Is this a democratizing force that will empower the previously unempowered? Or will the continuous consolidation of global industries simply result in trading one era's group of elites for the next? Some observers suggest that changes in corporate governance requirements are weakening chief executives and promoting a democratizing trend, while others note that power is concentrating among a few key board members, private equity firms, and hedge fund investors, and suggest that power is shifting from managers back to owners. But the global picture is mixed. After the collapse of communism in Russia, leaders wrested economic and political control out of the hands of one small group—the top leaders of the Communist Party and members of the Politburo—and experimented with passing it on to a much broader group. Today, however, much of the economic power that was ultimately grabbed by a few oligarchs and their allies is being reclaimed by the state.

Mills had little hope in the prospects for achieving a perfect balance of power between elites and the masses. It is, of course, the role of government and systems of law to manage that balance. Our attention, therefore, turns next to government elites, national and international, operating at a moment of profound historical change that has called into question many of the most fundamental assumptions about the nature and role of the nation-state.

5

GLOBALISTS VS. NATIONALISTS:

POLITICAL FAULT LINE
FOR A NEW CENTURY

> In the absence of justice, what is sovereignty but
> organized robbery?
>
> —ST. AUGUSTINE

History will record that, for eight years at the beginning of the twenty-first century, George W. Bush was the most powerful person on earth. It is sometimes difficult to make sweeping assertions about who sits atop the pyramid of power in a given human pursuit. In religion, the pope is undoubtedly the top Catholic, but multiple imams and rabbis also have widespread influence. Rex Tillerson may run the largest private energy company in the world, but, as we have seen, he may be less powerful than Saudi oil minister Ali Al-Naimi. Bill Gates may still by many measures be atop the information technology world, but today the buzz says Google is "hotter" than Microsoft on the innovation front, and the field is so volatile that a new technological breakthrough could dethrone the Seattle software mogul at any time. In other words, while it is possible to name the princes of the knowledge economy, crowning a single king is much more difficult.

But there is only one commander in chief of what is by far the world's most powerful military, and he also happens to be the chief executive of the world's richest nation—one with a GDP three times higher than the runner-up, Japan. The president of the United States has extraordinary power to conduct the business of the United States as he or she sees fit, despite the carefully constructed checks and balances provided by the Constitution via the carefully crafted roles it prescribes for America's bicameral legislature and its Supreme Court. Members of the president's cabinet serve at his or her pleasure; indeed, presidents have the option of changing the structure of the cabinet, of firing and hiring new members, and of determining who serves on influential advisory committees like the National Security Council, the Homeland Security Council, or the National Economic Council. Today there are more than three thousand such presidential appointees, a number that has swelled from roughly six hundred just thirty years ago. In this way, the president's greatest power may in fact be his or her ability to mete out authority to those around him, granting and withholding power. As former secretary of state Colin Powell said to me, "In our system it is hard to overstate the centrality of the president. Others advise. The Congress can block. But he is the initiator and the key decision maker. I've seen presidents who didn't fully realize this even as they were entering office. And often when I read commentaries about what is happening in our government, they underplay the responsibility the president has either through his actions or through his decisions not to intervene."

Bush proved the extraordinary power of his position by deciding to launch a global war on terror and invading two countries without anything resembling a formal declaration of war from Congress. When a U.S. president is joined in office by a Congress controlled by his party, as Bush was for his first six years in office, exceptional power is made more extraordinary and in some cases virtually unchallengeable. International disapproval of his actions, or even a majority of Americans opposing his policies, cannot stop the occupant of this office in those circumstances. There is no truer measure of real power than the ability to impose one's will on resistant constituents or, as Bush has done, on a resistant world. "This is the George W. Bush administration," one top Republican observer in Washington remarked. "Sure, the roles that Vice President Cheney and Donald Rumsfeld played were big. But what they did, what roles they played, how far they were allowed to go, that was ultimately the president's decision . . . and the outcomes are ultimately his responsibility."

The power of the modern president, especially when it comes to foreign affairs, is clearly not what America's founders had in mind. When John Adams observed, "There is danger from all men. The only maxim of a free government ought to be to trust no man living with power to endanger the public liberty," he was articulating a view shared by many of his brethren who shaped the new institutions and laws of the United States in the late eighteenth century. Indeed, the first impulses of the leaders of the new republic were reflected in the Articles of Confederation, which created only a very weak chief executive, vesting most powers in a single legislative chamber in reaction to what were seen as the abuses of the British monarchy. In this spirit was the American Congress empowered to declare war, approve executive appointments, and cast the deciding vote in choosing the president if no candidate had a majority in the electoral college.

Over time, presidents have asserted their primacy in numerous ways, from the gradual expansion of the executive branch and the budget and thus the influence associated with it, to the modification of concepts such as "executive privilege." These moves to consolidate power in what Bush administration officials like to call the "unitary executive" effectively do what was considered anathema by America's founders: place the president and those in his office above the law by placing them beyond the investigative powers of Congress. For its part, of course, America's congressional leaders have proved themselves to be periodically so capricious, ill-informed, self-interested, partisan and—not infrequently—much worse in their regard for the law, that presidents have benefited from considerable public support for the expansion of the chief executive's role and prerogatives. Nothing makes for strong presidents like weak legislatures.

THE POWER VACUUM

The pattern of arrogation of authority by the president and abrogation of responsibility by Congress is not only repeated throughout history; it also echoes patterns that have led to the concentration of political power among the few in the United States, especially when it comes to shaping America's global role.

For example, the top job in the U.S. political structure is actually not the president. It is the voter. But voters cede power when they fail to meet their responsibility as citizens to understand and deliberate on the choices before them. About 40 percent of Americans eligible to vote did not bother to do so in the 2004 presidential elections, and nearly 60 percent did not vote in the midterm elections two years later. According to the 2007 Pew Survey of Americans' knowledge of current affairs, it is clear that many do not take their broader civic responsibilities very seriously either. Only about two-thirds of Americans could even name the vice president; four times as many Americans could identify singer Beyoncé Knowles as could identify Senate Majority Leader Harry Reid; and three times as many could identify Indianapolis Colts quarterback

Peyton Manning as could identify Secretary of Defense Robert Gates. Only half knew that religious violence was behind most of the current fighting in Iraq, and less than a third could identify Sunnis as the principal group in conflict with the Shiites in a country that had dominated American headlines for five years prior to the polling. Less than a third could name the president of Russia. And only about a third of Americans, according to a Canadian government study cited in *The Economist*, have passports, suggesting that their preparation for "overseeing" the greatest power of the global era is sadly lacking. With this kind of base of knowledge, or rather of ignorance, voters either make themselves more easily manipulated or they simply opt out of the system of government, removing the main check on the power of the president.

The fact that most international issues fail to resonate with voters has also given Washington decision makers a sense that they can conduct their international policy making essentially within the confines of a small specialist community. This is the abrogation factor at work. Something like one-third of U.S. congresspeople and almost two-thirds of their staff don't have passports. Even these full-time professionals in the policy-making community seem to have opted out of being fully engaged participants in shaping America's international role—or they are laboring under the misconception that they can make constructive judgments about America's role in the world without actually venturing out into that world. Four of the five presidents elected between 1976 and 2006 had virtually no major international policy experience. Is it any wonder that the debate regarding the consequences of major international actions is so inadequate, or that those actions seem to be so uninformed by history or an understanding of regional affairs? As one very prominent political consultant said to me, "Americans tend to act based on what they believe rather than what they know, and they like leaders who have similar impulses."

Into the void created by congressional abrogation come marching those who would influence these issues—not surprisingly, a group containing a far higher concentration of those with global interests and one that is able through other tools of power and influence to arrogate disproportionate influence to themselves.

One such group, the subject of my last book, *Running the World*, is the international policy community in Washington. This is a very small, tightly knit group of influentials, many of whom have known each other and worked together for most of their careers. The group who have served or are likely to serve in top foreign policy and national security positions and those who have the greatest influence among them number no more than a few hundred. Most have attended or taught at a handful of elite universities (to identify a few: former defense secretaries Donald Rumsfeld and Frank Carlucci were undergraduate roommates at Princeton; Henry Kissinger and Jimmy Carter's national security adviser Zbigniew Brzezinski rivaled one another at Harvard; Madeleine Albright's father taught international affairs to Condoleezza Rice). Members of this set typically belong to the Council on Foreign Relations and other groups that link them closer together, and they often work together for administration after administration. Also, as a consequence of their domination in the top U.S. policy jobs, they are the few with the greatest ties to the foreign policy elites of governments around the world—which in turn makes them that much more valuable in Washington.

To run for president, candidates need teams of top advisers, not just for advice but also as "validators" who can demonstrate the candidate's competence in, for example, international affairs. Not surprisingly, the best validators are those who have held high positions in the past. Consequently, those who have done so are the most likely to do so again. As noted in *Running the World*, it is one of those communities in which the best credential for entry is already being a member. The result is a highly interconnected group of decision makers and a remarkable concentration of power in a small circle.

This power extends beyond the halls of the executive branch. We have seen the influence levied by firms like Goldman Sachs within the top echelons of the U.S. government, but it is worth underscoring yet again the revolving door that allows policy makers to leave top firms to go into government and then to reenter those firms. This is one way that the financial community maintains its influence. Perhaps it is not surprising that each of America's recent secretaries of the treasury has subsequently taken a senior position in the financial world: former secretary John Snow at Cerberus, former secretary Paul O'Neill advising Blackstone, former secretary Lawrence Summers at D. E. Shaw, former secretary Robert Rubin at Citigroup, former secretary Nicholas Brady at his own firm, Darby Overseas Investments. The reality is that a senior policy job in government is one of the most direct ways to a remunerative position on Wall Street, in the defense sector, or elsewhere in the corporate community. While that might fall into the "news from nowhere" category—presumably all these individuals must work somewhere after they leave government—it does not diminish the equally important fact that big Wall Street firms and corporations with long rosters of former government officials have disproportionate influence on policy decisions.

We need look at only a few examples to get a sense of the impact of this connection between elites in different power clusters. At the time of this writing, Goldman's board includes Stephen Friedman, the former Goldman CEO and current chairman of the President's Foreign Intelligence Advisory Board, and James Johnson, the former head of Fannie Mae and top adviser to Democratic presidential candidates. Within Goldman we find a wide variety of former top government officials including, to name a few, the former undersecretary of state Bob Hormats, the former undersecretary of the treasury John F. W. Rogers, and the former New York Fed chairman Gerald Corrigan.

Look at top firms besides Goldman and the results are the same. The board of Morgan Stanley includes former White House chief of staff Erskine Bowles, former National Economic Council chair Laura Tyson, and former SEC chief accountant Donald Nicolaisen. The board of Citibank: former CIA director John Deutch and former treasury secretary Robert Rubin. The board of Lehman Brothers: former Ex-Im Bank chairman John Macomber and former Rear Admiral Marsha Johnson Evans. And perhaps most impressively stacked with former government officials, the board of American International Group: former secretary of defense William S. Cohen, former chairman of the president's Council of Economic Advisers Martin Feldstein, former U.S. trade representative Carla Hills, former UN ambassador Richard Holbrooke, former chief Security and Exchange Commission accountant Michael Sutton, and former "energy czar" Frank Zarb.

Of course, the list does not stop at America's borders; the lists of international leaders with ties to major financial institutions is a long one as well. Former British prime minister John Major joined the Carlyle Group after his term in office, and former Peruvian prime minister Pedro-Pablo Kuczynski joined Credit Suisse First Boston. I chaired a panel at Davos in 2006 featuring the prime minister of Pakistan, Shaukat Aziz, who described during our chat in the green room how helpful his years at Citigroup had been in preparing him for political office.

Even with the most assiduous efforts at avoiding conflicts of interest on the part of these individuals and the many others who pass through the revolving door between the government and corporate communities, one can see how the worldviews of two such integrated communities must begin to blend together. With such a small group atop America's policy-making apparatus, and such a high likelihood that many of its members will work with the most internationally engaged and highly remunerative business organizations before and/or after their tenures, it is clear why the agendas of a few major global corporations resonate at the most rarefied levels of the U.S. government. This, then, is among the forces that fill the void created by the ignorance of the American public and many of its elected representatives. And it produces direct results, one of which is legislation that is overly favorable to financial institutions. To choose one example that was controversial at the time of this book's writing, private equity firms managed to persuade Congress to treat their "carried interest" in companies as capital gains rather than ordinary income, resulting in a substantial tax break (15 percent instead of up to 45 percent). Many, even a few financial leaders such as Warren Buffett, viewed this as so egregiously inequitable that an opposition movement has formed against it.

Because of America's international reach and power, the revolving door to the financial community is a phenomenon with global consequences. It is no accident that this group is broadly predisposed to policy prescriptions such as open borders, less regulation, and lower taxes. It also favors debt restructurings and bailouts for bad loans, as in the cases of the Brady Plan after the Latin debt crises of the 1980s and U.S. intervention to avert financial catastrophe in Mexico during the Tequila Crisis of late 1994 and 1995. In many respects this is not simply because one group influences another. It is because there is only one group, with its individual members moving from one set of jobs to another. Given that this group is globally sophisticated, well educated, intelligent, and successful by any measure, it is not surprising that much of what they advocate is also smart and worth implementing. But where is the counterweight in the system? Where is the oversight that is democracy's due to the many who are affected by these decisions—such as the taxpayers who must foot the bill for bailouts or pick up the slack created by corporate tax breaks for rich investors in private equity firms? It is hard to imagine the role of supervisor being played by a Congress that for the most part understands neither finance nor the global scene, and it will clearly not go to an executive branch that draws on this closed community for most of its top decision makers.

As Thomas Friedman said to me one afternoon in his office just two blocks from the White House, "Here, now, the asymmetry in knowledge about how the global economy works between legislators and businesspeople and technologists is as wide as the Atlantic ocean; that is, how many legislators have you met who you think have anywhere near the grasp that you or the average multinational CEO does today about how the world works? So these national governments have a problem—how can you regulate something you do not understand, and what is more complex than the inner workings of the global economy? And if government can't do it . . . it's only natural that the business community steps in. Whether that is what was originally intended or whether that is in everyone's best interests is a matter open for debate."

GANGSTERS FOR CAPITALISM?

As Kevin Phillips chronicles in his book *Wealth and Democracy: A Political History of the American Rich*, money is the lifeblood of American politics. The interests of the monied have always played a great role in setting the American political agenda and influencing the behavior of presidents and all those around them. Phillips describes how the rich have shaped policy throughout U.S. history, from the great profits enjoyed by American corporations as a result of wars they supported (share prices increased ten or even twenty times for some war suppliers during World War I) to the wealth held by top officials, like the ten members of Warren Harding's cabinet who were collectively worth more than $600 million. He cites Franklin Roosevelt's observations in a letter to one of Woodrow Wilson's top advisers: "The real truth . . . is, as you and I know, that a financial element in the larger centers has owned the Government ever since the days of Andrew Jackson—and I am not wholly excepting the Administration of W.W."

A similar concern about the connections between money and power was expressed almost simultaneously by Major General Smedley D. Butler, two-time recipient of America's highest military award, the Congressional Medal of Honor, and one of the most outspoken iconoclasts in U.S. military history. Popular with pacifist and anti-Fascist groups in his day, Butler's comments might be lost to history were they not so resonant with similar critiques that are heard today.

> I spent thirty-three years and four months in active service in the country's most agile military force, the Marines. I served in all ranks from second lieutenant to major general. And during that period I spent most of my time being a high-class muscle man for Big Business, for Wall Street and the bankers. I was a racketeer, a gangster for capitalism . . .
>
> Thus I helped make Mexico, and especially Tampico, safe for American oil interests in 1914. I helped make Haiti and Cuba a decent place for the National City Bank boys to collect revenue in. I helped in the raping of half-a-dozen Central American re-

publics for the benefit of Wall Street. The record of racketeering is long. I helped purify Nicaragua for the benefit of the banking house of Brown Brothers and Co. in 1909–1912. I brought light to the Dominican Republic for the sugar interests in 1916. I helped make Honduras "right" for American fruit companies in 1903. In China, in 1927, I helped see to it that Standard Oil went its way unmolested.

Such connections exist to this day. Butler's testimony echoes arguments of current vintage that both of our recent Gulf Wars have been fought for the benefit of oil companies to ensure that production remained uninterrupted and that threats to it were offset. These interventions have produced other beneficiaries who turn out to have considerable influence, like federal contractors such as the company once led by Vice President Cheney, Halliburton. In a similar way, during the Clinton and prior Bush eras, many pointed out that the financial bailouts associated with the emerging markets crash of 1997–98, with the Tequila Crisis, and with the savings-and-loan crisis of the late 1980s and early '90s greatly benefited the Wall Street colleagues and friends of Robert Rubin and Nicholas Brady, who also happened to be among the core groups they consulted in arriving at their decisions. Yes, these interventions also had important macroeconomic benefits, and the consequences of failing to undertake them would have been severe. But in such cases, political and economic elites are so intertwined that it is hard not to see elements of self-dealing.

Compounding this phenomenon is the fact that to a much greater extent than in most other countries (where political campaigns are publicly financed), America's system of campaign finance has what can only be described as a corrupting effect, making politicians dependent first on donors and only secondarily on voters at large. This in turn gives a special advantage to those who run large institutions and can use those positions, resources, and networks to play leading roles as fund-raisers. This has never been truer than today, when the leading candidates running for president in 2008 have had to raise more than $100 million each. The financial hurdles to the highest office in the United States are so high that it is inconceivable that one could surmount them without rich and powerful allies from both the private and the public sectors.

Having established lists and mechanisms and networks of fund-raisers at her disposal made it easier for Senator Hillary Clinton to pick up where Bill Clinton's fund-raising team left off. Having access to donors like Vinod Gupta also helps. Gupta, head of tech firm InfoUSA, reportedly had his firm provide $900,000 worth of travel to Europe, the Caribbean, and Mexico for both President and Senator Clinton. The firm also gave a $3.3 million consulting contract to Bill Clinton and a big six-figure donation to his presidential library. (All this data became public thanks to a lawsuit by disgruntled InfoUSA shareholders who didn't think such largesse was in the company's financial interest.) Gupta also underwrote a $1 million turn-of-the-millennium party on the Washington Mall, a $250,000 donation to the Clinton Foundation, and more than $200,000 to the Democratic Party during Hillary Clinton's last Senate campaign. When asked what they got in return, besides the close relationship between Gupta and the Clintons, a spokesperson for the firm said, "There is just the obvious value of having a former president on your team and at your disposal for advice."

The Clinton experience is not unique. The biggest donor to the campaign and early presidency of George W. Bush was the Enron Corporation, the infamous Houston-based energy company that collapsed into bankruptcy in late 2001; Enron's law firm, Vinson & Elkins, was number two, and their combined donations totaled well into the seven figures. Enron's accounting firm, Andersen Worldwide, was fourth. The top ten donors to Bush's 2004 campaign, all with an excess of $300,000 in donations (from their PACs or individual employees and their families): Morgan Stanley, Merrill Lynch, PricewaterhouseCoopers, UBS-Americas, Goldman Sachs, MBNA Corporation, Credit Suisse Group, Lehman Brothers, Citigroup, and Bear Stearns.

What do the donors get in exchange? Access to senior officials, positions on presidential councils, top appointments for friends who share their views, seats on trade missions, interventions by U.S. officials to tailor elements of global regulations and tariff structures to the needs of specific industries whether through the WTO, via bilateral agreements, or through other channels, efforts to enforce intellectual property concerns and, from time to time, efforts to help play down conflicts that might threaten corporate interests. (This happens often with China, for example, when brewing political tensions produce efforts from companies like Boeing or Motorola or Citibank with large interests in that country to avert the kind of crisis or trade sanctions that would be most costly to them.)

Kevin Phillips, in assaying the corrosive effect of money on American politics and ideals, quotes former senator Bill Bradley, who while running for president in 2000 asserted that one reason money was too intertwined with politics was the result of "a failure to understand that democracy and capitalism are separate parts of the American dream and that keeping that dream alive depends on keeping one from corrupting the other." One of the most serious consequences of this phenomenon has been the conflation of "free markets" and "democracy" in America's policy prescription for the world. The two ideas are often seen as one and the same. Yet there are countless examples today of countries in which markets are getting freer but democracy is suffering—China comes to mind, as does Russia, as does most of the Middle East. In each of these places, business interests are happy to ignore the political plight of locals provided that returns can be earned. Advancing free markets is good and helps promote positive changes within society, and there are certainly challenges associated with the effective promotion of democracy. But failing to adequately address those challenges results, as we have seen, in the concentration of wealth and power among a few who, in turn, act in their own interests (as markets would expect them to do) without the counterbalances good governance would require.

THE RULES CHANGE BUT THE GAME STAYS THE SAME: POLITICAL ELITES WORLDWIDE

The connection between money and political elites has existed for centuries. Phillips notes that of fifty people cited by *The Wall Street Journal* as the wealthiest of the past millennium, thirty were rulers or major government officials, and another nine were bankers or agents to governments. Perhaps even more evocatively, Cullen Murphy's book *Are We Rome? The Fall of an Empire and the Fate of America* recounts the evolution of the Latin word *suffragium* over five centuries of Rome's ascendancy and decline. According to the analysis of the Oxford historian Geoffrey de Ste. Croix, the word originally meant "voting tablet" or "ballot," but over the years—as republican traditions faded and the system became one of transactions among networks of established elites—the word evolved to mean "pressure that could be exerted on one's behalf by a powerful man." Ultimately, as money became the means of leverage, the term came to mean "a gift, a payment, or a bribe."

When Silvio Berlusconi ended his first term as prime minister of Italy in 1994, the country was rocked by a scandal that echoed back to the ancient language of its capital. Pundits called the debacle "Tangentopoli" (bribesville). But it was not enough to stop the political career of Berlusconi, then Italy's richest man and number fourteen on the *Forbes* billionaire list, from returning to office in 2001. He was reelected by virtue of his drive, his outsized personality, and, not in small part, his ability to harness the power of certain of his holdings, which included a media empire that spanned three television networks, a film company, and Italy's biggest publishing group. Many of the current or former employees of these companies actually entered politics, joining Berlusconi's party. But more significant was the coverage that they gave the politician on his quest to return to office. According to independent calculations, during his run for office, Berlusconi's Mediaset television networks devoted eleven times more coverage to their principal owner than to his opponent. Italia One, one of those networks, tuned its coverage to the anticrime, anti-immigrant themes that were central to Berlusconi's campaign. When Canale 5, the least biased of his holdings, cited a Berlusconi blunder, Berlusconi personally called Enrico Mentana, its news chief, and complained about the story. His *Panorama* magazine supported his campaign, as did the family newspaper *Il Giornale*, run by Berlusconi's brother. On the verge of his election, *The Guardian* called his control of these media assets "the biggest conflict of interest in western democracy." Given his holdings and the state's ownership of the other three main television networks, Berlusconi would effectively have control of virtually all the significant broadcast assets in the sixth largest of the world's economies.

Berlusconi brushed off the concerns about his wealth with panache, arguing that not only did the country need his entrepreneurial skills but that his decision to serve as prime minister was in fact a sacrifice. "No, look, excuse me, but I have worked my entire life. I am doing the country a favor. I don't need to go into office for the power. I have houses all over the world, stupendous boats, including Murdoch's yacht, which I just bought. I have beautiful airplanes, a beautiful wife, a beautiful family."

Five years later, he undoubtedly felt even more sincerely that he had made a sacrifice when he was driven from office amid a swirl of scandal and accusations that he had misused his political power to protect himself from prosecution. Berlusconi's empire and networks—including his chief operating officer, who hailed from Morgan Stanley—could not keep him in office, thus suggesting the limits of even extraordinary wealth. Apparently, even his business acumen could not help him in running the country, indicating the difference in skill sets required for elites in business and politics. He had done himself too much damage through alienating the business community that might have seemed a natural ally. Italy's economy faltered under his leadership, and his quick temper and knack for producing comments that put off many in Europe's leadership (he once compared a German member of the European parliament to the boss of a concentration camp) made it easy for his opponents ultimately to bring him down. So too did rumors of scandal and self-dealing that remain unresolved to this day.

Berlusconi was a trailblazer in another area, crafting a stance that bridged the difference between nationalism and internationalism. He was pro-America—a supporter of Bush's efforts in the Middle East, for example—and proglobalization, yet anti-immigration and combative with his European colleagues. It is a stance others would emulate in response to a growing political divide in Europe and elsewhere: the increasing tension between nationalist and internationalist factions in society. For the most part, business is pro-internationalist, following capital flows and cheap labor. Labor is more nationalist, threatened especially by immigration and trade deals that might lead to the loss of jobs. Berlusconi's position was roughly in the middle, the center of this new continuum. Another who has taken a similar approach is French president Nicolas Sarkozy, who ran for office on his record of being tough on security, tough on immigration, and tough on parallel concerns like keeping Turkey out of the EU; yet he is also pro-Europe and more pro–United States and pro-Israel than any French leader in the recent past.

The connections between Sarkozy and leaders of the business and media communities run deep, extending back to his days as mayor of the upscale Parisian suburb of Neuilly-sur-Seine, and they have been carefully cultivated throughout his climb to the top of the French political scene. Sarkozy developed particularly close relationships with a number of media magnates, which were important in helping him defeat Socialist candidate Ségolène Royal for the presidency. Many of the ties are practically familial: Martin Bouygues, CEO of a global conglomerate that owns the leading French TV network, is a godfather to Sarkozy's young son, while Arnaud Lagardère, the head of a military contractor and media company that owns a number of newspaper and radio outlets, calls Sarkozy a "brother." Bernard Arnault, a billionaire and the chairman and CEO of Moët Hennessy Louis Vuitton, which owns the daily business journal *La Tribune*, attended Sarkozy's wedding. And shortly after France's 2007 presidential elections, the victorious president-elect Sarkozy decompressed for a few days on the yacht of his friend and supporter, billionaire Vincent Bolloré. Bolloré's enterprise, which today has annual sales in excess of $8 billion, includes interests in advertising, transportation, energy, and a number of media outlets. A reporter for *Le Monde* recalled that after one of Sarkozy's campaign rallies, the candidate remarked to a group of journalists, "It's funny, I know all your bosses."

Sarkozy breaks the mold of government leaders in France in several important ways. Not only is he the first French president whose father was not born in France (he was Hungarian), he is also the first born since the end of World War II. He also, due to an undistinguished early academic career, was unable to gain admittance to France's school for future political leaders, the École Nationale d'Administration (ENA). Working his way around that obstacle was formidable. As one French CEO told me, "We have a tradition of celebrating *égalité*, but in France, everybody is equal only up until high school. Then, when you get into high school, you start getting diverted into programs that lead you into the specialized universities which, as with ENA, are usually the only way to the top. But Sarkozy did it the only other available way: He worked his way into the hearts of the elites who did go to those schools, by being loyal and tough and hardworking. He has a great way with people he wants help from."

Sarkozy skillfully did what political elites must do in a party system: gain favor with the controlling business and political elites, work those relationships hard, and improvise where necessary. It is a pattern seen in virtually all members of the political superclass, and indeed, in most members of the superclass who seek to rise up in the context of established institutional hierarchies—whether parties, companies, religious organizations, or crime families. Performance is key too. On his path from mayor to member of parliament, to gaining right-wing leader Jacques Chirac's patronage and becoming budget minister, to being appointed spokesman for the party, the wiry and intense Sarkozy did what needed to be done to get ahead. Truly, he tried almost everything, including dating Chirac's daughter. When his advancement was going too slowly and he took another path, backing a rival of Chirac, he stumbled, but in stumbling was forced to reinvent himself and reshape the modern French right wing.

Regaining his footing and repairing his relationship with Chirac, Sarkozy became interior minister in Chirac's 2002 government and thus was able to help the Gaullists offer a conservative alternative to the hard-right policies of Jean-Marie Le Pen. He was the minister in charge when immigrant groups, feeling left out of the French economy, rioted in 2005. Using his media ties and skills and a boldness that was new to French politics, he promised to put an end to the problem by washing the "scum" out of the ghettoes with an industrial-power hose. He played on the French national unease with the influx of immigrants, mostly from northern Africa, and, in borrowing that stance from Le Pen, co-opted him, ultimately ensuring his victory over Royal.

Since election, Sarkozy has zigged back a little to the center, choosing to appoint a cabinet that is half female and picking as his foreign minister Bernard Kouchner, a darling of the left and cofounder of Médecins Sans Frontières (Doctors Without Borders). In so doing, he revealed his recognition of the importance of image and the media in modern politics, his flair for the dramatic, and his awareness of the growing political relevance of nontraditional groups like NGOs. These moves were all as innovative as his tough stance against immigrants was not.

At a time when EU expansion and globalization are raising questions about European identity—especially with regard to the admission of Turkey—it is not a little ironic that one of the most prominent leaders of Europe has Hungarian roots. After all, it was control of Hungary and rivalry with the Austro-Hungarian empire that was at the center of the last Ottoman (Turkish) invasions into the heart of Europe, culminating in 1683 in the Battle of Vienna. Those conflicts underscore that politicians and policies may change, but proximity and geography do not, and that, for Europe, the "clash of civilizations" with the Islamic world will always be a more pressing issue than for even the United States. This explains the intensity of intolerance there—the Danish cartoon controversy being such a powerful example—and why the new European nationalism of Sarkozy has such deep and ugly roots. It is a fascinating paradox. Pan-Europeanism looks very modern and antinationalist, but for many in Europe, it is also antiglobalist regionalism, a desire to preserve what is seen as European and to assert Europe's role in the context of a world that would make it much harder for individual states acting alone to do so.

This tension between internationalism and nationalism has become a defining issue for the global political superclass during its emergence over the past several decades. Evolving international structures, such as the official mechanisms of multilateralism (the UN, the international financial institutions, alliances and "working groups" from NATO to the G8 to the G20) and the informal ones (clusters of bankers practicing self-regulation or public-private partnerships grappling with issues like AIDS), and long-established national institutions are all struggling to define their roles in the global era. There is a recognition that national political institutions, traditions, and cultures are ill-suited to the exigencies of the new reality. At the same time, the day-to-day track for aspiring political elites requires working the national system, starting in the right place, gaining the favor of local higher-ups, finding a mentor, and landing key posts under his (or sometimes her) guidance.

Interestingly, in this respect, the political superclass operates for the most part—except for insurgents and coup plotters—in a much more closed system than does the business and financial superclass, largely because each national system typically has only a couple of party apparatuses in which to successfully function. All the incentives to gain political power lie in a domestic system, but once in power, leaders discover an unsettling reality. Many of the most vital issues with which they must deal, like those that are or have been on the front burner for Sarkozy, Berlusconi, and Bush, as well as leaders in the developing world, are international in origin and require international solutions. Achieving domestic results will require working outside the domestic system. Those who recognize the merits of international collaboration become the globalists. Those who resist it, often in order to be perceived as champions of local interests, are the nationalists. The nationalists frame compromises that are necessary for collaboration as dilutions of sovereignty, whereas the internationalists see them as essential to preserving national well-being in the global era. Nationalists seek to preserve the power of closed domestic political systems in a world of increasingly open economic systems. These tensions and divides are increasingly defining the global political landscape.

For many of today's political leaders, the solution is to walk a tightrope to the top, remaining loyal to national political systems while teasing out international gains that sometimes threaten national prerogatives. Perhaps no one faces as difficult a challenge in this regard as Chinese president Hu Jintao. Born in 1942—another leader who is a child of the post–World War II era—Hu grew up in a merchant family in the city of Taizhou. He was, according to his family, an obedient child who did well enough at school to gain a spot at Qinghua University, where he earned a degree in engineering. (As Bill Gates once pointed out, many Chinese leaders have earned degrees in engineering, a favored pursuit under the Communist regime, which has made it possible for people like Gates to be able to speak to them about scientific matters and appreciate their greater understanding than might be found in capitals like Washington, where the political elite is still dominated by lawyers.) By the time he left college, he had become a member of the Communist Party, and during the early part of his career he was working with the patronage of a party official named Song Ping, who had been tasked with identifying next-generation leaders.

By the early 1980s, his discipline had earned Hu a position atop the Communist Youth League, where he did well enough to win the approval and support of the general secretary of the Communist Party, Hu Yaobang (no relation). The elder Hu accelerated the career of the future president, engineering his appointment at thirty-nine to the party's Central Committee and at forty-two to the position of provincial party secretary—achievements that had never before been offered to anyone so young. In the latter role, Hu displayed a particular gift that resonates with the gifts of other political elites we have considered thus far, like "compassionate conservative" Bush and "nationalist-internationalists" like Sarkozy or Berlusconi: He was able to shape a persona in which he was perceived as different things by different people. As party secretary in Guizhou, he fostered an atmosphere that embraced intellectual diversity and seemed flexible and more open to ideas of reform. When he moved on from there to Tibet, where he oversaw the province at a time of pro–Dalai Lama protests in the streets of Lhasa, he showed his willingness to use force to eliminate the threat to Beijing's rule. His work in Tibet from 1989 to 1992 earned him appreciation in the inner sanctums of the Communist Party, the one electorate that matters in the Chinese system, and he was named a member of the Politburo standing committee. Just six years later, in 1998, Jiang Zemin named him vice president and therefore positioned him as his most likely successor.

Hu was not only able to appear both progressive and tough to the elders leading the party, he was also seen as a voice of the future and built a strong following among other members of his own generation. This balancing act, which led to his assumption of the presidency in 2002, has obviously been followed by many other, tougher ones: balancing China's voracious need for growth with its simultaneous desire for stability, the dynamism of its cities and coastal regions with the poverty of its rural areas, its dependency on outside capital and trade with its desire to remain in control of its own destiny, its impulse to be a global power with its desire to preserve a Chinese national identity, rampant capitalism with the desire to maintain elements of the Communist system. Hu has summed up his core approach to these challenges with the phrase "harmonious society," which uses a traditional Chinese virtue to frame his plan for addressing the inequalities that remain the greatest perceived threat to the country's internal cohesion. He has sought to promote some modest levels of democratic innovation at local levels in Chinese society while simultaneously sending a strong message that the country remains committed to one-party rule and the central role of the Communist Party. In this approach, there is either something for everyone, or something to inflame every critic. It's a fine line, and how well it works will be seen largely in a dimension of Hu's performance that is hard to gauge now—his role as the leader of the party elite, the elders, who will select the generation of leaders they intend to succeed them.

BEHIND THE SCENES: THE GLOBALIZATION OF THE SMOKE-FILLED BACK ROOM

Less visible than prime ministers, presidents, leading legislators, and foreign ministers among the global political superclass are those who make them possible, advise them, polish their rhetoric, spin their positions. In the past, perhaps few professions were so parochialized by the "all politics is local" observation of former speaker of the house Tip O'Neill. But today, the proverbial smoke-filled back room has itself become globalized with a handful of top political consultants advising leaders and aspirants around the world. They bring with them polling techniques, television marketing strategies, opposition research approaches, and a host of other tools that are starting to make elections worldwide look more similar. In so doing, they also are building ties between political parties in different countries, between their leaders, and between their ideologies—ties that are slowly creating something like global political coalitions.

While the Communist parties of the mid-twentieth century may have been trailblazers in this regard, they were hampered by a deeply flawed product and generally lousy strategies. (When you're forced to win hearts and minds at gunpoint, it suggests that your message may need a little more work.) Instead, the real breakthroughs in the 1990s were led by consultants and parties from the United States and Britain, whose efforts quickly extended out beyond that traditional English-language axis to help fledgling candidates in the former Soviet bloc, throughout Europe and Latin America, and on into Asia and Africa. The consequence is a group that complements in influence those with money: one that offers the words and the techniques that resonate with voters worldwide, that transfers lessons from one country to another, and is collectively responsible for either the dumbing-down of global political discourse, the enhanced "sophistication" of global political campaigning, or, as it seems likely, both.

As early as the 1930s, American pollster George Gallup traveled to Britain to promote his polling abilities, and throughout the second half of the twentieth century British politicians were visiting the United States to observe political campaigns and discuss strategy with their counterparts. Thatcher and Reagan's rapport extended to a discussion of managing their political situations, and Thatcher's successor John Major introduced U.S.-style presidential debates to Britain. Perhaps unfortunately for Major, his opponent in the 1997 election in which such debates were introduced was Tony Blair, who had dedicated himself to finding a new voice for the Labour Party and the new campaign "technologies" to go with it. The authors of "New Labour" turned to the group that had invented "New Democrats" in the United States: Bill Clinton and the small cadre of political consultants closest to him. Some already had established networks, such as Philip Gould, who had worked with the top Democratic pollster Stanley Greenberg and his collaborator and friend James Carville, the colorful, sharp-tongued Louisiana native made famous as Bill Clinton's political guru in 1992.

Gould has written:

> I was not a lone voice for Clinton within Labour. Margaret McDonagh, John Braggins and Alan Barnard, who were to hold senior positions in the 1997 election campaign, were all working in one capacity or another for Clinton. Jonathan Powell, then working for the British Embassy in Washington, now Tony Blair's chief of staff, was observing the Clinton campaign at first hand and building links that were later to prove priceless. Out of all this was born Millbank Tower [Labour Party headquarters] and the "war room" it houses; rapid rebuttal and the Excalibur computer [used to monitor opposition communications]; an obsession with message; and a tough unremitting focus on hard-working people and their concerns . . . At the time the message of Little Rock was not heard, but it could not be silenced. The Clinton experience was seminal for the Labour Party. Within five years almost everything that was written in my document had been implemented. Modernisation of Labour did not depend on Clinton, it would have happened anyway, but his election did give modernisation a road map.

Today, Gould is revered within political circles on both sides of the Atlantic as one of the players most instrumental in the creation of "New Labour." "He is a legend," said Anita Dunn of Squier Knapp Dunn, a top U.S. political consultancy. Dunn, who is one of the most thoughtful and highly regarded members of her profession's elite, went on to note that while the globalization of political consulting is a powerful phenomenon, it is primarily one that has been pioneered and dominated by top Americans, including Republicans like Frank Luntz, John McLaughlin, Richard Wirthlin, and her Democratic colleagues, Greenberg, Carville, and Mark Penn, the chairman of Burson-Marsteller and the chief strategist for the presidential campaign of Hillary Rodham Clinton. Gould is in a class by himself among non-U.S. practitioners of the profession. "I think," Dunn said, "he is the only non-American political consultant who could successfully come to the United States, which after all is the home of this sort of practice, and be a major success here."

Dunn herself recounted a conversation with representatives of a European social democratic party who were concerned that their candidate would not be able to hold his own in an upcoming presidential debate. They wanted to hire some pros to help him with his "debate prep," another term, like "war room," "rapid response" (or "rapid rebuttal"), and "opposition research" that has made its way from the world of American pols to the world at large.

Stanley Greenberg, whose firm Greenberg Quinlan Rosner has worked on dozens of international campaigns, cites among his most prominent clients Bill Clinton, Nelson Mandela, Thabo Mbeki, Tony Blair, Ehud Barak, and Gerhard Schroeder. In the connections among some of these is seen one fledgling trend that may gather momentum as such consultants and those associated with them fan out into an expanding network across the globe. Clinton, Blair, and Schroeder were all "new" voices for their center-left parties, and an effort was made among them to remain in touch, forming a kind of global "third way" alliance. At times this was joined by others, such as the Dutch prime minister Wim Kok and Italy's prime minister Massimo D'Alema, who joined the group at a meeting convened in Washington in the spring of 1999 by the Democratic Leadership Council, a centrist political organization that was closely associated with Clinton. The dialogue that produced this meeting was actually the result of a conversation that Blair had with first lady Hillary Clinton a couple of years earlier. Together these leaders discussed commonalities in their message and the extent to which their views were taking hold "from Latin America to Australia," and they sought to translate disparate parties into a more coordinated effort. While the defeat of Al Gore in 2000 derailed the effort by removing its most prominent member, the ties remain, especially along the Washington–London access, and via which British Prime Minister Gordon Brown retains close relationships with many ideologically sympathetic counterparts in the United States.

Another dimension of these global political networks is that political consultants do not work exclusively for political parties. Greenberg, for example, also derives a substantial portion of his firm's revenues from private sector organizations including Boeing, BP, British Airways, Sun Microsystems, Monsanto, UnitedHealthcare, the Business Roundtable, and the Organization for International Investment. Mark Penn oversees a PR business that lists among its clients Ford, Merck, Verizon, BP, McDonald's, and Microsoft; according to the firm's website, Penn "has helped to elect over 25 leaders in the United States, Asia, Latin America and Europe." Among the most prominent of these was his successful work in helping Tony Blair win a third term as Britain's prime minister. In fact, as great as his reputation is for serving as the pollster for the Clintons, he has also earned a reputation in the business community as "brilliant" and "exceptionally creative" for his work on corporate campaigns, including helping Microsoft shed its reputation as a corporate bully. Critics, such as competing pollster Mark Blumenthal, have suggested that Penn and his firm "have displayed a thirst for corporate work, often in conflict with the policy agendas of their political clients, that has long set the bar among Democratic pollsters." Among Democrats, Penn is seen as a particularly strong advocate for business views, but the conflict exists for virtually all consultants. One senior Democratic official called the accusation "perhaps one part truth and one big part sour grapes [because] Mark is the king of the hill right now."

Despite their corporate ties, these consultants typically seem more like rumpled academics. Greenberg, who got his PhD at Harvard and is married to Congresswoman Rosa DeLauro, has an intense but cerebral mien, with a good sense of humor and an uncanny knack for seeing the core issues at play in a political contest. He is an author and has worked for a wide variety of NGOs and not-for-profits, including the campaign to ban land mines. Penn, who also studied at Harvard, often appears in his jeans while hosting high-level Washington soirees at his Georgetown town house. He too is married to an influential woman, Nancy Jacobson, one of the Democratic Party's top fund-raisers. He is an author and widely sought-after commentator, and is known to those within the campaigns he has advised as a guy whose brain is often working so fast that he leaves some of his listeners in the dust. He has worked exceptionally closely with the Clintons, who highly value what one person in their inner circle called his "special genius." In fact, he was booted out as an adviser to Vice President Al Gore's presidential campaign in 2000 when, in response to Gore's question about whether there was any sign of "Clinton fatigue," Penn quipped, "I'm not tired of him. Are you?" Gore's other advisers, who worried that Penn was too close to the Clintons, pressed for and secured his removal. Gore went on to run his campaign, distancing himself from Clinton, and in retrospect, Democratic insiders believe he did himself in, losing the lift Clinton could have provided and the resulting votes that might have given him the edge in the close election with George W. Bush.

TANGLED WEBS AND TOTTERING INSTITUTIONS

Fulfilling the international and domestic obligations of their jobs is another difficult balancing act members of the political superclass must manage. This challenge is made greater by the fact that the formal mechanisms with which they must work internationally are so weak—some so ill-formed or imbalanced that they must search for new ones or pursue informal approaches. This is hardly new; international interaction has always been an important part of affairs of state. The difference today lies in the degree to which global markets have created codependent relationships between governments and investors, and the degree to which public sector control of key assets—of their currency, of their borders, of their culture—is eroding. Beyond these factors is a growing awareness of the importance of transnational issues, whether they pertain to global warming, terrorism, proliferation of weapons of mass destruction, trafficking in drugs or people or counterfeit money, or pandemics and other global health risks, to name but a few.

It would be a comfort were leaders able to turn to global institutions as forums in which these issues could effectively be addressed. But most such institutions are rickety relics of a sixty-year-old worldview, a product of the way the planet looked at the end of World War II or of the dynamics that shaped it during the cold war era. And most have failed to adapt well as circumstances have changed. Today, the World Bank and the IMF are embroiled in serious debates about their futures, about voting structures that give disproportionate power to the United States and Europe, and even about the viability of their business models. Regional development banks such as the Inter-American Development Bank, the Asian Development Bank, the African Development Bank, and the European Bank for Reconstruction and Development are also scrambling to adapt to a world in which most capital flows are from the private sector and governments are increasingly less inclined to borrow or follow the prescriptions of international advisers whose formulas have proved to bring only mixed results at best. The UN has been racked by scandal, the General Assembly is widely considered to be unwieldly and seldom productive, the Security Council—while occasionally effective—gives special place to five countries because they happened to win a war that was a lifetime ago, and many of the UN's component agencies are seen as failing to deliver the services they are intended to provide.

Senior IMF officials have been preoccupied in recent years with internal and external debates about the future role and relevance of the fund. In 2007, a group of eminent world citizens was asked to make recommendations about the future, but they steered clear of issues like the IMF voting structure—which gives the United States almost 20 percent of the votes even though it is now no longer a net donor nation, but gives China, the country with the world's largest reserves, less than 4 percent of the vote. They didn't deal with the fact that by tradition European countries get to choose the leader of the IMF (the IMF managing director through most of 2007 was Rodrigo Rato, formerly Spain's finance minister) and the Americans choose the president of the World Bank. These facts are galling to much of the rest of the world, particularly the countries that have traditionally been the IMF's biggest borrowers and the ones that have had to follow politically unpopular prescriptions in order to win IMF funds.

According to Rato and his colleagues, there are even bigger issues at stake. The IMF has traditionally sustained itself by lending money to governments and getting paid back the money plus interest. In 2002, its loan portfolio was more than $100 billion. By mid-2007, following a backlash against the fund led by countries like Argentina, who simply decided they did not want to dance the IMF's tune anymore, the IMF has a loan portfolio of only $13 billion. It will soon fall further when Turkey pays off its $8 billion debt. So the gray eminences of the fund were turning their attention to how to generate enough cash to keep the fund afloat. One possibility they considered was the liquidation of some of the IMF's gold reserves, the second-largest reserves of gold anywhere in the world. Reinvesting that money could provide funds to sustain the institution. To do what? To continue providing advice to countries, to help regulate global financial flows, to anticipate and relieve problems.

"It is still a vital role," noted Rato, "and we are the only ones who are in a position to play it."

But there is a broader question of whether countries will continue to authorize funding. The distance between the fund's Washington offices and Capitol Hill is a long way. Prodded for examples of what the fund was doing well that might resonate with Congress, Rato suggested that the fund's work in Iraq had been a big success and that financially the country was working better than ever. While this may be so, it showed a remarkable insensitivity to the interests or inclinations of a newly Democratic Congress. The IMF is viewed with skepticism by many on Capitol Hill as a money sink that provides funding to countries that end up hating the United States no matter what we do to help. It is viewed as a threat to sovereignty, a mechanism of much feared "world government," and as hopelessly inefficient.

Abroad, the World Bank and IMF are viewed with hostility because their programs are seen as insensitive, draconian, or supportive of the interests of the United States, Europe, Wall Street, or big business. During the 1997–98 emerging markets crisis, protesters in streets from São Paulo to Seoul decried them. One evocative poster in Brazil read "IMF: International Mother Fuckers."

The fund's leaders have clearly been frustrated. (Rato himself resigned his post early, citing "family circumstances.") The organization had an important function; as the only mechanism able to coordinate government policies, it would in fact be vital in a time of global financial crisis. But change was needed. Today, given the shift in capital flows and the fact that the sea of private capital has vastly overtaken in importance the sporadic bursts of government capital that once could move markets to help achieve IMF goals, the fund requires collaboration with an informal network of private financial institutions to do its job. "It works differently today," said Robert Rubin. "In financial crises, there is a critical role to play for the fund, but we also had to work systematically on the phone with the banks to try to induce people to a standstill mode or whatever we were seeking. We had to create for each situation we faced a kind of ad hoc structure built around the combination of the IMF, the Treasury, and the financial community. That's what we did." In short, an informal cluster of political leaders and private sector leaders, bringing together national and international actors, had to be manufactured on the fly to respond to the specific needs of specific challenges. While this approach offers flexibility and is manageable because of its "invitation only" nature, it is also not representative of broader global interests and suffers a bit from the learning curve problems associated with any ad hoc approach.

Luis Alberto Moreno, president of the Inter-American Development Bank, faces similar challenges with his institution, which is now almost fifty years old. The countries of the region are less inclined to borrow, the old business model doesn't work, and financial markets are driving capital flows to the region and setting the rules. The Americas have seen vastly increased flows of remittances, cash sent from family members in the United States back to their relatives in Mexico, Central America, or elsewhere in the hemisphere. These flows now exceed $50 billion a year. They are vastly more important to regional growth and development than the roughly $6 billion a year lent by the IDB. The bank may also soon face competition from a proposed "Bank of the South" that Chávez wants to establish as an alternative lending source for South Americans—one that is more on his terms and less on those of the United States. The rules and goals of such a bank would likely create further headaches for the IDB. "All the multilateral development banks are facing similar challenges," Moreno said. "It is important we realize that our system of international financial institutions is really at a turning point. It may not be the number one issue in many countries, but if we don't address it, millions of people, billions, will suffer."

James Wolfensohn, former Wall Street superstar and later president of the World Bank, observed to me, "I don't write off institutions like the Bank or the Fund or the family of international financial institutions, but there is no question that the weight they bear is much less than it was and that the world has changed much more than they have." Like others, Wolfensohn sees the ownership and management structures of these institutions as a problem. "There's absolutely no question this is an issue," he said. "It's true with the UN. It's true at the World Bank. We have two directors on the bank's board for forty-eight countries in sub-Saharan Africa—out of twenty-four directors overall—even though they make up a huge percentage of the bank's focus.

"I think the institutions have not changed with the world. I remember going seven or eight years ago to a G7 meeting. It was the first time they had asked Jiang Zemin, as the then president of China, to attend. There were six or seven large developing countries there, and I believe the Brazilian president stood up and he said how proud he was to be among all these famous men, and then he suggested that maybe the following year the meeting should be in Rio because there were so many more people in the developing world and that within forty years they would represent 40 percent of world GDP and it would be nice to have more of a say in what is going on. And I thought it was both funny and extremely valid because global institutions have not adjusted to the changes around them, and in particular the United States and Europeans have not adjusted. And they still think that the core group is the G7—or the G8 if the Russians are lucky enough to be invited—and that the notion of having China or India, two countries with a third of the world's population between them, two of the fastest-growing economies in the world, is just too exotic for them to take on."

Wolfensohn is back in the private sector now, operating from a small suite of offices in midtown Manhattan. He spends his time working for a small group of clients, pursuing his interests in the arts (an accomplished cellist, he was for many years the chairman of Carnegie Hall), and advising on international issues, as he did when he served as an emissary for the Quartet in talks between Israel and the Palestinians. He is a kind of prototypical superclass member, qualified for the group by virtue of his achievements in the private sector, the public sector, and the arts. When the subject turns to the relevance of global institutions, his intensity and frustration are palpable.

It is true for literally all with whom I have spoken about these institutions. They acknowledge that there is a central mission, a vital need for them to address issues of poverty and inequality, of global financial market management and shaping polices. But change comes rarely and slowly, and they worry that these institutions are becoming less relevant at a time when they are needed most, and that there is little will to take up the difficult work of reinventing them. Making them more effective will cut to core questions of ownership, of the international pecking order among nations, and of sovereignty—of effectively ceding sovereignty to these mechanisms of world governance when sovereignty remains the third rail in national politics worldwide.

Kishore Mahbubani, former Singaporean ambassador to the UN and currently dean of the Lee Kuan Yew School of Public Policy, one of Asia's most influential policy institutions, confirmed the need for institutional reinvention. "There has to be a big reshuffling of the deck in terms of global governance," he told me. "I mean, you cannot have a UN Security Council that represents the victors of the 1945 war. As a result, one thing I would say, by 2045 they will no longer be there in those roles, because between now and 2045 the world is going to change profoundly . . . it has already changed profoundly . . . And it is simple: If the changes are not going to happen, they will lose their legitimacy. The core question is who are they speaking on behalf of? . . . By the year 2050, three of the four largest economies in the world will be Asian: (1) China, (2) United States, (3) India, (4) Japan. How can you exclude them from appropriate ownership or leadership of the IMF or World Bank? How can you exclude some of the biggest countries in the world from meaningful roles in the UN Security Council or coordinating mechanisms like the G7?"

The former UN deputy secretary-general Mark Malloch Brown also believes the system needs an overhaul, arguing, however, that we should not be too quick to forget what does work. "You have to be really very hard-headed about what comparative advantages the UN system brings to the table in any given issue," he told me. "But we shouldn't overlook that these organizations have the ability to bring clean water to a couple of billion people or to close the investment gap in a country or to persuade the North Koreans to stop launching these missiles into the air. It just needs to be put into perspective . . . We are government organizations, but that is no longer enough . . . We are stuck between being where we started as a kind of intergovernmental civil service in the Anglo-Saxon tradition and some new role as a global advocate and entrepreneur."

AN INFORMAL AFFAIR: THE SOVEREIGNTY VS. DEMOCRACY TRADE-OFF

Implicit in this analysis is the fact that these institutions can't do it alone; they must work with the private sector and form new kinds of partnerships. From the perspective of the superclass, this means a number of things. First, the formal intergovernmental institutions are in trouble and thus the influence of their leadership as members of the superclass is waning. Second, the international issues that they should be dealing with are meanwhile growing in importance and are being dealt with increasingly through informal mechanisms. These mechanisms are created to fill a void and often funding gaps, but they shift power in ways that makes even the ungainly and inequitable governance structures of existing international institutions seem more egalitarian or at least more directly oriented toward the interests of people at large rather than businesses or the rich. Instead of institutions dominated by the victors of World War II and the leaders of the industrial West, you have individual governments or clusters of them or weak multilaterals collaborating with private sector leaders, or all of these collaborating with a few richly endowed NGOs, solving problems, allocating resources, setting rules. Governments may stretch limited dollars, but they give up autonomy. Further, they may fill small slices of the global governance gap, but without a clear mandate from those they are impacting or with a big imbalance that gives special leverage to the private sector or subsets of countries that offsets that of the multilaterals. And at the core of the groups filling that gap are members of the superclass: the elites who run the big financial institutions, the big investors, key corporate leaders, billionaires, philanthropists, and even a handful of superstar artists who can drive or shape NGO activities.

All that said, many of these activities provide important value and their existence is far better than the void they fill. A considerable number are found in the medical field: the global public-private partnerships that form the core of more than half the activities of the World Health Organization, for example; or the Global Alliance for Vaccines and Immunization (GAVI), which is 75 percent financed by the Gates Foundation; or the TB Alliance, which also has both public and private finance. Another example is a recent initiative of the Aspen Institute, the Overseas Private Investment Corporation (OPIC, a U.S. government agency), and the Palestine Investment Fund to create a Middle East Investment Initiative—"an international collaboration of leaders from the Palestinian, American and European private and public sectors"—to help fund the creation of jobs for Palestinians. The program is an outgrowth of discussions from Aspen's Middle East Strategy Group cochaired by Henry Kissinger and Madeleine Albright. Yet another illustration is a recent effort by the EU to develop greener aircraft, a 1.6-billion-euro project called Clean Sky that is half funded by governments. All of these particular programs certainly offer admirable goals, but with much of the funding coming from private rather than public sources, clearly the underwriters have influence, whether it is the Gates Foundation's seat on the GAVI board or the aviation industry's 800-million-euro stake in Clean Sky, thus shaping just how green the project may be, how fast it may develop, and where it will focus.

Joseph Stiglitz, who was chief economist of the World Bank, observed to me that "we have this sovereignty problem. Some governments don't like participating in international institutions because they can't control them. But in a democracy, no one can control everything. The only person who can ever be assured of getting his own way in a government setting is a dictator. As hard as it may be to swallow giving up sovereignty in order to empower these institutions properly, it is important to see that our conduct of international economic policy is often, in some ways, undemocratic. For example, we delegate the writing of intellectual property rules to a small group of trade ministers—who often know little about matters of either intellectual property or science. The ministers often do this in collaboration with the special interest groups they work with most closely. Now, are these the right people to be setting these rules? Or consider another case: letting the

IMF be in charge of sovereign debt restructuring is akin to letting private creditors run our bankruptcy system. In America, would we ever even contemplate such an institutional arrangement?"

He pauses for a second and then adds, "Too many people—other than those linked with special interest groups—have simply been disconnected from these issues of international economic policy. So the reality is that whether it is because institutions are too weak and insufficiently democratic, or because people aren't engaged enough in the process, we are leaving key decisions to the special interest groups and those that lead them." In the case of banks running debt restructurings, the financial institutions have an obligation to their shareholders to maximize repayment in a way that may run directly contrary to the interests of the citizens of the borrower country, who may prefer the country invest its limited capital in social or job-creation programs, for example. It may also be in the interest of developed nations to see such programs supported because they might promote stability, whereas the banks' focus on meeting obligations to them might actually produce stresses that promote unrest. This kind of tension is precisely what caused Argentina in 2001 to stop working with banks and the IMF to restructure their debt and essentially go it alone, without the blessing of the leaders of the international financial system. The country had a terribly rough time as a consequence, but eventually it bottomed out and has begun to recover on its own terms, and the decision by then president Néstor Kirchner to fly in the face of the public-private alliance at the heart of financial community has, in retrospect, become comparatively popular among his people.

Elites in the financial community have resisted suggestions that they be regulated by some new supranational entity or entities analogous to those found in domestic markets. They have pleaded for self-regulation and liberalized markets from the national leaders whose campaigns they financed and who depend on their collective judgment in the daily "market referendum" to which I referred earlier. And thus far, more or less, they have gotten precisely what they sought.

The centrality of such approaches can be heard in the earlier comments of Robert Rubin and in conversations with people like Timothy Geithner, a former Rubin protégé who is today president of the Federal Reserve Bank of New York. Inside the Fed's looming office building just three blocks away from the New York Stock Exchange, Geithner seems out of place. The offices are imposing and the building itself is designed in the monolithic style of a financial temple from an earlier era, but Geithner is very youthful looking, friendly, and slight. He is indeed comparatively young—only forty-two when appointed to the post in 2003. He served in the Clinton Treasury Department, where he played a key role in managing the international economic crises of the late 1990s and proved himself calm and effective even under difficult circumstances. Because of the New York Fed's role in managing relations with other central banks and the financial community, it has become a crucial cog in the global financial system.

Geithner acknowledged that a significant portion of the work done today to manage markets, from currencies to derivatives, must be done in conjunction with the leaders of the world financial community. "We have a convening power here," he told me, "that is separate from the formal authority of our institution and which can be a very powerful tool. There is a debate among economists about how powerful it is relative to traditional tools of, say, monetary policy, but I think history has lots of examples of the use of convening power in ways that were effective . . . The work with financial institutions during the Latin American debt crisis of the 1980s, the work on managing the potential fallout from the collapse of LTCM [Long Term Credit Management], the work following the Asian crisis that I was involved in at Treasury."

He emphasized that the role of central banks remains important and spoke admiringly of the work that the Bank for International Settlements (BIS) in Basel, Switzerland, has done to ensure that the world's top central bankers convene every two months to share perspectives and ideas. He observed that the "principal tables there now have twenty-six countries around them. China is always there." While he cited this as an example of strong collaboration among governments, it is also worth noting that only a fraction of the world's countries are involved and that the BIS is not an organization selected for this role by the voters in any country. Rather, these meetings are themselves part of the world's semiformal structure, which is evolving out of an agreement among the most powerful countries on how they would like to see the management of the planet's financial affairs handled. In the same vein, Geithner observed that this community of actors has become very interconnected and that he in fact probably speaks more often to them than to all but one or two key players in the U.S. Fed system. "I spend a lot of time with these central bankers and they have world-class educations and experience. They share similar training and perspectives; we speak a similar language."

Geithner suggested that within this community, collaboration with big corporate players is key. Recalling a situation in which he had to manage a crisis in the derivatives market, he said, "What we did is, we got the fourteen major firms in a room down the hall here with their primary supervisors, a group of the largest global institutions and their supervisors from five countries. And we said to them, 'You guys have got to fix this problem. Tell us how you are going to fix it and we will work out some basic regime to make sure there are no free riders to give you comfort, so you know that if you move individually everybody else will move with you.' And there is nothing written, no guidance, no regulation, no formal process. We did it without a formal request to us. We told everybody we were going to do it but we were not asked to do it.

"These fourteen firms," he continued, "accounted for something like 95 percent of all the activity in this market. The Fed, the SEC, the FSA, the Swiss, and the Germans were there. And those were the principals, and each firm brought three people, they had an executive committee of four firms that ran, almost weekly at the beginning, a conference call among the other firms. And the best thing about the process was that it was efficient, there was nothing written except letters from the firms laying out their commitments. There's no formal mechanism we could have used to force this on anybody so we had to invent it. I think the premise going forward is that you have to have a borderless, collaborative process. It does not mean it has to be universal, every jurisdiction or every institution. It just needs a critical mass of the right players. It is a much more concentrated world. If you focus on the limited number of the ten to twenty large institutions that have some global reach, then you can do a lot. It's interesting, actually. Of the fourteen big firms . . . [chairman and CEO of Goldman Sachs] Lloyd Blankfein jokingly called them 'the fourteen families,' like in *The Godfather* . . . The Japanese were not in it, which was interesting. It is really the Swiss, Germans, U.S., UK. Really mostly the U.S. and Europe. No Asian firms."

Geithner's predecessor, Bill McDonough, now vice chairman at Merrill Lynch, echoed his perspective. "Central bankers work together well because they spend a lot of time together," he told me, "such as at the frequent meetings of the major central bankers at the Bank for International Settlements and at the annual meetings of the IMF and World Bank. They learn why other central bankers are following particular policies. They become personal friends. That is especially helpful in crisis management, of which I had quite a lot when I was president of the New York Fed. For example, I spent a good portion of the night before the meeting with the private sector of Long Term Capital Management informing the central bankers of Europe what was happening and why. Being able to call them by their first names, as friends, made those conversations much easier."

Richard Darman, senior adviser at the Carlyle Group and chairman of AES Power, has observed from high atop the system the changes that have taken place, first in the public sector during the Reagan administration. "Coming out of the 1970s, and perhaps through the early '80s, two members of the G5 club of central bankers, the U.S. and the German, were especially powerful. They were sometimes called the 'G2.' Together, they could exert extremely important influence upon currency relationships and global financial markets.

"By the time I became deputy secretary of the treasury in early 1985, however," he continued, "the increase of private capital flows had already been sufficient to make clear that the role of the G2 in particular, and central bankers in general, was going to decline in relative importance. The powerful Fed chairman, Paul Volcker, came to realize, somewhat reluctantly, that his world was changing. Because even a widening club of central bankers could no longer control currency relationships, the central bankers needed to involve the treasuries and finance ministries from their respective countries in order to influence the full range of public policies that, in turn, influenced private flows and markets.

"At the time, I was part of the team that negotiated two of the key financial agreements of that era, the Plaza Agreement and the Louvre Accord. They represent significant deviations from the world of the old central bank club—not only because they were the product of a group that included finance ministries, but also because they addressed a whole lot of policy variables that were far beyond the traditional scope of central bankers. They reflect the fact that the club was expanding bureaucratically, geographically, and substantively in order to do the same old job in a bigger, more complicated world.

"By the 1990s, private capital flows had come to dominate so much that central bankers were borderline irrelevancies in terms of what they could do through intervention. Their regulatory powers gave them some control, but there were ways to get around much of their reach. So the 'club' expanded further to include a bunch of the financial players you have talked about. And those financial players themselves were increasingly globalized to adapt to the increasing scope and complexity of the real economic world. So what does it really mean now to be a member of such an expanded club?" Darman felt that the group itself has become somewhat broader than it was and less bound by traditional class distinctions like inherited position, but he acknowledged that it is still a small, small group with very significant impact world-wide.

The financial superclass is not, however, the only group filling the void created by the weakness of global institutions. As Thomas Fried-man pointed out to me, "We now have a whole set of issues that have arisen as globalization has intensified that require global governance, but there is no global government. So that creates a fundamental core problem. Not only is there no global government for all these issues which require global governance, there is not going to be global gov-ernment. Sovereignty is always going to trump that. So the question is, then, what fills that gap? Well, what fills that gap is to some degree NGOs, operating transnationally on discrete issues. What fills it is sometimes global coalitions; maybe it will be the Fair Labor Associa-tion, working to get governments to convene textile companies with NGOs to set a global standard for these companies about sweatshops. A new thing that is emerging to fill it in is supply chains, the whole re-lationship between Wal-Mart now, Nike, McDonald's, and the NGO community. For example, Conservation International worked with Mc-Donald's for several years on a set of standards for their supply—who buys more beef, bread, pickles, and tomatoes than McDonald's? So how its suppliers farm their land, whether they do it in an environmen-tally sustainable way, is a huge issue. I mean, that is global governance the way it is done in the world today."

Today estimates suggest that NGOs worldwide have total turnover in excess of $1 trillion a year, making them a force to be reckoned with. John Elkington, coauthor of a study on NGOs published by Sustain-Ability, says that amount is augmented by levels of public trust surpass-ing that of governments and business and that as a consequence, NGOs might evolve into "among the most influential institutions of the twenty-first century." The relevance of this group as part of a continuum of policy makers and influencers is highlighted in the environmental arena in Daniel Esty and Andrew Winston's *Green to Gold: How Smart Companies Use Environmental Strategy to Innovate, Create Value, and Build Competitive Advantage*, in which they write:

> Today, the governmental role is changing . . . as rule-makers and watchdogs expand both vertically and horizontally. By "ver-tical," we mean the different levels of government . . . Down the vertical scale, we find state and local officials who have been more aggressive enforcers of environmental laws than the fed-eral government . . . At a higher level, we see global agreements

like the Kyoto Protocol . . . The "horizontal" dimension refers to the emergence of new actors tracking environmental performance, such as NGOs . . . and bloggers with websites read by millions.

One of the largest and most influential members of this "horizontal" governance matrix is the World Wide Fund for Nature, a Swiss-based NGO with an annual budget of over $120 million and operations in ninety countries. On the one hand, the WWF leadership, including its president, Chief Emeka Anyaoku of Nigeria, and its international director general James Leape of the United States, is seen as enormously influential; they represent more than five million members around the world and an organization with more than four decades of history seeking to promote biodiversity and preserve the environment. WWF has invested over $1 billion in more than twelve thousand projects worldwide, has played a central role in helping to preserve species from the tiger to the lechwe antelope, and has lobbied for everything from the preservation of fresh water to sustainable development policies. But with a mandate to work closely with governments and corporations, the WWF has also run afoul of critics with other environmental organizations who cite the close ties between the organization's leaders and big business. There was a chorus of protest in 2003, for example, when a top WWF U.S. official, Kathryn Fuller, who also served on the board of U.S. aluminum giant Alcoa, refused to join other WWF International members in voting to oppose a major Alcoa hydroelectric dam project in Iceland. Critics also noted that Alcoa contributed $1 million to WWF, which was seen as a further compromise to its objectivity. Similar attacks have focused on relations between the organization and other corporate supporters, including France's Lafarge, a mining and quarrying company, and HSBC, the international bank, which gave the WWF over £35 million in what was, at the time, a record-breaking donation but that was seen by critics as an effort to buy cover for its investments in environmentally unfriendly forestry operations and dams such as China's notorious Three Gorges.

Defenders of the WWF correctly note that few organizations have done more to raise awareness of biodiversity and environmental issues, and that part of the reason for their success is their ability to work closely with governments and businesses. Yet critics suggest that this closeness is a compromise, and in this disparity of views lies one of the problems associated with the rise of NGOs as proxies for governments— their accountability is limited and they are inevitably driven by checkbooks, thus opening the way for further influence for the resource-rich members of the superclass.

This kind of public-private collaboration has become central to global governance in everything from managing the trade of counterfeit goods to managing energy market supply disruptions; from getting medicine to victims of epidemics like AIDS to restricting travel in the event of pandemics; from interdicting terrorists' financial flows to containing proliferation of weapons of mass destruction. Indeed, the number of such instances is growing as more and more activities become cross-border and thus, by definition, move beyond the jurisdiction of individual nation-states.

So on the one hand you have weak international institutions and on the other you have growing global governance needs. Informal institutions evolve. Some are public-private like those described by Geithner and Friedman. But others are public-public, such as networks of government representatives who collaborate to coordinate policies on everything from trade to security-related issues.

For example, senior officials from different nations find themselves linked together in clusters based on alliances—formed by virtue of history or circumstance or complementary missions and resources. They develop personal connections, both while in office and out, consistent with the perception and definition of our concept of superclass. Former EU trade minister Lord Brittain and former United States trade representative Charlene Barshefsky both spoke to me about the close ties they formed with their counterparts in the trade community and the fact that many maintain ongoing relationships today. As we will see in the next chapter, senior military officials speak in the same way about relationships developed within NATO or in joint military-to-military initiatives. Former national security adviser Sandy Berger told a similar story. "The national security advisers had a kind of club . . . I don't mean a club in a formal way, but in an informal way. I had a drop line in my desk to the national security advisers of France and England and Russia. We did a lot of business that way. That cuts across the bureaucracy, it cuts through the bureaucracy of foreign ministries . . . During Kosovo there were a lot of decisions that got made by my dealing directly with my counterparts in Chirac's office and Blair's office."

These political clusters (or "clubs," as many seem to identify them) form around specific tasks, although central alliances and historical relationships play a key role in defining them. In much the same way that the G5 aircraft links together leaders in the corporate world (and some in the public sector), the "G" groupings of nations create informal mechanisms that play a significant role in defining global policy outcomes and common agendas among participants. We have heard already how the G2 was important among central bankers before it was overtaken by the G5, the G7, and the G10. Among trade ministers, the United States and the EU were also the G2—the big dogs who, when working together, drove the rest of the world on many critical issues. On other trade issues, the Quad—the G2 plus Canada and Japan— was key.

This institutionalization of concentrated power is periodically challenged. For example, trade ministers met in Cancún, Mexico, in 2003 to try to advance the Doha Round of World Trade talks. Drawing on approaches used in the past, U.S. Trade Representative Robert Zoellick and EU Trade Commissioner Pascal Lamy tried to guide the meeting, seeking a compromise on agricultural subsidy reform that they had envisioned. But a group called the G20-plus, led by countries like Brazil, India, China, and Indonesia, resisted their pressure, instead reemphasizing calls for the United States and particularly the EU to eliminate distortionary trade subsidies for their farmers. (Such subsidies are important revenue streams for European and U.S. farmers who also fear being pushed out of the market by cheaper imports from overseas. For the developing world, however, they amount to an impenetrable barrier, allowing local farmers to sell their products at below-market prices that make it impossible for foreigners to compete with them.) One of the G20-plus leaders, Brazilian foreign minister Celso Amorim, came out of the meetings sensing a watershed, saying, "We emerge from this process stronger than we came into it."

The most famous of the G groupings is the G7, which was established in 1976 and includes the United States, Canada, France, Germany, Italy, Britain, and Japan. G7 finance ministers meet four times a year, with central bank governors attending three of those meetings. In 1997, Russia was invited to join the G7—creating the G8—although it does not participate in economic and financial meetings because of its comparatively small GDP. It does, however, participate in regular G8 ministerial meetings on energy, education, environment, development, labor, and health policy. Within the G7 and G8 there are also regular meetings of heads of state. In fact, from a global policy perspective, this group has become one of the most influential mechanisms of informal coordination on the planet.

For example, while the majority of world leaders who get face time with the American president see him infrequently and only a few may do so as often as once a year, leaders of other G8 countries have much more regular contact. In 2006, President Bush met privately with each G8 leader an average of three times in addition to the discussions that took place at that year's leadership summit in St. Petersburg, Russia. These bilateral meetings are not all business all the time. A state visit by Japan's prime minister Junichiro Koizumi in June 2006 was one of the more memorable of the Bush administration, culminating with a tour of the home of Koizumi's musical hero, Elvis Presley. After two days of discussions, military displays, and a state dinner in Washington, the pair took off on a field trip to Graceland in Memphis, Tennessee. On the way, "Don't Be Cruel" played over the Air Force One PA system and Elvis DVDs aired on monitors while flight attendants served the classic Elvis snack, fried peanut butter and banana sandwiches. At the estate, Presley's daughter, Lisa Marie, and ex-wife Priscilla, arrived to lead a guided tour for the special guests, though they let the heads of state share some "private time" together in the Meditation Garden, where Elvis and his parents are buried. Later on, standing in front of the famed Jungle Room, Koizumi was moved to put on a pair of Elvis-style sunglasses, swivel his hips, and belt out several bars of "Love Me Tender" for the press corps. Bush laughed but did not join in, and then sent the PM home with a jukebox loaded with Elvis hits.

Beyond the G7/8, there are other G groupings, each creating similar clusters for the leaders and top representatives of its member nations. Among these are the Group of 20, established in 1999 to fill in some of the gaps created by the still more powerful G7/8. This group, which meets just once a year, actually represents 90 percent of global GDP, 80 percent of global trade, and 60 percent of the world's population. The G24, which was established in 1971, meets twice a year to discuss development issues and includes a broad cross section of developing countries. The G77, founded in 1964, confusingly has 130 members and serves a similar purpose. There is also the G22 (the "Willard Group"), which was superseded by the G33, which in turn was superseded by the G20. There is even a "Non-G6," also known as the Oslo Group, which includes Canada, Chile, Indonesia, Kenya, New Zealand, and Norway.

Other alliances, from the Association of Southeast Asian Nations (ASEAN) to Mercosur to the Organization of African States to the Non-Alligned Movement, also fill in a void, providing caucuses that guide nations as they work within international institutions or independently. These meetings, like Davos or business meetings, provide the social glue for the members of the political superclass and help bridge differences in mission or relative levels of power.

Such glue is vitally important. As the former Singaporean ambassador to the UN Kishore Mahbubani observed to me, "The ASEAN countries are meeting within themselves regularly. The golf games that they have create the same kind of role that you have mentioned. Oh, yes. In fact, I say the reason why the countries of Southeast Asia have not gone to war is because of a four-letter Scottish word: golf."

Such collections of powerful states and powerful leaders—both informal and institutional—lead many to believe that globalization is driven by only a few nations, often in collaboration with financial and business leaders from the private sector. Indeed, based on what we have seen, it is easy to see how that impression is created. This suspicion has had a corrosive effect, creating a fault line between those who believe globalization is in their interests and those who do not.

THE GLOBAL NETWORK OF ANTIGLOBALISTS

Bill McDonough sat thoughtfully in his office at Merrill Lynch, a modern suite in a building that towers above the wound in lower Manhattan where the World Trade Center used to be. "There is a growing view," he remarked to me, "that the modern economy is benefiting the more successful at the expense of the less fortunate. In the United States, the lower half of income distribution has not been keeping up.

"I believe that in all societies, clearly in democracies where the electorate can change the government at the next election, more attention has to be paid to making it clear to all the people that they too can benefit, or at least that the educational system gives their children that opportunity. That is the American dream. But even in less democratic societies, governments govern over the longer term with the consent of the governed. If not, revolutions take place.

"In guiding globalization, government leaders, central bankers, and leaders of the business community simply have to do a better job of taking those actions needed to have all the people believe that the system benefits all."

Former U.S. ambassador to the UN Richard Holbrooke, one of the most distinguished and respected of the foreign policy leaders within the Democratic Party, observed that the consequences of the actions of the global elite have produced what might be characterized as an antiglobalist elite. These antiglobalists are not only far removed from the worlds of London, Wall Street, and all the makeshift international networks that fill the global governance void on behalf of the most empowered countries and economic entities—they actively oppose them. They "have nothing to do with that world of what you call the 'superclass,'" Holbrooke told me. "One of the points [Iranian president Mahmoud] Ahmadinejad made in New York according to people who saw him was his attack on the UN as being the Western creation. And when somebody at the Council on Foreign Relations meeting at which he spoke said to him, 'You know, all these countries in the UN oppose you,' he said, 'Wait a second. I just came from Havana [the latest meeting of the newly revitalized Non-Aligned Movement]. I was with 125 nation leaders who all denounce you guys.' So I mention that because there are different elites. This other group is the anti-Davos crowd. They're the antiglobalization people . . . So, yes, I agree with you that there are these elites and there are these networks, but they have also triggered the creation of these antinetworks."

At the core of the "anti-network" is a small group of leaders, linked by many shared characteristics and attitudes though they come from widely different regions of the world. They might be characterized as "nationalists," or opponents of the United States, or critics of Western-led globalization. They include Mahmoud Ahmadinejad, Hugo Chávez, and Vladimir Putin. Each has fought or been trained to fight for his country: Ahmadinejad was a soldier in Iran's war against Iraq; Chávez is a military man by training; Putin was a career KGB operative. In their view, globalization is old Western imperialism dressed up in new clothes, and they are reacting to it much as they were trained to react to such incursions. Given the flow of Western products and ideas into their regions as a result of globalization and the growing international influence it gives multinational corporations often closely associated with Western governments, it is easy to see why (though we can also see the irony in the fact that Western governments are concerned about those multinationals disconnecting from their historic roots). Consistent with these views that are fairly traditional in the context of their national heritages of skepticism toward Western influences, each took what might be considered a conservative path to an established elite in his country. Each is capable of great charm before his supporters and the media, and each is capable of equally great ruthlessness and cunning.

Perhaps most important, each of these antielites comes from a country that has a national idea of itself as a great state, a regional or an international leader. Iran is the seat of Persian civilization, once an empire that carried the Peacock Throne into the heartland of India. In many respects it is the greatest modern civilization the Middle East has produced and, still today, one of the world's leading oil producers. Venezuela also draws upon great aspirations and traditions. Home to "the Liberator" Simón Bolívar, the man who more than any other forced the end of colonialism in Latin America, Venezuela has also enjoyed special position and influence due to its own immense oil reserves. Russia, of course, is the superpower that collapsed onto itself, one of the great defining forces of the twentieth century and a country in which virtually every adult citizen was, in the early 1990s, forced to rethink much of what he or she had been taught about himself or herself and the world. Today, it too has renewed power because of its great petroleum, natural gas, mineral, timber, and other resources.

Although each of these countries has benefited from global markets, each also contains many who see the evolution of the global system as not giving them a place commensurate with their view of themselves. This in turn has been seized upon by their opportunistic leaders and their supporters, who have harnessed the reactionary forces the global era has produced among their countrymen.

It is interesting to note that with just a few adjustments, a couple of twists the other way, these countries could be among the great cheerleaders of the new era. No country in the Middle East other than Israel is quite as cosmopolitan as Iran. For years, experts were suggesting that its fledgling form of democracy would make it the likely cradle of political reform in the region. It has had a vibrant artistic tradition, an acceptance of academic dissent, and has allowed women more active roles than elsewhere in the Middle East. Russia produced the burgeoning of cowboy capitalism that created the oligarchs but that also showed exceptional vitality and flair for business among its elites. It has always been torn between its European and its Asian identities, but in the global era that could have put it in a remarkable position: a bridge eleven time zones long that could connect the dynamism of its Chinese neighbor with that of a united Europe to its west. Venezuela's oil was tapped by the Standard Oil companies, Venezuela's elites studied in the United States, and for periods in the middle and latter parts of the twentieth century there was no country in the region closer to the United States.

The phenomenon can be seen as comparable to the rich who have come to despise the excesses of the superrich in the United States. The backlash against U.S.-led globalization comes from a number of countries close to the phenomenon that are tapping into it—countries that have or had legitimate reasons to think they could be at the forefront of it all had things gone slightly differently. Their failure to achieve what others have stems from a range of missteps, including overreliance on natural resources, lack of emphasis on education, endemic corruption, and preservation of the prerogatives of local elites. And, sensing that they have been left behind, they are increasingly lashing out.

Today, Putin, Chávez, and Ahmadinejad do not have congruent agendas, but each seeks to consolidate power and to elevate his country's importance in the world. Despite their differences and the distance between them, they have found it suits their needs to work together. Increasingly central to their approach has been the politically popular choice of confronting the United States and blaming it for the ills of a world system that has left many citizens discontented. Almost one-third of Russians live below the World Bank poverty line and almost two-thirds describe themselves as unhappy. The great inequalities between the oligarchs and the masses feed their discontent. For Putin, the choice is to accept responsibility or to identify scapegoats beyond Russia's borders—most often Chechen rebels or the United States. His anti-U.S. rhetoric has reached unsettling cold war levels of late, to the point of comparing the United States to the Third Reich. Within two weeks of that controversial statement, he test-fired new missiles specifically designed to penetrate European and U.S. antimissile defenses.

Ahmadinejad has goaded the United States and Israel by convening groups of Holocaust deniers and calling for Israel to be "wiped off the map." He has confronted the international system by asserting Iran's right to develop its own nuclear program and has regularly assailed the United States. The country's leadership has specifically formulated its foreign policy as a response to "global arrogance"—code language for U.S. foreign policy. Iran has not just offered angry threats, nor has it only played the role of David against Goliath; it has recognized that in standing up to the United States, no matter how outrageous its approach, it speaks for many other countries that see the international system as not working for them. For example, its effort to develop its nuclear program unimpeded resonates with dozens of other countries that feel they have been made second-class citizens by exclusion from the "nuclear club," a particularly potent subset of the power elite.

Chávez and Ahmadinejad have exchanged visits to each other's countries. Iranian-brand cars are now manufactured in the Venezuelan city of Maracay. Chávez has played up his solidarity with his Iranian brother by also allying himself with Hamas, the Syrians, and other anti-Israeli forces. Pro-Palestinian flyers have appeared thousands of miles from the Middle East, on lampposts in Caracas. As one expert, Alberto Garrido, was quoted as saying, "The Venezuelan left has for decades considered alliance with Muslim countries as one of the ways to create a new civilization through the toppling of American values." Of course, Chávez has gone further with regular attacks on George Bush, calling him "Mr. Danger" and a "donkey." (He has referred to the secretary general of the Organization of American States—whom he views as a U.S. ally—as "an asshole from 'a' to 'e.'")

Chávez has built an alliance among leaders whose countries have struggled in the past several years and many of which are just now embracing indigenous peoples into their political systems, including Argentina's former president Néstor Kirchner, Bolivia's Evo Morales, Ecuador's Rafael Correa, Nicaragua's Daniel Ortega, and, of course, his grand patron and role model, Fidel Castro. He has re-created a kind of cold war spy vs. spy mentality in the region by funding anti-U.S. candidates and revived the old cold war development aid competition by pledging billions in aid to left-leaning nations throughout Latin America. He has helped Argentina pay off its debt to the IMF, helped Bolivia pay legal bills, pledged $1 billion in credit assistance to Ecuador, and with Ahmadinejad announced a $2 billion investment fund for the region. The aid he has actually spent is several times the $1.7 billion provided by the United States in the same period (most of which went to "the war on drugs"). And working with Putin, he has aped another cold war convention: tit-for-tat arms deals. In the wake of a $3.8 billion deal to send U.S. F-16s to Poland in mid-2006, Putin and Chávez arranged to send over a billion dollars' worth of Russian arms to Venezuela just a month later. As long as the price of oil is strong, these countries have considerable independent resources to underwrite their international initiatives—even if those resources could be better utilized to address desperate needs at home.

Pursuing their agendas to contest what they see as an unfair system, this core group has mimicked a pattern of the G8 (of which Russia is, of course, a member): The leaders from within this alienated axis meet with increasing frequency. Indeed, in one of the transcendent ironies of the current era, one might say that the path of those most opposed to globalization in its current (or apparent) form is to create a global alliance of antiglobalists. In 2006 alone, key leaders within the Venezuela-Bolivia-Cuba-Iran-Russia-Syria bloc convened something in excess of twenty times—not counting meetings like the UN General Assembly or the gathering of all nonaligned nations that took place in September. Chávez alone visited China, Russia, Belarus, Iran, Indonesia, Vietnam, Malaysia, Portugal, Qatar, Syria, Mali, Benin, Angola, Argentina, Brazil, and Jamaica—and has not only forged strong ties with political elites but developed considerable popularity as well.

Speak to these leaders, however, and they might say that their alliance is not antiglobalist, but a coalition against U.S.-dominated globalization. It is hardly a mere quibble. Because of the weakness of global institutions and the fact that they have been supplanted by informal structures that are typically dominated by Western governments or private sector institutions, they are responding to a genuine defect of global governance and a genuine reality in terms of the shape of global elites.

Many of these leaders are easy to condemn as thugs and racists and crooks. But to dismiss them without assessing why they enjoy popularity at home and abroad, without understanding the traction they have gained, without understanding the needs they speak to, is a mistake. It is a mistake being made every day by many among the world's political superclass. You can hear it in unilateral and unconstructive declarations that members of the group are part of an "axis of evil," or in the rolling out of tired cold war formulas in response to twenty-first-century problems. The divide caused by this system has begun to define political debate within and among nations in powerful ways. Whether you characterize it as nationalist vs. internationalist, populist vs. globalist, or anti-neo-imperialist vs. pro-American globalization, these issues are shaping debates on trade, use of force, global regulation, and immigration worldwide.

Global political elites face other challenges—those associated with having to respond to global constituencies as well as domestic, national ones. Earlier, I mentioned world leaders campaigning on Wall Street to maintain the favor of markets on which they depend, markets that hold daily referenda on their policies and provide the investment capital they need to achieve their goals. But such challenges take many forms.

Not too long ago, I visited Bogotá, Colombia, to meet with President Alvaro Uribe about his country's struggle to win a free-trade agreement with the United States. At the time, Colombia had been targeted by labor unions and human rights groups because of the high number of labor union leaders who had died in that country's civil conflict and the low number of prosecutions the government had thus far been able to pursue of the killers. Unions in the United States—with leaders like John Sweeney among the most nationalist members of the global political superclass—generally oppose free trade because of the threat they see it posing to domestic workers. In Colombia's case, they had found an issue that had traction with members of Washington's new Democratic majority, and were so far succeeding in their efforts to stall the deal.

We met in the Presidential Palace in Bogotá, a beautiful city tucked into a valley in the Andes. The palace was surrounded by spit-and-polish troops, some wearing spiked helmets evocative of the World War I soldiers of Kaiser Wilhelm. Inside we were warmly greeted by the president and his team. Uribe, who studied at Harvard and Oxford and whose English is quite good, had been tough on crime and tough on drugs, and was extremely popular with both the Colombian people and with the Bush administration, which saw him as one of their few allies in the face of the drug threat and, more important, the threat posed by his neighbor to the east, Hugo Chávez. Indeed, since the initiation of Plan Colombia, a joint effort by the United States and Colombia to combat drugs and help stabilize the country launched in 1999, Colombia had not only become America's number three recipient of foreign aid, it had forged what could only be seen as a kind of "special relationship" with the United States—one that Venezuela and Argentina had once had.

Uribe had done as he had promised. Thirty thousand paramilitaries had turned in their weapons. Almost six hundred had been extradited to the United States. The major drug cartels had been broken up, although many smaller ones had taken their place. Killings of union leaders had declined, and some of those killed were almost certainly active with the FARC and ELN rebel groups that had been waging war against the Colombian government for almost half a century. There were rumblings of progress in the dialogue with the unions. All this explained Uribe's high approval rating at home. What he couldn't understand was why he was having such problems sealing a trade deal with the United States.

Uribe is a tightly wound guy, and halfway through the meeting, having listened to a stark assessment of why the Democratic Party—the party of his friend Clinton, after all—was assailing him as a violator of human rights and generally making his life difficult, he leaped to his feet. He felt he was doing everything right. Indeed, he had hired a string of Washington consultants including Mark Penn and Joe Lockhart, former press secretary for Bill Clinton. Wasn't that the way the game was played? Shouldn't things be going better? He paced the room. He was angry and frustrated.

Though globally sophisticated, Uribe was still seemingly unprepared for the reality of being a political leader in the new era, in which he had constituencies in several countries, often with views and needs that were hard to reconcile. Colombians knew for the most part that he was fighting tough enemies in the only way possible. But Americans, far away from the civil violence, had a different view. They were less interested in the gains Uribe had acheived on the ground, more focused on remaining issues like violence against labor leaders that were relevant to U.S. politics. The new Democratic majority needed to give some kind of trade victory to unions that were important to their base and that had felt ignored and abused for too long.

Uribe fumed. "I hope people in the United States know that they have put me in a very difficult position. Don't they understand what this might mean for the United States in the region . . . for all we have achieved?"

The reality, as I discussed with some business colleagues as we flew back on their G5 (eating, for the record, Big Macs at forty-one thousand feet), was that "they" do not understand. "They" don't have to, because, for the most part, politicians still derive their power from within their borders. But increasingly, at the very top, the political superclass also depends on power centers far away. They are torn, as much as are their countries. They are divided, much as is the world today.

6

The Age of Asymmetry:

Decline of the Titans and the Rise of Shadow Warriors

> Every gun that is made, every warship launched,
> every rocket fired, signifies in the final sense a
> theft from those who are hungry and are not fed,
> those who are cold and are not clothed.
> —Dwight D. Eisenhower

In the early years of the cold war, a new idea took root in the American consciousness and its government operations: permanent war. The idea was proposed by several men simultaneously, most notably a gentleman who might be considered one of the founding fathers of the modern military-industrial establishment. Charles "Engine Charlie" Wilson, who was president of General Motors when World War II broke out, guided the company's massive war effort and helped set priorities for the U.S. economy during the conflict as director of the War Production Board. In this capacity, when an Allied victory seemed imminent in 1944, he argued that in order to avoid a postwar recession, the country would need to create a "permanent war economy." Less than a decade later, as secretary of defense, Wilson helped to usher in the "new look" reforms at the Pentagon that marked the beginning of such a transformation. Working with President Eisenhower, Wilson set out to modernize the U.S. defense establishment, rationalize spending, and make the chain of command more efficient.

Wilson was the first in a line of corporate chieftans to head the Defense Department. Following him in 1957 was Neil McElroy, the former president of manufacturing giant Procter & Gamble. McElroy took office just a few days after the launch of the Russian satellite Sputnik—the dawn of a new era in the cold war—and his term in office oversaw the continued realization of Wilson's "permanent war" agenda. McElroy managed a major and costly restructuring mandated by the 1958 Defense Reorganization Act. For each of the three years of his term, the annual Defense Department budget exceeded $40 billion, which amounted to 10 percent of GDP and substantially more than half the federal budget of $70 billion. (Although the United States spends more than ten times as much on defense today, the level of the official defense budget is "just" 4 percent of GDP, one and half percentage points below the historical average for the preceding forty-five years.)

The close relationship between U.S. secretaries of defense and the business community had begun with Wilson's predecessor, Robert A. Lovett. Prior to his appointment, Lovett was an investment banker at Brown Brothers Harriman (the same firm where Prescott Bush, a senator as well as the father and grandfather of two presidents, worked). Following Wilson and McElroy, both corporate titans, came Thomas S. Gates, who worked at the banking and investment firm Drexel & Company and later became president and CEO of J. P. Morgan Bank. Succeeding Gates was another rising star of the corporate world, Robert McNamara, who was president of Ford Motor Company at the time of his nomination to be secretary of defense. Such ties have continued for years, as has the idea of permanent war. In fact, the revolving door between government defense leadership positions and leadership positions in the defense contracting community has become a fixture of Washington life, one no less striking or enduring than the monuments on the Mall.

The threat of conflict with the Soviet Union, made manifest by the "police action" in Korea and competitive parries and thrusts from Iran and other proxies, provided a rationale for permanent war footing. That in turn provided a rationale for the United States to embark on a half century of record defense spending, without question the single biggest public sector investment of any society—at any time, for any purpose—in history.

Once the cold war wound down and a momentary period of "new world order" semi-euphoria had passed, the "rationale" for permanent war came roaring back. On September 11, 2001, in a spasm of national overreaction, the United States embarked on its "war on terror," the first-ever military campaign against a feeling. This new war was undertaken in an emotionally wrought, posttrauma environment and without much in the way of reasoned debate. (Indeed, at the time, debate itself was considered unreasonable and, to many, unpatriotic.) Defense expenditures skyrocketed, sending hundreds of billions of dollars directly to military suppliers and contractors.

Consequently, in a new era of corporate-bred secretaries of defense, questions began to arise. The business ties of virtually every defense chief in the post–cold war period, from former Halliburton CEO Dick Cheney to former CEO of G. D. Searle and General Instrument Corporation Donald Rumsfeld, prompted concerns about motives, relationships, the revolving door, and the connection among all these factors and America's military policies. It is clear from the blundering execution of U.S. operations in Iraq that the orchestrators of the war were hardly the supercompetent cabal that some critics have alleged. Still, there can be no disputing that the swift and instinctive reaction to 9/11 produced a revitalization in U.S. defense spending and a new ascendancy of America's defense elites, a revival that seemed unlikely as recently as the 1990s when budgets were shrinking and meaningful enemies seemed hard to find. Since they were so lousy at managing their own war, one might wonder how these leaders were so good at persuading the country to embark on the latest expensive chapter in the era of permanent war.

Three possibilities exist. One is that the threat from terrorists was so great as actually to warrant such spending. Another is that the interested parties mounted an effective campaign to advance their interests in a coordinated way. The third is that without much conscious coordination but with plenty of unconscious selection of messaging, agenda-setting, and aligned self-interest (the gold-plated power tools in the toolbox of superclass members everywhere), the result came to pass much as though it were actually the reasoned will of the American people at large.

THE TERRORIST THREAT IN PERSPECTIVE

With regard to the notion that the terrorist threat is on a par with those posed by past reasons for going to war, there is little in the way of validation. The facts undermine the arguments made by the Bush administration and others in the alarmist, sky-is-falling contingent, from terrorism experts whose relevance depends on the urgency of the threat to the wacky fringe of quasi-racist Islamophobes who dominate the right-wing media. The very rhetoric used to describe the threat has often departed the realm of the rational. As Zbigniew Brzezinski has pointed out, "Terror is a tactic, not an enemy."

When put in perspective, the numbers suggest that the terrorist threat is indeed something less than it has been made out to be. According to the State Department, there were approximately fourteen thousand terrorist attacks in the world in 2006, up from eleven thousand in 2005. The number of deaths associated with these attacks rose to roughly 20,000 noncombatants, from 14,600 a year earlier. While these numbers are striking, they pale in comparison to a host of other issues that might, in terms of toll alone, be considered more urgent threats. About the same number of children worldwide die of preventable causes every twelve hours as people die in acts of terrorism in an entire year. According to the UN, the same number of people around the world die of HIV/AIDS every three days as die of terrorism annually.

Even having said all that, the numbers on terrorism are still smaller than they might seem to be. Of the twenty thousand people the State Department says were killed by "terrorism" in 2006, two-thirds died in Iraq. In other words, roughly fourteen thousand non-combatants died in terrorist attacks as a consequence of a situation triggered by the United States in its unprovoked invasion of Iraq in 2003. Those deaths would likely not have happened if it were not for the invasion, which leaves us with a worldwide number of non-Iraq-related terrorist deaths at about six thousand.

Furthermore, virtually all those killed and injured in terrorist violence were not, in fact, Americans. In 2005 there were fifty-six U.S. civilian deaths due to terrorism, and in 2006 that number fell by half to twenty-eight. Of those, the majority were killed in Iraq. So the total number of Americans killed by terrorists outside Iraq in 2006 was about a dozen.

While this data may confirm that terrorism is a serious problem, it hardly suggests that it is a worthy rationale for the most sweeping reconstruction of the U.S. national security system in the past sixty years. It hardly seems to justify the hundreds of billions of dollars that have been spent on Iraq. Nor does it seem to warrant a wartime footing in Congress, where the defense budget request for 2008 called for $481 billion—66 percent higher than it was six years earlier and a larger amount in constant dollars than any year since 1985, the high point of Reagan-era cold war spending.

Is this a proportional response? And if not, why not?

Even in the worst year of U.S. losses to terrorists on record, 2001's horrific toll of 2,974 fatalities, almost fifteen times as many Americans died in automobile accidents, more than six times as many died of homicide, and more still died from either fire or drowning. Yet none of these larger threats to American life produced even a fraction of a fraction of the response mobilized against terrorism. Despite claims to the contrary, there is absolutely no chance that terrorists would threaten the fundamental existence of the United States or, in all but the most unthinkable, coordinated nuclear scenarios, even have a material economic impact in the context of the overall size of the U.S. economy. Even in the nightmare scenario of a nuclear weapon detonated in a major U.S. city, the nation would survive, despite what could be terrible losses. Furthermore, there is no reason to believe that, even inflamed by our interventions in the Middle East, terrorism poses as significant a threat as—for historical perspective—a life-and-death struggle with communism, Nazism, or Japanese imperial ambitions once did.

So what does the threat actually look like? Al Qaeda, the terror network responsible for the 9/11 attacks, has an indeterminate number of members with the best estimates at several thousand. Its budget is around $30 million a year, according to *The 9/11 Commission Report*. This is approximately the cost of one Chinook military cargo helicopter. Or, alternatively, it is, at the recent Iraq "spending rate," equivalent to what the United States spends in four hours in Iraq. That doesn't mean they can't spend the money more effectively than the United States does in Iraq (they could hardly fail to do so), but it does suggest some limits on their capabilities. In addition, while much has been made of the "power" of its network structure, the lack of a cohesive, full-time organization makes it hard to estimate Al Qaeda's true strength at any given time, and it makes it very easy for those who are inclined to do so to overestimate it.

Al Qaeda depends on the amplification of its apparent threat by the media and by overreactive governments like the Bush administration to achieve its greatest results—results that are seldom if ever a consequence of their direct action. For example, while the 9/11 attacks produced $16 billion in property damage in lower Manhattan, the U.S. reaction to those attacks has by some estimates cost in excess of $1 trillion and the lives of more than four thousand U.S. soldiers and tens of thousands of Iraqis, not to mention the cost incurred by the erosion of domestic civil liberties and the incalculable damage to America's reputation in the international community.

In short, we have made the terrorists bigger than they really are. And the question becomes, why? Could it have been a plot among conniving, cigar-smoking, business, political, and military leaders in a fusty back room? The answer is clearly no—not just because of the lack of planning masterminds among the people who made the war on terror what it is today, but because it simply wasn't necessary to convene that back-room meeting.

First, given that the U.S. political system at the time of the 9/11 attacks was in the hands of a government with the ideological views the Bush administration had toward the Middle East, the history it had with key regimes in that region, and its close ties to the oil industry and key defense contractors, no one should have been too shocked by the result: All the vectors of force from the relevant power players were pointing in the direction of the kind of militarized, unilateral adventure that materialized. In part, it was the consequence of a system where the incentive structure for politicians made adopting a war footing advantageous—and where the incentive structure of the military-industrial complex made supporting such a war footing profitable. It was also the consequence of the political mood in a wounded country, which made the United States open to such an approach, disinclined to lengthy debate, and eager for the appearance of action and strength. Furthermore, as bad as the Bush team has been at managing the war in Iraq and maintaining international alliances, it has proved exceptionally adept at managing the levers of American public opinion.

(I want to underscore that the above analysis is in no way a dismissal of the terror threat. It is a critique of the rationale and conduct of the "war on terror" and an illustration of the perilous predispositions that in part resulted from a defense economy and policy community built on the idea of permanent war. All the same, the threat posed by these amorphous networks of hostiles, particularly with regard to the proliferation of weapons of mass destruction and the stability of a few vulnerable states—Pakistan, Lebanon, Egypt, and a number of others—is exceedingly dangerous. An appropriate multilateral approach combining military, police, intelligence, political, and economic initiatives is certainly and urgently warranted.)

Recognizing the relative importance of terrorist groups and nonstate actors is also critical to U.S. and Western military planners. In fact, the biggest change in the structure of the global military-industrial superclass in recent decades is its shift in focus from conflicts of symmetry (the bipolar world of the cold war) to conflicts of asymmetry (the present in which the United States and the West are hugely, disproportionately powerful compared to the other nations and nonstate actors). While this may change over a number of years—if China continues its massive military buildup, or if Russia becomes more belligerent, or if the United States manages to alienate into existence a new alliance of enemies—it has to be expected that the next few decades will see a number of the confrontations in which the United States or its allies find themselves take the shape, as it was put by Vietnam-era analyst David Galula in 1964, of the fight between the lion and the fly: conflicts in which "the fly cannot deliver a knockout blow and the lion cannot fly."

This has produced some substantial shifts in the structure of the global military-industrial superclass: the decline in fortunes of some traditional players, the rise of others, a reemphasis on different skill sets and, as in the other clusters we have seen, a growing emphasis on global collaboration. There is still a global military-industrial superclass, but it is changing rapidly and future changes will likely raise questions about some of the doctrines and structures that today seem untouchable.

THE ROOTS OF GLOBAL NETWORKS

When the commander of the U.S. Pacific Command (PACOM) is in his large corner office at Camp Smith, in Oahu, Hawaii, his four-star flag flies high on the pole in front of the building. That flagpole might be seen, however, as the epicenter of something more than the world's leading military command. It is the centerpoint of a series of relationships—political, economic, and security-related—that tie the leaders of the U.S. military in the Pacific to their counterparts throughout their AOR (area of responsibility). In this respect, it is like other major U.S. defense operations: a very national undertaking with broadly global ties. One former PACOM commander told me that these connections were "increasingly [part of] the job. We have more direct ties with the people and leadership of the region than most other branches of the U.S. government. We have become the diplomats in many cases. We are tied to defense cooperation, which has a big business component. We may be powerful in many ways, but we also know security is increasingly a partnership deal . . . Through better cooperation comes strength. And at the heart of a lot of this are the historical and carefully developed networks of ties between me, my top guys, and the military leaders of the region." It is a comment I heard echoed by U.S. and foreign military leaders in every part of the world. War fighters find that, increasingly, they too are global networkers.

Tradition means a lot among military elites, in no small part because they share so much training and because history is such an important element of the institutions and culture that empower them. Every commander of PACOM, for instance, has been a naval officer; when President Bush announced his intention to name an air force officer to the post, it created such an uproar he had to reverse his decision. Of the last five PACOM commanders, four were graduates of the U.S. Naval Academy at Annapolis, which has a historical role as the principal training ground for professional naval officers in the United States. For example, one recent PACOM commander, Admiral Dennis "Denny" Blair, who served from 1999 to 2002, was a member of the Annapolis graduating class of 1968. His class also produced, among others, the current chairman of the Joint Chiefs of Staff Michael Mullen, former navy secretary James Webb, current marine commandant General Michael Hagee, and infamous marine lieutenant colonel and former National Security Council staffer Oliver North. The preceding class produced the chairman of the Joint Chiefs who came before Mullen, Marine General Peter Pace. Pace's vice chairman, Edmund Giambastiani, was the class of 1970.

The U.S. Military Academy at West Point and the U.S. Air Force Academy have similar records of producing the top cadre in their services as well as many senior government and corporate leaders. Many of their graduates also interact with the rising stars who later lead alongside them in graduate or professional programs at institutions like the National War College and the National Defense University in Washington, D.C., the Army War College in Carlisle, Pennsylvania, and the Naval War College in Newport, Rhode Island. Programs like these, found in every country, knit together leadership cadres in important ways. For example, Denny Blair was a Rhodes Scholar at Oxford at the same time as future president Bill Clinton, the man who approved his appointment to be what was then called CINCPAC (commander in chief, Pacific Command). Blair, a sixth-generation naval officer, was also a White House fellow, participating in a program designed to identify rising stars with an interest in public service. In his class of White House fellows in 1975–76 was the West Point graduate, former Rhodes Scholar, and future U.S. supreme allied commander in Europe, Wesley Clark.

Such training programs have been defining the future elite of the U.S. military for two hundred years. More recently, they have also started training an increasing number of young future officers from other countries. The Naval Academy, for instance, currently has students from Guyana, Honduras, Ireland, Malaysia, the Maldives, Mauritius, the Philippines, Singapore, Taiwan, and Thailand. West Point has a similar tradition, even having produced three former foreign heads of state: Anastasio Somoza, former president of Nicaragua; Fidel Ramos, former president of the Philippines, and José María Figueres, former president of Costa Rica (and former co-CEO of the World Economic Forum). These efforts at globalizing the networks of U.S. military elites have become an important tool of U.S. foreign policy for several decades. One such program, the International Military Education and Training Program, has grown dramatically since the early 1990s and now offers military instruction to representatives of more than 130 countries. These programs not only spread American military methods and ideologies but also benefit the United States in a variety of other ways, from generating goodwill to supporting U.S. weapons sales to establishing networks U.S. commanders can use.

One of the most controversial of such programs is the training program the U.S. military has run since 1946 for Latin American military leaders. Known for much of its existence as the School of the Americas, the program changed its name in 2000 due to its association with human rights violations committed by some of its graduates, often in the context of America's cold war struggle with perceived Communist threats. The program is now called the Western Hemisphere Institute for Security Cooperation, and its graduates include a stunning collection of notorious names: Argentina's former president General Leopoldo Galtieri, known both for the Falklands fiasco and for accusations concerning the disappearance of leftist opponents; the interim Argentine president Roberto Eduardo Viola, who spent nearly two decades in prison for human rights violations during that country's dirty war; the Ecuadoran dictator General Guillermo Rodríguez; the Salvadoran death squad leader Major Roberto D'Aubuisson; the Guatemalan general and former de facto president José Efraín Ríos Montt, whose regime was responsible for a long list of documented atrocities during that country's civil war; Panama's Manuel Noriega, who later ran afoul of his former sponsors in the United States; and Peru's discredited and corrupt spymaster Vladimiro Montesinos—to name but a few. It is easy to see, given the record of such men and the support they received from the United States throughout their careers, how the program could grow to be seen as a liability. Nonetheless, it also illustrates what a powerful and effective tool such training programs can be, having given the United States a network of powerful friends who shared U.S. views (or went beyond them) with regard to the Communist threat in the region during the cold war. Today's training programs serve a similar purpose, although hopefully with less toxic by-products.

Much like Harvard and Yale among the world's business leaders, these military programs carry a great deal of prestige abroad. General

John Jumper, who served as U.S. Air Force chief of staff during the George W. Bush administration, told me that "if you go to any of these countries, you will find them wearing the accoutrements of one school in the United States. The first thing they'll bring up is that they went to this War College or that War College. It is actually a bigger deal for them and their countries than it is for us."

In addition to training ties, military-to-military programs such as joint exercises, meetings under the auspices of key alliances, and other similar cooperation efforts are regularly cited by leaders as being essential. Admiral Dennis Blair said to me, "The mil-to-mil communications channels were often better than the political ones or the diplomatic ones. I remember when we started to tackle the crisis in Timor while talks via other channels were stalled, I could pick up the phone and talk to my Australian counterparts and find solutions, move things along. We had a long-established relationship. There was no false formality in our exchanges. We could cut to the chase."

General Anthony Zinni, the blunt-talking, street-smart marine who was the CINC at CENTCOM, the U.S. central command covering the Middle East, offered similar stories. One relationship that proved particularly significant was the one he developed with a rising Pakistani military officer named Pervez Musharraf during multiple visits to that country. When Musharraf later led a military takeover in Pakistan and became one of the most important leaders in the world to the United States, Zinni was asked on more than one occasion to draw on his close ties to help resolve sensitive issues.

A former member of the Joint Chiefs of Staff observed to me, "There are deep, dark secrets in this diplomatic process that I have never understood. We make it harder for ourselves than necessary. For example, on the military side, we have an association of South American air chiefs. They get together twice a year. Most of these guys just want you to teach them how to fix their C-130s that are from 1965. With just a pittance of spare parts that is pocket change compared to the money we spend around the world, we'd do wonders for these folks. But it's hard to get it done. Penny-wise and pound-foolish, I'd say."

Leaders find the military-to-military ties useful even when fissures exist in this network. Jumper points out that, in the midst of differences over Iraq, "during the height of our anxiety with the French, I talked to the French air chief once, and the message was simple: We'll get over this sooner or later. It introduces an element of stability that, when the time comes to reconcile, I think it makes it easier. And it keeps people from being nervous. And we have so much in common. For all of our issues with them, the French are there almost every time we are. They're not there unconditionally and they have to call home before they can do anything. It's not always wonderful, but it works better than people might guess judging from the headlines."

General Jim Jones, the outgoing U.S. supreme allied commander in Europe, provided another perspective on the current role of U.S. military leaders as members of the global superclass. Our conversation took place at one of the many coffee lounges at the Congress Center in Davos. When I asked him about the relevance of the tight relationships among transatlantic military elites to running an enormous and complex military alliance like NATO, he responded, "If one considers the current political relationship between the EU and NATO, it is clear that, at the political level, there is great difficulty in having any meaningful political discourse. Conversely, at the military-to-military level, there is no such difficulty. We know how to make the situation work, we know how to work together, and we know how to focus on the important military issues affecting interoperability. Such personal and professional relationships have been formed since the creation of NATO itself and today they spill over and benefit the EU as well. Those who select military careers tend to build on such relationships, which become very long-lasting."

Jones, a tall man who sat folded somewhat uncomfortably into a modern Euro-style chair, continued, "I would make a personal observation: relationships in the international political world don't appear to have the same personal bonding quality that is developed in the international military community. It also seems to me that personnel rotations, at the very senior levels, occur with greater frequency on the political-diplomatic side of things than they do in the military. It is probably unrealistic to think that the cohesion of the two groups can really ever be expected to be the same."

Citing specific instances from his recent career, Jones offered, "As an example, at the most recent summit in Riga, Latvia, at the last minute Turkey came up with a much needed force contribution for Afghanistan. I give credit to the Turkish Chief of Defense [CHOD] for having been able to convince his government that this was not only essential but the right thing to do. The Turkish decision, which came only after extreme military pressure, show that international military cohesion can be effective, most especially when critically needed.

"Another characteristic of working within the community of top military leaders is that in Europe, chiefs of defense are rarely heard in the media. In other words, their way of operating is mostly behind the scenes. In my farewell comments to the CHODS [of NATO], I pointed out that this was not an ideal situation and that they, as individuals and as a group, would be much more effective if they were able to have a more public role in terms of their national policies and those of the Alliance. There exists, I am painfully aware, a very real difference on our side of the Atlantic, as contrasted with the European side of the Atlantic, as regards what the chiefs of defense are permitted to discuss publicly. For that I am extremely grateful to my country. European CHODS are comfortable—excessively so, in my view—with letting their political masters do 'that kind of work.' In most nations it is either a matter of law or firm policy that this be so, rather than passivity on the part of the CHODS."

European military leaders with whom I have spoken were, true to Jones's observation, more reluctant than their American counterparts to go on the record. One senior British officer did tell me, though, that "for us all, working together can be a matter of the greatest urgency, of survival in the worst case. And the international system on the political side just doesn't work very well. So who is going to step in and fill the void if we do not?" It echoed a comment made to me by Colin Powell: "I have developed many good relationships, real friendships, over the years with senior officials, political leaders, diplomats, and military men. Maybe it is because I was in the army for most of my career, maybe it is because of the bond between soldiers which is great, but those [relationships] have been special and I have turned to them often when other channels were stalled. I think sometimes the problems we have in the international system, the weaknesses of that system, are offset and managed through informal channels, invisible ones that have proven to be vitally important."

GREEN IS NOT JUST THE COLOR OF THE UNIFORMS

Following his tenure at NATO, General Jim Jones, often candidly critical of some of America's plans in Iraq, spurned offers to become deputy secretary of state and to assume another command. Instead, he entered the private sector, where he was recruited to head a major energy policy initiative by the Chamber of Commerce. He also joined the board of Invacare Corporation, which sells medical products. In this respect, he was both like and different from many of his colleagues. Most go on to senior corporate positions. Indeed, many step into the revolving door and head into the defense industry sector—this despite assertions by many that the revolving door is less important than before, thanks to legislation designed to curb the potential conflicts of interest it produced.

From the perspective of the corporations, why not seek advice from the people who know the area best and who have the most hands-on experience? Said one senior executive of America's thirteenth-largest defense contractor, Science Applications International Corporation, "Who better to get to tell us the needs of troops on the ground, to work with us, than a guy like Tony Zinni?" On the other hand, a senior defense contractor observed, "Look, there's a lot of talk about a shadow government, and I am here to tell you it's real. On every level the connections between our company and the government are amazingly deep."

It's a delicate balance. Military leaders need to earn a living when they leave the armed forces, and they should not be penalized for having chosen to serve their country—nor should their country be deprived of their know-how or the experience for which the country has already paid. Having said that, it is a short trip from an inadvertent old boys' network to the military-industrial complex self-dealing that has—in the past, in countries all over the world—led to overspending, delays, overlooked flaws, and outright corruption. In its international form it has also had an impact on the important role that arms sales have in foreign policy, leading to the promotion of symbolic deals that sometimes involve weapons systems that may not be optimum for countries involved but have been advocated by well-connected interests in the defense establishment—as in the case of the $20 billion, ten-year arms deal the United States began to develop with Saudi Arabia in 2007 as a way of countering Iranian influence in the Persian Gulf. While the program had yet to be reviewed by Congress at the time of this writing, controversy was already brewing over the inclusion of precision munitions in the package—sought by Saudis, advocated by the U.S. manufacturers of the arms, but feared by others, including the Israelis, who see it as giving the Saudis a new and threatening capability.

At the heart of the challenge in striking a balance between military, industry, and government lies a system that has, as noted earlier, long blurred the boundaries between the public and the private segments of the defense industry. Take those past five commanders of Pacific Command. The predecessor of the current commander is Admiral Thomas

Fargo, a compact former submariner. (Fargo was such a clipped model of his breed that when Scott Glenn was researching the role of Captain Bart Mancuso for the movie *The Hunt for Red October*, he modeled him after Fargo, then a sub commander.) When Fargo left the navy, he became the president of Trex Enterprises and the chairman of Loea Corporation and Sago Systems—all high-tech defense firms. He also joined the boards of Hawaiian Holdings and Hawaiian Electric Industries, a utility on the same islands where PACOM is based.

Fargo's predecessor, Dennis Blair, not only became president of the influential Institute for Defense Analysis but also joined the board of defense contractor EDO Corporation and Tyco International. Unfortunately for Blair, when it was discovered that the Institute had completed a government report on the future of the F22 Raptor fighter jet project and that EDO was a contractor producing parts for the F22, a brouhaha ensued over the perceived conflict of interest. Few people have such impeccable reputations for ethical behavior as Blair, and close observers see it as a problem of not being sufficiently sensitive to appearances, but the situation illustrates many dimensions of the ongoing ties that exist and the problems associated with the ties.

Blair's predecessor was Admiral Joseph Prueher, now on the boards of Merrill Lynch, Fluor Corporation, Emerson Electric, the Wornick Company, New York Life, and defense contractor DynCorp International. Another recent CINC at PACOM, Admiral Chuck Larson, is on the board of Northrop Grumman, the world's number three defense contractor. This is business as usual and good business at that. There is nothing inherently wrong with it, but it helps maintain the power of those at the top, whether in the military, government, or corporate arena.

Not surprisingly, a similar pattern of connections exists at the boards of the top defense contractors. Take the "big three" alone: Lockheed Martin, Boeing, and Northrop Grumman. Lockheed Martin is the largest defense contractor in the world, a mammoth corporation that took in $36 billion in defense revenues in 2006. On its board you will find the former undersecretary of defense E. C. "Pete" Aldridge; the former commander, Strategic Command, Admiral James O. Ellis; the former deputy secretary of homeland security and coast guard commandant Admiral James Loy; and the former supreme Allied commander in Europe and vice chairman of the Joint Chiefs of Staff Joseph Ralston. Second in the ranks of defense contractors is Boeing, with defense sales of $30 billion but an almost identical amount from commercial sales; thus its board is not as heavily laden with former military and defense de-

204 • S U P E R C L A S S

partment executives, although it does include General Jones (as well as a former White House chief of staff, a former commerce secretary, and a former assistant secretary of state). Number three, Northrop Grumman, has as board members Admiral Larson and General Richard Myers, former head of the Joint Chiefs of Staff; the former congressman Vic Fazio, a one-time member of the House Armed Services Committee; and the former National Security Council staffer and former chairman of the National Defense Panel, Philip Odeen.

The revolving door does, by its nature, revolve. Many drawn from the corporate world spend time high in the federal policy-making (and procurement decision-making) bureaucracies. When Donald Rumsfeld was replaced by Robert Gates, critics noted that he had been a board member of SAIC, TRW (a defense contractor that is now part of Northrop Grumman), and another contractor, the Charles Stark Draper Laboratory. But the current or recent high-level ties have also included Peter Teets: was president and chief operating officer at Lockheed, is now undersecretary of the air force; Gordon England: was vice president of General Dynamics and secretary of the navy, is now deputy secretary of defense; Michael Wynne: was a top executive at Lockheed and General Dynamics, is now secretary of the air force; James Roche: was vice president of Northrop Grumman, served as secretary of the air force from 2001 to 2005; Philip J. Perry: was a major lobbyist for Lockheed Martin, is now general counsel for the Department of Homeland Security (his wife is a daughter of Dick Cheney); and Rudy deLeon: was deputy secretary of defense and a senior vice president at Boeing.

Ties between political and industry power arenas are extensive and are not limited to top-tier positions. According to *The New York Times*, "Former Lockheed executives serve on the Defense Policy Board, the Defense Science Board and the Homeland Security Advisory Council, which help make military and intelligence policy and pick weapons for future battles." Nor do such ties always involve official titles and appointments: Boeing CEO James McNerney has sustained a friendly relationship with President George W. Bush since their days together on the Yale baseball team and has attended elite White House functions like an official dinner for Indian prime minister Manmohan Singh in 2005. Lockheed's CEO Robert Stevens was also among the 134 guests at the dinner, which was notable for an administration not given to social events. The following year Stevens attended an economic roundtable in Cancún and sat at Bush's side, near then Mexican President Vicente Fox and Canadian prime minister Stephen Harper.

The blending of military and defense industry leadership cadres is significant on several levels. Power is concentrated among a few people with similar backgrounds and, on key issues, similar outlooks about core concerns such as the size of defense budgets, which programs to promote and which to cut, or where the greatest imminent threats may lie. These similarities predispose those at the top to sharing special relationships based on aligned interests, which predispose them to certain behavior, such as the granting of special business advantages. This might be as modest as offering casual hints as to when programs will be bid out or what features will be especially valued in a proposal, or they may be tips about what is on the mind of key decision makers elsewhere in a process. It can come in the form of hiring valued friends or of placing ads that support particular political agendas.

Bernard Schwartz, one of America's leading defense industry CEOs for more than two decades, defended the revolving door: "If a uniform guy gets out of the service and he has a lot of friends, two years later when he is in business he is going to be able to call upon them. And so what is new? I mean business is like that, too. Human beings are like that. I do not see anything criminal about that necessarily. It is natural for it to happen that someone may say, 'I play tennis with a guy and I don't only play with him because he is a flag officer but, maybe once or twice during the course of our friendship, I'm able to say, Hey, you want to look at this, or maybe this is something you ought to buy, or we have an interest in this.' But I think that is human behavior. It is hard to legislate human behavior. I'm suggesting that something would be lost if we did somehow prevent individuals from investing something in the people that they trust and work with."

CONSOLIDATION AND CONCENTRATION OF MILITARY POWER

One of the most significant aspects of the defense industry in the United States today is the degree to which it has consolidated during the past decade. Beginning in the mid-1990s, reduced defense budgets and the glut of defense industrial capacity left over from the cold war led arms suppliers and contracting firms to merge at an unprecedented rate. Consolidation was welcomed and encouraged by the government, which offered reimbursement for transition costs, and by Wall Street as well. In less than a decade, what had been more than fifty major defense suppliers had been consolidated into only five or six dominant firms.

The executives of Lockheed Martin themselves have said that the concentration of power among military contractors is more intense than in any other sector of business outside banking. Since the attacks of 9/11 and wars in Iraq and Afghanistan, business has been booming. The top five U.S. contractors—Lockheed, Boeing, Northrop, General Dynamics, and Raytheon—have increased sales 10 percent a year every year since 2001. (The Pentagon's budget has grown by a nearly identical average of 11 percent during the same period.) In 2005 the profits of the top five rose 25 percent from the year before, to $12.94 billion.

While the United States far and away dominates the global arms market, several countries have made inroads into the industry, particularly Britain. Mike Turner earns a place on the list of military-industrial elites as the chief executive of BAE (British Aerospace), the United Kingdom's largest arms manufacturer and the third most profitable in the world. BAE is a global giant, employing nearly one hundred thousand people on five continents, and makes 26 percent of its sales in the United States—an anomaly in a market dominated by U.S. firms. It is the seventh-biggest military contractor in the United States—the only foreign Pentagon supplier to make the top ten—and as *The New York Times* reported, the company has special access to some of the Defense Department's most highly classified programs. (Of course, that privileged position may change following revelations that BAE allegedly bribed Saudi Prince Bandar bin Sultan to facilitate a $54 billion arms deal.)

Britain's defense industry is an exemplar of globalization and trade liberalization: The most open defense market in the world, it buys three-quarters of its arms through open competition, forcing British firms to compete with U.S. and European companies. Turner has consistently protested the system, saying it hurts Britain's indigenous industry, and has openly floated the possibility of merging with a U.S. firm. "If you add up what is spent on defense in Europe and the United States it's clear where our future is," he observed in 2003.

The industry's tendency toward consolidation, especially in the last quarter century, has strengthened the leadership class at its core, giving a few individuals greater influence. In 2006, only a dozen or so companies around the world accounted for the majority of international defense revenues. Before the end of the cold war, power within the industry was much more diffuse. But as the industry consolidated on an international level, the leaders of the largest firms emerged as a clique of powerful individuals, each with his own ties to government leaders.

One result of this concentrated network is that in addition to consolidating at an unprecedented rate, defense firms around the world are becoming more and more global in orientation. Cooperation among nations in certain aspects of arms production is nothing new, but in the past twenty years, international arms collaboration has expanded significantly in pace and scope. Not only are national companies trading more information and weapons with foreign governments than ever before, but they are also taking part in strategic alliances, joint ventures, and even mergers with their counterparts overseas. The transnational cooperation of the industry has been especially marked in Western Europe and has expanded to include many countries in the developing world as well, providing access to information and technology to develop national defense industrial bases.

While defense firms have become more integrated into a global network, they have also become more autonomous, taking the initiative in restructuring the international defense industry base—a role formerly taken by the state. Naturally, they advocate for the kinds of projects that suit them, either by virtue of what they are best positioned to produce, what produces the biggest margins, or what they perceive their best contacts within the military as being interested in. This in turn leads to a self-perpetuating process in which what was produced is likely to be most like what will be produced next. Incrementalism triumphs because it is more profitable and it builds on past efforts to sell an idea or the military doctrine underlying it. Thus again we see the pattern: a few leaders from a few big companies playing a dominant market role and assuming responsibility once held by public institutions for decisions affecting very broad cross sections of the public at large, including decisions that play a role in shaping a nation's defense doctrine. They are particularly active as advocates of big and/or expensive weapons systems such as carrier battle groups, major aircraft, and high-tech space weaponry, all of which are both profitable and offer maximum prestige to service leaders. Real change and reevaluation are resisted. Turning the military-industrial complex is a little bit like turning a battleship, in an age in which smaller, faster ships with smaller crews launching unmanned aircraft is probably a better way to go.

NETWORKS AMONG DEFENSE FIRMS

The interconnections among companies in the defense industry exist mainly on the national level, in a complex balance of cooperation and competition. For example, Lockheed and Boeing have been entangled in a lawsuit since 1998, when Lockheed sued Boeing for stealing proprietary data in order to win a contract, yet they continue to merge and collaborate on lucrative contracts such as a mammoth satellite launch bid in 2005. Likewise, BAE frequently engages in fierce competition with number two British contractor EADS (European Aeronautic Defence and Space Company) yet partners with it in joint ventures like a major missile manufacturing deal in 2001. Firms most often cooperate in the face of foreign competition, which is ever more common in the globalizing industry.

Yet, at the same time, the industry is increasingly dispensing with national borders and creating alliances to address a global market. When Ronald Sugar arrived at Lockheed, he placed a new emphasis on "building international partnerships with foreign firms." "We see the world as being connected," he told *The Washington Post* in 2004, "by financial, trade and security interests." Such partnerships can be complicated, especially with a U.S. Congress reluctant to share technology and domestic jobs. But if Turner of BAE has anything to say about it, such "protectionist sentiments" will continue to fade: "Notions of 'us versus them' have limited applicability in the global economy," he told a Washington, D.C., audience in May 2006. "Open markets help us all." (This is a direct contradiction with his earlier quoted concerns about protecting indigenous UK productive capacity. But despite the apparent disconnect between the two positions, they are linked in one fundamental aspect—they are completely consistent in the way they support the interests of BAE's shareholders and leadership.)

THEY'RE ALL IN A TINY ROOM

The top tier of the global military establishment—defense ministers, chiefs of staff—meet frequently in fairly intimate, officially orchestrated settings. The same is often true when the industrial sector is involved and arms deals are negotiated. Several venues offer an opportunity for the gathering of the military-industrial superclass—military professionals, civilian policy makers, arms manufacturers, and defense contractors.

Begun in 1962, the Munich Conference on Security Policy is one such forum for top-level officials to convene and collaborate on U.S.-European security and defense issues. The conference expanded greatly in 1999, to include representatives from Eastern Europe and Asia, as well as members of the media and the arms industry. One senior fellow at the Council on Foreign Relations calls it a "useful barometer of transatlantic relations." The list of attendees in 2006 was packed with power players, including Donald Rumsfeld, then defense minister of France Michèle Alliot-Marie, EADS CEO Tom Enders, the U.S. senator John McCain, *Die Zeit* editor Josef Joffe, NATO secretary general Jaap de Hoop Scheffer, and the Booz Allen Hamilton VP James Woolsey. Comparing it to other events like Davos, Bilderberg, or meetings of the Trilateral Commission, Richard Holbrooke told me, "For my personal interests, the Munich security conference is by far the best because it's very focused. That is a real meeting of the international national security elites. Originally just U.S. and Europe, but now it includes India, Israel, China comes, and they pack two hundred people into a room smaller than this one, so you're jammed in with Don Rumsfeld, Angela Merkel, John McCain, Hillary Clinton, and the ministers of defense and King Abdullah and President [of Georgia] Saakashvili; they're all in a tiny room . . . The discussion is serious, focused, and sustained. That's my favorite conference." The meeting revolves around debates over central issues, such as how NATO's mission should evolve, or the sensitive matter of how it should work out of its historical theater of operations, or how to address the future expansion of NATO capabilities into Eastern and Central Europe. It also has important implications for arms deals, as discussions range from questions of systems interoperability to the merits of deploying antimissile defenses and new weapons platforms—even as those discussions advance pending sales and prime buyers for new ones.

The Shangri-La Dialogue is another important venue for defense and military policy makers in the Asian-Pacific region. Begun in 2002, the dialogue aims to serve as "the best available vehicle in the Asia-Pacific region for developing and channelling astute and effective public policy on defence and security." The conference is organized by the International Institute for Strategic Studies (IISS) and sponsored by leading defense and arms manufacturers—BAE, Boeing, EADS, Northrop Grumman, and Mitsubishi, among others. (The board of IISS comprises a number of cross-cluster, global figures: David Ignatius, the *Washington Post* columnist; Thomas Pickering, formerly a VP at Boeing, undersecretary of state for political affairs 1997–2001, and a lieutenant commander in the navy; Robert Ellsworth, a VP at IISS, a former Kansas congressman, the ambassador to NATO 1969–71, an assistant and deputy secretary of defense 1974–77, a board member of General Dynamics, and a member of the Council on Foreign Relations.) Officials from twenty-two countries, including nine defense ministers, were present at the 2006 meeting in Singapore. IISS also runs the Gulf Dialogue, which brings defense and foreign policy authorities from the Middle East to-gether with global powers like the United States, China, and Russia. These meetings offer important forums where the ties at the core of military-to-military cooperation (so important, even in humanitarian interventions, as in the aftermath of the 2004 tsunami that devastated much of Southeast Asia's coastal regions) are cemented and new ones formed. Like other meetings of elites, they become venues in which conventional wisdom is shaped—in this case about threats, about the reliability of partners, about elements of existing military doctrine within an alliance.

THE PRIVATIZATION OF THE MILITARY: A TWO-WAY STREET

As of this writing, there are approximately 170,000 U.S. troops on the ground in Iraq. Less well-known is the fact that there are another 125,000 trained contractors, many armed and playing roles traditionally allo-cated to the national military. These guns for hire are typically former military personnel, but they have moved over to a rapidly growing in-dustry—one that has taken firms like North Carolina–based Blackwater, for instance, from virtually nothing to a reported $100 million in rev-enues in just a decade. The firm, run by an ultra-right-wing heir to an auto parts fortune named Erik Prince, has won diplomatic security con-tracts with the State Department worth, over a multiyear period, three-quarters of a billion dollars in just the past three years. (Blackwater also cashed in on Hurricane Katrina, winning contracts worth a quarter of a million dollars a day.) Prince, a former navy SEAL who has donated ap-proximately $200,000 to Republican politicians, took a company that made firing ranges and transformed it: As of this writing, Blackwater has personnel working in nine countries worldwide, a fleet of more than twenty aircraft, and a database of more than twenty thousand ad-ditional troops on standby. In fewer than ten years, Prince created a company that is today seen as a pioneer among private military firms, or PMFs.

PMFs are the less visible relatives of traditional fighting forces, but they are becoming a potent participant in the dynamic of military-state relations. In his study of the privatized military industry, P. W. Singer describes the rise of PMFs as "an overall global pattern," with opera-tions "on every continent except Antarctica, including relative backwa-ters and key strategic zones." PMFs are essentially private companies hired by governments to provide a wide range of military and security services. These include servicing of advanced weapons, facility protection and personnel security, translation, interrogation, and training for military and police forces; they usually exclude actual combat. PMFs have been around since at least the 1950s, when the United Kingdom and South Africa created similar groups of mercenaries to train and fight in the Middle East, Angola, and Sierra Leone; the United States also hired private contractors to train Vietnamese military and police forces in the 1960s and '70s.

There are now about thirty-five major PMFs in the United States, including now familiar names such as Kellogg, Brown and Root (Halliburton), DynCorp, and Trident, in addition to the infamous Blackwater. These firms often have ties to larger defense conglomerates; Northrop Grumman owns Vinnell Corporation in Fairfax, Virginia, for instance. Vinnell exemplifies the history and current function of PMFs in the United States: Founded by retired military officials, it has been operating in Saudi Arabia for more than thirty years, with the primary responsibility of training the Saudi National Guard—a force of one hundred thousand servicemen who protect the monarchy against potential threat from the standing army. Chalmers Johnson, author of *The Sorrows of Empire*, writes that, over just the past few years, Vinnell has "constructed, run, written doctrine for, and staffed five Saudi military academies, seven shooting ranges, and a health care system, while training and equipping four Saudi mechanized brigades and five infantry brigades. Saudi Arabia has, in turn, funneled hundreds of millions of dollars into major defense corporations to equip those forces."

The implications of such relationships are significant. If PMFs do in fact represent "the new business face of warfare," governments will no longer have a monopoly on violence, and state power will be greatly undermined. Crucially, private firms are also exempt from legislative or public oversight. Indeed, L. Paul Bremer, the U.S. administrator in Iraq, decreed that individual contractors were immunized from prosecution in Iraq, placing them beyond the reach of the law—where some have allegedly operated. (In the United States, contracts require the approval of both the State Department and the Pentagon.) This allows leaders to "short-circuit democracy by turning over important foreign policy tasks to outside, unaccountable companies." Or, as one journalist describes it, heads of these companies can "ignore the consequences and fudge the responsibility." (As the PMF phenomenon grows, states will have to adjust their foreign policies to account for their presence and to better control them.)

Blackwater's employees include a number of top former Pentagon and intelligence community officials, among them the former Bush administration counterterror official Cofer Black, the former Pentagon inspector general Joseph Schmitz, the former associate deputy director of the CIA's operations directorate Robert Richer, and the former top CIA Latin American operative Rick Prado. A fall 2006 article in *Harper's Magazine* described how the revolving door has worked for Blackwater:

> Richer is a former head of the CIA's Near East Division and has long served in Amman, where, for a period beginning in 1999, he held the post of station chief. For years he was the agency's point man with Jordan's King Abdullah, with whom he developed an extraordinarily close relationship. "There have been some ups and downs in our relationship with Jordan, but the king has always been on good terms with the CIA," said a person familiar with the situation. "The king's primary relationship is always with the CIA, not the American ambassador."
>
> . . . After Richer retired, sources say, he helped Blackwater land a lucrative deal with the Jordanian government to provide the same sort of training offered by the CIA. Millions of dollars that the CIA "invested" in Jordan walked out the door with Richer.

Many of the Blackwater troops on the ground in Iraq—troops that had central missions like the protection of Paul Bremer—are paid substantially more than U.S. military personnel; they often make in a month what soldiers make in a year, with some earning considerably more than U.S. cabinet secretaries.

A critic within a top fifteen contractor sees something different: "Here's what has happened over the years: Guys have gotten smart. They discovered they could do job X within a government for government wages but that if they did it in the private sector they would make much more. So they moved, and through their influence they moved the resource flows from those paying for government work to those hiring somebody else to do it."

Overseas, there are strikingly different perspectives on "privatization" of the military. During the massive reforms of the 1990s, Chinese military leaders in the People's Liberation Army (PLA) became avatars of change in the name of their self-interest. In fact, it is widely believed that one of the reasons Hong Kong's transition was so smooth and its role as a capitalist entrepôt was so carefully preserved is that senior

Chinese military officials needed Hong Kong's functioning banking system to preserve and build their own personal wealth.

The newfound appreciation for capitalism that overtook the PLA during the 1990s has made a number of them members of the global superclass, including Ren Zhengfei, now president of Huawei Technologies, who turned a $9 million loan from a state bank into one of China's leading international telecoms. Huawei, offering itself as a low-cost rival to big-name suppliers from the West, capitalized on knowledge obtained by Ren when he served as a technical researcher in China's military. The PLA also supported the company, much as Russia's former KGB leaders nurtured, at least for a while, oligarchs like Mikhail Khodorkovsky. The army needed state-of-the-art communications capabilities, and to the extent that senior military officials also profited financially from the growth of this firm, all the better. Ren, who spent a decade in the army, reportedly runs the company along military lines and keeps a low profile, but he is having a harder time staying below the radar now that the company's revenues exceed $11 billion. Other PLA holdings in the 1990s ranged from the plush Palace Hotel in Beijing to securities firms like the failed J&A Securities, and included other prominent enterprises such as Great Wall Telecom, China Poly Group, China Carrie Enterprises, and China Xingxing Group.

Late in 2006, the Chinese government took this trend to its natural conclusion, announcing plans to fund privately owned—as opposed to government owned—military equipment producers, thus promoting competition and innovation, and giving the PLA a better choice of products and services when it comes to their core mission. Companies like Shaanxi Baoji Special Vehicles, which makes armored personnel carriers, and a host of high-tech firms have stepped in to fill this role, often accepting in the process billions in grants and tens of billions in contracts, all intended to help China close its defense technology gap with the West. This comes at roughly the same time that China is announcing record military spending, with the 2007 budget the highest in five years. The increase, officially to nearly $45 billion, is almost 18 percent more than in 2006.

Said a senior partner of one of the West's top private equity firms active in China, "There's twists upon twists on all this. The PLA creates new enterprises in order to get its top guys rich. The government cracks down on the ties when too much money is being made and corruption stories spread. Then, these companies are cut loose to become more truly private, more independent and, often, more successful. What happens next is illustrated by a dinner I attended not too long ago in

Shanghai when, sitting with the CEO of a big tech company and talking about an upcoming set of meetings in Beijing, he said, 'Why do you bother even to see those old men anymore? We are the future of power in China.'"

PERMANENT WAR'S BOTTOM LINE: A COUNTRY AND AN ALLIANCE BEYOND ALL OTHERS

Even in the face of China's rise and its recent increases in defense spending, and despite the hue and cry in the West about the threat this represents, the PRC still has a long way to go to catch up with the undisputed leader in global defense spending: the United States. On the basis of dollars invested alone, more than fifty years of "permanent war" have confirmed America's status as the world's one true military superpower. According to the highly respected Stockholm International Peace Research Institute (SIPRI), of the roughly $1.2 trillion in global defense spending by governments in 2006, $529 billion, approximately half, was spent by the United States. Approximately 80 percent of the total was spent by America and its NATO allies. After the United States, according to SIPRI data, the top four spenders are Britain at $59 billion, France at $53 billion, China at $50 billion (note the discrepancy with the "official" figure cited on page 213), and Japan at $44 billion. Only the top thirteen spend over $10 billion a year each. Similarly, of the *Defense News* top 100 ranking of global defense contractors in 2007, seven of the top ten are from the United States, and the other three are headquartered in Britain, the Netherlands, and Italy. All of the top twenty are from NATO countries.

SIPRI also has an Arms Transfers Project that looks at who is selling weapons to whom. According to that project, the top year for major arms sales was 1982, during the cold war, when five countries—the Soviet Union, the United States, France, Britain, and Italy—were responsible for 82 percent of such transactions. Global arms sales have since trailed off and are now about half of what they were twenty-three years ago, yet five countries still dominate: the United States, Russia, France, Germany, and the Netherlands. Among these, Russia leads the pack, due to its price advantages and the fact that many arms purchasers are emerging nations for which price rather than technological sophistication is key. Within the Russian arms operation, though, there is a concentration of buyers. From 2001 to 2005, a full 43 percent of Russia's sales went to China, and 25 percent went to India. Thus, these two emerging giants were responsible for over two-thirds of all Russia's export demand.

Given its domination of the private arms industry, America's prospects for retaking the top position among arms sellers on SIPRI's lists look good, with the country virtually tied with Russia for market share. During 2001–05, 36 percent of U.S. sales went to Greece, Israel, Britain, and Egypt, but India and Japan are moving up on the list. The Indian relationship is seen as particularly important because of the potential size of that market but also because India is now a vital counterbalance, both to an increasingly martial China and to a politically unstable Pakistan. Just as military-to-military cooperation among leaders helps promote sales, so do sales help promote long-term political and diplomatic ties. Alliances drive arms sales and arms sales drive alliances. If Japan, as seems likely, adopts a more traditional military stance going forward, and others in Asia seek to counterbalance China's massive recent spending increase in arms, the market for U.S. sales in Asia would be expected to grow even further. A more forward-leaning Japanese military, as an example, is much more likely to buy the kind of American aircraft they are used to from manufacturers such as Boeing and Lockheed, or augment their fleets of ships featuring advanced defense systems manufactured by Northrop Grumman or Raytheon. Thus, a policy step that the Japanese might take after close consultation with the United States would probably have commercial consequences of direct relevance to the United States and to the leaders and the shareholders of big defense contractors. If this leads to a spiraling upward of other defense budgets in the region, whether in South Korea or Taiwan, two countries that are also big U.S. arms customers, the benefits cascade outward.

SIPRI's estimate of major conventional arms sales as a percent of global trade is only 0.5–0.6 percent, itself a fraction of total defense-related sales. This underscores that, in terms of global significance, this is not just a numbers game. Arms sales amount to transfers of the ability to project force and thus alter the balance of power regionally and internationally. Perhaps it is not surprising that as a consequence, they are the product of such close collaboration at the highest level of political, military, and commercial elites, core groups of the global superclass.

THE FLY AND THE LION

The lesser-known members, or "shadow elite," of the world's militarily powerful are inherently harder to locate geographically or demographically. They include illegal arms traders and terrorist leaders, among others—criminals whose activities transcend borders and cause international instability. Despite their lack of visibility, these individuals have global impact: Potentially using or supplying weapons of mass destruction, they can alter the fates of nations.

Many of the headlines and much of the attention in the arms business are associated with the most expensive or destructive weapons. William Langewiesche's *The Atomic Bazaar*, for example, chronicles one of the most destabilizing, power-shifting phenomena in global security: the acquisition by poor countries of nuclear weapons technologies. Langewiesche calls the acquisitors "the nuclear poor" and rightly notes that their possession of such weapons gives these countries and their leaders much greater leverage internationally. (Indeed, Bill Clinton once characterized nuclear weapons as North Korea's "only cash crop.")

But the story of how these weapons technologies were trafficked brings into focus several of the most important trends affecting the global arms marketplace: the growing significance of illegal trafficking in weapons or weapons technologies by actors who ignore international regimes, and their ability to ignore those regimes because they have failed or are failing. The effective negation of the Nuclear Non-Proliferation Treaty's (NPT) leverage as a mechanism for limiting nuclear weapons in the hands of just a handful of nations is the most egregious of these. With the acknowledgment of the acquisition of nuclear capabilities by India, Pakistan, and North Korea in recent years and the possibility of acquisition by Iran, it is clear that without teeth, the relevance of the regime is fading, spurring on the race by small nations and even nonstate actors to acquire the technology.

This in turn led to the likes of Pakistan's Abdul Qadeer Khan, who was discovered to be at the hub of an illegal global trade in such weapons. In the mid-1970s, determined to counter the threat of newly atomic India, Khan stole reactor blueprints from a lab where he worked in the Netherlands and launched his country's own nuclear weapons program, forging his identity as "father of the Islamic bomb." In the years since, Khan has established a global network for nuclear proliferation and has been charged by courts in Europe and South Africa with conducting business with secret or unsanctioned nuclear programs of at least six countries: India, Pakistan, South Africa, North Korea, Libya, and Iran. Much remains unknown about the full scope of the Khan network, however, and though Khan himself is currently under house arrest in Islamabad, President Bush's 2004 assertion that his administration had "put [the network] out of business" seems overly optimistic at best. In August 2006, Steve Coll reported in *The New Yorker* that, like Khan and his many anonymous associates, "the entrepreneurial engineers who have emerged as agents of nuclear proliferation covet privacy and rarely explain themselves. Yet their motives and beliefs—professional pride, greed, fear of exposure, and, occasionally, political conviction—have had, in cases such as Iran, Libya, and Pakistan, as much influence on the nuclear balance as the decisions of Prime Ministers or Presidents." Indeed, one senior U.S. official situates Khan's destabilizing role in the twenty-first century as "up there" with Hitler and Stalin in the twentieth. Even without a military title or CEO status, men like Khan have the capability to shape world events to an extraordinary and terrifying extent.

International terrorists constitute a similar, critical component of the shadow class of the military-industrial cluster. They are much more directly involved with the use of force and violence than their counterparts in the arms trade, and the effects of their actions can be no less momentous. In addition to notorious characters like Osama bin Laden, there are others with (purportedly) similar sway in their respective networks: Ayman Al-Zawahiri (Al Qaeda), Ramadan Abdullah Mohammad Shallah (Palestinian Islamic Jihad), and Sayyed Hassan Nasrallah (Hezbollah) top a long list of individuals whom American authorities consider masterminds. The focus on the top guys is, however, partially a result of the media and the public's impulse toward giving a movement a face, personalizing it. While leaders like bin Laden certainly qualify as superclass due to their iconic status, resources, networks, and political links—there are others who remain anonymous. From bin Laden's disappearance into the mountains between Afghanistan and Pakistan, to the vanishing of other key leaders, the facelessness and interchangeability of the players suggest that, in the case of terrorism, networks are more important than individuals. The killing of Abu Musab al-Zarqawi, for example, did little to weaken the lethal force of Al Qaeda in Iraq. Ironically, the preferred terror technique of many Middle Eastern terror groups, suicide bombing, is not just an effective way of delivering pain to an enemy; it is a metaphor for the movement. Individual identities are extinguishable, expendable.

Recently, as the attention given the so-called war on terror has mobilized intensive study of terror networks, it has also become clear that an important part of the capability of these organizations rests in the "terror supply chain": the ability to tap into illicit networks of arms merchants, money launderers, drug smugglers, and even peddlers of counterfeit goods to get cash, move it, direct it to weapons purchases, buy false papers, cross borders, bribe officials, do whatever it takes to bring a plan to fruition. *Foreign Policy* editor Moisés Naím, in his definitive work on the subject, *Illicit,* describes "thousands and thousands" of recombinant networks that can be drawn on to support a particular mission and extend, for cash, the capabilities of terror groups and other illicit enterprises.

The Libyan-born, Venezuelan-raised Naím, sitting in the living room of his comfortable Bethesda, Maryland, home, discussed with me the shadow elites of a global arms trade that seems impossibly remote. "This is a huge economy. This is immensely important and for many, hard to see," he said, "but it is what is happening in many countries. In many the degrees of separation between the legal and the illegal are two or three or none. Go to Russia and find a company that does not have three or four degrees of separation from a criminal entity.

"These are new elites," he continued, "very powerful financially and politically. They don't go, and don't need to go, to Davos. They do not belong to any of these circles but often they are financially better endowed and politically more influential than some of the new power elites that appear in business magazines and the fancy-party sections of newspapers. Some of them control regional governments, city councils, or have major influence in the military in more than one country and have governments in their pockets. You know what these people have that the Davos crowd does not have? Guns. So all these financiers from New York and London, the big hedge-fund guys, they probably have very big, big pockets, but they do not have guns and thugs and they are the currency in many parts of the world today." Naím refers to places like many so-called weak states in which outlaws rule and the outlaw with the best access to the best weapons is often dominant. If Colombia's rebels and their drug lords, or the drug lords along the U.S.-Mexican border, have access to more cash and as a consequence to better technology, they can outplay legitimate forces in those countries and buy or intimidate political leaders as suits their objectives.

Among the superclass of the arms dealer community, Naím cites Viktor Bout, called by some "the Bill Gates or Donald Trump of modern gunrunning." In the chaos of the early post-Soviet period, Bout bought a number of outdated Soviet aircraft and, under a complex front of fake businesses and subsidiaries, began a chartered weapons-transport service. In the 1980s and '90s he ferried arms (as well as diamonds, frozen fish, and even UN peacekeepers) all over Asia and Africa. From bases in "permissive jurisdictions," he supplied small arms, bombs, and missiles to an unknown number of violent clients from Hutu militias in Rwanda to the Taliban in Kandahar—including an estimated $50 million worth of weapons destined for Al Qaeda. While we can never know for certain the magnitude of Bout's influence, the arms he supplied undoubtedly affected the balance of power in several civil wars and aided the development of more than one lethal terrorist organization.

Until recently, another member of the same tier of shadow elites was sixty-one-year-old Monzer al-Kassar, a Syrian arms dealer who, thanks to his adopted residence and lifestyle of luxury in Spain, was called the "Prince of Marbella." Al-Kassar was undone early in June 2007 by two operatives linked to the U.S. Drug Enforcement Administration who claimed they were seeking to buy weapons for FARC (Revolutionary Armed Forces of Colombia), Colombia's most notorious terror group and one with deep links to the drug trade. Apparently, al-Kassar promised to deliver eight thousand machine guns, 2 million rounds of ammo, 120 rocket-propelled grenade launchers, 2,400 hand grenades, and surface-to-air missiles to the agents. In addition, like any major arms corporation would do, he promised to provide trainers to help enhance the productivity of his clients, offering special insights in the construction of improvised explosive devices. And in keeping with the trend in rent-a-soldiers, he offered a thousand fighters as well. Supposedly the total price tag for the deal was $8 million, but that payoff proved to be just a trap for al-Kassar when he was picked up at the Madrid airport. Al-Kassar has long been seen as a vital link in the networks that empower terrorists, one with a special appetite for anti-American causes, a charge he has always denied.

As dramatic as the stories are about missile launchers and loose nukes, it is worth noting in the context of the global arms business that by far the deadliest segment of the arms trade is small arms. The *Small Arms Survey 2006* reported that one million small arms and light weapons were procured by international militaries that year, with Russia, the United States, Italy, Germany, Brazil, and China the leading exporters. (The United States and the EU alone were responsible for 75 percent of total annual production.) It is only a $4-billion-a-year business, and strikingly, military consumption is only a tiny fraction of the entire trade, with between seven and eight million guns traded legally each year and millions more traded via illegal channels. But whereas deaths from terror attacks were twenty thousand in 2006, total homicides related to small arms were ten times that in the preceding year.

The survey emphasizes that almost half of those killed are young men, and that in places like Colombia with high levels of gun violence, the average life expectancy of males is three years shorter than it would be were it not for the gun violence. According to the UN Office for the Coordination of Humanitarian Affairs, these weapons, which account for only one-fifth of the global arms trade, "maim and kill far more than any other conventional weapons." For an exemplar of small arms' lethal power, one needn't look farther than the Russian-designed Kalashnikov rifle, better known as the AK-47, which alone has killed many millions since its introduction during World War II and which has become the weapon of choice for militants around the world. It and other small arms were the most commonly used weapons—and in some instances the only weapons used—in the 101 major conflicts fought worldwide between 1989 and 1996.

Here again, a failure of governments to act has created the void that has enabled this most dangerous segment of the arms industry to burgeon. A survey by the UN and a host of NGOs found that many states have out-of-date laws, and almost one hundred have "failed to enact what is considered to be a minimum step toward implementation" of small arms controls. Further, it is estimated that the vast majority, perhaps nine out of every ten weapons traded, originated with a state-sanctioned deal. In short, the networks tying the legal arms trade to the black-market trade are producing mayhem and death on a mind-boggling scale. Every year approximately sixty thousand to ninety thousand people are killed in military conflicts by small arms. But it is not in the interests of the powerful to target this problem. Why? Because it is a problem that does not resonate with political or business leaders. It is a problem of the poorest—and one from which global arms producers are profiting.

Ironically, or fittingly, such neglect feeds the anger of the small against the large, pushing people toward shadow elites and away from their corporate and first world counterparts. This creates the environment of asymmetry that is so baffling to many of today's military-industrial elites. The richest and most powerful have perfected a system that gives a few countries—or more accurately, one country and a few people within that country—huge dominance over all the others. But their system also leaves them unprepared and, if Iraq is any indication, almost impotent to face the threat that the fly poses to the lion.

7

THE INFORMATION SUPERCLASS:

THE POWER OF IDEAS

Men will never be free until the last king is
strangled with the entrails of the last priest.
—DENIS DIDEROT

It is no accident that terrorists, who have been around since the dawn
of history, have risen to such prominence during the information age.
Information flows provide the ultimate force multipliers for those who
are otherwise, in terms of raw strength, relatively weak. In fact, the
principal weapons of the terrorist are the television camera, the website, and the newspaper headline. An explosion or a gunshot is the
germ, but the media is the carrier that turns an isolated tragedy—one
that would have made relatively little impact in the days of slow-travel-
ing news—into an epidemic of fear and reaction. Men with roadside
bombs or explosive vests threaten only those they directly attack. Terrorists who can exploit information flows threaten societies.

What was more devastating on September 11, 2001: the destruction
of two buildings in lower Manhattan, or the repeated images—beamed
around the world—of those two iconic edifices crumbling? Al Qaeda
purposely targeted symbolic buildings. If the main objective of terrorism is to create maximum fear, then selecting images that live in the
imagination, that are central to our sense of order, and then destroying
them in a spectacular way is an optimal approach.

Manipulating imagery has become a key skill of terrorists and insurgents in the information age. If Hamas encourages young Arabs to
hurl stones at heavily armed Israeli soldiers in front of the cameras, the

images are persuasive either way: The Israelis are being taunted and appear helpless and weak, or they respond as they are trained and appear excessively violent. If Osama bin Laden or Ayman Al-Zawahiri appears on a videotape, he not only underscores the international community's inability to capture him, but he always, automatically, gets global media attention. Such appearances can serve to set the terms of debate, call supporters to action, and provoke hostile reactions. Perhaps even more than actual attacks, these cameos have become Al Qaeda's primary means of advancing their aims outside of the Middle East.

In this respect, the shadow elites that have risen to superclass status because of their global influence are not just bomb makers or gunrunners; they are master semioticians, individuals who manipulate the media as adroitly as any politician or celebrity (despite their lack of PR consultants). But the information tools at the hands of shadow elites go beyond managing news imagery or making media appearances to call attention to themselves. They use the Internet to expand and maintain networks with one another, to build a virtual global alliance of those who share their views, in much the same way teenage girls share gossip and fashion ideas on MySpace.

Rita Katz and Josh Devon of the SITE Institute, which tracks terrorist entities on the Web, have written that "the Internet has helped fragmented networks merge to form a global jihadist community that transcends national, age, gender and physical boundaries . . . The Internet has given birth to a new generation of jihadists who never travel to Afghanistan or Pakistan or Yemen or Sudan or Somalia to attend an al-Qaeda boot camp." They describe one notorious instance, when a British citizen named Younis Tsouli, screen name Irhabi007, independently assisted multiple terror groups—including Abu Musab al-Zarqawi's Jam'at al-Tawhid wa'al Jihad—by posting and circulating propaganda, including manuals on cyberattacks. He also was found in possession of information about potential targets sent to him by terrorism-associated individuals in the United States.

In their work at the SITE Institute, Katz and Devon have identified and tracked jihadist message boards and identified critical links in the worldwide terrorist Web presence. One example of these is the Al-Fajr Media Center, which "coordinates the distribution of the most messages from jihadist leaders, official communiqués, movies and other propaganda through the most important forums." The group simultaneously serves Al Qaeda and numerous other jihadist groups in the Middle East; its online releases have included an insurgent video of a downed Black Hawk in Iraq, the latest speeches by Osama bin Laden and his lieutenant, Ayman Al-Zawahiri, and videos of attacks on Brown & Root–Condor (a subsidiary of American private contractor KBR) in Algeria.

In this way, are the directors of a group like the Al-Fajr Media Center as powerful as active terrorists? More powerful? Aren't they the ones who provide the structure for global networks and the real ammunition for movements that are more political than military or criminal? Don't they influence more people across borders than even senior leaders on the ground in Iraq, for example?

I believe they do. The nature of power is changing. While for the most part power is highly concentrated—especially in mainstream media and information technology businesses—the information age has built-in democratizing components. Distribution used to be the barrier to entry in the media world, whether in movies, on television, on radio, or in newspapers. Building a distribution network, from theater chains to delivery vans, required a significant capital investment. Today, though, the means of distribution are available to all at no charge, making it possible for small, resource-poor groups to reach out and affect millions around the world. Thus a grainy video called "Evolution of Dance," featuring a guy doing the history of dance in six minutes—a bit of comedy fluff—was seen on YouTube by nearly thirty-five million people in six months: a trivial example, but one with significant implications.

FRESH AND YET STRANGELY FAMILIAR

Bloggers and other Web citizens have started to rival major media outlets in their impact, breaking stories and fueling movements. According to Alexa.com, a "web information company" that ranks sites by user frequency, some of the more popular blogs worldwide are Webring: The Individualists Ring, which states its purpose as supporting a "strong sense of individualism and opposing firmly any form of collectivization"; LewRockwell.com, "an anti-state/pro-market site run by the president of the Ludwig von Mises Institute"; and the Marxists Internet Archive. These sites channel the political passions of many millions of people around the world. Much like DailyKos.com, TalkingPointsMemo.com, and a handful of others that led the mobilization of liberal democrats in the United States in recent years, they have the potential for real political impact.

Nonetheless, for all the Web offers to empower the weak or to support those who cater to niche needs, look at the top-rated websites on the Alexa list as of mid-2007: They are all in the hands of undisputed members of the superclass. Some may be part of a new establishment, younger and more recently rich, but their business practices and their bank accounts and their roles in society sure look like those of elites gone by. Number one on the Alexa site, for example, is Yahoo!, a publicly traded member of the S&P 500 that has annual sales in excess of $6 billion, and that, until recently, was run by a CEO who used to head Hollywood's long-established Warner Bros. studio. Number two is Microsoft's MSN, run by the company controlled by one of the world's richest men, Bill Gates. Number three is Google, which has more than ten thousand employees, a market capitalization of $160 billion, and annual revenues of $12 billion. YouTube, at number four, is owned by Google (bought for $1.65 billion), and live.com, at number five, is owned by Microsoft. Number six, MySpace, is owned by Rupert Murdoch's News Corporation, one of the world's most powerful media companies. It should be noted that Gates, Murdoch, and Google founders Sergey Brin and Larry Page are all not only among the world's richest people; they also regularly appear among the top ten of the "new establishment" as defined by lifestyles magazine *Vanity Fair*. In other words, would you like a little superclass with your so-called democratizing Internet revolution?

That does not of course mean that the Internet is not a revolutionary force. It is almost certainly the most revolutionary development in human culture in many decades, driving globalization, changing social interaction, altering the nature of power, enabling the creation of wealth, transforming marketplaces. It is precisely one of those disruptive historical developments that we have seen stir up elites of the past and create new members. How it does this differs from story to story, across the many varied enterprises made possible by the Web, from a traditional selling platform like Amazon.com to something palpably new, like a social-networking site.

Elly Page has been the research director for this book, and in 2004, while still a student at Harvard, she witnessed one such revolution as her classmate Mark Zuckerberg presided over the inception of the website Facebook. "At the time, the phrase 'social networking' had barely even entered the lexicon," she recalled, "so it wasn't immediately obvious what the site was for. Any Harvard undergrad could post a profile—a page with their name, dorm, extracurricular activities, interests, and so on—and then they could do what every nerd who suffered socially in high school dreams of—they could link up with 'friends' to show everyone how popular they were.

"The site was an instantaneous hit. Word of it spread by cell phone, IM, e-mail, and even by mouth, and in a matter of days, everyone knew about it. In a matter of a week or two, almost every undergraduate was a member.

"It was hard to identify the appeal at first, but it was clearly addictive. For one thing, there was something thrilling about creating your own identity and sending it out into the world, something satisfying about being able to present yourself in whatever way you wanted. In that way it provided a venue to advertise yourself, but more importantly, it provided information on other people—even people you didn't know. You could find the classmate who happened to like the same obscure music as you, or who came from your hometown. You could keep track of who was friends with whom and who was dating whom. It opened up a whole new world of Internet 'stalking.' Maybe most important of all, it gave you something to do when you didn't want to work. In any case, almost overnight, Facebook became a major part of daily social life at Harvard. Without really realizing it, students started spending hours on the site—instead of, say, actually interacting with one another."

And that was only the beginning, the first flicker of a phenomenon that has made Facebook one of the most highly trafficked—and highly valued—sites on the Web. As of 2007, Facebook had more than fifty million members around the world, with an additional 200,000 signing up every day. Alexa's list of most visited websites placed Facebook at number fifteen in the world, and the purchase of a 1.6 percent stake in the enterprise by Microsoft put the value of the company at $15 billion—and made Zuckerberg, who dropped out of Harvard to preside over the skyrocketing growth of his brainchild, worth some $5 billion. Not bad for a twenty-three-year-old.

Does this explosion make Zuckerberg a member of the superclass? Well, yes, it does, given our definition. In fact, there is no realm in which we have been able to watch the creation of new superclass members as closely as we have in the Internet world. We watched the rise of the geeks and thought that this was something different—but was it really? How do these new technology elites compare to their superclass brethren? Educational background provides little distinction. Among the information revolution pioneers who attended Stanford as graduate or undergraduate students are the founders of Yahoo!, the CEO of Microsoft, the creators of Google, the founder of Intel, the founder of Netflix, the founders of Hewlett-Packard, the cofounder of YouTube, the cofounder of Sun Microsystems, the founders of Cisco, and the founder of WebEx. Among those who attended Harvard: the founder of Microsoft, the founder of Facebook, the cofounder and chairman of Sun Microsystems, and the chairman and CEO of Viacom. From MIT: the cofounder of Texas Instruments, the cofounder of Qualcomm, the founder of Lotus, the founder of Infoseek, the founder of 3Com, and the cofounder of Intel. This is of course only a partial list.

Naturally, many Internet pioneers went to other schools, but the point is that this elite did not spring up a long way from the origins of other elites. The apple, as it were, did not fall far from the elite tree. Furthermore, in many cases, once their ideas took root, alumni connections brought them into direct contact with funding sources from the same schools, who became parts of networks that were vital in nurturing the new industry. Subsequently, when the companies grew and went public or were sold, this newly enriched elite connected to the elites of Wall Street and became central players at places like Davos or the Allen & Company meeting in Sun Valley or the Technology Entertainment and Design (TED) conference. And many have then sought to use the money they made for political influence, on behalf of both their business interests and candidates who share their views.

This pattern has been followed in country after country. Though the occasional new idea generates a newly minted sensation who breaks the mold, the elite of the information era have largely followed the paths and patterns of other elites. They have even exhibited the kind of overreaching and produced the kind of backlash seen in the robber baron days: the antitrust cases against Microsoft, Oracle, and others; the investigations into the backdating of options at Apple Computer; the congressional hearings into censorship deals between the Chinese government and Yahoo!, Google, and Microsoft; record companies filing suit against file-sharing websites like Napster and Kazaa; television networks going after YouTube. And these clashes have not happened only in the United States. There has been major opposition to Internet sites in China, trials and convictions of Internet moguls in Asia and in Europe, and the targeting of many once sound investment deals and practices that, following a market downturn, were revealed to be something else and sometimes nothing more than pure scams.

Among the most dramatic of these stories is the rise and fall of Takafumi Horie, who, in his midthirties, has followed the most stunning trajectory of any Internet billionaire. Horie built a social-networking site called Livedoor into a giant among Japanese Web enterprises, following the model of U.S. start-ups and even mimicking the elite-university-dropout model of Gates, Zuckerberg, and others when he left Japan's number one school, Tokyo University, in order to pursue his vision. Horie's aggressive business tactics in his management of Livedoor rocked the staid Japanese establishment—a group already uncomfortable with his rock-star style and his repeated shows of disrespect for the status quo. Only two years into the enterprise, he was accused of stock manipulation through accounting misstatements, totaling perhaps $40 million. He was tried in 2007 and sentenced to thirty months in prison. Once over $1 billion, his net worth has fallen to a paltry $100 million or so.

Yet Horie remains undaunted. He argues that the establishment turned against him, in part because he tried to buy a baseball team and part of a much larger more established company called Fujisankei Communications Group. "The people who found me the most offensive are mid-managers with a stake in the old system—those in their 40s and 50s," he told *The New York Times* early in 2007. "Those people have invested decades in their companies . . . They don't want the world they believed in and guarded until now to break apart, not after they've toiled for twenty, thirty years without enjoying its benefits. They're going to let this punk smash it all?" Many note that not only was Horie's sentence unusually harsh but that there is some hypocrisy in a system that punished him for his comparatively minor misdeeds when much more deep-seated and dubious accounting practices have dogged Japan's biggest companies for years. This, and the way the media has piled on to his case, have left many wondering whether there is some truth to his assertions that he simply upset Japan's rigid establishment more than it could bear.

Horie certainly speaks to the more pernicious influence of the superclass, driven less by nefarious plan than by unbridled and unthinking self-interest. I once observed senior executives of a big technology company as they bald-facedly asserted that they wanted Chinese market share and would be willing to trade their Internet know-how—in particular their ability to help the Chinese censor Web usage—for that market share if they could. This was a big company, and they well understood the ramifications of their decision. There was no gray area. They were deliberately crossing a bright line.

New technology firms have made other compromises to achieve continued growth, encountering culture shocks as they are forced to respond more to the requirements of shareholders than to their own muses. A common story of the information age is the saga of the entrepreneur who must ultimately step down so that "professional managers" can take his or her company to the "next stage." Since the company's capital is often largely concentrated within the handful of financial institutions that I discussed earlier (investment banks, private equity companies, and venture capital funds), one can see how the tech "revolution" quietly fell into the hands of the existing power elite.

One prominent Internet pioneer with whom I spoke became rueful and somewhat guarded as we approached the subject of tension between old and new elites. He had faced the challenge of blending the culture of his company into that of a more established organization, one of those still popular deals that enabled those who were part of "old media" to be transformed by the ideas of "new media" and to stimulate reinvention. (Instead, many of these marriages have been rocky ones, business versions of Samuel Huntington's "clash of civilizations.") "It was natural," mused the CEO. "We should have known that better, perhaps. And it was full of challenges. But it is also the way progress is made, right?" He seemed to suggest that the old would inevitably reach out to the new, that they would try to change each other, and that, like a cold front meeting a warm front, thunderstorms might ensue.

Bob Wright, on the other side of the old/new divide, has a long history in the media game. I met with him in his offices at 30 Rockefeller Plaza in New York, where, from 1986 until early 2007, he ran the National Broadcasting Company. In an industry that traditionally has fickle relationships with its top executives, Wright had remarkable staying power, largely due to his record of building NBC from a television network into a widely diversified media company. (Under his leadership, NBC Universal encompassed the network, Universal movie studios, various cable holdings, international holdings such as Telemundo, and various new media outlets.) Although passing on the reins of NBC, he remains a vice chairman of General Electric. Easy to talk to, well liked, a lawyer by training, Wright in his early sixties is one of the senior statesmen of the global media business.

When speaking about new media, though, he seemed genuinely perplexed. It is clear that he and his colleagues know that everything about their industry is changing, but they don't yet know what the business model is. It is striking. These are the best minds at the pinnacle of the industry, nearly two decades after the introduction of the World Wide Web, and there is very limited forward visibility even at the highest levels— even from a suite high atop one of New York's most famous office towers, with stunning views of the city below. "Say we do, I don't know, twenty, sixteen large films a year and another ten smaller films, twenty-five or thirty [total], and we sent those to Japan today, we'll only be able to air four or five of those to the third biggest economy in the world," Wright told me. "On the other hand, the Internet capacity is unlimited but also unfettered from a regulatory point of view. So if we want to look on the glass half full, there is an opening ability to communicate to a much larger crowd than we're used to, and . . . we just have to figure out how to be part of that communication process . . . When I first came in here the issue was, is broadcast going to survive? Are newspapers going to survive? Are magazines as they were then going to survive? And the answer is yes and no. Our principal income comes from our cable television networks, not from NBC, and our film business is still pretty good because there's a lot of ways to distribute them and television's going to be part of that around the world. The broadcasting business is still a pretty good business, but it isn't what it was, and it is harder and harder. But everybody that is in the traditional media business has to acknowledge that this is a frighteningly complex scheme that we're getting involved in."

Pamela Thomas-Graham, a Harvard-educated former McKinsey consultant who writes murder mysteries in her spare time, worked with Wright for years as the CEO of CNBC. Then, and during her subsequent stint as group president at the Liz Claiborne fashion company, she too saw the challenges posed by new media, especially as it impacted the business with which she was most familiar, the news industry. From her office in New York's garment district, she told me, "There has been this elite, and in general that elite has been fairly discreet, and fairly clubby, and some of it has been fueled by media and kind of the ownership of media news organizations. But now with the rise of blogs and the democratization of the news industry, such as it is, those elites are being penetrated by people in Iowa who just happen to have the time and the resources to try to connect all these little dots. So it's interesting that scale is being turned on its head in some ways, particularly in the news business."

New media elites have not only upended the mainstream news establishment, they have fundamentally altered the industry. The rise of the 24/7, updated-by-the-second blogosphere, for example, has made speed and timeliness ever more critical in news reporting. This too poses challenges, when broadcasters have to verify stories and sources in record time in order to remain competitive. As Thomas-Graham recalled, "One of the things I was trying to instill at CNBC was the fact that, as a news organization, you've got to be able to make the right judgment call.

There is a moment when your interests and those of your source clearly diverge and you've got to be the journalist at that point."

It is a fine line to walk. It has been a particular challenge at organizations like CNBC, which itself represented a revolution in live, narrowly focused stock market coverage, where the connections between real-time news reporting and real-time market trading have produced a new kind of symbiosis between reporters and the field they are covering. Markets rise and fall based on whether broadcasters report that they are heading up or down. The key media personalities become exceptionally powerful. Said Thomas-Graham, "Some people wrote their PhD theses on the CNBC effects on market performance. And it was real, I mean it continues to happen on certain programs. I'd say Maria Bartiromo and Jim Cramer are two that actually really do, I think, have impact because they're both extremely well plugged in, and because everything's happening in real time."

A former U.S. official who served in the top tier of government for over four decades recalled listening to a panel of tech experts, including Google head Eric Schmidt, eBay CEO Meg Whitman, then chief of Yahoo! Terry Semel, CEO of InterActiveCorp Barry Diller, and Wikipedia founder Jimmy Wales. "An amazing panel, and they all were talking about these technologies, and everyone was on the edge of their seats. And I thought this was all irrelevant, that none of these guys were the actual inventors. They're the CEOs who are administering them. The next generation is being invented now by some nerd, who can't get a date, in his garage.

"The question is," the official wondered, "what is the political effect of the new media networks on events? Is it good or bad? And here they split. Eric Schmidt said information dissemination is always good, and he then defended the extremely important decision Google had taken to cut a deal with the Chinese on the grounds that 97 or 98 percent of all the stuff on Google worldwide would still be available in China for the sake of 2 or 3 percent. Other people on the panel laughed at him and said that was a commercial decision, and he held his ground, but from the audience came voices saying, 'You're wrong. This can be used as a force of evil. The modern Goebbels is lurking out there somewhere using it.'"

AN ASCENDANT VOICE OF CHANGE IN THE MIDDLE EAST

In the rapidly changing landscape of information technology, even traditional media are being used in revolutionary ways, allowing for the emergence of unconventional media elite members like Sheikh Hamad bin Thamer Al-Thani. Al-Thani is a member of the Qatari ruling family and a distant cousin of the current emir, Sheikh Hamad bin Khalifa Al-Thani. He began his career in the Ministry of Information and eventually reached the position of first undersecretary to the minister of information. Following the ministry's abolition in the mid-1990s, he was seized with the idea of starting an independent news organization in the vein of the BBC or CNN. Qatar's emir saw the station as a chance to elicit support from the West so as to dissuade a possible invasion from its larger neighbors. In 1994, the channel was established, and by 1996, Al Jazeera was being broadcast across the region.

The station was planned to be self-sufficient, funded by advertising revenue, but many governments in the Middle East, particularly the Saudis, have taken a negative view of the channel due to its criticism of their policies and have pressured companies not to advertise on Al Jazeera. Consequently, the station has continued to be supported largely by the government of Qatar. The channel has an "opaque" relationship with Sheikh Hamad bin Khalifa Al-Thani, but as Hugh Miles put it in *Foreign Policy*, the emir has thus far "kept his fingers off the station," and Al Jazeera has thrived under his aegis. The station purports to offer a Middle Eastern view of world affairs and was originally held up by the West as a beacon of independent reporting, especially its coverage of controversial issues such as women's rights. But recently Al Jazeera has been attacked by the American administration for giving too much air time to terrorists, including Osama bin Laden, and the Iraqi insurgency (media coverage that, as mentioned earlier, provides the ultimate force multiplier for the relatively weak). The station's antagonism of the U.S. regime even led President Bush to contemplate bombing the station's Doha headquarters in 2004.

The American-led invasion of Afghanistan following the 9/11 attacks truly lifted the station into the international spotlight. Al Jazeera was the only television station that was allowed to report from inside Taliban-ruled Afghanistan, and as a result many news agencies around the world depended on the station for images and information. Notable scoops included the American bombing campaign, the Taliban's destruction of ancient Buddhist statues, and exclusive videos of Al Qaeda and Taliban leaders. Having made a name for itself, the station has expanded its operations to include an English-language website and new offices in London, Kuala Lumpur, and Washington. It plainly wants to compete with CNN and the BBC; it has hired many journalists from these organizations and recently began airing an English-language, twenty-four-hour news station. It has also sparked the establishment of a number of competitors in the Middle East, including the Saudi-backed Al Arabiya television station.

NEW MEDIA MONKEY-GLAND INJECTIONS: A QUICK SHOT OF SIZZLE

The established media giants of the past are often, as noted earlier, in the position of incorporating new media innovations to serve the interests of existing elites. It is the equivalent of what Richard Burns, my former business partner, used to call "a monkey-gland injection," an effort to revitalize the organization in a single action. Every newspaper with a hope of surviving is now a Web business; sports empires are built on fan bases that are expanded through video games; columnists become bloggers. The biggest and most successful media executives of today are thus those who are best able to continually reinvent their companies and, to some extent, themselves. No one has done this more deftly, or while generating more debate, than Rupert Murdoch.

As chairman and chief executive of News Corporation, Rupert Murdoch owns roughly 30 percent of the company and a majority holding of voting stock, which gives him virtually complete control. The voting structure results in News Corp. being, according to *Time* magazine, "one of the few megacorporations controlled by a single individual." The company itself was, in mid-2007, worth almost $70 billion even before its successful takeover of *The Wall Street Journal*, by far the most influential daily business newspaper in the world. Australian by birth, Murdoch followed the path of colonial elites of the era and went off to Oxford University, then he returned to Australia to begin building his media empire, buying up a series of local and national newspaper businesses. By the end of the 1960s, Murdoch had established himself as one of the leading newspaper barons in the world with his ownership of London's *News of the World*, and not long after strengthened his global market share by acquiring the *Sun*, the *Times*, and the *Sunday Times* (of London). He continued to expand his print empire into the 1980s and broke into the American market with the purchase of the *New York Post*.

In 1985, Murdoch became a nationalized American citizen to fulfill the requirements of the U.S. media ownership laws—recognition on his part of the preeminence of the U.S. information industry in the information age. He had gained full control over 20th Century Fox production studio and the Fox television network the previous year, which solidified his position as one of the most influential individuals in the world. Through these outlets, the driven yet often warmly charming Murdoch oversaw the creation and distribution of a solid string of hits including the *Alien* movies, *Titanic*, *The Simpsons*, and the global *American Idol* franchise. News Corp. has major stakes in satellite television services including DirecTV in the Americas, the assorted Sky services in Europe, and the Asian STAR TV. Finally, the corporation also owns HarperCollins publishing house. In 2006, Murdoch aligned himself with Ahmet Ertegun, the founder of Atlantic Records, who held Turkish citizenship, to skirt a Turkish media ownership law in his bid to enter the Middle Eastern market. Through these holdings, Murdoch has a huge level of influence over the information and entertainment that reaches hundreds of millions of people.

These achievements aside, Murdoch is probably best known for revolutionizing television news, with the creation of the self-proclaimed "fair and balanced" Fox News Channel in 1996. The station is currently the most popular twenty-four-hour news station in the United States, ahead of fellow billionaire Ted Turner's CNN. Journalist James Poniewozik has written: "Fox taught TV news that voice, provocation and fun are not things to be afraid of. And for better or worse, probably every TV news program outside of PBS has been Foxified by now. The explosive graphics on your newscast . . . The 'Free Speech' opinion segments on the new *CBS Evening News*: that's Fox . . . You may tell yourself you don't watch Fox News. But as they used to say in the old Palmolive commercials: You're soaking in it."

While other media conglomerates may be larger and more profitable, few are as powerful as Murdoch's News Corp., in part because Murdoch actively seeks to use his power to advance his political views. The analogy with military elites is clear: Having the ability to project force is one thing; having the will to use it is another. Murdoch has the will to use his influence and regularly does. There is an understanding that Murdoch generally has the ability to affect the editorial opinions of his newspapers. For example, according to *The Guardian*, not a single one of News Corp.'s papers opposed the invasion of Iraq at the beginning of 2003. Murdoch's involvement in the output of his media outlets was, in fact, the main point of criticism by *The Wall Street Journal*'s editorial board, which resisted Murdoch's bid for their owning company, Dow Jones, in 2007. Other reports suggest that when attempting to take over Warner Communications during the mid-'80s, Murdoch directed reporters at the *New York Post* to dig into the background of

Warner's Steve Ross to help with the legal process involved in the attempted acquisition. He also repeatedly pushed stories that would help and blocked projects that he felt would hinder his business interests or the interests of political allies. But one individual close to Murdoch for many years told me, "He is incredibly complex and the story is not a simple one. He has saved countless businesses that would have folded in other hands, and if he were such an ideologue would he have backed Blair or Hillary Clinton or gotten along so well with the Chinese government?"

When it comes to politics, Murdoch is consistently pragmatic about whom he supports in elections and does not belong to either party in the United States. Despite the conservative slant of many of his outlets (Fox News Channel and the *New York Post* are perhaps the two most prominent), he recently hosted a fund-raiser for Democratic presidential candidate Senator Hillary Clinton, as well as a retreat attended by Bill Clinton and Al Gore. The former chairman of the FCC Reed Hundt noted that "he has a far better understanding of how to influence government than anybody else I've ever met in the media." The former New York City mayor Ed Koch recalled receiving a personal phone call from Murdoch when Koch was running for the mayoralty in 1977. When Murdoch informed him that he would be endorsed by the *Post* the following morning, "I said, 'Rupert, you just elected me.' And he had. The *Post*'s endorsement transformed my campaign. I wouldn't have won without it." Murdoch's accumulation of personal power was confirmed by his close friend Irwin Stelzer of the *Sunday Times*: "They say Rupert talks to Tony Blair to protect his company [News Corp.] . . . Maybe there's a small element of that, but that's not what drives him. It's about affecting events."

For now, Murdoch is well placed to do just that, though he rules in an industry where change is the only constant and he will have to change with it to maintain his position. News media, in particular, have evolved considerably in the last five years, not only with the rise of Internet news and blogs, as discussed, but also with reporting that is increasingly entertainment-oriented in nature. Indeed, more Americans in the eighteen-to-twenty-five age bracket get their news from Jon Stewart's "fake news" program *The Daily Show* than from any other source. (Keeping in step, Murdoch's Fox News Channel introduced *The ½ Hour News Hour* in 2007 to compete with Comedy Central's popular parody.) In the global era, overlapping networks of entertainment celebrities have more than star power—they have the power to affect real-world outcomes, political and otherwise.

PRO BONO

Some musicians and actors are known around the world. Their images plaster magazine covers, they sell millions of records, they bring in hundreds of millions in box-office sales. Their every move is fodder for speculation, in celebrity tabloids, on TV, and throughout the Web. They are more famous and better recognized than almost anyone else on the planet—such is the power and reach of popular culture.

A select few of these celebrities have transcended their pop culture status and aspired to use their unrivaled visibility to generate greater influence. Musicians like Bono or Peter Gabriel or Bob Geldof have become regulars at elite assemblies like Davos, but they can also be found behind the scenes, working with government leaders to advance causes like bringing aid to Africa. Bono, for one, has been a whirlwind in recent years, guest editing an issue of *Vanity Fair* on Africa, creating programs to raise awareness through highly identifiable "red" products that raise money for African causes, and pressing government leaders for debt relief for developing nations. Geldof has done likewise, helping to organize massive worldwide concerts like the Live Aid events, which harnessed the power of multiple pop stars to bring attention to the plight of the world's poorest.

How informed are these celebrity ambassadors? Are entertainers suited for policy work and grounded in the substance of the issues? Said one former top official of a multilateral development agency, "I've seen these guys in action and their commitment is impressive. Naturally, they are not development professionals, but what they bring in passion and access to the media is vitally important. In one instance, I remember vividly watching Bono work the back halls at the G8 Summit in Gleneagles, Scotland, and I was really struck by how up to speed he was. Geldof was there too and, though he worked hard, he was not in the same league as Bono." Bono is far more than just a well-intentioned celebrity with a craving for attention. As one European development official said to me at last year's World Economic Forum, "It's easy to snipe, but I don't think there is a single public official who has done more to raise awareness of Africa or to mobilize action than Bono. If he ended up winning the Nobel Peace Prize it would not be such a great stretch."

Other celebrities—like Angelina Jolie, Nicole Kidman, and Michael Douglas, to name a few—have actually been designated as UN ambassadors. While some have used the position for photo ops, Jolie has gotten credit for her energy and intelligence in approaching the plight of children in the developing world (far beyond her propensity for adopting a few of them). Recognizing the importance of her mission, the prestigious Council on Foreign Relations recently granted term membership to Jolie, almost certainly the only current term member without a college education.

British minister of state for foreign affairs for Asia, Africa and the UN Mark Malloch Brown was in 2006 asked by *Time* magazine to profile Jolie for its "100 Most Influential People in the World" issue. He described his meeting with her: "There was, with my wife Trish, much chuckling on this. The story is that she wanted to meet me for a briefing before she went to Davos last year. The article actually could have been much funnier, but it read that somehow I had been standoffish and she insisted on meeting me at this London hotel, about which, of course, I got to hear my locker-room friends all roaring about with disbelief. In reality, the funniest aspect was that Trish called me from a broken-down car with a sick daughter, Maddie, on her way back from a doctor in the winter snow of Westchester, and said, 'Where are you? I suppose you are doing something great.' I said, 'Actually, I am in a hotel room with Angelina Jolie!' But fun aside, when we spoke, I was impressed with her knowledge and her commitment."

Malloch Brown also described the G8 Summit at Gleneagles: "I was there last year with Kofi [Annan, then the UN secretary general]. Bono is genuinely knowledgeable with his stuff. And with his smart guy advocate allies, they were really making a difference. They got Kofi to help arrange one last go at how to engineer a trade breakthrough there for the poor countries. But just imagine the hotel room with these two, Bono and Kofi . . . Ultimately, it is just a handful of celebrities like this who, in their spare time from their entertainment jobs or their roles as queens or princesses or whatever, are smart enough to use what they have very well. The question is, are they representative of something broader? Are they a missing link between these detached global elites and mass opinion and mass culture? I think they are obviously filling a vacuum."

The motto of my junior high school in Summit, New Jersey—and countless other schools, I would warrant—was "knowledge is power." But in the current era, celebrity is power. With modern information technologies, celebrity amounts to the ability to command the attention of mass audiences. Just as terrorists try to commandeer that visibility, to capture the new global means of distributing information for their purposes, so can celebrities turn the fact that the cameras and the reporters seek them out into power. For David Beckham or Cristiano Ronaldo, for Michael Jordan or Tiger Woods or any big-name star endorsing a product, this is the power to generate revenue for a client, to draw consumers to merchandise or services associated with them. For others, it can be the power to raise awareness of an issue, to fuel passions and initiate action and mobilize resources, as have Bono, Bob Geldof, Angelina Jolie, and Shakira, the Colombian pop star and UNICEF ambassador. When Shakira tells Chilean president Michelle Bachelet, "Education is not a luxury, it is a right everyone should have," it may not ring with new insight, but it has many more times the impact than a thousand experts would have.

SAVING THE WORLD ONE IDEA AT A TIME

Not all of the world-class activists who might be found at Davos or other elite retreats are rock stars, of course. In fact, few are as easily distinguishable as Bono might be as he slips through the crowds in his tight leather pants wearing his trademark wraparound shades.

It is a pity, actually, because it might save needless embarrassment. I recall vividly an evening function several years ago in Davos during which I was standing next to a compact, friendly, bearded man whose badge was obscured but who was holding court among the group of business and government leaders with whom we were both chatting. Warm and emphatic on the subject of the environment, he spoke English with a Mexican accent. During a lull in the conversation, I introduced myself, hoping to elicit a clarification from him as to who he might be. Another in the group—a garrulous woman who was also Latin, if I recall correctly—recognizing that I was moments away from making an irredeemable fool of myself, said, "Oh, don't you know Mario?"

There was apparently not much of a flicker of recognition from my eyes, and she then said, "This is Mario Molina. He won the Nobel Prize in Chemistry."

I shook his hand, but it was more evident than I would have liked that I had not heard of him. "He is the one who discovered that we were destroying the ozone layer," the woman went on, and then quietly, in the kind of slow whisper saved for children you are trying to spare embarrassment, she added, "He has helped save the world."

Molina was exceptionally kind during the remainder of the conversation but was soon swept off in another direction, heading to an evening conclave of several Nobel laureates. There, he characteristically underscored that despite the progress made since he and co-Nobelist Sherwood Rowland wrote their groundbreaking 1974 article in *Nature*, explaining how the use of chlorofluorocarbons (CFCs) was leading to depletion of the protective ozone in the atmosphere, much more needed to be done to avert the potentially catastrophic consequences of climate change.

Several years later, at another such event I happened to attend, I heard former U.S. Vice President Al Gore refer to Molina as not only a genuine hero of the effort to preserve the environment but a man with a special ability to bring people together. Gore said that Molina, the only Mexican-born scientist to win the Nobel, was the sole person he knew, for example, who got along with both the mayor of Mexico City and the president of Mexico, bitter rivals who had recently competed in a hotly contested election to occupy Los Pinos, that country's presidential palace. Mexico's president, Felipe Calderón, underscored the power of the image that has evolved around Molina as a result of his actions; when trying to describe the image he sought for Mexico going forward, he said at Davos in 2007, "We want to revert the image of the guy leaning up against a tree snoozing with his sombrero pulled down over his eyes to the Mexico of Nobel Prize scientist Mario Molina and Golden Globe–winning director Alejandro González Iñárritu."

Molina has said that growing up in Mexico City, he found that science was not highly valued as a pursuit for a young boy, and that he had to work to offset the image problems that this lack caused him. But just two years after completing his studies as an undergraduate in Mexico and then as a graduate student in Germany and the United States, he permanently altered not only the way the world would perceive him but how it would perceive itself when, working as a postdoctoral fellow for Rowland at the University of California at Irvine, he became the principal author of their article demonstrating that emerging concerns about the impact of chlorofluorocarbons from refrigerators and aerosol cans were warranted, and predicting the formation of what has become known as the "ozone hole." At the time of the article's release many, even in the scientific community, were skeptical. But, as noted in Molina's Nobel citation, "Many were critical of [their] calculations but yet more were seriously concerned by the possibility of a depleted ozone layer. Today we know that they were right in all essentials. It was to turn out they had even underestimated the risk." The Nobel Committee went further in describing the work, noting reverently that through the international agreements that ultimately resulted from their research and which banned the chemicals that were doing the damage, the work of Molina, Rowland, and their corecipient, Professor Paul Crutzen of the Max Planck Institute for Chemistry, "contributed to our salvation from a global environmental problem that could have catastrophic consequences."

Recent scientific data has demonstrated that the Montreal Protocol, the treaty that led to the reduction of ozone-depleting chemicals, has actually worked. "Compelling evidence" has been cited that suggest ozone is being lost "less quickly" and that, within several decades, actual recovery of the damaged atmospheric layer might begin.

What is only implied by the data, however, are the political and economic dynamics involved in turning scientific conclusions into global action. It is in those dynamics that the likes of Molina and his colleagues transcend the distinction of being elite scientists and meet our criteria for inclusion among the members of the superclass—which is to say not only impacting the lives of millions across borders but doing it on a regular basis. It requires something more than just being innovative or rigorous or capable of elegant scientific reasoning. It also requires the ability to translate discoveries and conclusions into action.

Molina meets this requirement and, indeed, is a superb example of what might be called the scientist-activist, a number of whom certainly qualify to be members of the superclass, ranging from the likes of Anthony Fauci of the U.S. National Institutes of Health, who was at the vanguard of scientists working to both combat and raise awareness of AIDS, to J. Craig Venter, an evangelist for the benefits of mapping the human genome, to those on the darker side of the use of their scientific skills, such as Pakistan's A. Q. Khan.

The scientific community is built more than many other groups around the idea of global networks, cooperation, and communication, which makes having global influence that much more natural. But, as in Molina's case, merely discovering and then sharing an idea is not enough. In the mid-1980s, as the debate leading up to the Montreal Protocols was heating up, major business groups such as the Alliance for Responsible CFC Policy, comprised of more than five hundred organizations in the United States, mobilized to blunt the efforts of Molina and others seeking to ban or limit the production of the products they produced. This group noted that CFC sales in the United States at the time were more than $750 million and said that the annual sales of goods and services "dependent" on these products was $27 billion. Powerful economic cases were being made, and political opposition to change was being mobilized. However, because of the activism of Molina and his colleagues in promoting their findings, and because of their continual research into new dimensions of the brewing crisis (such as demonstrating that the ozone depletion discovered over Antarctica was a result of the impact of extreme cold in the atmosphere on the CFCs), incontrovertible evidence was produced and then publicized via active use of the media. It is a formula that has been used similarly in recent years to promote the data substantiating other dimensions of climate change, notably those associated with the manmade causes of global warming.

Molina remains an activist. In August 2007 he wrote an article in the *Financial Times* to commemorate the twentieth anniversary of the Montreal accord, urging that the treaty be expanded to seize "the opportunity to reduce climate emissions by many times the reductions mandated under the Kyoto protocol on climate change." He went on to emphasize the impact of collaboration among the scientists and policymakers who produced the international agreement, which virtually eliminated ozone-depleting substances in the developed world and substantially reduced them elsewhere. Current estimates suggest these measures will within six decades prevent more than six million skin-cancer deaths in the United States alone, producing over $4 trillion in health benefits. That is a disaster the size of the Holocaust prevented, thanks to the powerful combination of science, activism, modern information technologies, and responsive political systems. And it clearly underscores the special place scientists can have among the superclass.

THE REENCHANTMENT OF THE WORLD

Today, confounding centuries of anticipation of the arrival of an era in which science trumped the historical dominance of faith-based institutions, the power of religion is combining with the power of modern media to facilitate a religious rebirth. This, in turn, has re-energized and empowered an important component of the global superclass: the religious leaders of the information age.

For most of of the twentieth century, conventional wisdom and an expansive body of literature posited that modernization would create more secular societies. In the early 1900s, the sociologist Max Weber called this phenomenon "the disenchantment of the world": Capitalism would replace godly worship with devotion to the dollar, and the spread of science and literacy would undermine the turn to God to explain the unknown. In midcentury, President Kennedy was elected after proclaiming his belief "in an America where the separation of church and state is absolute . . . where no public official either requests or accepts instructions on public policy from the Pope, the National Council of Churches, or any other ecclesiastical source."

Popular support for a government free from religious influence coincided with conspicuous signs of atheism and spiritual doubt, and not only in the United States. The Harvard theologian Harvey Cox described in 1965 "the loosing of the world from religious and quasi-religious understandings of itself" in his controversial book *The Secular City*. The following year, *Time* ran a cover story entitled "Is God Dead?," which observed: "Nearly one of every two men on earth lives in thralldom to a brand of totalitaranism that condemns religion as the opiate of the masses—which has stirred some to heroic defense of their faith but has also driven millions from any sense of God's existence. Millions more, in Africa, Asia and South America, seem destined to be born without any expectation of being summoned to the knowledge of the one God." Of course, there was something else in the supposed question, a classically American implication that everyone else must be wrong. But the question was a real one. To many, religion increasingly seemed as ancient and distant as the stories that it venerated. As a consequence, as religious elites were losing their flocks, they also seemed to be losing significance in the global power structure.

But by the early 1970s, many areas of the world began witnessing a backlash to secularism, and with it the reemergence of powerful religious leaders. The religious reversion was especially marked in the Middle East and Southeast Asia: In Iran, the secular and Western-oriented Shah saw his power diminish through the 1970s, culminating in the revolutionary ascension of Ayatollah Khomeini in 1979. Similar movements toward more religious forms of nationalism took place in India, Pakistan, Bangladesh, and Sri Lanka. A "born-again" Baptist president, Jimmy Carter, was elected in the United States, and Americans tuned in en masse to the televised sermons of evangelist Jerry Falwell and other broadcast ministries. Catholicism blossomed in the developing world during the reign of modern history's most popular pope, John Paul II, and by the late 1980s, his Communist adversaries not just in Poland but throughout the world faltered and collapsed. The trend in religions' political victories continued through the 1990s, with the rise of the Taliban in Afghanistan, and into the twenty-first century, with the victory of Hamas in the Palestinian elections and Christian conservatives in the United States. These political movements reflected a more general transformation: In many parts of the world, people were becoming more religious. The chief rabbi of Great Britain argued, "Religion is no longer marginal to international politics. After a long period of eclipse, it has reemerged with immense and sometimes destructive force."

Economic globalization, urbanization, education, and the spread of democracy have brought about not secularization but a spiritual reawakening in many parts of the world. A number of polls reveal this rise in religious observance and adherence: The two largest sects of Christianity, Catholicism and Protestantism, could both claim larger percentages of the world's population in 2000 than they could a century before. According to a 2005 compilation of sources, 84 percent of all people consider themselves religious. The trend may vary somewhat by geographic region—Europe, notably, remains decidedly secular with a mere 21 percent of its people claiming that religion is "very important" to them—but overall the picture is one of an increasingly religious world.

The result is a pronounced concentration of power among religious leaders. Just a few religions are dominant, and it is their leaders who have the greatest global followings and influence. Christianity dominates the world scene by far, with 2.1 billion estimated adherents, followed by Islam at 1.5 billion, Hinduism at 900 million, traditional Chinese religion(s) with 394 million, and Buddhism with 376 million. Fewer than a dozen religions have more than ten million members. (Of course, within the biggest religions there are important divisions. Catholics and Protestants are no longer killing one another with the frequency that shaped the history of the Reformation, but still the differences are great. The divisions within Islam, primarily the conflict between Sunnis and Shiites, which dates back to a dispute over who should succeed Mohammed to lead his followers, are as profound and deadly today as at any time since they first triggered violence in the seventh century.)

In light of the resurgence in religious adherence, particularly Christianity and Islam, cultural critics have had to rethink the complex relationship between religion and modernity. In many respects, the rise of religions as vibrant, mass movements has been aided, not impeded, by globalization. Information technology and the communications boom have helped religious groups and their leaders spread their message around the world, attracting new followers and securing networks among existing ones. Television, radio, movies, and especially the Internet have become extremely effective tools of modern proselytizing for religious groups from Muslims to Mormons. This use of communications technology, moreover, is hardly a one-way flow of information, as traditional proselytizing is usually conceived, but rather allows for the exchange of ideas among preachers and adherents. In this way, the increased connectivity characteristic of globalization fosters religious pluralism.

Modern Christianity provides one example of the possibilities for diversity and transnational scope within a single religion. "Consider what went on last Sunday," wrote the historian Mark Noll:

> More Roman Catholics attended church in the Philippines than in any single country of Europe. In China, where in 1970 there were no legally functioning churches at all, more believers probably gathered for worship than in all of so-called "Christian Europe." And in Europe . . . the church with the largest attendance last Sunday was in Kiev, and it is a church of Nigerian Pentecostals. Last Sunday, more Anglicans attended church in each of Kenya, South Africa, Tanzania, and Uganda than did Anglicans in Britain and Canada and Episcopalians in the U.S. combined. And several times more Anglicans attended church in Nigeria than in these other African countries. In Korea, where a century ago there existed only a bare handful of Christian believers, more people attended the Yoido Full Gospel Church in Seoul than all of the churches in significant American denominations like the Christian Reformed Church. In the United States, Roman Catholic mass was said in more languages than ever in American history. Last Sunday many of the churches with the largest congregations in England and France were filled with African or Caribbean faces. As a final indication of global trends, as of 1999 the largest chapter of the Jesuits was in India, and not in the United States as had been the case for many decades before.

Modern Christianity has witnessed another phenomenon in the proliferation of massive churches. The largest in the world, Yoido Full Gospel Church in South Korea, serves over eight hundred thousand worshippers; every Sunday, the church in downtown Seoul holds two services, each attended by more than twelve thousand people. According to the Megachurch Research Center in Bolivar, Missouri, there were ten non-Catholic megachurches in the United States in 1970; in 2005 there were 282. Rick Warren, author of *The Purpose-Driven Life* and pastor of the fifteen-thousand-strong Saddleback Church in Orange

County, California, is often identified as the inventor of the modern megachurch. Tired of hellfire sermons and empty rituals, Warren opened Saddleback in 1980, intending to draw in the "everyman" parishioner. He has since spread his vision of "purpose-driven" faith on a global scale; he took a tour of thirteen countries in 2006, including a stopover in Seoul, where he spoke to a crowd of one hundred thousand. Warren has identified the megachurch as a potential means of global problem solving: "Nothing comes close to the size of churches," he says. "[They have] the broadest distribution network, the most volunteers, local credibility—all these different things that make the church poised to deal with these issues of spiritual emptiness and corrupt leadership and poverty and disease and illiteracy, which are problems that affect billions of people, not just millions."

Already in the United States, megachurches function not only as places of worship and community gathering, but also, according to *The New York Times*, they often operate "almost like surrogate governments," providing a variety of social services including counseling and schooling. Indeed, these churches have the potential to rival national governments and secular civil society organizations in their capacity to address global challenges. Churches becoming involved in global affairs is nothing new, especially in the Christian tradition of proselytizing that drove much of the age of exploration and today inspires liberation theologians in Central America and religious freedom advocates in China. Their power is manifest similarly in the ability of the leaders of Islam to issue fatwas—commands to the faithful that know no borders, such as the one condemning writer Salman Rushdie after publication of *The Satanic Verses*, which was considered to be deeply sacrilegious. Or, likewise, the calls for protests and revenge that extended across the Middle East and into Europe in response to Danish cartoons that appeared to lampoon the prophet Muhammad. New information technologies enable religious leaders to call for action or to pronounce decisions with the weight of law in ways that have instantaneous global impact.

PASTOR OF PARTYING

A cadre of religious leaders worldwide stand out for their ability to harness modern information technologies in order to expand their influence, generate revenues, and gain international stature. It is worth examining a handful of cases to look for patterns, to compare them to other global elites, and to attempt to discern how their roles or the roles of those like them may evolve in the future.

Luis Palau has made a number of names for himself—he is the "international evangelist," or "the Billy Graham of Latin America," or, most recently, pastor of "party hearty Evangelism." Beginning in 1999, Palau's Christian evangelical enterprise, already famous for drawing crowds in the hundreds of thousands around the world, changed formats in order to reach even larger audiences. The Luis Palau Association began hosting massive festivals in open venues where families and friends could mingle, almost unconsciously absorbing the message of Jesus Christ subtly inserted among gospel concerts and celebrity guests. One newspaper described it as "stealth evangelism": "His festivals offer no displays of religious symbols, no robed choirs, no clergy onstage, no solemn Bible readings or long-winded prayers." The Palau ministry is aptly called "Livin' It." Unlike Billy Graham, with his staid, sermon-focused stadium crusades, Palau advertises his events as informal, interactive, and fun. Many of the festivals feature rock bands and skate parks. In 2003, Palau even put on a spring break festival in Fort Lauderdale—an ideal location for attracting college students who might be engaged in less-than-saintly behavior. The event drew more than three hundred thousand people.

Palau is a prime example of religious leadership that transcends national borders and reaches millions. He has taken his ministry to seventy countries, broadcasts a regular radio program on more than 2,100 stations in forty-two countries, and heads an organization with staff members on four continents. His is an unlikely success story, however. He was born in Buenos Aires, Argentina, to an affluent family of devoted churchgoers. Palau could recite Bible verses at a young age, but he didn't accept the faith as his own. According to him, he discovered God one night when he was twelve, as he sat with a camp counselor in the mountains of southern Argentina, in the middle of a rainstorm. Six years later, while working full-time as a bank teller, he began preaching on the side to help support his mother and five sisters. By 1957, at age twenty-three, he had launched his own ministry, complete with tent sermons and radio programs.

Palau came to the United States in 1960. He met his wife, Patricia, at a seminary in Portland, Oregon, and the pair returned to Latin America as missionaries for Overseas Crusade, traveling and preaching with their four sons. Palau's big break came in the 1970s when he crossed paths with Billy Graham, for whom Palau worked as an interpreter and apprentice. For Palau, Graham was not only a mentor, he was a major source of funding in the formative years of Palau's ministry. Today, Palau's events carry a significant price tag—a recent festival in Washington, D.C., cost $3.5 million, paid in large part by corporate funders including Pepsi and Amtrak. (John H. Dalton, the former secretary of the navy, was the festival chairman.)

In addition to his extensive global network of believers and corporate sponsors, Palau's influence now and then extends into the political sphere. He has had personal contact with President George W. Bush on a number of occasions, most recently when he accompanied Bush on an official visit to China in autumn of 2005. During the visit, the two rode to church in a limo together, chatting about the condition of Christianity in China. Palau has also been among a handful of spiritual advisers called upon by the president in the wake of national tragedies. In October 2005, President Bush invited him to speak at a memorial event for victims of Hurricane Katrina, and ten days after 9/11, Bush included Palau in a meeting of "faith leaders," a gathering held hours before he was to address Congress on the state of the nation following the attacks. According to *Christianity Today*:

> Palau, who took notes at the meeting, said Bush drew a comparison between himself and the country. Bush told the gathering, "I was a sinner in a need of redemption and I found it." The President was referring to the difficult time earlier in life when he was a heavy drinker and lacked a sense of purpose. But the gospel became clear to him through a conversation with evangelist Billy Graham.
>
> Bush told the group that the nation was staggering and needed to get back on its feet. He said the devastation in New York challenged the nation to look deep into its heart. "I think this is part of a spiritual awakening in America," the President said.

Palau has interacted with the president on less solemn occasions as well. He gave the official opening prayer at a White House reception for Hispanic Heritage Month in October 2001, an event with a star-studded cast including White House counsel Alberto Gonzales, the pop singer Gloria Estefan, and Rey Ordóñez of the New York Mets, among others. Elites and messages blended, amplified, and supported one another. Politicians gained from the association with the divine, clergy gained from the association with national power, and celebrities multiplied the power of both. It was a kind of trifecta for power cultivation in hyperreligious information-age America.

THE TELEMUSLIM

Christian evangelicals in the Americas aren't the only ones using modern media to spread their faith and influence. Amr Khaled, an Egyptian accountant turned Muslim TV superstar, regularly reaches millions through televised sermons and Web-based proselytizing. Based on audience numbers and website hits, he is more popular than Oprah Winfrey, and in the Muslim world, according to the popular weekly *Al-Ahram*, boasts "the kind of following you'd expect of a movie or pop star." He has no official religious credentials but has managed to attract a devoted audience of millions—mostly young, educated, and upwardly mobile—stretching from the Middle East to Romania to Ireland. From his position of incredible influence and visibility, Khaled has emerged as a powerful figure in shaping Muslims' relations with the West.

Khaled grew up in Alexandria, Egypt, in an upper-middle-class family that was traditional though not religious. He discovered the Koran as a teenager and became increasingly devout while completing his studies at a secular university, but he continued to pursue a career in accounting. Khaled made his first religious speech, impromptu, during a relative's birthday party at a social club. It was hugely popular and led to weekly lectures—mostly practical advice for contemporary Muslims—which led to a four-episode religious talk show that he produced with a high school friend. No network would buy it, so Khaled made two thousand copies of the tape and handed them out to Cairo street vendors, who sold them in stalls alongside slippers, posters, and knick-knacks. Sales exploded, and Khaled had to make an additional fifty thousand tapes before a Saudi-owned satellite network took notice and offered him a contract.

Khaled's appearance on the show is often reminiscent of his days as an accountant; he eschews long, flowing robes for stylish, tailored suits from European designers. Interviewers have remarked on other obvious signs of a comfortable lifestyle—his Bulgari watch, his new Nokia PDA. Khaled's lectures, consciously modeled after those of Evangelical Christians in the United States, blend pragmatic self-help and life management advice with conservative Islamic messages. Many attribute his popularity with young Muslims to his combination of stern words and a smile—softening the harsh, hellfire messages of conservative Islam with a friendly face. ("He is so tender and most adorable," gushed one female fan.) The thirty-nine-year-old Khaled also uses language that young people find more accessible than that of older, traditional clerics. He sprinkles his lectures with Egyptian slang and includes female listeners when addressing his audience, which is unusual for Muslim speakers. And, not incidentally, he is a skillful showman. From *The New York Times*: "In the best traditions of United States televangelists, the Khaled style on stage is a big seller. With eyes shut tight the preacher will summon a message as though from the depths of his soul. His face contorts. There's a rush of emotion. His voice rises to an excited squeal. In a trice he brings his audience back down again, his voice dropping to a near whisper."

On Khaled's website, which received twenty-six million hits in 2005, his followers can download videos of his lectures, chat with one another, and even buy Khaled-brand sweatshirts. (It is the third-most-popular Arabic site on the Internet and ranks among the top one thousand in the world, close to *The Washington Post* and Al Jazeera.) Several mobile phone companies in Arab countries offer Khaled minisermons via text message.

Fame takes some getting used to, and Khaled is still learning. He reportedly gives his phone number to anyone who asks and takes calls from total strangers. One reporter recalled a dinner with a number of wealthy German Muslims who dug into their platters of kebab while Khaled happily chatted away with a teenage girl in Lebanon who had called him out of the blue. According to a colleague, Khaled once ran up an $8,000 phone bill in less than a month, talking to fans. He clearly revels in his followers' admiration, but the anecdotes also reveal a distinctly quirky, absentminded element to his character. A *New York Times* reporter recalls Khaled's career as an accountant as "the most amazing detail of his life," given that "he had trouble keeping track of things. He went missing in airports, wandering off to examine sweaters at duty-free ships or to find Boss shirts, his favorites. He told me he 'lost' an oversize suitcase with 25 expensive European suits on his way back from Saudi Arabia after Ramadan, and I watched him lose his 4-year-old son, Aley, in Heathrow Airport during the only 10-minute interval he was responsible for watching him."

Rick Little, an American adviser to the UN and CEO of an alliance of social entrepreneurs called ImagineNations, said of Khaled, "When you look at the reach of what he's doing, the millions of young people he's touching, I don't know anybody, I don't know of another single individual in the region who is having the impact on young people that Amr is having." Little first learned about Khaled while researching a book on Jordan's Queen Rania, one of Khaled's close friends. She is but one of Khaled's many influential connections—powerful figures in both political and business sectors, including the president of Yemen, the British foreign minister, Saudi oil magnates, and the Nike Corporation. He has been approached by European governments to help combat domestic Islamic extremism, and after the violent controversy over Danish cartoons of Muhammad in 2006, he organized a conference in Copenhagen to engage Muslim and Christian leaders and young people in dialogue about free speech and religious tolerance.

Khaled clearly has powerful and wide-ranging influence over his followers. Many Muslim commentators say he is the single major force behind the dramatic increase in young women who wear a *hijab*, for example. (He has told audiences that to remove the headscarf is "the biggest sin, the biggest sin, the biggest sin.") Recently, Khaled has placed greater emphasis on the link between his moral messages and larger societal and regional goals: his Web- and TV-based program *Life Makers* encourages young Muslims to improve their world and start an Arab revival—premised on what he calls "faith-based development." The renewal of Islamic values, he believes, is the only way to counter the appeal of violent fundamentalism like Osama bin Laden's, which draws Muslims disaffected by rising poverty, joblessness, illiteracy, and political oppression. "I believe that every one hundred years the world's thoughts change," he said, "and extraordinary people appear who carry new ideas to humanity."

DISSIDENT SPIRITUALITY OR SUBVERSIVE CULT?

The mass appeal and growing influence of religion are not limited to mainstream, established faiths. Falun Gong, a spiritual movement that combines elements of Buddhism, Taoism, and breathing rituals called *qigong*, remains one of the most mysterious and controversial "fringe" beliefs, and its founder, Li Hongzhi, is similarly an enigma among the world's most powerful religious leaders. He believes that aliens live on Earth; he has also said that he is a superhuman who can walk through walls, cure cancer, and practice telepathy. To his followers, he is the "Living Buddha." To the Chinese government, he is the subversive head of an "evil cult."

Li created Falun Gong, also known as Falun Dafa, in China in 1992. Clusters of followers, taking part in classes and the movement's trademark meditation exercises, cropped up around the country, and when Li published the Falun Gong bible, *Zhuan Falun*, in 1996, it became a best seller. The following year, threatened by the movement's popularity, Chinese officials banned the publication of Li's books and began an assault on his followers. (Li fled the country and is now a permanent resident of the United States.) In 2000, Amnesty International reported that in one year at least seventy-seven Falun Gong practitioners had died in custody—in "suspicious circumstances," showing signs of torture or other mistreatment. The human rights monitor and other media reported that the Chinese government was systematically arresting and detaining all identified followers, keeping them jailed until they renounced their beliefs. The number of Falun Gong members is disputed—more than one hundred million, according to spokesmen of the sect, two million by official Chinese estimates. (External sources, including *Time* and *Asiaweek* magazines, put the number in the "tens of millions.") And the battle between those followers and the Chinese government continues to rage.

The sect's response to oppression reveals a key component of its power. At government buildings in Beijing and Chinese consulates around the world, Falon Gong members hold regular gatherings, usually silent demonstrations or vigils, to protest their persecution. Protesters, though peaceful, are often armed with props such as graphic posters, fake blood, and cages, purporting to show how they are treated by the Chinese. The first of these demonstrations, in China, was perhaps the most striking: In April 1999, more than ten thousand of Li's followers gathered around Zhongnanhai, a government complex, and stood in silent, meditative protest—the largest organized show of opposition since Tiananmen Square, and by all accounts "entirely unexpected" by government officials. It is the ability to "spontaneously" organize such protests that has so unsettled the government. They are concerned about the group's potential to trigger massive unrest without warning— and this in a country in which central authorities in some places cling tenuously to control (last year there were over eighty thousand public disturbances recorded in China). "Falun Gong had lots of ways of communicating to the public," said a vice president of cosmetic maker Mary Kay Inc., which was caught up in an extensive protest by the group in 2003 after it was disclosed that the company had banned the religion among its Chinese workers. "We didn't know their network even existed until we saw it front and center." Its informal network of Internet sites and print media connects small cells of followers around the globe and gives the group's leader the ability to rally large numbers at a moment's notice. "It spooked the leadership because Li was able to mobilize so many so quickly without being detected," said a China scholar at UCLA. "It represented the end of social control in China."

THE PRAGMATIC FANATIC

The religious leaders who enjoy superclass status have taken various routes to power. Some have simply cleaved to tradition, with such conservative fervor as to distinguish themselves while deftly managing an ascension within the power structures of their faiths. Unlike the elite of the information age, who have used tools and strategies akin to the entrepreneurial classes of the age before them, these traditionalists are more like the elites found in most political classes and in many corporations: They have found the right mentors, built power bases, carefully adapted to changing political situations, and hidden their ambition even while focusing relentlessly on the next goal.

One such leader is arguably the most important figure in the Middle East today. Ayatollah Ali Khamenei, the Muslim cleric and supreme religious leader of Iran, wields more authority than anyone else in his pivotal nation. Khamenei's power is formalized under the Iranian constitution of 1979, which dictates a government based on *velayat-i faqih*, or "rule by expert jurist," giving him the final word over all other leaders and bodies, clerical or political. His approval is required for an elected president to take office, and he has the power to declare war, choose the heads of the military and judiciary, and appoint more than half of the Guardian Council—a body with veto power over the Iranian parliament. His place in the Iranian power structure was well represented at Ahmadinejad's inauguration in 2005, when the newly installed president made a very public sign of obedience: bending down to kiss Khamenei's hand.

Unlike most religious leaders, Khamenei has significant direct experience in government. He served two terms as Iran's president from 1981 to 1989, winning the 1981 election with a 95 percent vote. His predecessor and mentor, Ayatollah Khomeini, led the overthrow of the Shah, founded the Islamic Republic of Iran, and held the highest rank of cleric, a Source of Emulation. In modern Iran, a better mentor would be hard to find. As supreme leader, Khamenei has proved a model of political pragmatism in creating networks of strategic allies. He has strong ties to the Revolutionary Guards, the clerical regime's powerful military force, as well as the Basiji volunteer militia, a quasi police force dedicated to enforcing religious law in Iran. His position gives Khamenei the power to shape foreign and domestic policy and an avenue to promote the nation's Islamist agenda. He openly supports a more confrontational approach to the West, and has publicly condemned "the bitter and venomous taste of Western liberal democracy." He believes Iran has the right to pursue nuclear power but wants to avoid international reprisals that would threaten the stability of the regime. Officials say he has steadily built up support among fundamentalists while undermining the authority of more moderate, independent state leaders. President Ahmadinejad himself has acknowledged Khamenei's direct influence on his decisions; many believe the cleric had a hand in the president's famously provocative letter to George W. Bush in June 2006. According to *Time* magazine, Ahmadinejad and Khamenei meet weekly, in sessions described by observers as those of "a disciple with his leader." He is the force making the critical decisions in one of the world's leading oil-producing states, the key figure in determining how Iran will advance its nuclear ambitions and its regional goals, the final decision maker when it comes to providing support for Hezbollah and other powerful terrorist groups. He is therefore clearly very much a man of this world, even as he is seen as one of Iran's leading spiritual guides to the next.

There are others who use their faith or roles as spiritual leaders to augment various forms of power. As the head of Hezbollah, Hassan Nasrallah is a political leader and a terrorist, as well as a religious figure, much as Muqtada al-Sadr is a cleric and leader of a major Shiite militia in Iraq. Another example is the Grand Ayatollah Ali al-Sistani, the Iranian-born Iraqi cleric who has been such an important force in Iraq, one of the key figures who enabled elections in that country to take place and who, in fact, was instrumental in getting them to be held earlier than many in the country wanted. Each of these leaders affects the path of peace and stability, or instability, in the Middle East. Even the leaders of the world's greatest powers cannot hope to achieve their aims in the region without dealing with them in one way or another. The Dalai Lama, beyond being a media and celebrity favorite, is similarly both a spiritual leader and the spokesperson for the displaced people of Tibet with whom the government of the world's most populous nation must contend as it seeks to consolidate its hold over that mountain realm. L. K. Advani of India's opposition Bharatiya Janata Party draws on that party's close association with that country's Hindu majority.

As with other elites, the religious superclass also draws its power from collaboration and meetings with members of other clusters. Religious figures from Grand Muftis to Greek Orthodox leaders can be seen plying the halls of the World Economic Forum, an event that often has a number of programs with spiritual or religious components.

Far from seeing the death of God, the twenty-first century has witnessed a rebirth of interest in faith. Whether this reenchantment of the world is a reaction to uncertain times or the erosion of other elements of national identity, it is clear that like other cultural elites, the religious superclass is harnessing the tools of the information age to create something that is new, vibrant, and transformative, while at the same time reflecting many of the traditions, traits, and flaws of elites past.

How to Become a Member of the Superclass:

Myth, Reality, and the Psychopathology of Success

> The only way I can get to sleep at night is by imagining a secret cabal of highly competent puppetmasters who are handling the important decisions while our elected politicians debate flag burning and the definition of marriage.
>
> —Scott Adams

Conspiracy theory is the comfort food of politics. Actually, it is more than that. According to psychologists, it fills a fundamental desire to balance perceived causes with perceived consequences and thus satisfies our sense that big outcomes are not the product of happenstance. In an article on the proliferation of 9/11-related conspiracy theories, Patrick Leman, psychology professor at Royal Holloway, University of London, argues, "If we think big events like a president being assassinated can happen at the hands of a minor individual, that points to the unpredictability and randomness of life, and that unsettles us." Conspiracy theories are in fact "psychologically reassuring," says Michael Barkun, author of *A Culture of Conspiracy: Apocalyptic Visions in Contemporary America*, "because what they say is that everything is connected, nothing happens by accident and that there is some kind of order in the world."

The Internet may well be one of the principal drivers of globalization as well as a powerful tool for knitting together communities of elites, but it has also proved to be a special boon for other crowds—those with so-called fringe views who, previously isolated, are now able to connect with others who apparently share those views. As a consequence, the Internet has ushered in a golden age of conspiracy theorists. In the wake of the death of Princess Diana, thirty-six thousand websites sprang up devoted to finding alternatives to the official explanation of her death. Type "9/11 conspiracy" into Google, and you get millions of hits. The immediacy of Internet communication, moreover, means that paranoid theories and myths can reach vast numbers of people around the world in record time. For example, in 2004, a man from a small town in England posted online a video called "9/11: Pentagon Strike," which claimed that on September 11 the Pentagon was hit not by a commercial airliner but by a missile. Within days, the video had been viewed by hundreds of thousands of people. Within weeks, millions around the world had downloaded it.

As more and more ideas are shared, they alter one another, blending and morphing. Barkun writes about the integration of old-fashioned theories about Jewish control of the world with worries about space aliens. One theory posits that the *Protocols of the Elders of Zion* was produced by "the Rothschilds and the reptile-Aryans." Barkun has determined that in the past twenty years "virtually all of the radical right's ideas about the New World Order had found their way into UFO literature."

A Very Short History of Things That Didn't Really Happen—And Their Very Real Consequences

Among the most popular conspiracy theories throughout history have been those about small groups of people, perceived elites or enemies, who were working together in secret to undermine the existing order or to impose their will on the masses. It is natural for those who feel powerless to speculate about where the power lies.

In 431 BCE, at the beginning of the Peloponnesian War, the Athenian Thucydides recorded his countrymen's suspicions of conspiratorial plotting by Spartan oligarchs: "He who succeeded in a plot was deemed knowing, but a still greater master in craft was he who detected one." Throughout the Middle Ages and into the Renaissance, there was an especially vigilant effort to detect signs of the ultimate conspirator, the devil. In AD 962, in Metz, France, hundreds of cats were burned because they were believed to be witches in disguise; Pope Gregory IX later made this particular conspiracy theory doctrine when he denounced black cats as diabolical in 1233. Witches themselves and their familiars (and pets) were dunked, drowned, stoned, and burned in great numbers during the sixteenth and seventeenth centuries—perhaps two hundred thousand witches and hundreds of thousands of cats in that time.

Throughout history, Jews have been seen as a threat by many peoples, including the Romans, Catholics, Protestants, Muslims, Nazis, Communists, and just about everyone else. Legends about Jewish practices and plots produced draconian responses. The Romans destroyed Jerusalem and killed as many as one million Jews in the year 70, followed by similar slaughters in 113 and 132. Starting in the fourteenth century, some of the more famous conspiracy theories about Jews and Jewish practices emerged. In 1321, when it was asserted that local Jews had poisoned the wells in Guienne, France, five thousand were burned alive. When, later in the century, relatively fewer Jews than Christians died of the Black Death, likely due to different sanitary and dietary habits, they were blamed for it, and tens of thousands of Jews were burned.

While some degree of paranoia may be inherent to the human psyche, many historians trace the first real "grand conspiracy" to the French Revolution. In 1792, two deputies named Jacques-Pierre Brissot and Armand Gensonné stood before the National Assembly and announced that a shadowy "Austrian Committee" of the king's advisers was plotting to destroy the revolutionary regime. They had very little evidence, but the idea alone and forcefulness of their speech inspired fear and uncertainty among the assembly and panic throughout Paris. As a result of their warning, the city "was placed on a war footing, patrolled continually, and illuminated throughout the night." Over 90 percent of the executions carried out in the following two years—the Reign of Terror—were against individuals suspected of sedition or collusion with enemies of the republic. According to one historian, "The obsession with conspiracy became the central organizing principle of French revolutionary rhetoric. The narrative of Revolution was dominated by plots."

In a particularly memorable written attack, a French Jesuit named Abbé Barruel first blamed the French Revolution on the Masonic Order, then changed his mind and blamed it on the Jews. (This connection between two conspiracies helped to trigger what now amounts to two centuries of conspiracy theories involving either the Freemasons or the Jews.) Later in the century, Jews were again faulted when Czar Alexander II of Russia was assassinated, and over two hundred riots against the Jews, called pogroms, took place. At the turn of the century, in

1905, the Russian secret police, the Okhrana, adapted an earlier anti-Semitic novel about Jewish plans to control the world into what they christened the *Protocols of the Elders of Zion*, thus promulgating a false secret conspiracy via a real one. Throughout the twentieth century—in Russia, Hitler's Germany, and even today in the Middle East—this forgery has been used to incite violence against the Jews as a reaction to their alleged plot to seize power.

Fears of secret plots punctuated the decades of the twentieth century. After 1917, the Bolsheviks were consumed with fear of counter-revolutionary conspiracies. In 1934, Smedley Butler testified that he was approached by a bond salesman named Gerald McGuire seeking assistance in deposing President Franklin Roosevelt. The U.S. Congress's McCormack-Dickstein Committee, which heard his testimony, later became the House Un-American Activities Committee, the vanguard of the red scare in the 1950s. While the United States was in a real struggle with Communist Russia, the assertion that Communists were everywhere and intent on undermining the United States was vastly exaggerated (in much the same way that the terror threat is exaggerated today). Particularly targeted by the committee was the movie industry, which was asserted to be infiltrated by Communists—and perhaps not incidentally, Jews—as a means of warping American culture.

Conspiracy theories about plotting elites have, of course, been helped by the media, whether it is books like Dan Brown's *The Da Vinci Code*, a worldwide best seller, with its interlocking conspiracy theories involving Knights Templar, the Illuminati, and Opus Dei; or movies like *JFK*, offering Oliver Stone's paranoid vision of the events around the assassination of President Kennedy. Brown's next focus was a novel about another favorite of conspiracy theorists, the Freemasons.

WHEN IS A TROWEL JUST A TROWEL?

Allegedly the oldest secret society in the world, Freemasonry attracts conspiracy theories like moths to a flame. Over the years, Masons have been charged with paganism, occultism, and Satan worship, and have been blamed for fomenting revolution everywhere from Franco's Spain to Nazi Germany to Soviet Russia to Red-fearing America. Recent criticism of Freemasonry has focused on the veiled influence of its most powerful members, fueling sensationalist portrayals in popular media like Nicolas Cage's 2004 film *National Treasure* (in which Cage hunts for legendary treasure guarded by the Masons) or *The Man Who Would*

Be King, in which a Freemason (played by Sean Connery) inherits a kingdom because he wears a masonic symbol linked to Alexander the Great, himself a Mason.

The international fraternity was founded in London in the early eighteenth century but traces its founding principles to the construction of the Temple of Solomon around 950 BCE and even earlier to Greece and Egypt. Its founders in England were actually real masons, individuals highly esteemed over the centuries for having the unique skills required to build cathedrals, churches, palaces, and other symbols of power. Though not a religion, Freemasonry requires that its members swear allegiance to a Divine Being—in whatever form they choose—and biblical lessons and principles are central to the society's "system of religious philosophy." Fraternal members have a system of secret "grips and passwords" to identify one another and engage in secret rituals during closed meetings. The society revolves around four cardinal virtues—fortitude, prudence, temperance, and justice; and seven liberal arts—geometry (source of the iconic G in many Mason designs), arithmetic, rhetoric, logic, grammar, music, and astronomy. Masonic symbols have been sighted in the layout and street plan of Washington, D.C. (inverted triangles), as well as the design of the Pentagon and other federal buildings (pentagrams). Some claim that the one-dollar bill contains extensive Masonic imagery: The eagle on the back of the note is the symbol of St. John the Evangelist, patron saint of the Freemasons; its thirty-two feathers represent the number of degrees in Scottish Rite Freemasonry; the arrows in its left talon refer to King David, father of Solomon; the olive branch in its right is associated with Solomon himself; the thirteen stars above its head symbolize the tribes of Israel; and the Latin motto *"E Pluribus Unum"* suggests the Mason fraternity. The unfinished pyramid with a triangle containing an "all-seeing eye" is also alleged to be a Masonic symbol.

Since its establishment in 1717 with the founding of the Grand Lodge of England, in London, Freemasonry has endured a rocky history. Its members were condemned by Pope Clement XII in the 1730s, initiating Catholic-Mason animosity that still exists today. In 1826, the mysterious disappearance of an anti-Mason activist named William Morgan fueled the creation of an anti-Masonic movement in the United States—including a short-lived political party that fielded a presidential candidate in 1828 and 1832. The twentieth century brought the greatest challenges to the society, however, especially under the Nazi regime: During the postwar Nuremburg trials, the chief prosecutor and U.S. Supreme Court justice Robert H. Jackson (a Freemason himself) said,

"It is not generally understood that among the earliest and most savage of the many persecutions undertaken by every modern dictatorship are those directed against the Free Masons." Discrimination against Masons continued in the United States during the cold war and later, when the order joined groups like the Council on Foreign Relations and the Trilateral Commission in the minds of critics who feared its members had undue power to conduct covert policy.

As with most conspiracy theories, there are some grains of truth in the sensationalist tales of the Masons. To be sure, Freemasons have historically had a number of powerful and influential figures among their ranks: Fourteen U.S. presidents were Masons, including Presidents Ford, Lyndon Johnson, and Reagan, along with numerous vice presidents, cabinet secretaries, Supreme Court justices, and other top government officials. The links between Freemasonry and American politics go back to the nation's founding: Nine of the fifty-six delegates who signed the Declaration of Independence were Masons, as were thirteen of the thirty-nine signers of the Constitution, including George Washington and Benjamin Franklin. The first presidential oath of office was administered by a so-called grand master of Masons, Robert Livingston, and used a King James Bible owned by St. John's Lodge in New York. This same Bible, moreover, was subsequently used for the inaugurations of Presidents Harding, Eisenhower, Carter, and George H. W. Bush, as well as the dedications of numerous Masonic buildings and events.

Franklin, a member of the Masons from the age of twenty-six and a grand master at age twenty-eight, once said that the "grand secret" of the Masons "is that they have no secret at all." That is very much the message of the day for the Masons, who have been trying to open up and soften their image in order to attract new members. Today the society's aging membership hovers between four and five million worldwide, with around 1.7 million residing in the United States—down from four million in the early 1960s. Guilds have initiated advertising and recruiting drives, emphasizing the fraternal and personal aspect of Freemasonry. They focus on the charitable component of the society, which has at least two hundred foundations or other philanthropic programs in the United States alone and funds everything from nursing homes to charter schools. (American Masons contribute around $750 million a year.) Nonetheless, like many of the organizations asserted to be ancient and powerful clubs of elites, today most of the Masons themselves are just as ancient, and the organization is a shadow of its former shadowy self.

CAN IT BE CONSIDERED AN ACADEMIC ELITE SOCIETY IF GEORGE W. BUSH WAS A MEMBER?

Behind the locked iron doors of a dark, windowless tomb in New Haven lies one of the most well-known academic secret societies in America. Skull and Bones, a social club at Yale University, has over the years cemented its status as, in the words of Yale alumna and Bones scholar Alexandra Robbins, "an incubator and meeting point for rising generational elites." Its members have included future captains of industry, influential academics, sports stars, Supreme Court justices, prominent politicians, and presidents—including George W. Bush. George W. is in fact one of a long line of Bushes who have enjoyed Skull and Bones membership: grandfather Prescott Bush, great-uncle George Herbert Walker Jr., father George Herbert Walker Bush, uncle Jonathan Bush, and cousins Ray Walker and George Herbert Walker III.

Skull and Bones was founded in 1832 by William H. Russell, a wealthy Yalie (not to be redundant) who imported the idea of a secret student society from Germany, where he had studied abroad for a year. Originally called the Eulogian Club, the group taps roughly fifteen new members, or "knights," every year, maintaining an active membership list of about eight hundred at any given time. (It began admitting women in 1992, following a bitter legal dispute between the society's members and its corporate board that made *The New York Times* editorial page and involved a restraining order from the New Haven Superior Court.)

One of the most infamous aspects of the group is the gruesome, cultish rituals that it allegedly conducts. Depending on whom you ask, these involve everything from mud wrestling to fake murder to kissing a skull—one that, according to legend, was robbed from the grave of Geronimo by Prescott Bush. The first round of initiation for new knights includes a tamer sort of rite: a naming ceremony, in which incoming members are granted secret names by which they will forevermore be known by fellow Bonesmen. These include traditional names, handed down from member to member, which are taken from myth and literature—Thor, Uncle Remus, and Hamlet, for example. Some names are determined by the characteristics of the newcomers, such as Magog, which traditionally goes to the initiate with the most sexual experience. (Among those who have taken the name Magog: President William Howard Taft, Olympic swimmer Don Schollander, and, supposedly, President George H. W. Bush.) Some initiates are invited to choose their own name. Revealingly, according to Robbins, when George W. Bush was presented with this opportunity, "nothing came to mind," and the Yale junior was dubbed "Temporary."

As *New York Observer* contributor Ron Rosenbaum says, "Skull and Bones is not some ordinary frathouse; the initiation was just the beginning, the first of a lifelong series of bonding rituals that helped forge the powerful Bones Old Boy network—a network at the heart of the heart of the American Establishment. Historically, the people who had done so much to shape America's character in the world—the Tafts, the Luces, the Stimsons, the Harrimans, the Buckleys, the Bundys and the Bushes, among others—had their character shaped in the Tomb of Skull and Bones."

Conspiracy theories about Bones have blamed them for funding Adolf Hitler, infiltrating the CIA, controlling American media (including, notably, owning publishing house Farrar, Straus and Giroux), choreographing the Bay of Pigs invasion and the Kennedy assassination, and generally running the United States.

David Brooks, a conservative columnist for *The New York Times*, has a slightly different take on the intrinsic power of the group:

> My view of secret societies is they're like the first-class cabin in airplanes. They're really impressive until you get into them, and then once you're there they're a little dull. So you hear all these conspiracy theories about Skull and Bones.
>
> And to me, to be in one of these organizations, you have to have an incredibly high tolerance for tedium 'cause you're sittin' around talking, talking, and talking. You're not running the world, you're just gassing.

Brooks's skepticism of the group dovetails closely with what I have gathered from speaking to those close to it. In the end, it is a lot of hot air.

The "Ex-Presidents' Club"

Many of the conspiracy theories of today revolve directly around the institutions and gatherings of the superclass. One such organization that provokes feverish speculation is the world's largest private equity firm, the Carlyle Group, which manages more than $56 billion and has offices in eighteen countries. In fewer than twenty years, the firm has amassed a portfolio of companies that have more than $87 billion in revenues and employ more than 286,000 people around the world. The most impressive—and for many inclined to think that way, suspicious—statistic about Carlyle, however, is its roster of prominent employees: The former secretary of state James Baker, the former secretary of defense Frank Carlucci, the former White House budget director Dick Darman, the former head of the FCC William Kennard, and the former chairman of the SEC Arthur Levitt have all been on the firm's payroll. But it gets better: The former British PM John Major, the former Philippines president Fidel Ramos, and former president George H. W. Bush have also served at the company, mostly in senior advisory positions. Even the younger Bush had a stint on the firm's board in the early 1990s. According to Dan Briody, author of Carlyle exposé *The Iron Triangle,* "Conspiracy theorists that obsess on secret societies and outlandish plots overlook the more insidious and destructive effects of a company like Carlyle. By insinuating itself into the very fabric of the world's economic structure, Carlyle has accomplished more than any Trilateral Commission or Masonic society could dream. They have made themselves part of the international community's cash flow. Millions of people are invested in Carlyle and don't even know it."

Briody's book is itself something of an attempt to dress up conspiracy theories with legitimacy. The paragraph above, for instance, blends sensationalism with overstatement and misstatement, alleging that one private company has exceeded in influence organizations reputed to have world governance aspirations. According to Brody, this was done by making "themselves part of the international community's cash flow," which to some sounds, no doubt, like something very mysterious, although I suspect for anyone with half a brain for business the question arises, "What else were they supposed to be doing? They are an international private equity firm. That's what international private equity firms do." The assertion that millions of people are invested in Carlyle and don't even know it offers another example of dramatic language capturing less than the whole story. In a country of pension funds and mutual funds and 401(k) programs, it is fair to say that hundreds of millions of people are invested in countless thousands of companies that they don't know about.

Look closely and a rather different picture emerges: that of a remarkably successful investment organization which, as a consequence of its success, the nature of its business, the rise of its industry, and its unique position among financial firms in the capital of the most powerful country on earth, is very influential. Cofounder David Rubenstein and his management team have not exactly hidden in the shadows; newspaper articles and business magazine cover stories about them and their deals appear regularly.

Though its investments range from soda pop to dot-com start-ups, Carlyle is best known for its stake in the defense industry. It was founded in 1987 by William Conway Jr., Daniel D'Aniello, and Rubenstein, two corporate insiders and a Washington lawyer who initially invested in a motley but successful bunch of deals: an airline-catering company, a health food chain, and a biotech firm, among others. Then Frank Carlucci joined the firm, and in 1990 Carlyle started buying up defense-related assets, beginning with the $130 million purchase of BDM Consulting. Defense acquisitions have since provided some of Carlyle's most rewarding deals. One of its most famous was that of United Defense, a Virginia-based contractor and weapons producer that Carlyle acquired for $850 million in 1997. Carlyle later took the company public—at a profit of nearly $240 million. Its $73 million purchase in 2003 of a majority stake in QinetiQ, a British defense technology firm, earned Carlyle more than half a billion dollars when the company went public in 2006—a return of 800 percent.

The Washington headquarters of what has been called, in something of an overstatement, "the Ex-Presidents' Club" are located midway between the White House and the Capitol building, making it easy for critics to complain about its potential for undue influence in the political establishment. The firm undoubtedly contacts government officials on behalf of its companies—just as Carlucci did when United Defense was negotiating a major contract with the Pentagon. (He purportedly made a phone call to Jacques Gansler, head of acquisitions. Carlucci is also good friends with former defense secretary Rumsfeld, whom he has known since their days on the wrestling team at Princeton.) "The problem comes when private business and public policy blend together," Peter Eisner, director of the Center for Public Integrity, told *The Guardian* in 2001. "What hat is former president Bush wearing when he tells Crown Prince Abdullah not to worry about U.S. policy in the Middle East? . . . The informality involved is precisely a mark of Carlyle's success."

One of Carlyle's cofounders told *The Nation* in 2002 that "no one wants to be a beneficiary of September 11," yet the firm has profited immensely from America's "war on terror." Its investment in the U.S. Information Services (USIS), a private investigative company, is a classic example: "Since 9/11, USIS's acquisition of contracts has exploded," one Carlyle employee told Dan Briody. "All the new FAA, Customs . . .

all those employees being hired [for homeland security] are being investigated by USIS. They also have contracts with all the major airlines, and the contract companies who provide airport security. I do not exaggerate when I say that Carlyle is taking over the world in government contract work, particularly defense work." The terrorist attacks of 2001 exposed another aspect of the firm that hyperstimulated conspiracy theorists—among their investors (who include George Soros and Prince Alwaleed Bin Talal) were members of the bin Laden family. Shafig bin Laden, one of Osama's numerous brothers, was in fact attending a Carlyle conference in Washington on the day of the attacks.

For all the big names connected to Carlyle, they are not that different from the big names associated with other major companies. Such names offer both experience and, of course, access. As one top-level Carlyle employee was quoted as saying, on the subject of a lunch held by defense secretary Rumsfeld in 2001 (which was attended by former defense secretaries Frank Carlucci, William Cohen, Caspar Weinberger, William Perry, and Dick Cheney): "Cabinet-level people are a small fraternity who all stay in touch. Once they've reached that global 50,000-foot view, they tend to stay there." These people are part of the community of global elites in much the same way that many other former high-level government officials are, or the way that the leaders of other big private equity firms such as Blackstone are. The fact does not need to be overstated, nor does it require conspiracy theory lily-gilding. That Carlyle's investment decisions influence the lives of over three hundred thousand employees worldwide (with their families, perhaps 1.5 million people), plus countless investors, competitors, and others, reflects quite a bit of power indeed, but only a few members of Carlyle's top management have influence across all their holdings. That Rubenstein is one of the richest men in Washington, that he and his partners and advisers are a powerful global network unto themselves, with the ability to invest their money, to support political candidates, to be at the table in "agenda-setting" situations, and even to host their own big meetings that attract some of the most influential people in the world is another dimension to that power.

What is more striking is not that they are supplanting the exclusive world government cabals of past conspiracy theories but that they are part of a larger community. They join the leaders of a host of other companies, financial institutions, foundations, and other organizations that inevitably have more clout than average citizens, small businesses, and even local politicians whose fates they may influence and who have little ability to counteract them.

One individual who is very close to Carlyle told me, "In a way, I don't mind the swirl of rumors. Most of them are ludicrous. Most of the people who they suggest have the most sway around here—the big names—are largely window dressing at this point. But it gives us a little mystique, and that doesn't hurt in our business. We are often presumed to know more than we do. What we are really is very mundane, very disciplined business guys, bean counters. It has made a lot of money for a lot of people and that does translate into power—though not the dime store novel stuff that many of these wild theories and books like *The Iron Triangle* suggest."

The Big Events: Less Than Meets the Eye?

Plug the words "Bilderberg" or "Trilateral Commission" or "World Economic Forum" into a search engine and you will see the dark side of the Internet: crudely designed websites with names like PrisonPlanet, CounterPunch, Crystalinks, and Infowars. Each trades in allegations and headlines that make supermarket tabloids look like *The Economist*: "Al Qaeda–Bilderberg Connection?" "Trilateral Commission: World Shadow Government," "Corrupt Government, Conspiracy, New World Order, No Future."

In fact, these three organizations and others like them are an important part of the story of the superclass. They are places to convene, places to network, places to cultivate relationships, places to share views. To paraphrase Mark Malloch Brown, they are the village greens of the global elite. In addition to Bilderberg, the Trilateral Commission, and WEF, the more prominent venues include the Boao meeting on Hainan Island, Carlos Slim's Fathers and Sons retreats in Latin America, the G50 meetings, the Joint Annual Meeting of the IMF and the World Bank, the Munich Conference on Security Policy, the Club of Madrid, the Fortune Brainstorm meeting at Aspen, the Allen & Company retreat at Sun Valley, and the Bohemian Grove. The list of meetings changes and grows as others seek to convene clusters of the superclass, recognizing that, as noted earlier, the most precious commodity in those circles is access; such meetings are among the few places that offer and even facilitate access to many of the world's most sequestered and elusive leaders. The reality of these meetings and what they reveal about the informal mechanisms of power is much more interesting than the hyped-up conspiracy theories and their hysterical visions of total control.

The World Economic Forum

One antiglobalist website, NewsWithViews, recently wrote, "5,000 feet up in the Swiss ski resort of Davos, Switzerland, the rich and powerful CEOs that create wealth and jobs are meeting to discover the 'state of the world.' While networking is key and business is accomplished, so too is the political agenda that is far different from the one found in the U.S. Constitution and Bill of Rights. With the blessing of its Republican and Democratic leaders, America is being pulled into a global framework of states that are now 'interdependent' as all of the barriers between the nation-states have been torn down."

Interest groups frame their critiques somewhat differently, as Friends of the Earth did in 2001: "Business leaders go to Davos to set out their agenda for neo-liberal economic globalisation. Friends of the Earth is going to expose their unaccountable dealings. We will also be planning how to change the course of the global economy towards a sustainable future. The WEF fat cats might have the wealth and the ears of the powerful. But we have public sympathy and justice on our side."

While the most extreme antiglobalists never fail to entertain with their lively imaginations and feverish prose, there are somewhat drier, more mainstream critiques as well, such as that framed by Jeff Faux of Washington's Economic Policy Institute: "Davos is . . . the most visible symbol of the virtual political network that governs the global market in the absence of a world government. It is more like a political convention, where elites get to sniff one another out, identify which ideas and people are 'sound' and come away with increased chances that their phone calls will be returned by those one notch above them in the global pecking order." Faux refers to a "constitution of Davos," suggesting an orchestrated plan, a social compact among leaders of the global leadership class that has produced what he considers to be bad deals for the world's workers.

As Davos approaches forty, it has certainly established itself as the biggest of the world's elite meetings, the most visible and consequently perhaps the most controversial. From the perspective of the outside world, the controversy centers on concern that high in the Swiss Alps decisions are being made that will affect the lives of millions, perhaps in a negative way, without their input. From the perspective of those within Davos, controversy centers on whether the meeting has grown too large, too unfocused, remained too Eurocentric, and whether it is perhaps on the cusp of irrelevance (or past it). Even within the organization of the World Economic Forum itself, now generating more than

$85 million a year in tax-free revenue, there are controversies about who will replace forum founder Klaus Schwab, and whether the organization can ever stabilize itself given years of internal turmoil, often fostered by Schwab's mercurial personality.

The facts about the meeting are well known. At the age of twenty-seven, the German-born Schwab left a career in engineering to earn a degree at Harvard's Kennedy School of Government, where he took an interest in the role of business leaders in public service. To that end, he returned to Switzerland and in 1971 launched what initially became the Foundation of the European Management Forum, a symposium for European business elites to share ideas on social responsibility and international peace. In 1987, the foundation changed its name to the World Economic Forum (WEF) and since then has expanded in size and diversified to include elites from around the globe and from every arena—politics, culture, religion, media, and civil society (although women, Asians, Africans, and others from the developing world continue to be underrepresented). Emphasis shifted from educating business leaders on management strategy to providing a premier networking opportunity for leaders of all kinds. As Henri Schwamm, former vice president of the WEF board, noted, "The strategic thinking at the origin of Davos would henceforth abandon its intellectual roots to embrace the thinking of big names."

The forum has played a role in a handful of important moments in history. At the annual meeting in 1988, for example, the prime ministers of Turkey and Greece signed the Davos Declaration, pulling their nations back from the brink of war. In 1995, Israeli foreign minister Shimon Peres and PLO chairman Yasser Arafat came to an agreement on Gaza and Jericho while attending the WEF. Some of the most potentially significant such encounters, moreover, take place behind the scenes. An influential French businessman recalled hearing about a below-the-radar meeting between president of Iran Mohammad Khatami and UK foreign secretary Jack Straw during the 2003 Davos. Unable to hold official talks due to political constraints, the two exchanged cell phone numbers and met discreetly in Secretary Straw's hotel suite.

Other potentially landmark incidents have similarly taken place outside of official meetings. In 1996, the Russian Communist Party leader Gennady Zyuganov made a crucial appearance at the conference, during which he wooed the powerful, mostly Western audience and primed them to see him as the next Russian president. As David E. Hoffman describes, Zyuganov, who was leading early polls in the upcoming elections, "stole the show in Davos," rubbing elbows with the elite of the elite and giving numerous press conferences and interviews. Throughout, Zyuganov presented himself as "a kindler, gentler Communist who would respect democracy and some kinds of property"— the perfect candidate to succeed Boris Yeltsin. The handful of other Russian elites present at Davos—among them the oligarchs Boris Berezovsky, Vladimir Gusinsky, and Mikhail Khodorkovsky, and the politician Anatoly Chubais—watched in dismay, fearing a Communist takeover. The American billionaire George Soros feared it too and reportedly told the bankers and businessmen over coffee, "Boys, your time is over." Chubais recalled, "I saw many of my good friends, presidents of major American companies, European companies, who were simply dancing around Zyuganov, trying to catch his eye, peering at him. These were the world's most powerful businessmen, with world-famous names, who with their entire appearance demonstrated that they were seeking support of the future president of Russia, because it was clear to everyone that Zyuganov was going to be the future president of Russia, and now they needed to build a relationship with him. So, this shook me up!"

It was at this moment, according to Hoffman, that Chubais and the Russian tycoons "decided on the spot to try and save Boris Yeltsin." Chubais phoned Moscow to alert others to the situation. He then held a press conference in which he denounced Zyuganov's "classic Communist lie" and warned that his election would "lead to bloodshed and civil war." The oligarchs set aside differences and held several private meetings in Davos hotel rooms, where they strategized over how to defeat the Zyuganov threat. The result was the "Davos Pact": an agreement between Chubais and the oligarchs that he would lead the anti-Communist campaign and they would fund it—and him—generously. The subsequent months saw a massive media offensive as "money poured into advertising campaigns, into regional tours, into bribing journalists"—all supported by the oligarchs (who owned the major TV stations and newspapers) and orchestrated by Chubais. Yeltsin's subsequent victory over Zyuganov later that summer changed the course of Russia and can be traced back in part to the events that took place in an otherwise sleepy alpine village that February.

The connections made or fortified at Davos help make things happen later on. So it shouldn't be surprising that the most publicized events there—besides mildly controversial statements and minor scandals—are the parties. On a single night at the 2006 convention, evening events were held by Infosys, the Schwab Foundation, Goldman Sachs, Coca-Cola, *The Wall Street Journal,* and Google. The Google party in particular has generated the greatest hype in recent years; hosted by

Larry Page and Sergey Brin at Davos's Kirschner Museum, the bash drew a crowd of the crème de la crème that included the American actor Michael Douglas and the Israeli politician Shimon Peres, and featured a vintage wine list of similar stature. The Google duo are not your typical computer nerds but have achieved a reputation for coolness approaching that of movie stars. At a *Forbes* party in 2006, one young woman watched rapt as Brin removed his outerwear to reveal "sculpted biceps framed by a tight, black T-shirt."

Informal events in and around Davos have become so ubiquitous, in fact, that one of the repeated complaints from participants is that they have become the real show. The formal agenda features hundreds of sessions covering a massive amount of global and intellectual territory, from "Iraq: Uniting for Stability" to "The Fate of the Universe and the Search for Life"; from "CEO Salaries: How High Will They Go?" to "Why Do Brains Sleep?" Meanwhile, throughout the meeting, the most important delegates are seen popping into the Congress Centre to deliver their official remarks and then slipping out the back door, heading into big black SUVs and off to another corner of the mountain town. AOL founder Steve Case said, "You always feel like you are in the wrong place in Davos, like there is some better meeting going on somewhere in one of the hotels that you really ought to be at. Like the real Davos is happening in secret somewhere." This view, that there is another cabal somewhere inside the cabal, would no doubt strike the conspiracy theorists as ironic. (Or it would if they had a sense of irony to begin with, which they typically do not.) But it is a problem that has begun to trouble even the organizers, who acknowledge that most of the big-name attendees are in the meeting hall only when they speak and then retreat to the Belvedere or the Kongress or the other A-list hotels and do their real work in their suites.

Old Davos hand Moisés Naím suggests that a few informal events at Davos have become the real power centers. "The main reason," he says, "why people go to meetings is because of the activity in the corridors outside the meetings. Many participants don't much care about what goes on in the sessions. They care more about what—or more precisely, who—they can get in the corridors. The masterful genius of Davos is that the organizers have recognized this preference and have created all sorts of opportunities and places for people to mingle. Then there are the private meetings that take place outside the formal program and are very often where most of the relevant action takes place.

"For example, there are some privately hosted dinners that have become very important over the years. I have been attending Davos for eighteen years and what you discover over the years is that these private events are so important that there are some evenings when you cannot find anyone of importance and the reason is that they are in one of these dinners. One hosted by Pepsico is legendarily good. Another of the most interesting and respected dinners is hosted by Victor Halberstadt and his wife, Masha, who is an accomplished painter. [Halberstadt is a long-time Bilderberg organizer and professor at the University of Leiden in Holland.] Sometimes Halberstadt will have a chef flown in especially for the dinners. He deftly runs it like a salon: At some point early in the dinner he interrupts and says, 'Let's start this,' and welcomes everyone, describes with great humor who they are and what they have recently achieved, and then provokes an always fascinating discussion. So for example he says, 'Jean-Claude Trichet [president of the European Central Bank], tell us, how do you see Europe's main economic vulnerabilities?' or to [*Financial Times* columnist] Martin Wolf, 'What do you think will happen to the Chinese currency?' or 'You, Mr. Minister of Finance of Turkey, what are the repercussions of the Iraq war in your country?' and so on. The dinner has a strong European flavor, as it normally includes the CEOs of Heineken, Royal Dutch Shell, Phillips, and other major European firms. But Victor always manages to also attract the smartest Russians, Americans, and Middle Easterners at the dinner, as well as some of the most interesting academics and media leaders. It is not just who goes to that dinner but the extraordinary way in which he manages to have everyone exchange very interesting information that you would not otherwise get just reading the newspapers or going to the formal sessions."

Klaus Schwab himself is keenly aware of the event's evolution and is constantly testing the formula and tinkering with it. Sometimes he drives his staff mad with the pace at which he produces new ideas; he has gone through a long string of senior managers who have all ultimately come to realize that it is his show. Complex, he is a committed intellectual; he truly loves the exploration of what he perceives to be the great issues of the day in which the forum engages. He is an avid lover of art and genuinely interested in the creative process.

When asked how the forum has changed over the years, Schwab, sitting in his modern, serene office with a glass wall framing the breathtaking view of Lake Geneva, doesn't hesitate: "I think that the forum has become much more multistakeholder. We have integrated quite a number of additional groups like the NGOs and also religious leaders. We have about thirty religious leaders attending each year, and the spiritual approach they bring has become more reflected in some of our discussions. We also are recognizing the changes in our audience and what they are interested in. If I were to do two sessions now, one on the WTO and one on brain research—one on how maybe in twenty or thirty years we can implant memories into people—I think today of those two, maybe 70 percent of our delegates would choose the brain session and 30 percent would choose the WTO.

"One challenge for us has been to maintain acceptability—not legitimacy, but at least acceptability. You have to show that there are concrete results to your actions, which is a dilemma. So we had to build up capacity to create a validity for what we are doing. We had to create a number of public-private partnership initiatives which show in a very concrete way—like our global disaster initiative or our global health initiative and so on—that we are not here only to provide a platform for dialogue, but there are concrete, even if they are sometimes small, positive results. Take for example the global health initiative . . . It is probably the most extensive global network to fight tuberculosis, AIDS, and malaria. And we are doing it by interconnecting companies on a local level, with the NGOs and with governments. We are active in twenty-six or twenty-seven countries now. So we reach today millions of people, providing some with the opportunity to be tested or treated and so on."

Schwab, who has helped define the concept of the modern global elite, who has literally been the person determining who meets the criteria to become a "Davos Man," feels elites are changing too. "I think in order to belong to an elite," he says, "you have to fulfill two requirements. You have to be a powerful person, whatever that may mean, because elite means to me to have influence on others. You also have to command a powerful institution or organization. I would also say elites are changing rapidly. Of course there will also be a few people who are especially powerful, who have high salaries and positions, and so forth, but there is increasing volatility. One day they are the incarnation of power. The next day they are out. So you still have an elite, still a group with special, even great influence. But every few years there is very substantial change among them."

His rationale for the relevance of the forum is based on his understanding of an epochal transformation. "In 1856, just 150 years ago, you had for the first time in the States more merchandise transported by rail than by canals. You had the invention of the pipeline. The first transatlantic cable. This was a kind of compression of time and space, and with it people really moved from local identity to national identity. Accordingly, you had to create the necessary structures, national governments, big national companies . . . which afterwards became big international companies. Now what we have today is a similar revolution in which we are moving from a national dimension to a global dimension. And, at the same time, for the same reasons, old power structures don't work anymore. I don't think we ultimately need to create a common view. I think in a global context this will make proposals for governance much more under attack. I think we have to have a global trusteeship and within this there needs to be more room for variations in terms of interpretation of universal values.

"If you deal with issues like global warming from the perspective of defending national interests, you will have trouble making progress to resolving the issue in a very satisfactory way. So what I think we are helping to build . . . what we need . . . is much more in the way of informal global networks, very purpose oriented, very focused. How do you get legitimacy for those networks? Even if they do not have a mandate, they are very closely monitored, so that is something. So beyond that we have two key principles: one is to agree on a set of values and to approach those with what I call intellectual integrity. We are not influenced by special interests. We are like a university. We find a problem and we try to find a solution. This is absolutely necessary. As soon as we will be accused of defending specific interests, then we lose our legitimacy in the eyes of all those people who are not represented by those interests. The second condition is to show concrete results."

Schwab's analysis reveals the complexity of the man and the institution. The World Economic Forum is an organization dominated by and paid for by big corporations: perhaps thirty lead sponsors who each pay in the neighborhood of $300,000 a year in fees, another group of around a hundred who pay approximately $150,000, and as many as two thousand members paying up to $30,000 a year to attend. It could easily not address issues like AIDS or global warming or spiritual issues or Africa or poverty; yet it does, and that is why Bono comes to be among, as he puts it, "the fat cats in the snow."

The willingness to create such coalitions is a positive development. But Schwab's assertion that through transparency and monitoring these efforts gain something like the legitimacy they might derive from having a genuine mandate is a bit of a rationalization. First, there are limitations on the transparency of the processes involved, whether they involve identifying priorities within the discussions at the forum or determining how plans will be followed through. Many players are, after all, private-sector actors. Second, business groups tend to act in the interests of business. Consequently, if a coalition is dominated by business they may do some good—sometimes a lot of good—but only to the extent that it serves their corporate interests. And that is why legitimate public governance mechanisms with real mandates are needed to set these priorities.

Schwab has, through Davos, developed legions of supporters. The former Saudi Arabian ambassador to the United States Prince Turki Al-Faisal, for example, says, "I recommend Davos not just for my government but for my friends, as well. I think when people get together they tend to end up doing things together, and that is good. When you remove the barriers that politeness or civil practice impose on people and establish rapport with one or a group of people, you find that you turn to them when you have other ideas or you need to do something. I saw that in a group I cochaired with them called the C-100 [the Council of 100 Leaders, created to promote dialogue between Western and Islamic worlds], which brought together people from inside and outside. And the forum was so important because you could tap into sources of funding at the conference you couldn't find anywhere else."

Schwab also has his critics, of course, even among those who attend Davos. In my experience, you have to take such critiques with a grain of salt. There is much ego in these crowds and sometimes a small snub or a failure to remain at the center of the Davos limelight from year to year is cause for unhappiness among the elites who attend. Nonetheless, there are legitimate issues raised in their criticisms. For example, one American who has been a top Wall Street executive and a high-level government official said to me, "I won't go to Davos unless I have to. I think it is awful, a tedious mob scene, but we are part of that world whether we like it or not. It's the liberal internationalist world. However, it has no real policy implications. It is a big show these days and Klaus, well, Klaus is a complicated businessman, the great P. T. Barnum of our time, and he has created in Davos the world's greatest Ponzi scheme."

Philippe Bourguignon, a former co-CEO of the World Economic Forum, offered a more balanced view. "Davos played this role in at least developing awareness among leaders, governments, and businesspeople. Like HIV/AIDS or global warming. But I think today it has also become in some ways a big missed opportunity. It still clearly has a role, but this role could have a much greater impact. I wouldn't say it is bad, it has just missed a step. People like [former French president Jacques] Chirac look at Davos and they see a club of rich, global leaders whose only motivation is economics, business, and not human things. And he just hated it. He considered it a threat to France. Once we tried to get him together at the meeting with Lula, the Brazilian president, who wanted to do a dialogue at Davos with him on emerging country versus developed country issues, and we tried and tried but Chirac just refused to go. Not only didn't he do it, he convinced Lula to meet with him outside of Davos one week after the meeting. It wasn't the substance of the issue he objected to. It was Davos."

Bourguignon sees pockets of opportunity within the meeting, places where the hubbub of the "big show" is far away and real work can get done. For example, he says, "There is a group in Davos called the International Business Council. They are especially interesting because it is a very good group, just the biggest business leaders. It is one hundred people, but because it is only one hundred the quality is high. Secondly, it is more of a global mix with America, Europe, Asia and so on . . . very global. And it has everything from pharmaceuticals to heavy industries through digital. And it produces some of the best discussion. By the way, I don't think that political leaders are less important at Davos just because economics is more important than politics. It is because the political leadership is just not as good. They don't get it and therefore they have become less influential."

One place where he has seen political leaders remain influential by using conventional tactics is China, where the forum tried to set up a meeting to address the glaring lack of Asian participation at Davos. The only problem was that the Chinese government absolutely refused to permit discussions about certain sensitive subjects. At first, because the forum would not capitulate, the Chinese created their own Davos (the Boao Forum), but later the forum agreed to what one insider gently referred to as a more "collaborative" stance, and they formed a partnership that led to forum events and an office in China. Although, said one forum insider, "The jury is still out on whether that will take . . . and that's really the biggest issue there is for the continued relevance of the forum in a world economy where so much has moved East."

The Carlyle chairman and former IBM CEO Louis Gerstner told me, "I was a member of the Trilateral Commission and Bilderberg. But I never went to Davos. Some forums, like the Council on Foreign Relations or the America-China Society, these are very constructive, useful ways for you to share your views with people who have a common interest. It is just like going to a chess club or a bridge club. There are people who share a common interest and you get a reward for contributing, for being a part of it. But in a big meeting like Davos, I believe, there is a very seriously diminishing return . . . and I think that may be true at times for Trilateral and Bilderberg as well. What difference have they made?"

This sentiment was often echoed in my conversations. Bob Kimmitt, currently deputy secretary of the U.S. Treasury, said, "I have participated in almost every one of those events, and I find they are very, very useful settings for relationship building, for setting up bilateral meetings, to get a little bit away from the world of action to the world of ideas. The intersection between public and private sector at these events can be important . . . At Davos or Bilderberg and some of the others where people from both worlds get together . . . sometimes we can use those settings to help get things done, to help get the message across. But generally we find the most effective way to get things done is to complement the public side of these events with bilateral meetings, with exchanges that are private. It is all about knowing how to use them and about keeping expectations at the right level."

When Samuel Huntington coined the term "Davos Man," he was lamenting the emergence of an elite without a country. He described this group as having "little need for national loyalty"; they "view national boundaries that thankfully are vanishing, and see national governments as residues from the past whose only useful function is to facilitate the elite's global operations." Huntington's idea has evolved over time, and today it is often used in blogs, books, essays, and newspaper columns to describe not just global citizens but a group intent on forcing its view of the world on everyone else. Sometimes it takes on a lighter context, emphasizing the social hobnobbing that goes on during the WEF meeting, as in an observation from the BBC, for example: "And so they walk around—tie or no tie—to do what Davos man does best: Networking and schmoozing." Not surprisingly, Davos and "Davos Man" are both less and more than they are cut out to be. They are less in that Davos is a big, unfocused bazaar, full of a broad mix of people, some extraordinarily powerful, some much less so, some leftover power players from past eras, some who must have come in via someone's luggage. Davos rarely produces big breakthrough events and is in truth an unlikely venue—teeming as it is with reporters—for meetings of secret cabals.

But Davos is also more, in that perhaps five hundred to one thousand of the people who attend truly are members of the global superclass. It is the largest gathering of them that takes place anywhere. It is also, thanks to the wonderful, obsessive, complex, and quirky brain of Klaus Schwab, a place where they don't just talk business. Sometimes his commitment to the notion that the forum really can improve the state of the world seems vaguely delusional—a kind of altitude-induced messianic dizzy spell that at times comes off as dilettantism. But social and spiritual issues are on the program and they don't have to be. Yes, perhaps this is in part to calm the protestors and defuse criticism. But the great power of this group, as we have seen, is not that of coconspirators but that of agenda-setters. Bringing these issues to the attention of elites has, gradually, palpably helped change their agenda. The recent "mainstreaming" of AIDS and later global warming as widely held concerns are the two best examples.

Davos is a phenomenon: bustling, fascinating, boring, chaotic, important, gross, earnest, and proof that one man with vision and energy can make a difference. That it is growing a bit wheezy as Schwab nears retirement raises questions about its future, but Huntington and others were certainly right to note its significance in the early years of the global era. If Schwab hadn't invented it, somebody else certainly would have.

Bilderberg and the Trilateral Commission: Two Gatherings of Old Men

In fact, others have created important global forums, and many rival Davos or have at one time or another. Most are smaller and more exclusive. And today, as international meetings become commonplace among every group of leaders, many of the legendary ones are losing their sheen.

Bilderberg in particular attracts a special breed of critics. An excerpt from the promotional materials associated with *Bilderberger: The Timetable of the New World Order* (2006), by German author Andreas von Rétyi, illustrates the genre, perhaps not as melodramatically as some others but with a similar thrust:

> Our world history is not the result of coincidences, but rather precise planning. More than half a century ago a powerful group was formed to take the fate of this planet into hand and steer the world in the direction of a secret brand of internationalism. Numerous crucial events in politics and economics can be traced back to subtle manipulation by Bilderberg. Their goal: total global control.
>
> The "high priests of globalization" first met in 1954 under strictest secrecy for the first time in the Netherlands hotel de Bilderberg. Since then "Bilderberg" meets once a year in the most distinguished hotels of the world. What is discussed there behind locked doors, remains strictly secret, but we have no choice. Whatever the Bilderberger decides will shape our future.

They rank among the central organs of a world-wide shadow government.

The annual meeting of the Bilderberg Group has provided ample fodder for conspiracy theorists since its founding by Prince Bernhard of the Netherlands in the mid-1950s. By 1964, it was accused of orchestrating support for Socialist Gaston Deferre in the French presidential elections. In 1971, critics claimed that Bilderbergers had been given advanced notice of Nixon's New Economic Policy, which allowed them to make $20 billion in profits. And in 1974, critics charged the group with coordinating the military coup in Portugal.

Bilderberg emerged in the 1950s as a private initiative by European political and business leaders who were concerned about America's commitment to Western Europe. The group was composed of business leaders, diplomats, academics, military chiefs, and senior government officials, reportedly including top-level members of the intelligence community.

Bilderberg does its best to stay under the radar. There is no official Bilderberg website, and the BBC reported in 2004 that a phone call to the listed number for the Bilderberg Group, based in Leiden, Holland, yielded an anonymous voice mail message reciting back the number and giving no further information. The organization keeps the location of its annual meeting under wraps and its participants, roughly 150, including a handful of journalists, are sworn to silence about what goes on inside. In 2006, the venue—Brookstreet Hotel in the tiny town of Kanata in Ontario, Canada—was entirely shut down, barricaded by heavy metal gates, and swarming with police who had special-issue Bilderberg passes. Even the security is secret. Local police told an Ottawa reporter that security was being handled by Global Risk Holdings, but when the reporter reached the president of GRH, he was told, "Never heard of that conference. What is it? What do they do?" Indeed, trying to break through the wall of secrecy has created a cottage industry of Bilderberg sleuths, from the British Tony Gosling to the American James Tucker (founder of American Free Press and author of *Jim Tucker's Bilderberg Diary*), the French Pierre and Danièle de Villemarest and William Wolf (authors of *Facts & Chronicles Denied to the Public*), and the Belgian Geoffrey Geuens (author of *Tous Pouvoirs Confondus* [All Powers Confounded], which contains an extensive history of Bilderberg).

The four-day Bilderberg meeting in Kanata attracted the usual crowd of spectators and protestors, each with various theories about what was going on inside. Speculations about the group's agenda included world domination, a merger of Canada with the United States and Mexico, the suppression of technology for fuel-efficient cars, and hiding the cure for cancer. One protestor, a filmmaker from Texas who claimed to have an insider source, shared his theory on Bilderberg: "It's a group of very powerful individuals whose objective is to create one world government," he said, "based on an economic model from the Middle Ages . . . a postindustrial model where you have slaves and slave owners." A fellow protester who had camped out at the hotel's entrance agreed that the high rollers inside were up to no good. "They're ruining our planet," he said. "They're suppressing free energy . . . They're forcing farmers to switch to genetically modified seeds. They want to control everyone. No freedom, no democracy."

Contrary to the mystique and the mythologies surrounding the conference, former and current participants readily assert that Bilderberg does not in fact set the global agenda. "Crap!" pronounced Lord Denis Healey, one of the four founding members, when asked about the conspiracy theories. "There's absolutely nothing in it." One former senior U.S. official who has been a regular participant for more than a decade said that the Bilderberg meeting had far greater relevance when it was first established in the 1950s but that it had since become worthless as far as effecting change. "There is nothing that happens at Bilderberg that affects events after Bilderberg," he said. Discussions with veteran Bilderbergers suggest that the group has become largely outdated and obsolete; its members no longer represent the global power elite in the way they once did. Participating political leaders consist mostly of ministerial-level officials and former bureaucrats, while members from the business and finance community are for the most part CEOs of old-guard corporations and banks. Emerging power players in technology and new media are almost entirely absent. "None of the telecom giants come to Bilderberg," the former U.S. official confirmed. "None of those people would bother going. They'd say, 'Who are these old farts?'" The event is almost exclusively transatlantic, with rare representation from Asia, Latin America, the Middle East, or Africa.

Victor Halberstadt, who has organized many of the meetings over the years as its secretary-general and still works closely with the organization, denies that it has become merely a forum where influential people can regularly meet in a private setting and discuss issues of mutual interest. Halberstadt is one of those habitués of the elite world who literally know everyone; he cannot walk across the floor of the Congress Center in Davos without being stopped every moment, and yet he has maintained a sense of humor and proportion about it all. He is a special sort of figure among the members of the superclass, a node, a facilitator of connections, and one who has risen to a position of considerable influence and access as a consequence. (He also serves on the Goldman Sachs International Advisory Board, on the Supervisory Boards of Koninklijke KPN, TNT, and Concertgebouw, and as a nonexecutive director of PA Holdings Ltd. and RHJ International.)

"I find the world government accusations absolutely laughable," Halberstadt said. "For the past few decades I have observed what happens in some of these rooms and corridors, the disagreements, the divisions. These conversations often serve a useful purpose; the world's history demonstrates the continuous appearance of many such forums. If they didn't exist, new informal clubs would immediately be created, as now happens through the Web."

Said one Bilderberg regular, "I've been to most of the last twelve [meetings]. It's nothing. It's a group of 120 very senior people. By senior I mean old. I'm not joking about them being old, by the way. Rockefeller is in his nineties. The original idea of Bilderberg was a classic example of the power elite. A small number of Europeans and Americans would meet in total secrecy somewhere in the world when they really mattered and try to reach a consensus. That was in the '50s . . . and the consensus they tried to reach was within an existing framework of NATO and the Marshall Plan. Bilderberg and the Trilateral Commission are absolutely meaningless except as individual network opportunities. Oprah Winfrey has more influence than anyone who goes to Bilderberg at this point."

The Trilateral Commission, another private policy group, has about 350 members from Western Europe, North America, and Pacific Asia (with a handful of Triennium Participants from other regions). It was founded in 1973 by David Rockefeller, who asserted the need for a forum in which to share European, American, and Japanese views. Rockefeller was chairman of the Council on Foreign Relations at the time, as well as chairman and CEO of Chase Manhattan Bank; given these facts and his family history it is small wonder that the group, created with the active help of future U.S. national security adviser Zbigniew Brzezinski, became a lightning rod for conspiracy theories.

Trilateral meetings were first held in 1975 and continue to this day, with the Japan leg of the group now expanded to include more countries from throughout the Asia Pacific region. As of 2006, the chairmen were Tom Foley, the former U.S. speaker of the House; Peter Sutherland, the former WTO director-general and chairman of both BP and

Goldman Sachs International; and Yotaro Kobayashi, the chairman of Fuji Xerox. Former and current members comprise a wide range of former U.S. presidents, Federal Reserve governors, cabinet secretaries, senators, CEOs, bankers, journalists, academics, and their counterparts worldwide. Most of the attendees with whom I spoke were becoming gradually disenchanted with the group. Four different people called it an "old men's club."

"The Trilateral Commission is a joke," said one especially dismissive former member, who was a senior official in several Republican U.S. administrations. "It's a bunch of has-beens who do not have power except to convene themselves—and to feel a little bit more important because they convened themselves." The meetings, according to the official, consisted of "useless presentations and levels of abstraction that are unconnected with reality."

THE CLINTON GLOBAL INITIATIVE AND THE POWER OF GLOBAL PHILANTHROPY

If anything has rocked the world of elite gatherings and had a genuine impact in the past several years it has been the Clinton Global Initiative (CGI). First convened in New York City in September of 2005, the event brought together business and government leaders and experts to "discuss solutions to major world problems." It is a project of the William J. Clinton Foundation and former president Clinton, with a stated mission to "increase the benefits and reduce the burdens of global interdependence; to make a world of more partners and fewer enemies; and to give more people the tools they need to build a better future."

What has set CGI meetings apart is not the attendees, who look very much like the people you might find at Davos, but rather the approach. The objective is to promote action, to get participants actually to commit resources to solving problems. It addresses the core issue of action that Schwab cited as being so vital to legitimizing such an organization. In fact, Schwab's reference to that fact is no doubt a reflection of the importance he grants to the CGI. Several different executives of the World Economic Forum with whom I spoke said they felt Schwab saw the CGI as a potential threat, assuming, perhaps more effectively, a space that Davos had sought for itself as a gathering that formulates and effects global projects.

Illustrating the power of the idea, during the 2006 event, participants made 215 pledges totaling $7.3 billion, all targeted toward problems—poverty, global warming, and pandemics, for example—that have been established as priorities by the CGI. The largest of these was a $3 billion commitment from Sir Richard Branson to direct a portion of the future profits from his transport business to fight global warming. Skeptics suggested that many of these commitments would have been made even without the "catalytic" role played by Clinton and his team, and others took particular aim at the Branson pledge as a noncommitment commitment, given that it was pledging as yet unearned profits and it reserved the right of Branson to choose where the cash might go. Yet virtually everyone with whom I spoke sees the Clinton effort as a breakthrough and a big step away from the talkfests that most global conferences have become.

The CGI is tapping into a particular gestalt, the rise of the new philanthropists and of a new era of engaged activism by some members of the superclass and big companies. This trend is also reflected in the establishment of the Bill and Melinda Gates Foundation, combining $30 billion commitments from both Bill Gates and Warren Buffett, two of the world's richest men. This is not entirely an accident. Not only was Clinton the president who presided over the dot-com boom that made so many members of the new superclass rich (like Gates), and not only has he emerged as perhaps the world's most prominent advocate for what might be called "enlightened globalization," but ties between the Clinton Global Initiative and the Gates Foundation include links between key leaders at Gates and the Clinton administration. The foundation's CFO, Alexander Friedman, was a White House fellow and assistant secretary of defense, while its number two executive, Sylvia Mathews Burwell, served as deputy White House chief of staff. (Burwell was also a protégé of the man whom many consider Gates's mentor on globalization, Bob Rubin, and initially worked for him in the Clinton administration.)

Thomas Friedman was effusive in his praise for the Clinton event. "This is as close as you will get to global government," he said. "I was thinking about it as I was looking around the room and here you have these leaders from all over the world. And let's say Branson pledges $3 billion to fight global warming—that is really a government-level, government-size commitment. That is a form of transnational governance and it is filling a void.

"These things like Davos," he observed, "really started out as business networking, that was really the original impulse. But Klaus quickly realized that 'I have really got something here. I have created a form of global governance and I can use it for a lot more than to help Microsoft and ING get rich. I can leverage this thing.' And then Clinton sees that and he does kind of his own offshoot under his own brand. And what he does is he gets your superclass into a room and he gets them to sign commitments. I mean, literally, when you go, you see these guys come out and they sign a document. They actually go and take something big, like a diploma, like a government declaration, and they sign it. [Leading U.S. venture capitalist] John Doerr goes up and Richard Branson goes up and they literally sign 'I will do this.' It has the feeling of an act of law. In fact, John Doerr said a funny thing. He said to Clinton, 'I am used to you signing the laws.'

"This could have been the UN," he continued. "They could have been countries signing. But the countries haven't stepped up . . . with some of these international issues, [they] aren't really in the position to do so politically. In fact, it is interesting to compare. The UN General Assembly was meeting at the same time as the CGI. Both were going on. Who did more? UNGA [UN General Assembly] was a talking shop where Hugo Chávez was accusing the president [Bush] of being the devil and Ahmadinejad was promoting his idea that the Holocaust was a myth, and meanwhile, the Clinton Global Initiative was enlisting government-level commitments from individuals in order to provide governance, in this case social safety nets."

Richard Holbrooke observed in kind, "Right now it is clear that Bill Clinton is the most influential private citizen in the world. You can like it or hate it. You can marvel at it or wring your hands at it. But he is astonishing right now. And on the issues I work on—AIDS, for example—he is making a huge impact."

California's Superclass Summer Camp

Scores of events each year, from air shows to industry conferences, from awards ceremonies to birthday parties of the very prominent, end up attracting members of the superclass. These elites do, after all, have more in common with each other than they do with anyone else, and they are constantly strengthening and refining the networks within their evolving universe. Even if the global superclass is defined as narrowly as we have defined it, a group of approximately six thousand people, it is still large enough that most members know only a fraction of the others. Consequently, all these meetings are important nodes for connections, for sharing views, for shaping views, for setting agendas, and for making the connections that lead to deals or stronger coalitions to support their interests. They help ensure that chief executives and government leaders stay current with each other's views, and they help build consensus on issues from taxation to trade, to who is in and who is out. (In fact, the constant assessing and reassessing of the relative positions of various members of the elite is, I have found, one of the favored pastimes at these events.) Together, these assemblies help form the glue of the global community of leaders, providing the meeting halls and, as Mark Malloch Brown put it, "the village greens."

In this regard, the Bohemian Grove is "not a place of power. It's a place where the powerful relax [and] enjoy each other's company." As G. William Domhoff, a professor of sociology at UC Santa Cruz (which is located 150 miles from the Grove), puts it, "Despite the suspicions of many on the Right, and a few on the Left," the Bohemian Grove "is not a secret meeting place to plot, plan, or discuss—everyone there is too drunk for that kind of thing anyhow." The motto of the club, "Weaving spiders, come not here!" comes from Shakespeare's *A Midsummer Night's Dream* and serves as an admonition against discussing business or other "worldly concerns" at the Grove. Members are instead encouraged to focus on "the arts, literature, and other pleasures found within the portals of Bohemia." According to a recently revealed audio recording, one regular participant, the ever-colorful Richard Nixon, called it "the most faggy goddamned thing you could ever imagine."

The Grove, located on twenty-seven hundred acres of redwood forest in Northern California, is perhaps one of the most bizarre examples of an elite organization. For two weeks in late July, the camp is attended by around fifteen hundred all-male members of the Bohemian Club, a private social group founded in San Francisco in 1872. Press reports of the group are rare, since the ultrasecretive club shuns publicity, but by most accounts the Grove is like summer camp for rich and powerful grown-ups. Because of its high-powered membership— recent guests from the current U.S. administration include Dick Cheney, Donald Rumsfeld, Karl Rove, and George W. Bush—the group has also fueled its share of conspiracy theories. Critics on the left worry about political conspiracies and global policies plotted at the Grove, while critics on the right cite stories of homosexual rituals, devil worship, and child sacrifice. One of the most famous accounts of consequential happenings at the Grove identifies it as the site where the atomic bomb was first conceived and planned. According to Domhoff, the Grove's only atomic connection concerns a single member, who asked the club president if he could use part of the camp during an off-season month to meet with other individuals involved in the Manhattan Project—none of whom were Bohemians.

Membership at the Grove is highly selective and invitation-only. Initiation begins with a ritual called "the Cremation of Care," in which the Grove's members burn an effigy to rid themselves of worldly concerns. This ceremony contained a twist in 1996, when George H. W. Bush, Clint Eastwood, and Walter Cronkite, playing the parts of "Lakeside Frogs," croaked like the frogs in the famous Budweiser ads of the 1990s, substituting a tritone chant of "cre-MA-tion" for "bud-WEI-ser."

The Lakeside Talks, occasional informal speeches at the Grove, have historically given politicians an important platform for self-promotion. As one Bohemian put it back in 1963, "Well, of course when a politician comes here, we all get to see him, and his stock-in-trade is his personality and his ideas."

One particularly telling illustration of the importance of Lakeside Talks came with Richard Nixon's account of future president Dwight D. Eisenhower's appearance at the event: "In the summer of 1950, I saw him at even closer quarters at the Bohemian Grove." Nixon notes that "after Eisenhower's speech we went back to Cave Man Camp and sat around the campfire appraising it. Everyone liked Eisenhower, but the feeling was that he had a long way to go before he would have the experience, the depth, and the understanding to be President. But it struck me forcibly that Eisenhower's personality and personal mystique had deeply impressed the skeptical and critical Cave Man audience." Nixon later claims that a speech he gave at the Grove may have catapulted him to the nation's highest office: "If I were to choose the speech that gave me the most pleasure and satisfaction in my political career, it would be my Lakeside Speech at the Bohemian Grove in July 1967. Because this speech traditionally was off the record it received no publicity at the time. But in many important ways it marked the first milestone on my road to the presidency."

In 1995, then U.S. House speaker Newt Gingrich and former president Bush delivered a Lakeside Talk. (Bush reportedly spoke of how his son George W. would make a great president someday.) As Domhoff notes, perhaps the most striking change in the Lakeside Talks in the 1990s was the absence of any Clinton administration officials. In previous years, cabinet members from Democratic administrations were prominent guests and Lakeside speakers. Domhoff argues, "It is safe to say that the Bohemian Club's regular members are now solidly Republican."

One attendee at the 2007 meeting found it "relaxed . . . and a little strange." He noted that the various talks were not that much different from those you would find at other conferences, but that the setting—including the occasional pinup photo tacked to a wall and rather elaborate, heartfelt theatrical productions featuring participants—made it unusually relaxed and convivial, "much more fun than other meetings I've been to attended by the same people."

The Grove boasts a telling blend of members from the political, financial, and business clusters of the American elite. From a list of the top 1,144 corporations in America, the sociologist Peter Phillips found that 24 percent had at least one director who was a member or guest in 1993. For the top one hundred corporations outside of California, the figure was 42 percent. So while the vast majority of what goes on at the Grove is just fun and games (and a lot of drinking), it is inevitable that when elites get together, they will talk business. Domhoff notes that this sort of forced proximity breeds consensus, and he provides a social-psychological perspective on elite gatherings:

> First, the very fact that rich men from all over the country gather in such close circumstances as the Bohemian Grove is evidence for the existence of a socially cohesive upper class. It demonstrates that many of these men do know each other, that they have face-to-face communications, and that they are a social network. In this sense, we are looking at the Bohemian Grove and other social retreats as a result of social processes that lead to class cohesion. But such institutions also can be viewed as facilitators of social ties. Once formed, these groups become another avenue by which the cohesiveness of the upper class is maintained.

Even the more moderate of conspiracy theories usually ascribe an exaggerated amount of coordination, coherence, and influence to the groups they criticize. The individuals who take part in these institutions and who participate in certain elite events—clubs and conferences and casual dinners—probably do not have secret designs for world domination, but most likely do have common interests. They share similar goals and in many cases a similar view of the world and the direction it should take. In linking together with one another, they aim not to conspire as a group but to enhance their own power by advantageous associations. For that reason one finds that each sector—political, business, and military—has venues where its leaders gather and, in a sense, reassert their togetherness.

ASIAN AND LATIN AMERICAN "WANNABES" OR HARBINGERS OF THE SUPERMEETINGS OF TOMORROW?

The Boao Forum for Asia (BFA) was created as a regional alternative to the WEF in 1998 and has been attempting to hold comparable annual meetings in Hainan, China, since 2002. It follows the same basic format: one to two thousand elite participants, a hodgepodge of panel discussions, social gatherings, and other informal networking events. But by many accounts the BFA has yet to achieve the same status and relevance as its European doppelgänger. In 2006, the meetings lasted less than forty-eight hours, and other than a handful of current and former heads of state, there seemed to be a shortage of high-profile leaders and entrepreneurs. Such comparisons are not completely fair, of course, since the WEF has had a head start of nearly thirty years; BFA has surely made extraordinary progress since its first conference, at which a number of high-profile delegates were forced to take a bus from the airport while others were assigned hotel rooms with no running water. (Many resorted to eating at food stalls in a nearby village when the forum ran out of food.) Only five years later, the conference had an impressive roster of participants that included Bill Gates, Philippine president Gloria Macapagal-Arroyo, and Nobel Peace Prize winner Muhammad Yunus. It has a number of major corporate sponsors, including COSCO and Merrill Lynch.

The origins of BFA illustrate well the potential for deal making at informal elite gatherings—in this case, a game of golf. The former prime minister of Australia Robert James Lee Hawke, the former prime minister of Japan Hosokawa Morihiro, and the former president of the Philippines Fidel Ramos were golfing together in 1998 when they hit upon the idea of an "Asian Davos": a way to encourage cohesion and dialogue among Asian leaders, address concerns about the region's economic prospects, and echo the consolidating behavior of the European Union and North America. The idea held promise, but the former heads of state lacked funds. Conveniently, however, their golf outing happened to take place on grounds owned by an enterprising businessman. Jiang Xiaosong, a Chinese real estate developer, had a large swath of property in Boao, in China's Hainan Province; he was also the son of a famous Shanghai actress and had cultivated close connections to top-tier government officials in Beijing. He immediately suggested Boao—at the time a tiny, ancient fishing village—as the perfect location for a convention center and luxury resort to accommodate the forum. After a few trips by Jiang to Beijing, then vice president Hu Jintao told Ramos and Hawke that the Chinese government would support their project.

Said one former U.S. cabinet official with whom I spoke, "I got there the first time and I thought I had landed in the wrong place. The island was drab, the occasional palm tree and of course the Chinese had dressed up the road from the airport. But the hotels were underwhelming and it was only about a day or a day and a half long and it just wasn't there yet, wasn't what they wanted it to be. It was a Davos wannabe . . . although knowing the Chinese, they will stick with it, and China is so important to so many people, they will go, even if it is a trip to the armpit of Asia." In this comment, the meeting is a kind of metaphor for modern China and an illustration of the conflicts the leadership faces. The country and its top officials understand that the only way to stave off social chaos and instability is to continue to attract foreign capital and grow. Capitalism is for them the only way to salvage and preserve what is left of communism. Boao is still unformed and seemingly somewhat unfocused due to this schizophrenia. Discussion topics are typically uncontroversial, the one way the organizers can guide a discussion of foreigners, and its island location keeps it out of the spotlight of the rest of the country. Nonetheless, said the American official, "They are making an effort." In her eyes, the tensions it reveals are vitally important to the future of the region and the world, which is one reason that this fledgling meeting and its emerging competitors elsewhere in Asia are drawing increasing interest.

In the same way that Boao illustrates tensions between economic and political forces within China, Latin America's Fathers and Sons meeting is emblematic of the superclass dynamic in that region. The fact that the Latin American version of such an event is attended by the kind of plutocratic families that have dominated Latin societies for two centuries reveals why Latin America is falling behind. Few countries in the region have shown much appetite for the kind of reforms that will produce upheaval, growth, the birth of a middle class, and competitors to the elites who comfortably rule the roost.

The force behind the gathering is Carlos Slim Helú, one of the richest men in the world. As noted earlier, Slim is by far the dominant force in Latin American telecommunications, controlling over 90 percent of the phone lines in Mexico and providing service to eight out of ten of that country's cell phones. Slim took advantage of the privatization of Mexico's phone networks during the Carlos Salinas era, buying key assets and building his share—primarily through controlling interest in Teléfonos de México, Telcel, and América Móvil—to its currently estimated value well in excess of $50 billion. He has been criticized for his near monopoly control over the Mexican telephone industry and the fact that his rates are disproportionately higher than those in countries with more competition.

One close acquaintance of Slim's describes him as "unusual for a Latin business leader. He actually reads books. Most of these guys, they are good with numbers, good at their family businesses. But he is an intellectual and he has very broad interests. I think that is the reason that he started this meeting . . . also I think because Davos was faltering in terms of Latin participation . . . and also, largely, of course, because he thought it suited his interests."

Calling the gathering "Latin American Businessmen: An Encounter Between Fathers and Sons," Slim created a forum for elites in Latin America's network of still predominantly family-owned or -controlled empires. The telecom billionaire paid for the entire event himself and orchestrated the schedule, which according to one participant was "quite work intensive, a little time for tennis or golf but lots of panels on business issues, sharing experiences, initiatives that were important to Slim" (like the restoration of Mexico City's historic center), and mingling at Slim's own house. According to a preliminary program from the first meeting, attendees included groups from Argentina, Brazil, Chile, Colombia, Ecuador, Mexico, and Venezuela, and the group of countries expanded in following years.

One participant noted that he thought one of the strangest sights at the all-male meeting was when someone felt it was time to dance: "You know, it is fathers and sons and nephews, that is the meeting, right? It is a reflection in a way of Latin machismo culture that it is so limited. But, still, when the music went on and with no women there, a number of the guys started dancing with each other, partying it up." Networking takes all forms.

HOW TO BECOME A MEMBER
OF THE SUPERCLASS

No understanding of the superclass would be complete without taking a closer look at the "who" behind the exclusive meetings and power command posts. I have done just that by conducting a kind of super-class census, creating a list of over six thousand names from around the world. Each individual on the list has influence over the lives of millions across international borders. Each is actively involved in advancing his or her interests. The group includes, as noted at the outset of the book, leaders of the biggest companies, the biggest banks and investment firms, governments and political parties, military organizations, media organizations, religious groups, NGOs, as well as members of the shadow elites, those whose influence stems from illicit or unconventional means, from terrorists to the most important bloggers.

Such a list is, of course, imperfect. Whereas a broken clock will be right twice a day, a list like this is doomed to be inaccurate as soon as it has been completed. Positions change. Organizations merge. Power ebbs and flows. Publishing such a list immediately generates debate about who's in and who's out, and obscures the bigger issues involved.

Nonetheless, by compiling such a list we can get a rough picture of the demographics of the group: gender, countries of origin, educational background, and how these traits might change in the future. To some extent the data is a product of the analytical categories chosen. If I had decided that government leaders were dramatically more important than business leaders, I would have had many more on the list. If I had decided that CFOs typically met my criteria, I would have had many more businesspeople. Instead, the list reflects as much as possible some basic truths about where power is concentrated in the modern world, the rise of the financial, business, and information elites, the relative decline of military and government elites, and the first stirrings of change as the geographic base of the elites starts to show signs of shifting.

Even accounting for disagreements, it would be nearly impossible to deny that this is a story of homogeneity and of imbalance. The data reflects a fairly straightforward picture of just what the average person needs to do if he or she aspires to become a member of the superclass.

There are eight key rules to follow:

1. *Be born a man.* There is no group as disproportionately under-represented among the members of the superclass as women.

On a planet where 51 percent of the inhabitants are female, the global power structure is extraordinarily imbalanced: Only 6.3 percent of the superclass is women. Interestingly, the few female superclass members with whom I spoke are convinced that women have what it takes to lead and are certain that a male-dominated system is responsible for ignoring the promise of girls and women in many countries worldwide. But, still, they regularly argued that few women are willing to make the necessary sacrifices to enter the ranks of the powerful; they also seemed to relish their special status as female leaders and did not seem particularly eager to share the honor.

2. *Be a baby boomer.* It is the boomers' time to rule. Despite the rise of the new, younger IT elite, only 3 percent of the superclass is under forty; 45 percent is over sixty. The median age of the members of the superclass is fifty-eight. The generation born in the decade after World War II has seized the reins and is likely to hold the balance of power for a while, especially given extended life and work expectancies.

3. *Trace your cultural roots to Europe.* No country has even half as many superclass members as the United States, which is home to almost 17 percent of the superclass, four times what you would expect based on population alone. North America and Europe together make up half of the superclass. The countries of the Asia Pacific region make up only a third. Only ten countries are responsible for 57 percent of the group: the United States, China, Britain, India, Brazil, Russia, Germany, Japan, Mexico, and France. That said, the fastest-growing groups are in the emerging world, especially Asia, and if you count North America as part of a transpacific community, the balance tips the other way.

4. *Attend an elite university.* Taking a globally and sectorally representative sample of three hundred members of the superclass drawn randomly from the list, we find that nearly three out of ten attended one of just twenty elite universities, led by Stanford, Harvard, and the University of Chicago. As a rule, the superclass is much better educated than the population at large. Whereas only 9 percent of Americans have a postgraduate degree, 47 percent of the superclass does. Only 2 percent are like the Skype founder Janus Friis, the Danish entrepreneur who does not have even a high school diploma; 91 percent of the superclass have an undergraduate degree. And if you are from the

emerging world, you are much more likely than your country-men to attend a university in the developed world: Over 41 percent of superclass members from developing countries did so.

5. *Go into business or finance.* Sixty-three percent of the superclass is from either business or finance. Top business executives make up about half of the group and top financial and investment executives another 13 percent. Second on the list are those holding government or multilateral offices, with 18 percent. Military and defense representatives account for 7 percent of the group, with religious leaders contributing 4 percent, slightly less than the cultural leaders identified. Almost 2 percent of the group are members of what I have categorized as the shadow elite.

6. *Have an institutional power base.* There are very few individuals on the list who are simply so rich or so influential that they do not require an institutional power base to achieve global influence. And even they use institutional mechanisms—publishers, movie producers, investments in institutions—to project their power. It is estimated that less than 2 percent of the members of the superclass are not also associated with a company, a government, a military organization, a fund, a church, a media outlet, or even a shape-shifting terror or criminal network from which they derive and through which they project power.

7. *Get rich.* Virtually all of the world's nearly one thousand billionaires made the list by definition. In addition, as we have seen, political leaders in the United States as well as members of cultural elites from J. K. Rowling to Shakira to Bono all bring in annual incomes in the millions. Though wealth does not automatically translate into power, it is estimated that approximately 60 percent of the superclass are millionaires.

8. *Be lucky.* Demography is not destiny. There are plenty of sixty-year-old, Harvard-educated American millionaires who are not members of the superclass. In fact, as noted earlier, many of this latter group of also-rans, while doing well, are extremely frustrated by that fact and can't figure out why the meritocracy they have promoted all their lives has left them as bridesmaids to the ultrasuccessful. The answer, as we have seen, is—at least partly—luck. It's hard to cultivate, but it is a sine qua non for entry into the superclass.

THE PSYCHOPATHOLOGY OF SUCCESS

So demography is not precisely destiny. Nor is luck enough in itself. There is therefore a ninth rule to follow if you want to be a member of the superclass: You've got to want it bad. So bad, as the song goes, it's driving you mad.

In study after study done of the successful and the powerful, common traits emerge that are not exactly in keeping with our common notions of what is well-adjusted. That's not to say that powerful individuals are all raving loons. Quite the contrary: The vast majority are extraordinarily high functioning. (Although, in a group that includes Hugo Chávez, Mahmoud Ahmadinejad, Kim Jong Il, and a number of terrorists and other sociopaths, it must be admitted that there are a few superclass members whom you might think twice about inviting over for dinner.)

There are certain psychological traits that are more common in leaders than the general population. While unsuccessful people often let their neuroses impede their success, successful people often use their pathological traits to propel themselves forward. For this reason, obsessive personality types are often found among leaders. They are the list makers, the workaholics, the detail-oriented, and sometimes the micromanagers who grind down those around them. According to the psychologist, anthropologist, and consultant Michael Maccoby, obsessives are

> self-reliant and conscientious. They create and maintain order and make the most effective operational managers. They look constantly for ways to help people listen better, resolve conflict, and find win-win opportunities. They buy self-improvement books such as Steven Covey's *The 7 Habits of Highly Effective People.* Obsessives are also ruled by a strict conscience. They like to focus on continuous improvement at work because it fits in with their sense of moral improvement. As entrepreneurs, obsessives start businesses that express their values, but they lack the vision, daring, and charisma it takes to turn a good idea into a great one. The best obsessives set high standards and communicate very effectively. They make sure that instructions are followed and costs are kept within budget. The most productive are great mentors and team players. The unproductive and the uncooperative become narrow experts and rule-bound bureaucrats.

While being a team player is often a key ingredient to great success, in his article "Narcissistic Leaders: The Incredible Pros, the Inevitable Cons," Maccoby cites a resurgence of CEO superstars such as Bill Gates, Andy Grove, Jeff Bezos, and Jack Welch—individuals who claim the limelight and are leading change in much the same way as other singular figures in history. Maccoby describes the narcissistic as opposed to the obsessive personality:

> Throughout history, narcissists have always emerged to inspire people and to shape the future. When military, religious, and political arenas dominated society, it was figures such as Napoléon Bonaparte, Mahatma Gandhi, or Franklin Delano Roosevelt who determined the social agenda. But from time to time, when business became the engine of social change, it, too, generated its share of narcissistic leaders. That was true at the beginning of this century, when men like Andrew Carnegie, John D. Rockefeller, Thomas Edison, and Henry Ford exploited new technologies and restructured American industry. And I think it is true again today.
>
> But Freud recognized that there is a darker side to narcissism. Narcissists, he pointed out, are emotionally isolated and highly distrustful. Perceived threats can trigger rage. Achievements can feed feelings of grandiosity. . . . Consider how an executive at Oracle described his narcissistic CEO Larry Ellison: "The difference between God and Larry is that God does not believe he is Larry." That observation is amusing, but it is also troubling. Not surprisingly, most people still think of narcissists in a primarily negative way. After all, Freud named the type after the mythical figure Narcissus, who died because of his pathological preoccupation with himself.

Another psychological challenge facing the superclass is the distortions associated with power. Northwestern University's Adam Galinsky has done a number of studies in this area, demonstrating that those with great power are more likely to act in a more "risk-seeking" fashion. Conversely, those without power are less likely to take risks. This explains a bit of the nothing-succeeds-like-success phenomenon and the trend toward ever greater concentrations of power.

One psychiatrist with whom I spoke identified another potential psychopathology of the supersuccessful. They literally become addicted to the endorphins their brains produce as a consequence of their high-stress, high-return jobs. Running a country, a company, an army, or a church is kind of an extreme sport, and when you face high-stakes situations daily, you produce endorphins daily—and you grow dependent on them. Thus, the psychiatrist noted, when politicians leave office they often go into periods of depression that she asserted not only look like withdrawal but actually are withdrawal.

There is a conventional wisdom in Washington that the traits that make someone likely to be a successful candidate for president of the United States are among the traits you would least like to see in a president of the United States. You have to be very narrowly focused on the task of becoming president for much of your life. You therefore have to be blindingly ambitious. More often than not, you have to discard traditional notions of balance in your day-to-day existence. It is hard to be in permanent, lifelong campaign mode while also being a devoted parent or spouse. You have to place the business of politics ahead of the knowledge needed for governing. You have to want the job perhaps a little too much to be willing to give up so much of your privacy and to be so exposed to mean-spirited, politically motivated witch hunts or worse. There is narcissism involved, to be sure, offering yourself up to fill the most powerful post on earth. And obsession. And addiction to the positive feedback you get from crowds.

This pattern is mimicked in many members of the superclass. After all, they are not just successful, they are typically successful beyond what the vast majority of people dream of or even desire. They are one in a million. This raises the question: Are these the people to whom we want to default the leadership of the global community? In many respects they may be the best and the brightest, but they are also among the most relentlessly self-interested, the most committed to preserving whatever it is in the status quo that got them to where they are. Narcissists may make great chief executives, but poor listeners with empathy deficits are not necessarily the people you would trust to manage or shape the future of a system that is essentially self-balancing when it balances at all—especially when international issues like global warming and the proliferation of weapons of mass destruction mean that the survival of the planet (or substantial parts of it) is at stake.

In the end, the picture we are left with of the superclass is a human one: idiosyncratic, imperfect individuals driven to succeed, a constantly evolving group that retains many traits that are recognizable in the elites of the past. Conspiracy theorists may be frustrated that among them there are so many divisions and inefficiencies, so few secret handshakes and coded messages, but perhaps they will find some solace in the fact that the aligned interests of large segments of the superclass often produce the same outcomes that dark conspiracies might: a world that often seems to favor those who need favor the least, that empowers the powerful and ignores even the most urgent needs of the weakest. We cannot help but see ambiguities, as some leaders are avatars of needed change while others are insensitive to the inequities they are exacerbating, or even the crimes they are committing. At the same time, the group is strikingly homogeneous, for the moment, primarily a bunch of older white men from one side of the Atlantic or the other. Asians are gaining ground among them. Women are still woefully underrepresented. And most of the people of the world have no plausible near-term chance of joining their ranks or counterbalancing their power. That is as it has been for past elites—and, as for them, it is a source of tension that will dictate both their future and ours.

9

The Future of the Superclass—And What It May Mean for the Rest of Us

> With the rich and mighty, always a little patience.
> —Spanish peasant's proverb from
> *The Philadelphia Story*

I am pretty sure that the most dangerous mind-altering substance on earth is oil. Much like a few glasses of wine or certain drugs, a little oil causes people to drop their guard, lose their inhibitions, and believe the lies of whomever they are with. This intoxicating effect has gotten the United States and much of the world into more than a little trouble. Country after country has found itself, despite its better judgment, falling into bed with the darnedest people. The Saudis and the Iraqis, Iranians and Russians, Venezuelans and Nigerians, professed special friends—dictators, thieves, and worse—have drawn their customers close, whispered sweet nothings about strategic relationships, used us and abused us (while they did the same to their own citizens).

It has happened time and time again. But I had never witnessed the beginning of one of these dysfunctional relationships until a dinner a few years ago, which was attended by a dramatically unappealing character that everyone in Washington seemed to want to seduce.

Teodoro Obiang Nguema Mbasogo was and continues to be the president, dictator and supreme authority of the small West African nation of Equatorial Guinea. Since engineering the overthrow of the previous dictator, his uncle, Obiang has shown himself to be brutal. He has also been accused of being corrupt. U.S. investigations into Riggs Bank in Washington disclosed that millions of dollars had been paid in from

Equatorial Guinea. According to a Senate Report, some of the money was said to have been paid into accounts owned or controlled by Obiang.

Obiang actually represents an improvement on his uncle, who killed or drove into exile about a third of the country's people and was famed for drowning out the screams of victims he had gathered in a soccer stadium by playing "Those Were the Days" on the loudspeaker system. The uncle had a number of colorful nicknames, including "the Sole Miracle of Equatorial Guinea," which is outrageous, insulting, and just plain wrong. The sole miracle of Equatorial Guinea was discovered in 1995—it was oil.

The country is sitting on an ocean of petroleum, so much that today production is worth more than $3 billion a year. That kind of wealth could be a boon for the people of the impoverished country, most of whom scrape by on less than two dollars a day. Instead, it has been a boon for the oil companies pumping it (ExxonMobil, Marathon, and Chevron, among others), the companies supporting them (Halliburton, for one), and the elite, who have derived from it mansions, fancy cars, and fat bank accounts. It has also been seen as a boon for the United States, as it seeks to reduce its dependency on Middle Eastern oil. Equatorial Guinea is the third-largest producer in sub-Saharan Africa after Nigeria and Angola, and together the nations offer what is being billed as an alternative to the corrupt, dangerous, terrorist-supporting countries of the Middle East. That they too are corrupt and dangerous suggests that perhaps we are more concerned about the very high cost of maintaining relationships with Middle Eastern regimes—ones that may not be dependably pro-American.

The cost of maintaining a relationship with Obiang's government is much lower. The cost is simply not caring.

That price was willingly—no, enthusiastically—being paid at the dinner I attended. It took place in a small, lovely dining room in one of Washington's poshest hotels, with perhaps fifty guests, maybe a dozen of whom were with Obiang and his wife (one of several). Many of the rest were there with one goal in mind: get their hands on some of the oil money.

I am certain that their focus was on the fact that the country had billions in revenue coming in and needed good advice as to how to manage it. It is quite likely that many were not fully aware of the details of the Obiang regime. But the policy pros in the room should have known better, as should the Bush administration, which has embraced Obiang and turned a more or less blind eye to the fact that the dictator has tortured his people, crushed his opponents, overseen an oil boom that has not benefited most of his country, and is courting the Chinese as well because they, like the United States, "don't get too involved in internal matters."

Toasts were made welcoming Obiang and saluting the promise his oil boom would usher in. Obiang spoke blandly for a few moments, offering thanks for the reception. Then, one by one, the ambitious among the luminaries and the Washington insiders shifted their focus to networking, shaking the dictator's hand, exchanging cards with his retinue. If Paulo Coelho or someone equally spiritual had been there, I suspect he could have seen bits and pieces of mortal souls flitting out the window with each soft-spoken entreaty.

It was clear that week in Washington, in that room and others like it, that Teodoro Obiang, a dubious character at best, was well and truly part of the global superclass. He had massive political and economic power, influence over countries much greater than his own, close ties with major oil companies, Moroccan bodyguards and a fleet of Ukrainian attack helicopters. He was the real deal.

It was fascinating to see, actually. After years of watching from the peanut gallery as generations of American leaders embraced one wrong guy after another because it suited their strategic interests of the moment, here I was at ringside, witnessing the current generation of leaders from the most powerful country and the most powerful companies in the world do the same thing. I could even, on some level, understand why. Isn't a stable bad guy better than an unstable, terrorist-supporting one? Maybe it's just that America is desperate for alternatives to the Middle East. And if you are Exxon or Chevron and trying to earn returns for your shareholders, aren't you obligated to do deals with lizards like Obiang?

It is just such self-interested impulses that drive so many of the deals struck among the members of the superclass and cement so many of the relationships. Which is precisely why the group, for all the good that it does, for all the invaluable leadership it affords, ought not to be relied upon or defaulted to as a watchdog for global public interests. Fox, meet henhouse. Henhouse, be sure to recognize a fox when you meet one.

Obiang is an extreme case. Oil is a particularly pernicious drug. But the pattern of aligning interests is followed in countless circumstances to varying degrees all the time. In some respects, it is a source of great progress. In other ways, however, it is the source of great harm.

The challenge, then, is that the members of the superclass are the most powerful people on earth, and when their interests align there are few contemporary forces comparable to them. Because they have more power, they have shaped the system to dovetail with their interests more than others could have. As Joe Stiglitz told me, "You don't need to have a conspiracy once you have set the rules." Whereas other tin-pot tyrants would be ostracized, undermined, or worse, Obiang is given the red carpet treatment by American members of the superclass, complete with champagne. Equatorial Guinea's halfhearted attempts to investigate corruption hardly changed the status quo, and one U.S. ambassador was tossed out of the country for "practicing witch-craft," yet as recently as 2007 the United States found itself able to characterize its relationship with Obiang's fiefdom as being "positive, constructive."

IN PRAISE OF OUR ELITES VS. THEIR ELITES

So how do we react to the emergence of the global superclass? The first step is to understand it. This means understanding what it is and what it is not, what good we derive from it and what problems its existence may create or exacerbate. This means also understanding how it differs from what we have had in the past and how it may change in the future.

In the course of this book, I have attempted to address these is-sues, laying the groundwork for what I hope is a balanced assessment of this group and its implications. In these final pages, I would like to recap the core points and to explore where they may lead us.

To begin with, we must resist the temptation to reflexively attack elites. As Richard Darman said to me during one of our conversations, "'Elite' sounds pejorative. You have to be careful there." He is right. Of course, "elite" does not sound pejorative if you are attending an "elite" school or are accepted into an "elite" company. "Elite" sounds bad only when it is a code word for referring to the other guy who has what you want and what you may even feel is out of reach. This is, in some ways, the critical issue. Elites are tolerable if we feel that what they have is within everyone's reach—intolerable and a reminder of systemic fail-ures or injustices otherwise.

But elites are much more than tolerable. They are natural, having existed in every society, in every era, and in every area of human pur-suit. And they are desirable. They are leaders, innovators, risk takers. They are the ones among us who excel, possess vital experience, and serve as essential connections among centers of power. Moreover, in the global age, many members of the global elites are pioneers, shedding the blinders and the bonds of national ties, helping to create new markets and new opportunities, stimulating growth, putting in place the infrastructure and initiatives that are linking together previously distant societies. From such initiatives, led by the business, financial, and media elites that comprise over two-thirds of the superclass, grows tolerance; from such openings also come net benefits even to the poorest in the world. If the rising tide is not lifting all boats equally, if huge imbalances remain and some are growing worse, it is also true that the number of people in the world living in extreme poverty has fallen by nearly 20 percent over the past twenty years. Improvements are being made, and if we are to criticize this group for what we see as wrong with the system they have played a disproportionate role in shaping, then we must also give them credit where we see progress.

Furthermore, the global elites of the early twenty-first century are different from those that came before. Far fewer have inherited their positions than in centuries past. Many more, consequently, are self-made, living proof that opportunities exist within the system. Further, many more derive their power from the private sector than in the past, many more from entities with global operations, many more from entities that are traded on open markets and subject to the disciplines they impose.

These are all positive developments, signs of human progress, and important to note and consider if we are to weigh the influence and role and merits of the superclass fairly.

DISPROPORTIONATE CONCENTRATION OF POWER

This group mirrors elites of the past in that its members possess a hugely disproportionate share of the power on earth. Indeed, this is what defines them as members of the superclass. And because they operate globally, with few or no institutional means of counterbalancing their influence, they are dramatically unlike past elites who rose up within nation-states and who, when they overreached, were reined back via traditional mechanisms like the use of force or the leverage of law.

Just as elites occur naturally, so too do concentrations of power. In this regard, the ubiquitousness of the Pareto principle is really quite breathtaking. The 80/20 rule (again: for many phenomena, 80 percent of consequences stem from 20 percent of the causes) applies across the spectrum. In horse racing, 20 percent of the jockeys typically win 80 percent of the races. In the breeding of championship rabbits, 20 percent of the herd produce 80 percent of the show rabbits. In a Bose-Einstein Condensate, 20 percent of the atoms produce 80 percent of the activity. The rule has been cited as pertaining to distribution of words in texts, concentration of oil reserves between large and small fields, and the sizes of things in nature from particles of sand to meteorites.

As we have seen, a similar principle also applies to the main drivers of power supporting the superclass, starting with the wealth distribution that caused Pareto to formulate the principle in the first place.

Wealth: The richest 10 percent of the population owns 85 percent of the world's wealth. What is more, data suggests that there is an 80/20 rule within the 80/20 rule (among the richest, just a few are the very richest): The richest 2 percent in the world own half of all global wealth. The world's billionaires, less than 0.000015 percent of the world's population, own wealth equal to nearly *twice* that owned by the poorest 50 percent.

Finance: The top 100 financial institutions in the world manage nearly $43 trillion, or about one-third of the world's global financial assets. Of ten thousand hedge funds worldwide, the top one hundred, just over 1 percent, control an estimated 60 percent of the industry's $2 trillion in assets. One investor, Fidelity, with nearly $2 trillion in assets, owns 10 percent or more of one hundred of America's largest companies.

Business: The world's 250 biggest companies account for more than $14 trillion in annual sales, equal to about one-third of global GDP. The top two thousand employ over seventy million people around the world.

Religion: Out of roughly four thousand religions worldwide, only about a dozen have more than ten million adherents. Only two, Islam and Christianity, claim more than one billion followers each, and together they account for one-third of the world's population.

Force: The United States and its allies in NATO, comprising roughly 12 percent of the world's people, account for more than 80 percent of all military expenditures. The United States and Russia alone, accounting for less than 10 percent of the world's people, control more than 90 percent of all operational nuclear weapons.

Politics: In a world of almost two hundred countries, just a handful dominate multilateral political processes, whether through ownership and voting rights in international financial institutions, or veto power in the UN Security Council.

Such concentrations, moreover, produce self-reinforcing behaviors, whether it is more money going to the most successful funds, or weapons treaties granting certain favors to those who already have the most weapons. Power often leads directly to more power.

Another key factor at work is that the most powerful people are closely connected to other powerful people through networks that reinforce power, access, and reach. One metric of such networks is overlapping board and institutional relationships. We have seen how the top board members and managers from the top five companies alone have direct influence over 150 companies and over twenty institutions of higher learning through board, advisory, and executive positions. We have seen how the revolving door cycles between governments and the financial world, the national security community and defense contractors.

We have also seen that these elites are in regular contact with each other. They not only have available to them better means of transport and communications, but because formal and informal global mechanisms exist to link them—from the G8 to the "new nonaligned" club of antiglobalists, from Davos to Boao, Bilderberg to Carlos Slim's Fathers and Sons meeting. We have also seen consolidation tying these groups together and making the world's biggest players even bigger, from Mittal Steel's string of acquisitions to News Corporation's domination of the media industry. And, with the growth of private equity and the ownership circle of big institutions, we have seen a few megainvestors acquire more and more influence over other large, influential, international entities, as in the case of Fidelity or SAFE, the bank that manages China's unprecedented reserves.

So in our world of highly concentrated power, there is a community of several thousand who in a sense hold the keys to the planet. They are the superclass: linked by networks and meetings, across clusters and across borders, most speaking a common language, most reading the same newspapers and traveling to the same resorts. You'll find them aboard private jets, in executive suites, and in the seats of political power. And as you observe them, you will see that the group does not look at all like the planet it dominates. Not only is power concentrated within the hands of a few, but the few themselves are concentrated in a few places in the world, predominantly white, overwhelmingly male. A few thousand very similar people whose hands are on the world's most important levers of power and influence, closely connected with one another and sharing interests on issues from market regulation to taxation, from freedom of movement to easy access to workers, from who should possess weapons of mass destruction to who should not.

Who needs conspiracies, indeed?

AGENDA-SETTING

Of all the powers the superclass possesses, one of the clearest and most important is the ability to set agendas for the rest of us. These individuals can't necessarily always make final decisions, they can't always project force, they can't always even agree. But in their own organizations, as presidents and chairmen, chief investment officers and commanders, they can set priorities, guide critical asset allocation decisions, and determine who among their subordinates will have the most influence. And in the context of meetings like Davos, where specific outcomes, despite Klaus Schwab's protestations to the contrary, are few and far between, what they can do very well is shape a majority view among participating elites—or tap into the zeitgeist of the elite—and thereby set an agenda for the companies and governments they control and influence the agenda-setting of others that follow them, compete with them, or emulate them.

Both Schwab and Victor Halberstadt have said to me that the best such organizations can hope for—and something of real significance that they believe is a very worthwhile outcome—is to help leaders shape and set their agendas. Indeed, in the case of meetings like Davos, if you are a big enough sponsor of the event, you really can help create a program agenda that can shape the global agenda. World Economic Forum staff meet throughout the year with these so-called strategic partners to ensure that their biggest concerns are covered in the program. It is one of the benefits of sponsorship.

David Sanger, the chief Washington correspondent of *The New York Times*, has commented to me that he sees "agenda-setting" as the central role that major newspapers and media outlets play. They choose the lead stories, choose where to devote coverage, bring issues into the public eye through reporting and editorials. A clear example is Iraq. For most of the Clinton era it had faded into the background as an issue. Then, because the major media outlets focus so narrowly on top leaders like those in the White House, when a few in the administration decided to reintroduce Iraq as a threat, the media followed—and Baghdad was back on the front pages.

In a similar way, major private equity firms set market prices because there are only a few that can do the big global deals, and they all speak to each other. They can deny it. It doesn't have to be illegal collusion. (Although it might be. Watch for regulators looking for that in years to come.) But it will happen more and more often as those big private equity players increasingly coinvest, collaborate, and share risk. The buzz around big industry events from the Allen & Company retreat to the TED (Technology, Entertainment, Design) Conference will also shape a view as to what's hot and what's not that has a knock-on effect in terms of investment decisions.

Agenda-setting can take many forms. It can simply be reflecting the broad impulses of this group to support the market end of the government-market continuum. For example, the financial community's agenda for the IMF almost unquestioningly embraces policies of fiscal discipline with inadequate attention to social issues, even those that are directly linked to political sustainability of vital reforms in developing countries. It's not that the core idea was wrong; it is that the balance was off. The same can be said of the Washington Consensus. The Washington Consensus is full of merit, yet its reforms were not sufficiently broad or balanced in scope. It did not focus enough on creating the new stakeholders of globalization by enabling the poor to accumulate and develop assets more rapidly, nor did it prioritize giving them the training and the access to capital they would need to do so— and thus it sowed the seeds of inequity in places like Chile and Brazil and the populist revivals that have occurred throughout Latin America and in Russia. When the agendas that are embraced produce results for the powerful much more rapidly or to a much greater degree than they do for the disenfranchised, it is a warning sign.

The superclass does not rule by dictate or direct control, nor does it exercise power through conspiracies or cabals. It has a thumb on the scales and exerts influence, not as a unified group but via its most powerful, activist, or motivated subsets. Has big oil influenced energy policy so that the world has remained dependent on its product for too long? Have the big automakers dragged their feet on major technological breakthroughs that could have produced significant mileage gains? Have major banks promoted policies that enabled debtor countries to pay them back without sufficient regard to the social consequences or the political instability that might be engendered? Have the biggest defense contractors helped foster a mind-set of permanent war that has pushed the world's biggest defense consumer, the United States, to outspend its nearest rival ten to one? Do the views of the biggest churches influence national and international politics disproportionately so that it is even possible to conceive of a divide between "Christian" and "Muslim" worlds? Have we embraced the "market revolution" for a quarter century without sufficient concern for its effect on those without the means or access to compete in the marketplace? Clearly, the power curve has been at work in each of these cases and the connections are there, visible in a not purely circumstantial way.

INFORMAL MECHANISMS OF GOVERNANCE

It should be acknowledged, however, that the meeting of the minds of superclass members goes beyond agenda-setting to effective decision making. This is particularly true where the gaps left by weak and dysfunctional international institutions, or by the absence of legal jurisdiction or enforcement mechanisms create a void to be filled.

The reaction to America's unilateral decision to invade Iraq in 2003 triggered widespread criticism for understandable reasons. So too did the decisions of the administration to selectively apply international law and principles of justice in its treatment of prisoners. The overwhelmingly negative global reaction was completely reasonable, much as it would be were a bully to impose his will on the weak in any community. The United States argued that given the threat posed, it could not wait for the broken, lethargic United Nations to work—a fair complaint about a lousy system. That said, when the most powerful act without the consent of the community or, possibly, against the interest of the community, it is inevitable that discontent and tension result.

But when a handful of private equity players price a market, or a handful of financial institutions and the central banks of a few governments determine how a new market is going to be managed (by them), or even when public needs are left to be met by a few rich companies and people, there are incomparably fewer complaints, although the phenomenon is much the same and the consequences of these actions touch arguably more people.

There is a notion that many big decisions are made by "the market" in the global economy, as in the case of gasoline prices mentioned earlier. But we have seen that the market is just one factor among many, some within the control of business and government elites, that influence those prices. It is fair to look further and ask: Did the market really decide that it wanted cars that were not fuel efficient or women's shoes that caused a lifetime of foot pain or television programming that would addle the brain of a lower primate or "American-style democracy"? Or did the people who sell those things—and their close associates who regulate those sales and those who provide financing—have a hand in it? And if businesses make decisions about where to locate factories based on cost-benefit analysis (because their shareholders measure their successes in profits), aren't they sending a message to governments that they want to see lower labor costs, lower taxes, infrastructure that reduces shipping costs, and so on? In global marketplaces when all things truly are equal, such as the case of unskilled or relatively unskilled labor, the investor clearly has the upper hand. The message is compete or be passed over. The world may well be flat or flatter, but the playing field is hardly level.

It is undoubtedly true that many informal mechanisms of global governance—whether the small committees of the most powerful governments or public-private collaborations between powerful governments and private organizations—fill gaps and make growth and globalization profitable. But when the interests of all are resolved by the actions or inactions of a few, or the system offers the few influence unavailable to others with more constrained resources or access, it is inadequate. It would not have been acceptable if the EU had granted the power to work out all economic and foreign policies to England, Germany, and France because they were the biggest countries. Nor should New York, Massachusetts, and Virginia be constitutionally enabled to impose their will on Rhode Island or South Carolina.

It is a positive development that top business and government officials have close ties, and that when seeking to achieve a global goal they can turn to one another with ease. But if the goals are set in the councils of the few, you end up with distorted results. When the political leader leaves office and goes to work for the big defense contractor, and a friend who has made the trip in the other direction replaces him, whose views are advanced and where is there a space for dissenting voices? When a private conference call among big financial institutions is the way an international financial crisis is managed, that may be the height of efficiency. But the crucial questions remain: Whose views are represented in that negotiation? Who is at the table? Who is not?

ELITES VS. THE DISENFRANCHISED

For the past seven years, activists have organized the World Social Forum, a "counter-Davos," to take place in a developing country at the same
time as its Swiss counterpart. (It began in Pôrto Alegre, Brazil, and has
since convened in India, Venezuela, Pakistan, and Kenya.) Each year, a
couple of thousand organizations participate in seminars and work-
shops that would boggle the mind even of Klaus Schwab. The WSF is
often even linked to Davos via satellite for teleconferences that prove
rancorous, as one did during the very first such event when Hebe de
Bonafini, the spokesperson of the Madres de Plaza de Mayo, called
George Soros "a hypocrite and a monster." It has been attended by as
many as one hundred thousand participants.

The existence of the two events underscores the fact that influence
does not come from organizing seminars. It does not even come through
numbers (the World Social Forum may have fifty times the registration
of Davos). It comes through access to the levers of power.

The WSF participants come from unions and left-wing political parties, environmental groups and indigenous rights activist organizations.
They argue that they speak for the masses—but most of the masses
have little idea who they are or what they are doing. The billion people
who live on a dollar a day may periodically benefit from the efforts of
people at Davos or in Pôrto Alegre, but for the most part they are as politically impoverished as they are economically impoverished. Even those
who can and do vote in local elections often lack the information to make
the best use of their vote. (However, comparatively well-educated populations have been known to make bad choices with alarming frequency
as well.)

We should be as troubled by their lack of political resources as we
are by their lack of other basic needs. How can a global system prioritize asset allocation if those who need the assets the most are unable to
be heard unless a movie star adopts one of them or a rock star passes
through town? It is great to have Bono or the Gates Foundation or the
Clinton Global Initiative speak for them. It would be better to give
them the means to speak for themselves.

While globalization may lift up the relative position of the poorest
somewhat or reduce the number of them living in absolute poverty,
they remain at the bottom of the power food chain, still effectively
without a change in their relative status in terms of influence. At the
same time, if reforms and changes that have led to faster development

have also led, as they have, to the shrinking of middle classes in almost every emerging country except India and China, then the distribution of power in the world is adversely affected. The disenfranchised remain disconnected, and the middle classes, the basis for stability and traditional political power, shrink, while the richest get a much bigger piece of the pie—and with it more influence. So progress by some income distribution metrics does not automatically translate into progress in terms of power distribution.

ELITES VS. WOMEN

I will admit that among the biggest surprises to me as I did the research for this book was people's reaction to the fact that women are so egregiously underrepresented among the global power elite. In an era in which women are increasingly successfully playing leadership roles in companies and countries, the facts are still remarkable. As of 2007, there were only thirteen women chief executives among *Fortune*'s top five hundred, twenty-six among the top one thousand. Michelle Bachelet of Chile, Ellen Johnson-Sirleaf of Liberia, Micheline Calmy-Rey of Switzerland, Tarja Halonen of Finland, Cristina Fernández de Kirchner of Argentina, Borjana Krišto of Bosnia and Herzegovina, Mary McAleese of Ireland, Gloria Macapagal-Arroyo of the Philippines, and Pratibha Patil of India are the only women currently serving as heads of state worldwide. A handful of others, led by Angela Merkel in Germany, Helen Clark in New Zealand, Portia Simpson-Miller in Jamaica, and Luisa Diogo in Mozambique, serve as heads of government. In congressional bodies the story is much the same: Around the world, women held on average only 17 percent of parliamentary positions in 2007. The U.S. Congress fell below the global average, with 16 percent female members in the House and Senate. Yet wherever I went, whether I spoke to men or women, there was hardly a stirring of outrage at this obvious failure of the notion of representative government.

Geeta Rao Gupta, the president of the International Center for Research on Women, spoke to me about the phenomenon. "I have seen it too," she said, "and I am surprised it persists to this day. Or perhaps I am not. We still live in a world in which in many countries girls are devalued, uneducated, not even given access to medical treatment that is available to boys. There are many organizations like the one I lead, the ICRW, which are working to address this, and good progress has been made in some areas. But it is an uphill struggle in no small part because of the imbalances in the global power structure that you have spoken about.

"As for the absence of outrage," she mused, "while I find it perplexing myself . . . we are up against a lot of history, a lot of socialization of the idea of gender roles. That doesn't make it any less unfair, though. It doesn't excuse it."

ELITES AND MOBILITY

Today's global elites are certainly more mobile and open to new membership than the elites of the past. There are proven paths to the top that nonelites can aspire to. Indeed, as I have noted, there is much more fluidity among the ranks of elites than there has ever been.

That said, these paths are only comparatively more open than in the past. If 90 percent of the members of the superclass have university degrees and only 0.06 percent of Ethiopians or only 0.1 percent of Guineans go to college, the open door effectively slams shut. But even in relatively better-off countries, education is the big impediment to upward mobility—whether to the superclass or simply to a better life. Only 6 percent of South Koreans attend university, and only 3 percent of Chileans do. In fact, in the world's least developed countries, only 67 percent of boys and only 61 percent of girls are even enrolled in primary school. Naturally, for those who do make it to university, the ones who can actually attend the elite schools that make up such a substantial portion of the feeder system to the superclass are few and far between, and typically from wealthy families. And from those schools how many make it to elite employers that are the fast track to the superclass?

Ibrahim Dabdoub of the National Bank of Kuwait observed, "The biggest issue in the Middle East and the rest of the developing world is education, the quality of education. This is, in my opinion, the major factor that keeps the Arab world lagging behind despite the boom that we have recently enjoyed. With all the money we have now because of oil price hikes, we could do much much more than we have, but we have not, and it will cost us in the long run. We have third-class education in terms of quality. We have lots of quantity, but not enough quality, and so the question becomes, Where will our leaders come from? How will we compete globally if we cannot produce more students who might someday be effective as global leaders?"

INSTITUTIONS VS. INDIVIDUALS

The rise of global institutions—dominated by transnational corporations but including global nongovernmental organizations, churches, media networks, and shadow alliances among terrorists or criminals—is a driving factor in the emergence of the global superclass. When the chief executives of big companies became responsible for global rather than national operations, when their growth started coming from abroad rather than from home, those CEOs became global citizens and global power brokers. Indeed, it is the rise of powerful, high-functioning, rich, global organizations that is at the heart of many of the challenges that international systems face today. National governments are increasingly like the Liliputians trying to bind the giant Gulliver to the ground. Acting alone, they can't achieve their goal of influencing the behavior of entities that now can choose between domiciles and foreign direct investments, based on the active competition of governments for their favor. Acting together, they may—for a time—but their own orientation, where power is derived from reflecting the will of a local population often in the context of local issues, is not suited to such collaboration. The result is a world of loping Gullivers, among whom only a few very big governments have anything like the stature or resources to measure up to them in terms of global influence.

One senior government official from the Middle East with whom I spoke argued that the members of the superclass were not truly elites because they did not derive their influence from something intrinsic to them or their families, but from the organizations for which they worked. It was a complaint I heard several times in preparing the book, but my response remains the same: The superclass is a power elite. Just as C. Wright Mills observed that the U.S. power elite in the 1950s was no longer the inherited old money of early America, but that they had been supplanted by corporate elites tied to big companies, "war lords," and other power clusters linked to big institutions, so it is with this group.

They are elites because they are powerful, not powerful because they are elites. And in almost every case, large organizations have, for obvious reasons, vastly more power and resources than do individuals. Thus virtually all of the members of the superclass are atop the global power pyramid because they also occupy a top position within an institutional power pyramid—or because they can influence them by directing their capital, their views, or their networks of supporters in one way or another.

THE EMERGING SUPERCLASS:
A COMING CULTURE SHOCK?

Although there are almost no circumstances in which anyone would call Steve Schwarzman average, he is in many ways an average member of the superclass. He is white, American, male, at the time of this writing sixty years old, and the chief executive of a global firm that he and partner Pete Peterson built from nothing. He is active in the arts, serving as chairman of the Kennedy Center, influential in politics, and attended Yale and Harvard Business School. He has an exceptional network of influential colleagues and friends, and access to leaders worldwide. His firm also owns forty-seven companies with more than $85 billion in revenues; he made almost $2 billion when the company went public in 2007. When he celebrated his sixtieth birthday, the entertainment was provided by Rod Stewart and Patti LaBelle. Okay, so in some ways, he is perhaps somewhat above average, even for the superclass.

The question is, will Steve Schwarzman be a typical member of the superclass if he is still active in, say, twenty years? This is hard to predict, but given the fact that China is the world's most rapidly growing major economy, that it is fueling growth throughout Asia, and that India—soon to surpass China in population—is not far behind, it seems more likely that as Schwarzman celebrates his eightieth birthday, the average member of the superclass will be the son of Li Ka-shing, the chairman of both Hutchison Whampoa Limited and Cheung Kong Holdings, Asia's richest investor, and as of 2007 the ninth-richest man in the world, with more than $23 billion.

The younger Li was born in 1966 and today is chairman of Hong Kong's leading telecom company PCCW and Pacific Century Group. In 2007 Richard Li ranked 754th on the *Forbes* billionaire list and was worth $1.3 billion. American educated—although he did not finish his degree at Stanford—he earned initial fame starting STAR TV for $250 million and later selling it to Rupert Murdoch for $950 million. He has since invested heavily in technology and real estate. PCCW is the world's largest provider of television via the Internet, one of the trends that NBC's Bob Wright felt would ultimately transform the global media business. While Li's career path has not been without its challenges, he remains not only an heir to the region's richest man and a powerful figure in his own right, but he has carefully networked into the global elite. He holds positions such as a "governor" of the World Economic Forum's Information Technologies and Telecommunications Group, a councilor to Washington think tank the Center for Strategic and International Studies, and an adviser to Harvard's Center for International Development. He is also a dual citizen of Hong Kong and of Canada, making him even more literally a model for the transpacific superclass of tomorrow.

By 2028, Li will undoubtedly be joined in these ranks by many from the rising class of Chinese business superstars. In considerable contrast to the United States and Europe, as of this writing almost half of the twenty-five richest people in China are under forty-five. Only four are over sixty. The richest as of 2007, Yang Huiyan, is twenty-six. Many of these rising stars are also active globalists in the vein of Richard Li. Shi Zhengrong is an Australian whose solar energy company, Suntech, is listed on the NASDAQ stock market. William Ding Lei runs NetEase. com, also NASDAQ listed, which offers many Chinese an Internet portal to the world. Zhang Cheng Fei, of Nine Dragons, defers to his older sister and one of China's richest women, Zhang Yin, in the management of a company that is one of the world's leaders in the manufacture and sale of paperboard.

While China's economy may falter during the coming two decades, it is difficult to foresee any credible scenario in which the number of Asian companies among the world's most important does not rise. As the region's economies grow, so too will the number of its elites, who already are included among the world's richest. According to Merrill Lynch and Capgemini, dollar millionaires in China increased by 6.8 percent to 320,000 in 2005 and their average net worth was $5 million. Between 2006 and 2007, the number of billionaires vaulted up from 15 to 106. Chinese were among the largest sources of newcomers to *Forbes*'s rich list in 2007, lagging just behind India and Russia. In short, the region's elites are likely to make up an ever-growing share of the global superclass.

What might this mean? On the one hand it could mean that the superclass will be less cohesive than it has been in eras in which it was dominated by representatives of Western countries with common cultural and historical backgrounds, as it is today. On the other, it could mean that in order to compete, to take advantage of the opportunities of the global economy, to assume more prominent roles in the global community, more and more Asian business leaders will work to remove obstacles to communication with established leaders. This can already be seen in the growing number who speak English or who have been educated in Western schools.

But it would be naïve and more than a little condescending to think that the rise of Asia among the world's power elite will result in the westernization of Asian leaders. Quite the contrary, it is more likely that the lure of Asia's rapidly growing markets will result in more and more Westerners adapting to growing Asian influence. China is already exhibiting that influence in its global quest for resources, building ties with countries in Africa, Latin America, and elsewhere. It is doing so, moreover, through a different approach to investment and government-to-government relations than found in competitors like the United States—one that is more values-free and is all about the deal. As former national security adviser Sandy Berger observed, there has been a "tremendous shift of power and influence from West to East and the real American dominance, which existed for the last fifty years, is certainly not sustainable. We're throwing our weight around, but the weight is comparatively lighter. And the Chinese and others are getting savvier and savvier about how they cultivate international relationships, which they do in a way that is quite different from ours."

If the superclass exerts influence by agenda-setting and shaping conventional wisdom, not through a set process of control but simply through the alignment of interests around a given issue, what will happen when the culture of those with the influence changes? Won't the conventional wisdom change too? It is likely that it will. Many may embrace the idea of a world in which the Asian approach of trying to stay nonjudgmental about internal issues offsets the Western proselytizing tradition. China and India have not in modern history been global imperial powers seeking to impose their will far beyond their borders (though they certainly have had border issues). To the contrary, India was a colony of such a power, and parts of China found themselves under the heel of imperial powers. They seek influence, of course, but their approach and priorities are different.

While the United States and the Europeans have surely gone too far in attempting to influence other nations' internal affairs, often in a strikingly hypocritical and inconsistent way, that does not necessarily mean it would be a good thing for the world's community of leaders to become less values-oriented. There is right and wrong in the world and it is the responsibility of members of the global community to seek to identify and eliminate the wrong when it poses a threat to peace and stability. Sometimes it is appropriate to judge and to use influence to try and change abhorrent or dangerous behavior. But the world's power elite may be shifting in a somewhat different direction.

Will other values change? Regarding best practices? Regarding how we weigh stability versus democracy or the role of the individual versus that of the state? It is quite possible that if the fastest-growing groups within the superclass hail from the cowboy economies of the emerging world, this may produce more tolerance for corruption, for example. Or it may be that a more go-slow approach to global warming will be adopted given the resistance of emerging economies to pay for environmental technologies and higher environmental standards, especially as the West was never constrained by these concerns during its period of rapid growth.

My sense is that what will happen will be like much else that takes place within the world of the superclass. There will be thousands of individual and small-group dynamics—negotiations, tugs-of-war—that will gradually have the cumulative effect of pulling groups together. As the center of gravity shifts, some of the core values will shift as well to be more acceptable to the growing number of influential figures with Asian views. But it also seems that the concentration of capital resources in the developed world, the leverage of having that capital, and the nature of markets will likely combine to act as a check against behaviors investors find worrisome (such as corruption or reckless policy making, for example). These factors will shape the second major change in the superclass during the next twenty years, as those from regions that were less dependent on global markets and international standards become more exposed to and dependent on those forces. The future is not just more Asian, therefore. It is full of emerging elites that will act according to the same standards all players in global markets must adhere to. China's struggles to enforce safety regulations on the products it exports are a perfect illustration of how this happens. Its failure to effectively enforce intellectual property protections suggest another area in which the teeth of the marketplace have yet to sink in and change behaviors.

GLOBAL GOVERNANCE VS. GLOBAL GOVERNMENT

In a number of areas, members of the superclass have stepped in to help fill the void in global governance. Business leaders engage in what is essentially self-regulation, unelected clusters of the most powerful in national governments effectively drive governments' decision making on global issues, and empowered individuals direct private resources that have become the sine qua non of development capital flows— these are all important strands of the connective tissue binding the global community. The superclass confronts issues that many national governments and multilateral organizations cannot or will not address.

Throughout history, many have reflexively reacted against the idea of global government as a betrayal of local or national identity, a shifting of decision making farther away from home and therefore away from local interests. Such distrust has been strengthened due to the fact that the only effective mechanisms for imposing such governance have been empires, which asserted the will of the few over the many, and the generally feeble or defective twentieth-century international institutions that have had few effective enforcement mechanisms associated with them and that have often lacked either initiative or coherence. There have, however, been champions of the idea of more effective mechanisms of global citizenship—from ancient times through Dante, Hobbes, Kant, and in the last century through Bertrand Russell, Einstein, and Gandhi—suggesting that the idea is sustained by an appeal greater than the abuses and missteps of several thousand years could subdue.

The selective enforcement of the law and the selective protection of the basic rights of individuals are among the most dangerous recurring impulses of unprincipled leaders throughout history. This concept has been used to justify holding certain people or certain institutions above the law and others beneath and unprotected by it, or to claim that national laws and values no longer need to be adhered to beyond national borders or along the divides that separate civilizations. The result is the collapse of moral order and the potential for great horror. Ultimately, as the generation that emerged from World War II seeking to establish a global system governed by law and common principles saw, the global community must redress and undo these imbalances for the sake of its own preservation. Injustice threatens social stability. And injustice is amplified by the fact that today's mechanisms of government are effectively obsolete. In a world of global movements and threats that don't present their passports at national borders, it is no longer possible for a nation-state acting alone to fulfill its portion of the social contract.

Of course, even the international organizations and alliances we have today, flawed as they are, would have seemed impossible until recently, notably the success of the European Union—a unitary democratic state the size of India. The evolution and achievements of such entities against all odds suggest not isolated instances but an overall trend in the direction of what Tennyson called "the Parliament of Man," or "universal law."

For these reasons, I am optimistic that progress will continue to be made. But it will be progress into a strong headwind, as it undercuts many national and local power structures and cultural concepts that have foundations deep in the bedrock of human civilization, namely the notion of sovereignty.

Long accustomed to dismissing as an impossible and perhaps even dangerous fantasy the idea of global government but recognizing the need to better manage global issues, many have focused on the idea of global *governance* as an alternative. Typically this substitution of a few letters is a kind of code that means fulfilling government roles with mechanisms that either lack the full traditional power, authority, or mandates of governments, or with hybrids that involve both governments and other actors such as the private sector or NGOs, or some combination of all these.

The arguments in favor of such approaches have many important merits. Mechanisms of global governance are more achievable in today's environment. As conceived of or in practice, they draw on the legitimacy of participant entities such as states, plus the capability and diversity of nongovernmental participants to achieve a quasi-governmental feel and to fulfill their goals. They are also generally less hierarchic and more network driven, a sign for many that they are better suited to our globalized times. Certainly, they are often creative with temporary solutions to urgent problems that cannot wait for the world to embrace a bigger and more controversial idea like real global government.

These examples exist on many levels. One is the welter of multilateral, national, and private authorities that collaborate through the connections between organizations. For instance, Internet domain names are managed through an association of ICANN (Internet Corporation for Assigned Names and Numbers), CENTR (Council of European National Top-Level Domain Registries), the World Intellectual Property Organization, the United Nations, and the private sector. The process has been complex and sometimes tense, but it has produced a number of global agreements on the management of key elements of the global electronic commons that is the Internet. In ICANN, the Internet pioneer Vint Cerf sees an emerging model for what global governance institutions might look like: "We have something of an interesting experiment because it is a multistakeholder organization. It includes governments, private sector, civil society, and the academic world. The attempt to draw those different sectors together in order to do policy development has certainly been a lesson if nothing else. There has been an enormous amount of tension among those various interested parties. We have competitors who are trying to cooperate to make policy. Of course, they are very hesitant to do anything that would damage their business interests. As we continue to see this erosion of national boundaries, I wonder whether we will see multistakeholder structures showing up that are not solely of governments."

The notion of such hybrid networks of institutions and actors is a promising one, and it is a central concept in the evolving public debate on these issues. It is linked to views such as those in the dean of Princeton's Woodrow Wilson School Anne-Marie Slaughter's *A New World Order*, which explores how we can make more effective use of international networks of government agencies and officials. It also echoes views that are increasingly acceptable to the international community of businesses as well—because the investment in hybrid networks emulates the way international business strategic alliances regularly work today. Some speculate that this approach will win support from the private sector (as we have seen, the ascendant force in the global superclass) to help bring order to the potential chaos of the unregulated global marketplace. Richard Darman speculates that "we will reach a stage where companies, facing a choice between multiple regulating authorities worldwide that are not in coordination and a more coordinated regulatory arrangement, will themselves become a force for the very institutional developments they say they currently oppose . . . Is it going to be a series of ad hoc connections, topic area by topic area . . . that will develop that way first exactly because nation-states do not want to see sovereignty threatened? Probably yes. Is there a stage at which some global authority starts to have serious taxing power, which will be, in fact, a precondition to having some fundamental change in political and governing power worldwide? I do not expect that in my lifetime."

Darman is not alone in this view. Virtually everyone whom I interviewed about the superclass fell in the range of "not in my lifetime" and "never" on the question of progress toward real and effective institutions of international government. This was true from Asia to Latin America, Europe to the Middle East and the United States. At the same time, all had come to accept the idea that new mechanisms of global governance were needed.

Members of the global superclass may see this trend as a challenge, given their current dominant role in shaping the informal mechanisms of global governance to their advantage. They may well feel threatened by efforts to create other mechanisms in which their power is compromised or challenged by interest groups that do not share their goals. On the other hand, some among them will see the world as Darman does, gradually recognizing that order and legitimacy are the allies of both business and of those who seek social stability. This tension will be as important to the future of the superclass as it is to the world.

Is a Crisis Inevitable?

Beyond that tension, however, is the threat of even greater instability. As one European business leader observed to me, "If the elites make these decisions, if these elites are as influential as they seem to be, countries may be protecting sovereignty but people are going to end up divided worldwide. If the global decisions that take place out there serve only the powerful, and many of the people making the decisions are not elected or chosen by the people, the average person is going to recognize they have less influence. So it won't just be unfair, it will produce a backlash. People will say, I don't want to be part of the world because I can't control it." Such views will continue to be exploited by populists like Venezuela's Chávez, and such accusations will continue to make the fault line between internationalists and nationalists/populists among the most volatile on the planet.

The current global system seems to many people to be fundamentally unjust: The richest get much richer and the great majority of others struggle to remain in place. For much of the period of the greatest wealth creation known—the 1980s and '90s—the message to the poorest nations from leading countries and their friends in the financial community was that austerity today produces benefits tomorrow. But for all the merits of such an approach on an economic level, it was politically unsustainable; it was also in some very real ways immoral, suggesting that paying back major financial institutions automatically ought to take priority over meeting the most urgent human needs. It was a question of balance—of how much austerity how fast, of how much for the people and how much for the banks. And in many, many places, from Argentina to Southeast Asia, the balance was wrong and it produced political instability and ultimately the discrediting of the IMF and the leading money lenders in the eyes of many.

The balance has also been off in the progress of global trade liberalization. Freer trade, which benefits everyone, has been threatened by the fact that those who advocated it were not sensitive enough to the dislocations it causes. The view effectively was, "Let's focus today on what helps the big guys, and the little guy will be helped over time." Or, "Let's focus on the deals today; we can get to the environment later." I have been a part of those discussions while in the government and since and have said such things. And I have been, as were my colleagues and counterparts elsewhere in the world, wrong. Not in thrust or ultimate goal, but in emphasis.

Similarly, critics see the incredible imbalances that exist on the security side as the overreaching or the self-dealing of the powerful. Why should just a few nations have nuclear weapons? I know why I don't like the idea of a state sponsor of terrorism run by a dangerous guy like Mahmoud Ahmadinejad acquiring nuclear weapons. I even know why I would support strong multilateral measures to keep him from getting them. But I can't for the life of me figure out a logically or ethically sound rationale for why the United States should be allowed to have such weapons and small countries should not—especially given that the United States is the only country to have actually used nuclear weapons, twice, on civilian populations. I suppose it makes sense from the perspective that they are an acknowledged evil and job one is to contain their spread, after which we will eliminate them where they are. But the efforts to eliminate them where they are have been too slow and not very serious. (Indeed, the problem is being exacerbated by the fact that the United States is developing a new generation of nukes.) Only by showing that they are committed to an equitable outcome will the powerful nations tamp down opposition and accusations of hypocrisy. This hostility is reinforced over and over as the most powerful violate international laws with impunity and consolidate influence and advantage in what are supposed to be representative institutions of global governance. We are risking backlash.

It has happened throughout history. While it seems impossible now to imagine a real divergence from the popularly perceived course of progress over the past fifty years, we should remember that it was also impossible to foresee the fall of the Soviet Union or the reversals that have threatened democracy in America in the first years of this century. (It was likewise difficult to imagine how America's reaction to 9/11 could produce a global backlash *against America.*) The internationalist-nationalist tensions have already produced reactionary efforts among the new nonaligned, but they are also informing more mainstream efforts, such as the efforts of Nicolas Sarkozy to present himself as the internationalist-nationalist: pro-EU, but anti-immigrant and anti-Turkish EU accession. The emergence of such hybrid positions is likely to change the agenda for the agenda-setters. How the balance of their power tips the scales is the key to whether they will be able to forestall cascading public reaction against real and perceived global imbalances, or whether they will be able to respond to the threat in advance and constructively rein in the impulse to overreach—the irresistible impulse that has been the downfall of elites throughout history.

ON BALANCE

The real story, therefore, is not about the likes of Teodoro Obiang, accidental member of the superclass. It is about the elites who embrace him or enable him. In past eras, most elites were national and their support could dictate the future of princes and prime ministers, the fate of coalitions within their borders, the rise and fall of individuals and initiatives that had a domestic power base.

But the center of gravity of elites has shifted. Today, the most powerful elites are global citizens tied more to international finance than national politics. Obiang without the international oil companies is nothing but a dime-store dictator. Without a sponsor like the United States or China—nation-states that are so dependent on global resources to fund their economies and militaries that old distinctions between domestic and international interests have no meaning for them—Obiang and his ilk are no different from a thousand warlords, gangsters, or ward politicians who claim a small piece of turf until someone more ruthless comes along.

If the richest and most powerful individuals in the world are now predominantly globally oriented, globally dependent, globally active, then an important shift has taken place in the world's balance of power—away from national governments and away from national interests narrowly defined. And we have seen that this transformation is more than hype. Globalization is not just some kind of fad or geopolitical flavor of the month. In every one of the clusters we have examined, it becomes clear that the most powerful are the most global.

As I have noted, today, for the first time, more than half the revenues of the largest companies, like the ones that make up the S&P 500, are international. For the few major defense contractors that remain after years of consolidation, global markets are key to growth and, of course, global tensions the engine of demand for their products. All of the biggest media companies are seeking global reach and in so doing seeking to influence global cultural norms to suit their commercial interests. The great religions are transnational, and those religions that remain trapped within national borders wither and lose influence. Even the most powerful nations, like the United States, China, and the other countries of the G8, are heavily dependent on international investment flows, international borrowing, and international trade for their growth. Most developed nations are aging and face demographic crises that only immigration can solve. Elections may be local, but national political leaders must think internationally very quickly. Even the leaders of small countries are so dependent on foreign investment flows that to some degree they report simultaneously to their people and to Wall Street traders. Indeed, this is also true for leaders of powerful countries.

The power elites of C. Wright Mills's era were primarily Americans with American interests. Their country had become a global power, but international issues were still literally foreign. Permanent overseas engagement was something new that these elites were just learning to understand both militarily and commercially. Transnational corporations came to dominate, the result of progress in technology and cold war alliances that established the infrastructure and the economic momentum toward what we now call the global era. And as these national elites succeeded in this enterprise, their interests shifted.

National elites remain. But for the most part, on most issues, they are trumped by the scale, resources, networks, and power of their more globally oriented rivals. Tensions remain between the two, and the national elites have tradition and cultural ballast to help them hold their ground. But the handwriting is on the wall. Protectionism or reactionary nationalism may reassert itself, perhaps with devastating consequences, perhaps for decades to come. But it is likely that these reactions will be seen as transitional spasms, growing pains, as people struggle to come to grips with the redefinition of core ideas like sovereignty, community, identity, local, and foreign.

To a large extent it is up to the global power elites themselves to determine how long and how destructive those spasms will be. If they use their influence to create a global system of rules that exacerbates inequalities and is as patently unjust as is the current system, crisis is virtually inevitable. However, if they recognize that it is in their central interest to move away from approaches that offer today to the rich and powerful while offering the promise of a distant tomorrow to the poor and the disenfranchised, then they may avoid the fate of past elites that were brought down due to their overreaching, greed, insensitivity, and shortsightedness.

The critical issue is balance. Where democracy may have been wanting, we have felt that freer markets might somehow make up the difference. But time and time again we have seen that market mechanisms and dictatorship—or oligarchy, or illiberal democracy—go hand in hand. We have learned the hard way that the institutions or accoutrements of democracy are not enough if they are not accompanied by the culture of democracy. So do markets become illiberal if they offer the appearance of free competition without a level playing field, without truly equal opportunity for all. The answer does not lie in the reflexive protection of national sovereignty. This impedes the creation and empowerment of those mechanisms of international governance— some perhaps new and very different from what past generations have come to expect—that are essential to rebalancing freedom and justice, to rebalancing the power of the superclass and the power of the masses, worldwide.

Nor does the answer lie in a world without global elites. For all their deficiencies or for all the deficiencies of the system they have helped create, many in this group have made enormous contributions to the well-being of the planet. We will always want and need leaders. The measure of our success in redistributing resources within our global system will be the degree to which we can balance our need for such leadership and for the incentives that help the best among us rise to greatness. We must recognize that society, including those elites, has to make the needs of those least able to help themselves its number one priority. Further, we must recognize that this is not purely an economic issue: Justice depends on those poor having not just a political voice but also a fair share of political power—power in which the measure of one's influence is not altered by economic factors, in which that power is a birthright of every individual.

The great challenge of this century and perhaps the centuries ahead will be to accept that the era of the nation-state as we have known it, born in the seventeenth century and brought to fruition over the following 400 years, has ended. While national governments will and certainly should remain a vital part of the global system, they are no longer enough, no longer adequate to fulfill their basic promises to their people. In a global world, we cannot protect people's rights only through actions within national borders. Build that fence along the border. It will prove to be the Maginot Line of globalization, a pathetic reminder of the folly of past wars and the failure to rise to new challenges.

In the same way, reducing the importance of national borders while not recognizing the impenetrability of economic and social boundaries that separate the majority of the world's people from control of their destiny is a formula not for the first years of globalization but for the last. If the people at large do not become stakeholders in globalization, then they will become its enemies—and its undoing.

Sitting far away from those disenfranchised, whether during a fondue lunch in a small restaurant in Davos or atop an office tower in Santiago, perhaps flying far overhead in a custom-fitted Gulfstream jet, the members of the superclass are, in the end, the people who can do the most to eliminate those threatening divides. Until they do, using their financial or institutional levers as businesspeople or the power of the government, military, media or cultural institutions they lead, the process and the promise of globalization as an opening and leveling force will remain incomplete, and the good it can bring will remain at risk. But the superclass cannot do it alone. Nor will they. History has shown that. Without the emergence of countervailing power centers to represent and ultimately institutionalize the will of the people at large, we will continue to get only partial solutions.

History is the story of a negotiation between the rich and powerful and the less fortunate but still dangerous: a bargaining over the price that must be paid for stability. The poor and weak are never at the table. In era after era, the deals brokered have been inadequate, with the rich winning today and gaining an advantage in the future, while the poor get crumbs today and only the promise of a better life generations hence. It is a lousy deal and it has never held for long. The questions, then, that we and the superclass must ask are, Who will make the first moves for change this time? What form will they take? Will elites once again be deposed by other elites, acting in the name of the people but actually representing their own narrow interests? Or will progress finally offer lasting proof that true stability lies in balance: between freedom and justice, between growth and equity, between market and state, and between the few who would lead and the rest of us from whom the legitimacy of leaders must flow?

NOTES

INTRODUCTION: THE POWER ELITE ON THE PROMENADE

5 *Coelho has sold more than one hundred million copies* Dana Goodyear, "The Magus," *New Yorker*, May 7, 2007, 38.

6 *"Davos man"* Samuel Huntington, "Dead Souls: The Denationalization of the American Elite," *National Interest* 75 (Spring 2004): 5–18.

6 *When founded in 1971 by Klaus Schwab* "Frequently Asked Questions," World Economic Forum, www.weforum.org/en/about/FAQs/index.htm.

7 *His central claim was that at the top tier* C. Wright Mills, *The Power Elite* (New York: Oxford University Press, 1956), 4.

8 *Eisenhower captured much of Mills's spirit* "Text of Eisenhower's Farewell Address," *New York Times*, January 18, 1961.

9 *the U.S. military is only 1.5 million* "Fiscal 2007 Department of Defense Budget Is Released," Department of Defense news release, February 6, 2006.

9 *the defense budget exceeds $425 billion* Ibid.

9 *the earnings of only the fifty most profitable U.S. companies* "Fortune 500," *Fortune*, April 30, 2007.

10 *Mark Malloch Brown . . . recalled a Davos reception* Mark Malloch Brown, interview with the author, October 2006.

11 *One of the first to observe this phenomenon* Walter B. Wriston, *The Twilight of Sovereignty: How the Information Revolution Is Transforming Our World* (New York: Scribner, 1992), 46.

11 *Christopher Lasch observed* Christopher Lasch, *The Revolt of the Elites: And the Betrayal of Democracy* (New York: Norton, 1995), 35–36.

11 *American free-trade skeptic Jeff Faux*   Jeff Faux, *The Global Class War: How America's Bipartisan Elite Lost Our Future—and What It Will Take to Win It Back* (Hoboken, N.J.: Wiley, 2006), 1.

12 *As Prince Turki Al-Faisal*   Prince Turki Al-Faisal, interview with the author, September 9, 2006.

13 *After all, Marx had*   Karl Marx and Friedrich Engels, *The Communist Manifesto*, 1848.

14 *Mills had in fact seen evidence*   Mills, *Power Elite*, 8.

15 *the average American CEO makes 350 to 400 times*   Krishna Guha and Francesco Guerrera, "America's Elite Is Pulling Further Ahead," *Financial Times*, December 20, 2006.

17 *Some $7 billion had been committed*   Beth Fouhy, "Clinton Initiative in New York Secures $7 Billion to Fight Global Woes," Associated Press, September 22, 2006.

17 *in the era of record gifts to philanthropy*   Yuki Noguchi, "Gates Foundation to Get Bulk of Buffett's Fortune," *Washington Post*, June 26, 2006.

18 *he began to describe Davos in terms of its mythology*   Paulo Coehlo, interview with the author, January 25, 2006.

19 *the famous story of the young man*   Kenneth L. Fisher, *100 Minds That Made the Market* (New York: Wiley, 2007), 80.

20 *I heard more resonances with what Mills wrote*   Mills, *Power Elite*, 27.

CHAPTER 1: EACH ONE IS ONE IN A MILLION

24 *new aircraft typically come equipped*   "More Than 100 Gulfstreams Now Have EVS System," *Weekly of Business Aviation*, October 4, 2004.

24 *As Moss says*   Brian Moss, interview with the author, December 2006.

25 *When the "standard" private jet isn't enough*   Lauren Sherman, "Priciest Private Jets," *Forbes*, March 8, 2007.

25 *the used 767 that Google's bargain-hunting Larry Page*   Kevin J. Delaney and J. Lynn Lunsford, "Wide-Flying Moguls: Google Duo's New Jet Is a Boeing 767-200," *Wall Street Journal*, November 4, 2005.

25 *Now Boeing has begun booking orders*   Eugenia Levenson, "Pimp My Jet," *Fortune*, April 16, 2007.

26 *the custom versions of the double-decker*   "Airbus Superjumbo for Private Use," BBC News, June 19, 2007, news.bbc.co.uk/2/hi/business/6768237.stm.

27 *real estate mogul Donald Trump's plane*   Stephen McGinty, "Any Rows and You're Fired, Scotland!" *The Scotsman*, April 29, 2006.

29 *Stephen Kaplan and Joshua Rauh*   Steven N. Kaplan and Joshua D. Rauh, "Wall Street and Main Street: What Contributes to the Rise in Highest Incomes?" University of Chicago, Graduate School of Business, and National Bureau of Economic Research, NBER Working Paper No. 13270, July 2007, 32.

30 *Sherwin Rosen wrote a landmark paper*   Sherwin Rosen, "The Economics of Superstars," *American Economic Review* 71, no. 5 (December 1981): 845–58.

30 *Lawrence Summers explained it* Lawrence Summers, interview with the author, October 2006.

33 *more than fifteen hundred with annual sales* Scott DeCarlo, "The World's 2,000 Largest Public Companies," *Forbes*, March 29, 2007.

33 *In 2007, for example, global GDP* "The World Factbook—World," Central Intelligence Agency, www.cia.gov/library/publications/the-world-factbook/geos/xx.html#Econ.

33 *the top 250 companies in the world* DeCarlo, "World's 2,000 Largest Public Companies."

34 *of this group—166 in total* This comparison and a similar conclusion were the basis of a report by Sarah Anderson and John Cavanagh, "Top 200: The Rise of Corporate Global Power," Institute for Policy Studies, December 2000, i.

35 *The world's two thousand largest corporations* DeCarlo, "World's 2,000 Largest Public Companies."

35 *the total market value of the assets traded* McKinsey & Company, "Mapping the Global Capital Markets Third Annual Report," McKinsey Global Institute, January 2007, 7.

35 *In 1983, the top five hundred companies* Jeffrey Kentor, "The Growth of Transnational Corporate Networks: 1962–1998," *Journal of World Systems Research* (December 2005): 267.

35 *In 1962, the one hundred largest corporations* Ibid., 266.

36 *Siemens, a German engineering conglomerate* From company websites, www.siemens.com and www.hp.com.

36 *Not only do markets like the United States* McKinsey & Company, "Mapping the Global Capital Markets Third Annual Report," 8.

36 *According to* Forbes, *there were twenty-one banks* DeCarlo, "World's 2,000 Largest Public Companies."

36 *the richest 10 percent of Americans* Edward N. Wolff, "Changes in Household Wealth in the 1980s and 1990s in the U.S.," in *International Perspectives on Household Wealth* (Northampton, MA: Edward Elgar, 2006), 124.

36 *In just a few years, hedge funds have grown* David Cho, "Hedge Funds Mystify Markets, Regulators," *Washington Post*, July 4, 2007.

36 *these ten thousand funds are, according to some estimates* Cho, ibid.

37 *A 2006 study by United Nations University* James Davies, Susana Sandstrom, and Edward Wolff, "The World Distribution of Household Wealth," United Nations University—World Institute for Development Economics Research, December 5, 2006, 26. For the purposes of the study, the authors defined wealth as "the value of physical and financial assets less debts."

37 *Though within that top 10 percent* Ibid.

38 *according to a 2007 report by Merrill Lynch and Capgemini* Merrill Lynch and Capgemini, "World Wealth Report 2007," June 27, 2007, 2.

38 *between thirty and forty with weapons of mass destruction* "Countries with Weapons of Mass Destruction—Intelligence Threat Assessments," Federation of American Scientists, www.fas.org/irp/threat/wmd_state.htm.

38 *fewer than twenty with any kind of missile capability* Joshua Williams,

"World Missile Chart," Carnegie Endowment for International Peace, November 2005, www.carnegieendowment.org/npp/ballisticmissilechart.cfm.

38 *only nine with nuclear weapons capability* George Bunn, "The World's Non-Proliferation Regime in Time," *IAEA Bulletin*, 2004, www.iaea.org/Publications/Magazines/Bulletin/Bull462/nonproliferation_regime.html.

38 *only six armies with roughly five hundred thousand or more troops* Central Intelligence Agency, "World Factbook," 2007, www.cia.gov.

39 *there are perhaps forty-three hundred religions* www.Adherents.com.

40 *what one recent book characterized as "Richistan"* Robert Frank, *Richistan: A Journey Through the American Wealth Boom and the Lives of the New Rich* (New York: Crown, 2007).

40 *Carlos Slim Helú, one of the richest men* "Carlos Slim Becomes World's Richest Man," Reuters, July 3, 2007.

40 *According to* The New York Times*, Slim* Ginger Thompson, "Prodded by the Left, Mexico's Richest Man Talks Equity," *New York Times*, June 3, 2006.

40 *Rupert Murdoch controls media outlets* "The World's Billionaires: #73, Rupert Murdoch," *Forbes*, March 8, 2007.

41 *News Corp. can reach the vast majority* "Turn On, Tune In, Switch Off," *McClatchy-Tribune Business News*, April 14, 2007.

41 *The president of the United States has ultimate command* International Institute for Strategic Studies, *The Military Balance*, 2007 (London: Routledge, 2007), 28.

41 *The United States spent more than $630 billion* Christopher Hellman, "U.S. Security Spending: How Much Do We Really Spend?" Center for Arms Control and Non-Proliferation, October 1, 2007. Figure includes authorized federal defense budget for FY2007 and appropriations for military operations in Iraq and Afganistan.

41 *Edward C. "Ned" Johnson is, as of this writing, the CEO* John Waggoner, "Fundline: The Buzz at Fidelity," *USA Today*, October 3, 2007; Jia Lynn Yang, "How to Interpret Recent News Out of Fidelity," *Fortune*, March 5, 2007.

41 *The pope speaks for more than one billion* www.Adherents.com.

41 *his reassertion that the Catholic church is* Nicole Winfield, "Pope Reasserts Salvation Comes from One Church," *Boston Globe*, July 11, 2007.

41 *Wu Xiaoling governs the foreign reserves* Paul Maidment, "What's Behind the Surprise Rise in China's Forex Reserves," *Forbes*, April 16, 2007; "China's Forex Reserve Tops $1.43 Trillion," *People's Daily Online*, October 12, 2007.

41 *It has already extended its reach* Frederick Balfour, "China's $3 Billion Bet on Blackstone," *BusinessWeek*, May 21, 2007.

41 *Rex Tillerson oversees ExxonMobil's energy reserves* Joe Nocera, "A Change of Tune?" *International Herald Tribune*, February 10, 2007; DeCarlo, "World's 2,000 Largest Public Companies."

42 *H. Lee Scott, CEO of Wal-Mart* Anthony Bianco, "Wal-Mart's Midlife Crisis," *BusinessWeek*, April 30, 2007; DeCarlo, "World's 2,000 Largest Public Companies."

42 *Lakshmi Mittal's steel company* Peter Marsh, "Man of Steel with a Show-

man's Flair," *Financial Times*, December 23, 2006; "The World's Billionaires: #5 Lakshmi Mittal," *Forbes*, March 8, 2007.

44 *it is not so surprising to find a single street in London* Caroline McGhie, "Where £10m Is 'a Snip,'" *Sunday Telegraph*, June 28, 2006.

44 *Hong Kong, with its lavish Peak neighborhood* Matt Woolsey, "World's Most Expensive Homes 2007," *Forbes*, February 22, 2007.

44 *Once home to the Rockefellers and the family of Jacqueline Kennedy* Michael Gross, *740 Park: The Story of the World's Richest Apartment Building* (New York: Broadway, 2006), 7–11.

45 *"The world is pretty small"* Stephen Schwarzman, interview with the author, November 2006.

47 *Consider the following language about its variety* Blackstone website, www.blackstone.com, accessed April 2007.

Chapter 2: Ceteris Non Paribus

52 *the current foreign minister, Alejandro Foxley* Dennis Shanahan, "Chile's Hot Free Trade Pact with Oz," *Australian*, November 14, 2006.

53 *trade agreements with forty-seven countries* "Chile: Lots of Free Trade Agreements and Growth but at What Cost?" Oxfam, www.oxfam.org/en/programs/development/samerica/chile_regional_trade_agreements, March 2007.

53 *The term was coined by John Williamson* John Williamson, "A Short History of the Washington Consensus," Institute for International Economics, September 24, 2004.

54 *Just ask the Russians* Paul J. Saunders, "Why 'Globalization' Didn't Rescue Russia," *Policy Review*, February 1, 2001.

54 *The top 20 percent of Chileans* "Economic Indicators: Chile," World Resources Institute, earthtrends.wri.org/pdf_library/country_profiles/eco_cou_152.pdf, 2003.

54 *the worst inequality indicators on the planet* World Bank, "Table 2.7: Distribution of Income or Consumption," *World Development Indicators 2005*.

56 *His perspective was clear* Andrónico Luksic, interview with the author, 2006.

56 *"We cannot be complacent"* Alvaro Saieh, interview with the author, 2006.

58 *Cornell University economist Robert H. Frank* Robert H. Frank, "In the Real World of Work and Wages, Trickle-Down Theories Don't Hold Up," *New York Times*, April 12, 2007.

59 *It obviously troubled him* Andrés Velasco, interview with the author, 2006.

59 *"the group that has the most power"* Jorge Rosenblut, interview with the author, 2006.

61 *Marshall tackled the issue another way* Jorge Marshall, interview with the author, 2006.

63 Newsweek *editor Fareed Zakaria* Fareed Zakaria, "The Rise of Illiberal Democracy," *Foreign Affairs*, November/December 1997.

63 *As Harvard's Dani Rodrik has written* Dani Rodrik, "The Cheerleaders' Threat to Global Trade," *Financial Times*, March 27, 2007.

63 *Columbia University professor Joseph Stiglitz* Joseph E. Stiglitz, *Globalization and Its Discontents* (New York: Norton, 2002), 79.

64 *Mack McLarty, suggested that the issue* Mack McLarty, interview with the author, 2006.

64 *Moisés Naím, a former Venezuelan trade and industry minister* Moisés Naím, interview with the author, 2007.

65 *a new "gilded age"* Martin Wolf, "A New Gilded Age," *Financial Times*, April 25, 2006; Paul Krugman, "Gilded Once More," *New York Times*, April 27, 2007.

66 *"The World Is Not Flat"* Nancy Birdsall, "The World Is Not Flat: Inequality and Injustice in Our Global Economy," 2005 WIDER Annual Lecture, October 31, 2005.

66 *According to the United Nations* "The Inequality Predicament: Report on the World Social Situation 2005," United Nations Publications, August 2005.

66 *the richest countries in the world* L. Pritchett, "Divergence, Big Time," *Journal of Economic Perspectives* 11, no. 3 (Summer 1997): 3–17.

66 *the ratio between the GDP of today's richest country* Achin Vanaik, "Unequal Gains," *Telegraph*, December 22, 2005.

66 *The world's billionaires, those roughly one thousand individuals* "The World Distribution of Household Wealth," United Nations University—World Institute for Development Economics Research, December 5, 2006.

66 *In some places, the concentration of poverty* United Nations, "UN Human Development Report 2005."

66 *in the period between 1984 and 2004* Bob Davis et al., "Globalization's Gains Come with a Price," *Wall Street Journal*, June 3, 2007.

66 *The World Bank's Branko Milanovic* Branko Milanovic, *Worlds Apart* (Princeton: Princeton University Press, 2005), 39.

67 *with the Gini for all adults in the world nearly sixty-five* Ibid., 108.

67 *Professor James Galbraith* James K. Galbraith, "By the Numbers," *Foreign Affairs*, July/August 2002, 178–83.

68 *In the last two decades, income inequality* Birdsall, "The World Is Not Flat."

68 *Emmanuel Saez of the University of California* Thomas Piketty and Emmanuel Saez, "The Evolution of Top Incomes: A Historical and International Perspective," *National Bureau of Economic Research*, Spring 2006, 204. See also Emmanuel Saez, "Income and Wealth Concentration in a Historical and International Perspective," UC Berkeley and National Bureau of Economic Research, February 21, 2004.

69 *As* The New York Times *explains in its series "Class War"* Eric Konigsberg, "A New Class War: The Haves vs. the Have Mores," *New York Times*, November 19, 2006.

69 *Similar phenomena can be found in Britain* "The Super-Rich: Always with Us," *Economist*, October 19, 2006.

70 The Economist *explains that the meritocratic* Ibid.

70 *Matt Miller wrote* Matt Miller, "Revolt of the Fairly Rich," *Fortune*, October 30, 2006.

70 *he follows two individuals who both went to Harvard* A recent study at Ohio State University, by the way, undercut a core assumption about the "smart" part of the equation. Looking at more than seven thousand four hundred Americans, they found that although workers with higher IQs tended to earn more than the less gifted, they were no more likely to end up rich nor were they less likely to avoid financial calamity. Jay L. Zagorsky, "Do You Have to Be Smart to Be Rich? The Impact of IQ on Wealth, Income, and Financial Distress," *Intelligence*, vol. 35, no. 5, September 2007.

71 *Tom Hertz of American University* Tom Hertz, "Understanding Mobility in America," Center for American Progress, April 26, 2006.

72 *Nancy Birdsall calls the distinction* Birdsall, "The World Is Not Flat."

72 *the ratio of wealth held by the richest one-fifth* Sam Roberts, "In Manhattan, Poor Make 2¢ for Each Dollar to the Rich," *New York Times*, September 4, 2005.

72 *the average CEO of a large company* Jeanne Sahadi, "CEO Pay: 364 Times More Than Workers," CNNMoney, August 29, 2007, money.cnn.com.

72 *In 2006, the average take-home for the chief* Scott DeCarlo, "Big Paychecks," *Forbes*, May 3, 2007.

73 *Home Depot's Robert Nardelli* Josh Fineman, "Nardelli Exit Package Called 'Outrage,' May Heighten Pay Debate," *Bloomberg*, January 3, 2007.

73 *AT&T bid farewell to CEO Ed Whitacre* Dionne Searcey, "A Pension to Retire for: $158.5 Million Plus," *Wall Street Journal*, April 27, 2007.

73 *The median pay for CEOs of Britain's top one hundred* Brooke Masters, "A Campaign to Tighten Executive Pay," *Washington Post*, April 28, 2006.

73 *That same year, the head* Geraldine Fabrikant, "EU: U.S.-Style Pay Packages Are All the Rage in Europe," *New York Times*, June 16, 2006.

73 *One is the boom in stock options* "In the Money: A Special Report on Executive Pay," *Economist*, January 20, 2007.

73 *A 2006 study by finance professors Amir Barnea and Ilan Guedj* Amir Barnea and Ilan Guedj, "'But, Mom, All the Other Kids Have One!' CEO Compensation and Director Networks," McCombs School of Business, University of Texas, August 2006.

74 *Barry Diller opined in 2006* Krishna Guha and Francesco Guerrera, "America's Elite Is Pulling Further Ahead," *Financial Times*, December 20, 2006.

74 *Warren Buffett once ridiculed compensation panels* Joann S. Lublin and Scott Thurm, "Behind Soaring Executive Pay, Decades of Failed Restraints," *Wall Street Journal*, October 12, 2006.

74 *Steven Kaplan and Joshua Rauh argue* Kaplan and Rauh, "Wall Street and Main Street."

74 *Sherwin Rosen's theory* Rosen, "Economics of Superstars," 845–58.

74 *cofounder of Home Depot, told The Wall Street Journal* Lublin and Thurm, "Behind Soaring Executive Pay."

74 *"The lion's share of the executive's bonanza"* "In the Money," *Economist*.

74 *In June 2006, the Corporate Library* Paul Hodgson and Ric Marshall, "Pay for Failure: The Compensations Committees Responsible," Corporate Library, June 2006.

75 *One striking example of overpayment* Eric Dash and Amanda Cox, "Executive Pay: A Special Report; Off to the Races Again, Leaving Many Behind," *New York Times*, April 9, 2006.

75 *economist John Kenneth Galbraith* John Kenneth Galbraith, "What Comes After General Motors," *New Republic*, November 2, 1974.

75 *Bill Moyers framed the executive pay debate* Bill Moyers, "America 101," speech to the Council of Great City Schools, San Diego, California, October 27, 2006.

CHAPTER 3: LESSONS OF HISTORY

81 *According to* Institutional Investor's Alpha *magazine* Jenny Anderson and Julie Creswell, "Make Less Than $240 Million? You're Off the Top Hedge Fund List," *New York Times*, April 24, 2007.

82 *BP has directed hundreds of millions* David Mercer, "California, Illinois University Researchers to Team in BP-Funded Clean Energy Search," *International Herald Tribune*, February 1, 2007.

82 *political officials in China have committed* Agence France-Presse, "China to Spend 180 Billion Dollars to Boost Renewable Energy Use," *Sino Daily*, November 7, 2005.

82 *Bloomberg School of School of Public Health dean Dr. Al Sommer* Interview with the author, August 2006.

82 *To run for president in 2008* Thomas B. Edsall and Chris Cillizza, "Those with 2008 Ambitions May See a $100 Million Entry Fee," *Washington Post*, March 12, 2006.

82 *billionaire David Geffen* Chris Cillizza and Dan Balz, "Clinton, Obama Camps' Feud is Out in the Open," *Washington Post*, February 22, 2007.

82 *Israeli-American billionaire media mogul Haim Saban* Center for Responsive Politics website, www.opensecrets.org.

82 *For example, during the first quarter of 2007* Ibid.

83 *In fact, 40 out of 100 members of the Senate* Ibid.

83 *According to the Center for Public Integrity* Center for Public Integrity website, www.publicintegrity.org.

84 *Bill Gates and Eli Broad* David Herszenhorn, "Billionaires to Start $60 Million Schools Effort," *New York Times*, April 25, 2007.

85 *nearly three hundred commercial contracts worth more than $140 billion* David L. Aaron, remarks to U.S. Department of Commerce, December 8, 1999.

90 *statesmen that Henry Kissinger once admired* Henry Kissinger, *A World Restored* (New York: Universal Library, 1964), 213.

91 *Although Greece is known as the cradle of democracy* Sarah B. Pomeroy, Stanley M. Burstein, Walter Donlan, and Jennifer Tolbert Roberts, *Ancient Greece: A Political, Social, and Cultural History* (New York: Oxford University Press, 1999), 28–37. Also Thomas R. Martin, *Ancient Greece: From Prehistoric to Hellenistic Times* (New Haven: Yale University Press, 2000), 24–30.

92 *sometime around 1200 BCE* Martin, *Ancient Greece*, 30–31.

92 *Populations dropped 60 to 90 percent* Pomeroy et al., *Ancient Greece*, 37–39.

92 *The historian A. M. Martin argues* Martin, *Ancient Greece*, 46.

93 *12 to 20 percent of Greek families* Pomeroy et al., *Ancient Greece*, 96.

93 *In response to this disorder* J. B. Bury and Russell Meiggs, *A History of Ancient Greece to the Death of Alexander the Great* (New York: St. Martin's Press, 1975), 146.

93 *as in the case of Cypselus of Corinth* Nicholaus of Damascus, quoted in Martin, *Ancient Greece*, 80.

93 *The public response, in 590* Pomeroy et al., *Ancient Greece*, 165–68; H.D.F. Kitto, *The Greeks* (Chicago: Aldine, 1964), 99–101; G.E.M. de Ste. Croix, *The Class Struggle in the Ancient Greek World: From the Archaic Age to the Arab Conquests* (Ithaca: Cornell University Press, 1989), 282.

95 *All this and yet no kingdom in Europe* Jonathan D. Spence, *The Search for Modern China* (New York: Norton, 1999), 7.

95 *At the center of a carefully nurtured* Ibid. Also John King Fairbank, *China: A New History* (Cambridge, MA: Harvard University Press, 1992), 8; Paul Kennedy, *The Rise and Fall of the Great Powers: Economic Change and Military Conflict from 1500 to 2000* (New York: Vintage Books, 1989), 4–6; C. A. Bayly, *The Birth of the Modern World: Global Connections and Comparisons, 1780–1914* (Oxford: Blackwell, 2004), 32.

95 *Europe had nothing like Zheng's massive ships* Fairbank, *China*, 137–38.

96 *The ossified and centralized structure* Rinn-Sup Shinn and Robert L. Worden, "Historical Setting," in Robert L. Worden, Andrea Matles Savada, and Ronald E. Dolan, eds., *China: A Country Study* (Washington, D.C.: U.S. Government Printing Office, 1988), 18.

96 *"Considering the emperor's required role"* Fairbank, *China*, 141.

96 *The eunuchs took advantage of the situation* Spence, *Search for Modern China*, 16–18.

96 *And in Manchuria a chieftain* Immanuel C. Y. Hsu, *The Rise of Modern China* (New York: Oxford University Press, 1970), 21–24.

97 *Jonathan Spence writes* Spence, *Search for Modern China*, 28.

97 *According to the historian Immanuel Hsu* Hsu, *Rise of Modern China*, 35.

98 *what Spence calls "a depth and extent"* Spence, *Search for Modern China*, 69.

98 *"Had they been Tyrian traders"* Henry Adams, *The Education of Henry Adams* (New York: Oxford University Press, 1999), 201.

98 *The economy burgeoned* Louis D. Johnston and Samuel H. Williamson, "The Annual Real and Nominal GDP for the United States, 1790–Present," Economic History Services, 2006. Figures in constant 2000 dollars. www.eh.net/hmit/gdp.

99 *The term "millionaire"* Mills, *Power Elite*, 101–102.

99 *railroad and banking mogul Daniel Drew observed* Matthew Josephson, *The Robber Barons: The Great American Capitalists, 1861–1901* (San Diego: Harcourt, 1962), 59.

99 *The business historian Maury Klein writes* Maury Klein, *The Change Makers: From Carnegie to Gates, How the Great Entrepreneurs Transformed Ideas into Industries* (New York: Henry Holt, 2003), 2.

100 *"The man who dies thus rich"* Andrew Carnegie, in a 1989 essay quoted in H. W. Brands, *Masters of Enterprise: Giants of American Business from John Jacob Astor and J. P. Morgan to Bill Gates and Oprah Winfrey* (New York: Free Press, 1999), 25.

100 *"one fifth of all Pittsburgh men"* Peter Krass, *Carnegie* (Hoboken, N.J.: Wiley, 2002), ix–x.

100 *"hell with the hatches on"* Charles Morris, *The Tycoons: How Andrew Carnegie, John D. Rockefeller, Jay Gould, and J. P. Morgan Invented the American Supereconomy* (New York: Times Books, 2005), 205.

100 *"Blessed be the man who invented sleep"* Quoted in Krass, *Carnegie*, 57.

101 *He later wrote in his autobiography* Andrew Carnegie, *The Autobiography of Andrew Carnegie* (Boston: Northeastern University Press, 1986), 170.

102 *With this asset and several others* Krass, *Carnegie*, 411–13.

102 *He gave away $350 million in his lifetime* Ibid., 358–59.

102 *While families in Pittsburgh had to earn $600 a year* Ibid., 214–20.

102 *"It is a waste of time"* Andrew Carnegie, "Wealth," *North American Review* 148, no. 391 (1889): 653–65.

102 *In his autobiography, written after his retirement* Carnegie, *Autobiography*, 243.

103 *Carnegie offered a moving tribute* Krass, *Carnegie*, 251.

103 *In* The Prize Daniel Yergin, *The Prize: The Epic Quest for Oil, Money, & Power* (New York: Simon & Schuster, 1991), 35–36.

103 *"By creating new industrial forms"* Ron Chernow, *Titan: The Life of John D. Rockefeller, Sr.* (New York: Touchstone, 1992), 228.

104 *"More than anyone else"* Ibid., xvi.

104 *kerosene resulted in five to six thousand fatal accidents* Yergin, *The Prize*, 50.

104 *This was the kind of not-quite-legal advantage* Chernow, *Titan*, 133–42.

105 *John T. Flynn dubbed this "drawback" scheme* Ibid., 136.

105 *From 1872 to 1879, Standard bought refineries* Brands, *Masters of Enterprise*, 85–86.

105 *the company controlled 90 percent* Yergin, *The Prize*, 43.

105 *introduced the idea of employee stock ownership* Chernow, *Titan*, 227.

106 *Investigations and even an indictment* Ibid., 211–12.

106 *The trust, according to Yergin* Yergin, *The Prize*, 45.

106 *"a way of life and a creed"* Richard Hofstadter, *The American Political Tradition and the Men Who Made It* (New York: Vintage Books, 1989), quoted in Morris, *Tycoons*, 216.

107 *Between 1893 and 1901, Rockefeller's share* Chernow, *Titan*, 397.

107 *"He despised the rich"* Hofstadter, *American Political Tradition*, 270, 290–91.

107 *Roosevelt's government brought suit against Standard Oil* Chernow, *Titan*, 553–59. For the opinion's text, see *Standard Oil Co. of New Jersey v. U.S.*, 221 U.S. 1 (1910), laws.findlaw.com/us/221/1.html.

108 *the collective sales of these successor organizations* Scott DeCarlo, "The World's 2,000 Largest Public Companies," *Forbes*, March 29, 2007.

108 *His wealth of $900 million* Chernow, *Titan*, 556–57.

CHAPTER 4: THE MULTINATIONAL MOMENT

114 *"The industrial directors"* David Hoffman, *The Oligarchs* (New York: Basic Books, 2002), 112.

114 *Roman Abramovich, an associate of Boris Berezovsky* "Russia's 'Chelski' Tycoon Abramovich to Get Massive Dividend Payout," Agence France-Presse, July 28, 2003.

116 *Writing of the "corporate rich"* Mills, *Power Elite*, 147.

117 *Global branding is an important element* "The Best Global Brands," *BusinessWeek*, August 6, 2007.

119 New York Times *columnist Thomas Friedman related a pertinent conversation* Thomas Friedman, interview with the author, 2007.

120 *Take the world's ten biggest corporations* "Fortune Global 500," *Fortune*, July 23, 2007.

120 *in 2006 roughly six out of every ten dollars* Data compiled from company information, www.forbes.com.

120 *In fact, for the S&P 500* Michael Tsang and Daniel Hauck, "S&P 500 Record Stoked by Growing China, German Sales," Bloomberg, May 7, 2007, www.bloomberg.com/apps/news?pid=20601109&refer=news&sid=a2Gptvdd1_88.

120 *In 2007 the smallest company on the* Fortune *Global 500* "Fortune Global 500."

120 *The* Forbes *Global 2,000 companies* Scott DeCarlo, "The World's 2,000 Largest Public Companies," *Forbes*, March 29, 2007.

121 *After all, American GDP in 1956* Johnston and Williamson, "Annual Real and Nominal GDP for the United States, 1790–Present." Figures in constant 2000 dollars.

121 *The more than $100 trillion in assets* DeCarlo, "World's 2,000 Largest Public Companies."

121 *The $2 trillion controlled by the world's* Andrei Postelnicu, "GLG Partners Going Public in the U.S. Through Merger," Bloomberg, June 25, 2007, www.bloomberg.com/apps/news?pid=20601087&sid=aStPTvZ7Eef8&refer=home.

121 *The $2 trillion in buying power* Rik Kirkland, "Private Money," *Fortune*, February 19, 2007.

121 *The more than $1 trillion in reserves* Carter Dougherty, "More Risk for China on Investment Front," *International Herald Tribune*, January 25, 2007.

122 *the U.S. Chamber of Commerce* Jeffrey H. Birnbaum, "A Quiet Revolution in Business Lobbying," *Washington Post*, February 5, 2005.

122 *if you were to take just the top three* Data compiled from company information, www.forbes.com.

123 *Brookings, who made his fortune* Brookings Institution website, www.brookings.edu.

123 *This is especially the case in the politically* Gregg Easterbrook, "Ideas Move Nations," *Atlantic*, January 1986; Eloise Salholz, "A Think Tank at the Brink," *Newsweek*, July 7, 1986.

124 *on the left, the Center for American Progress* Marie Horrigan, "Analysis: Wealthy Progressives Pull Weight," United Press International, January 13, 2005.

125 *the Robin Hood Foundation* Jenny Anderson, "Big Names, Big Wallets, Big Cause," *New York Times*, May 4, 2007.

126 *the Harvard Business School class* Steven Syre, "Harvard MBAs of '79," *Boston Globe*, June 10, 2004.

126 *According to Schwarzman* Stephen Schwarzman, interview with the author.

127 *A* New York Times *op-ed* David J. Rothkopf, "Whistle Stops on Wall Street," *New York Times*, March 8, 1999.

128 *Joe Stiglitz argued in the same vein* Joseph Stiglitz, interview with the author, October 2006.

130 *From his office in Carlyle's duplex* Louis Gerstner, interview with the author, July 2006.

131 *Bill McDonough, vice chairman of Merrill Lynch* Bill McDonough, interview with the author, August 2006.

131 *The firm's annual revenues are now heading* DeCaro, "World's 2,000 Largest Public Companies."

131 *The top twenty-five executives in the firm* Roddy Boyd and Zachary Kouwe, "$16 Bil Sachs of Loot," *New York Post*, December 13, 2006.

132 *he almost had a 10.6-acre estate* Braden Keil, "Gimme Shelter," *New York Post*, March 15, 2007.

133 *It caused business commentator Kyle Pope* Kyle Pope, "Goldman Sachs Rules the World," *Los Angeles Times*, June 4, 2006.

133 *Vice chairman of Goldman Sachs International* Robert Hormats, interview with the author, September 2006.

134 *more than three-quarters* "Oil's Dark Secret," *Economist*, August 10, 2006.

135 *Within the realm of the NOCs* T. Wallin, "Saudi Aramco's Abdallah S. Jum'ah Named Petroleum Executive of the Year for 2005," *Business Wire*, April 25, 2005.

135 *He recently cited Saudi Arabia and China* "Aramco Stresses Ties to China," *Energy Compass*, July 15, 2005.

135 *Aramco exported 450,000 barrels* Simon Romero and Jad Mouawad, "Aramco Seeks India and China Ties," *International Herald Tribune*, February 18, 2005.

136 *a mission of "Saudi-ization"* Simon Romero, "Saudi National Oil Giant Becomes More Arabian; American Workers Still Play Vital Role," *International Herald Tribune*, March 17, 2004.

136 *Ali I. Al-Naimi, has been called the "Greenspan of oil"* Stephen Glain, "The Right Touch," *Newsweek International*, April 3, 2006.

136 *Yergin provided additional insights* Daniel Yergin, in interview with the author, September 2006.

137 *"the changing nature of corporate China"* Fu Chengyu, "Why Is America Worried?" *Wall Street Journal*, July 6, 2006.

137 *He is highly educated, first at China's* Boao Forum for Asia, "Fu, Chengyu President, CNOOC Chairman & CEO, CNOOC Limited," March 24, 2005, www .boaoforum.org/boao/eng-ziliao/200503/24/t20050324_3411547.htm.

137 *Fu was not assisted* Francesco Guerrera, "The Maverick Oil Mandarin," *Financial Times*, June 25, 2005.

137 *Nonetheless, the company is controlled* Ibid.

138 *Fu has sought to expand CNOOC's international portfolio* Enid Tsuiin, "CNOOC to Buy Offshore Nigerian Oilfield," *Financial Times*, January 10, 2006; Richard McGregor and John Thornhill, "CNOOC in Petronas Gas Deal," *Financial Times*, September 17, 2006.

138 *he served on the international advisory board* "John Browne, CEO, BP," CNN, May 12, 2004, edition.cnn.com/2004/BUSINESS/05/12/browne.profile/index.html.

138 *The son of a former BP manager* Terry Macalister, "BP Goliath Plays David," *Guardian*, November 28, 2005.

138 *the "Sun King" became the darling* Grant Ringshaw, "Tough Times for Browne and BP," *Sunday Times* (London), September 24, 2006; "BP Talks of Evolving Deals with NOCs," *Petroleum Intelligence Weekly*, November 1, 2004.

138 *"It's to do with economies of scale"* Macalister, "BP Goliath Plays David."

139 *the company has dedicated around $1 billion* "BP Plans China Investment," *International Oil Daily*, May 12, 2004.

139 *the result of his growing concerns* John Browne, "Small Steps to Limit Climate Change," *Financial Times*, June 30, 2004.

139 *Browne put in place measures* John Browne, "Beyond Kyoto," *Foreign Affairs*, July–August, 2004.

139 *"Best Impression of an Environmentalist"* Deborah Rephan, "BP Amoco CEO Wins Earth Day 'Oscar' for Acting Like an Environmentalist," Greenpeace press release, April 22, 1999.

139 *"I serve on these boards because"* "John Browne, CEO, BP."

139 *His other commitments included* BP website, www.bp.com.

140 *In 2004 and 2006, major energy companies* Megan Moore, "Energy and Environmental Giving in the States," National Institute on Money in State Politics, May 23, 2007, www.followthemoney.org/press/Reports/200705231.pdf.

140 *Teodoro Obiang, kleptocrat in chief* Terence O'Hara, "Ex-Riggs Manager Won't Testify About Accounts: Senate Panel Probes Money from Equatorial Guinea," *Washington Post*, July 16, 2004.

140 *At that time, Vice President Cheney* Michael Abramowitz and Steven Mufson, "Papers Detail Industry's Role in Cheney's Energy Report," *Washington Post*, July 18, 2007.

141 *"a Texas twang"* Jeffrey Ball, "The New Act at Exxon," *Wall Street Journal*, March 8, 2006.

141 *ExxonMobil provides 83,700 jobs* Nelson Schwartz, "The Biggest Company in America . . . Is Also a Big Target," CNN, April 3, 2006.

142 *provided Tillerson close relations* Dana Milbank and Justin Blum, "Document Says Oil Chiefs Met with Cheney Task Force," *Washington Post*, November 16, 2005.

142 *Tillerson is "well-connected"* Cathy Booth, "2003 Global Influentials," www.CNN.com.

142 *"We live in a global community"* Susie Gharib, "One on One with Rex Tillerson, Chairman & CO, ExxonMobil," Nightly Business Report, PBS, March 8, 2006.

142 *Tillerson has launched* Ball, "The New Act."

142 *Raymond became the bane of environmentalists* Ibid.

142 *Tillerson has made clear* Thomas Catan, "A Subtler Force at the Top of ExxonMobil," *Financial Times*, April 24, 2006.

142 *As* Fortune *wrote in 2007* Geoff Colvin, "Why Exxon Mobil Doesn't Care About Alternative Fuels," *Fortune*, April 30, 2007.

CHAPTER 5: GLOBALISTS VS. NATIONALISTS

145 *a GDP three times higher than the runner-up* Central Intelligence Agency, "World Factbook," 2007, www.cia.gov.

146 *more than three thousand such presidential appointees* Ken Silverstein, "Civil Service," *Harper's*, June 2007.

146 *"In our system it is hard"* Colin Powell, interview with the author, May 2006.

146 *When John Adams observed* David McCullough, *John Adams* (New York: Simon & Schuster, 2002), 70.

147 *presidents have asserted their primacy* See, for example, Reynolds Holding, "The Executive Privilege Showdown," *Time*, March 21, 2007.

147 *These moves to consolidate power* James Bovard, "Bush's Bogus Theory of Absolute Power," *Baltimore Chronicle*, April 6, 2006.

147 *About 40 percent of Americans eligible to vote* "Turnout Exceeds Optimistic Predictions," Committee for the Study of the American Electorate (CSAE), American University, January 14, 2005; "Bush, Iraq Propel Modest Turnout Increase," CSAE, November 9, 2006.

147 *According to the 2007 Pew Survey* "What Americans Know: 1989–2007," Pew Research Center, April 15, 2007.

148 *And only about a third of Americans* "The Unfriendly Border," *Economist*, August 27, 2005.

148 *Four of the five presidents elected between 1976 and 2006* Blogger and syndicated columnist Byron Williams makes this point in "What Exactly Is Foreign Policy Experience?" *Huffington Post*, December 26, 2006, www.huffingtonpost.com.

148 *One such group, the subject of my last book* David Rothkopf, *Running the World: The Inside Story of the National Security Council and the Architects of American Power* (New York: Basic Books, 2005).

151 *private equity firms managed to persuade Congress* Shawn Tully, "Private Equity: End of the Golden Age?" *Fortune*, June 18, 2007.

152 *As Kevin Phillips chronicles* Kevin Phillips, *Wealth and Democracy: A Political History of the American Rich* (New York: Broadway Books, 2002), 71.

152 *"I spent thirty-three years"* Smedley D. Butler, excerpt from speech delivered in 1933, from website of Federation of American Scientists, www.fas.org/man/smedley.htm.

153 *leading candidates running for president in 2008* Thomas Edsall and Chris Cillizza, "Money's Going to Talk in 2008: 'Entry Fee' for Presidential Race Could Be $100 Million," *Washington Post*, March 11, 2006.

153 *Having access to donors like Vinod Gupta* Chuck Neubauer, Walter F. Roche Jr., and Dan Morain, "Clintons Disclose Assets in the 8 Figures," *Los Angeles Times*, June 15, 2007; Matthew Mosk and John Solomon, "Largess to Clintons Lands CEO in Lawsuit," *Washington Post*, May 26, 2007.

154 *When asked what they got in return* Mosk and Solomon, "Largess."

154 *The biggest donor to the campaign and early presidency* Don Van Natta Jr., "Early Rush of Contributions Opened the Floodgates for Bush," *New York Times*, January 30, 2000.

154 *The top ten donors to Bush's 2004 campaign* Data from the Center for Responsive Politics, www.opensecrets.org.

154 *Bill Bradley, who while running for president* Phillips, *Wealth and Democracy*, 419. Brandeis quote, 418. Roosevelt quote, 420.

155 *Phillips notes that of fifty people* Ibid., 205.

155 *Perhaps even more evocatively* Cullen Murphy, *Are We Rome? The Fall of an Empire and the Fate of America* (Boston: Houghton Mifflin, 2007), 96–97.

155 *When Silvio Berlusconi ended his first term* "You Can't Win," *Economist*, November 26, 2005.

156 *According to independent calculations* Tony Barber, "Election Unease over Berlusconi's TV Coverage," *Financial Times*, March 31, 2006.

156 *When Canale 5, the least biased* Alexander Stille, "Silvio's Shadow," *Columbia Journalism Review*, September/October 2006.

156 *On the verge of his election* Rory Carroll, "Silvio Berlusconi Is Days Away from Spawning the Biggest Conflict of Interest in Western Democracy," *Guardian*, May 5, 2001.

156 *Berlusconi brushed off the concerns* Alessandra Stanley, "Berlusconi, the Rerun," *New York Times*, April 15, 2001.

157 *The connections between Sarkozy and leaders* Martin Arnold and John Thornhill, "The Will to Power," *Financial Times*, May 15, 2007.

157 *Martin Bouygues, CEO of a global conglomerate* Tara Patel, "Election of Sarkozy Produces Instant Winners on French Stock Market," *International Herald Tribune*, May 8, 2007.

157 *Arnaud Lagardère, the head of a military contractor* Charles Bremner, "French Media Seek Freedom from Power of President," *Times*, June 29, 2007.

157 *A reporter for Le Monde recalled* Doreen Carvajal, "Fears of Self-Censorship at French News Outlets," *International Herald Tribune*, June 24, 2007.

158 *was unable to gain admittance to France's school* Arnold and Thornhill, "The Will to Power."

158 *washing the "scum" out of the ghettoes* Jenny Barchfield, "Sarkozy Sends Strong Signal to France's Minorities in Government Reshuffle," Associated Press, June 20, 2007.

159 *for Europe, the "clash of civilizations"* Samuel Huntington, "The Clash of Civilizations?" *Foreign Affairs*, June 1, 1993, 22–49.

160 *He was, according to his family* John Tkacik, Joseph Fewsmith, and Maryanne Kivlehan, "Who's Hu? Assessing China's Heir Apparent, Hu Jintao," Heritage Foundation, April 19, 2002, www.heritage.org/Research/AsiaandthePacific/HL739.cfm.

160 *As Bill Gates once pointed out* For example, Bill Gates, speech presented at the Microsoft Government Leaders Forum Europe, February 1, 2006.

160 *By the early 1980s, his discipline* "China Risk: Political Stability Risk," *Risk Briefing Select*, from the Economist Intelligence Unit, May 2, 2007.

161 *he showed his willingness to use force* Melinda Liu, "The Man in Jiang's Shadow," *Newsweek*, Atlantic edition, May 6, 2002.

161 *his core approach to these challenges* Maureen Fan, "Cashing in on Communism," *Washington Post*, February 18, 2007.

163 *"I was not a lone voice"* Philip Gould, *The Unfinished Revolution: How the Modernisers Saved the Labour Party* (London: Little, Brown, 1998), 176.

163 *"He is a legend"* Anita Dunn, interview with the author, July 2007.

164 *Stanley Greenberg, whose firm Greenberg Quinlan Rosner* Greenberg's biography on Greenberg Quinlan Rosner's website, www.gqrr.com.

165 *Mark Penn oversees a PR business* Penn's biography on Burson-Marsteller's website, www.bm.com

165 *Critics, such as competing pollster Mark Blumenthal* Mark Blumenthal, "On Pollsters and Conflicts," www.pollster.com, May 1, 2007.

165 *he was booted out as an adviser* Anne Kornblut, "Clinton's PowerPointer," *Washington Post*, April 30, 2007.

167 *In 2002, its loan portfolio* "Overview of World Bank Activities in Fiscal 2002," World Bank website, www.worldbank.org/html/extpb/2002/Overview.htm.

167 *By mid-2007, following a backlash* Stephen Kirchner, "The redundant IMF," *Institutional Economics*, April 15, 2007.

167 *It will soon fall further when Turkey* Orhan Coskun, "Turkey No Longer Needs IMF," Reuters, July 27, 2007.

167 *"It is still a vital role"* Rodrigo Rato, meeting in which author was present, 2006.

168 *"It works differently today"* Robert Rubin, interview with the author, June 2006.

169 *These flows now exceed $50 billion* Eduardo Porter, "Flow of Immigrants' Money to Latin America Surges," *New York Times*, October 19, 2006.

169 *The bank may also soon face competition* David J. Lynch, "As World Bank Controversy Unfolds, Turmoil Takes Its Toll," *USA Today*, May 16, 2007.

169 *"All the multilateral development banks"* Luis Moreno, interview with the author, 2006.

169 *"I don't write off institutions"* James Wolfensohn, interview with the author, October 2006.

170 *Kishore Mahbubani, former Singaporean ambassador* Kishore Mahbubani, interview with the author, November 2006.

174 *Geithner acknowledged that a significant portion* Timothy Geithner, interview with the author, 2006.

176 *Richard Darman, senior adviser at the Carlyle Group* Richard Darman, interview with the author, 2006.

177 *John Elkington, coauthor of a study* Seb Bekoe, John Elkington, et al., "The 21st Century NGO: In the Market for Change," SustainAbility, 2.

177 *The relevance of this group* Daniel C. Esty and Andrew S. Winston, *Green to Gold: How Smart Companies Use Environmental Strategy to Innovate, Create Value, and Build Competitive Advantage* (New Haven: Yale University Press, 2006), 68.

178 *WWF has also run afoul of critics* Jon Swan, "Green Image, Grim Reality," *World Rivers Review*, vol. 18, no. 1, February 2003, 1.

178 *Similar attacks have focused on relations* John Vidal, "WWF in the Dock Over Island Quarry Deal with French Firm," *Guardian*, February 7, 2003. See also "Alcoa and WWF," from the SavingIceland website, www.savingiceland.org.

179 *Former national security adviser Sandy Berger* Sandy Berger, interview with the author, 2006.

180 *Brazilian foreign minister Celso Amorim* Hardev Kaur, "West to Be Blamed for Collapse of Cancún," *New Straits Times*, September 16, 2003.

181 *A state visit by Japan's prime minister* Peter Baker, "Bush Takes Koizumi for Tour of Graceland," *Washington Post*, June 30, 2006.

182 *Former U.S. ambassador to the UN* Richard Holbrooke, interview with the author, 2006.

185 *Almost one-third of Russians* World Bank, "World Development Indicators 2006."

185 *His anti-U.S. rhetoric has reached unsettling* Andrew Kramer, "Putin Likens U.S. Foreign Policy to That of Third Reich," *International Herald Tribune*, May 9, 2007.

185 *Ahmadinejad has goaded the United States* Michael Slackman, "Iran the Great Unifier? The Arab World Is Wary," *New York Times*, February 5, 2006.

186 *As one expert, Alberto Garrido, was quoted* Alberto Garrido, quoted in Simon Romero, "Iranian President Visits Venezuela to Strengthen Ties," *New York Times*, January 14, 2007.

186 *Chávez has gone further* Robert Collier, "Chavez's Anti-U.S. Fervor," *San Francisco Chronicle*, September 21, 2006.

186 *He has helped Argentina* Juan Forero and Peter S. Goodman, "Chávez Builds His Sphere of Influence," *Washington Post*, February 23, 2007, D1.

186 *working with Putin* Anna Smolchenko, "Chavez Praises Russia and Rifle," *Moscow Times*, July 27, 2006; Joshua Kurlantzick, "Crude Awakening," *New Republic*, October 2, 2006.

188 *Indeed, he had hired a string of Washington consultants* Joshua Goodman, "Colombia to Honor Bill Clinton amid Growing Democrat Scrutiny," Associated Press, May 25, 2007.

189 *Uribe fumed* Alvaro Uribe, meeting in which author was present, 2007.

CHAPTER 6: THE AGE OF ASYMMETRY

190 *Charles "Engine Charlie" Wilson* "Engine Charlie," *Time*, October 6, 1961; "The Testing of Engine Charlie," *Time*, February 2, 1953.

191 *McElroy managed a major and costly restructuring* "Toward Unification," *Time*, April 14, 1958.

192 *prompted concerns about motives, relationships, the revolving door* See, for example, Renae Merle, "Report Examines Defense Hiring," *Washington Post*, June 29, 2004.

193 *As Zbigniew Brzezinski has pointed out* Zbigniew Brzezinski, "Terrorized by 'War on Terror,'" *Washington Post*, March 25, 2007.

193 *there were approximately fourteen thousand terrorist attacks* U.S. Department of State, "2006 Country Reports on Terrorism," April 30, 2007. Also David McKeeby, "Terrorism Report Highlights Global Challenge," U.S. State Department press release, April 30, 2007.

193 *About the same number of children worldwide die* World Health Organization, "World Health Report 2005: Make Every Mother and Child Count," 2005, 106. Around 10.6 million children under the age of five die every year of preventable causes.

193 *According to the UN, the same number of people* UNAIDS, "Report on the Global AIDS Epidemic: Executive Summary," 2006, 4. An estimated 2.8 million people died from HIV/AIDS in 2005.

193 *Of the twenty thousand people the State Department says* McKeeby, "Terrorism Report Highlights Global Challenge."

193 *In 2005 there were fifty-six U.S. civilian deaths* Karen DeYoung, "Terrorist Attacks Rose Sharply in 2005, State Dept. Says," *Washington Post*, April 29, 2006.

193 *Nor does it seem to warrant a wartime footing* Anne Scott Tyson, "Bush's Defense Budget Biggest Since Reagan Era," *Washington Post*, February 6, 2007; James Dao and Steven Lee Myers, "Bush Warning on Spending Cools a Wishful Pentagon," *New York Times*, February 4, 2001.

193 *almost fifteen times as many Americans died in automobile accidents* Elizabeth Arias and Betty Smith, "Deaths: Preliminary Data for 2001," National Vital Statistics Report, U.S. Centers for Disease Control, March 14, 2003, 4.

194 *Its budget is around $30 million a year* National Commission on Terrorist Attacks, *The 9/11 Commission Report* (New York: Norton, 2004), 171.

194 *This is approximately the cost of one Chinook* Doug Holmes, "'Rocky' Road," *Boeing Frontiers*, July 2005.

194 *at the recent Iraq "spending rate"* Martin Wolk, "Cost of Iraq War Could Surpass $1 Trillion," MSNBC News, March 17, 2006.

194 *while the 9/11 attacks produced* Lloyd Dixon and Rachel Kaganoff Stern, "Compensation for Losses from the 9/11 Attacks," RAND Institute for Civil Justice, 2004, rand.org/pubs/monographs/2004/RAND_MG264.sum.pdf.

194 *the U.S. reaction to those attacks* Martin Wolk, "Cost of Iraq War Could Surpass $1 Trillion," MSNBC.com, March 17, 2006.

194 *more than four thousand U.S. soldiers and tens of thousands of Iraqis* "Faces of the Fallen," WashingtonPost.com, projects.washingtonpost.com/fallen, as of September 1, 2007. Iraqi fatalities from IraqBodyCount.org, www.iraqbodycount.org, as of September 1, 2007.

196 *Vietnam-era analyst David Galula* David Galula, *Counterinsurgency Warfare: Theory and Practice* (New York: Praeger, 1964), xi.

197 *when President Bush announced his intention* Thomas Ricks, "Pacific Command Nominee Withdraws; Army Pick Questioned," *Washington Post,* October 7, 2004.

198 *the International Military Education and Training Program* U.S. Department of State, "Military Assistance: International Military Education and Training," www.state.gov/documents/organization/17783.pdf.

198 *human rights violations committed* See School of the Americas Watch website, www.soaw.org, and Center for International Policy, "Just the Facts," www.ciponline.org/Facts/soa.htm.

198 *General John Jumper, who served as U.S. Air Force chief of staff* John Jumper, interview with the author, 2007.

199 *"The mil-to-mil communications channels"* Dennis Blair, interview with the author, 2006.

199 *General Anthony Zinni, the blunt-talking* Anthony Zinni, interview with the author, 2007.

200 *General Jim Jones, the outgoing U.S. supreme allied commander* Jim Jones, interview with the author, 2006.

201 *a comment made to me by Colin Powell* Colin Powell, interview with the author, 2006

202 *the $20 billion, ten-year arms deal* David Cloud, "U.S. Set to Offer Huge Arms Deal to Saudi Arabia," *New York Times,* July 28, 2007.

203 *Fargo was such a clipped model* Spencer Michaels, "Collision at Sea," *NewsHour with Jim Lehrer,* PBS, February 12, 2001.

203 *Unfortunately for Blair, when it was discovered* Jeffrey Smith and Renae Merle, "Leader of Panel That Endorsed Jet Program Has Ties to Contractor," *Washington Post,* July 25, 2006.

203 *Lockheed Martin is the largest* "Defense News Top 100," *Defense News,* 2007, www.defensenews.com.

204 *"Former Lockheed executives"* Tim Weiner, "Lockheed and the Future of Warfare," *New York Times,* November 28, 2004.

205 *Bernard Schwartz, one of America's leading* Bernard Schwartz, interview with the author, 2006.

206 *The executives of Lockheed Martin themselves* Weiner, "Lockheed and the Future of Warfare."

206 *The top five U.S. contractors* Jonathan Karp, "In Military-Spending Boom, Expensive Pet Projects Prevail," *Wall Street Journal,* June 16, 2006.

206 *The Pentagon's budget has grown* Fred Kaplan, "The Money Pit: Can the Pentagon Pay for the War and Its New Toys?" *Slate,* August 16, 2006.

206 *In 2005 the profits of the top five* Karp, "In Military Spending Boom, Expensive Pet Projects Prevail."

206 *BAE is a global giant* Information from BAE website, www.na.baesystems.com.

206 *as* The New York Times *reported* Leslie Wayne, "British Arms Merchant with Passport to the Pentagon," *New York Times,* August 16, 2006.

206 *BAE allegedly bribed Saudi Prince Bandar bin Sultan* Julia Werdigier, "British Company to Investigate Its Own Deal with the Saudis," *New York Times,* June 12, 2007.

206 *Britain's defense industry is an exemplar* James Boxell, "How BAE Can Call Itself Champion," *Financial Times*, June 22, 2006.

206 *Turner has consistently protested the system* "Paris Air Show 2003," AINonline, www.ainonline.com.

206 *In 2006, only a dozen or so companies* "Defense News Top 100," *Defense News*, www.defensenews.com.

206 *One result of this concentrated network* Ann R. Markusen and Sean S. Costigan, eds., *Arming the Future: A Defense Industry for the 21st Century* (Washington, DC: Council on Foreign Relations Press, 1999), 9.

207 *Lockheed and Boeing have been entangled* Renae Merle, "Lockheed CEO Sees a World of Potential," *Washington Post*, November 8, 2004.

208 *When Ronald Sugar arrived at Lockheed* Ibid.

208 *But if Turner of BAE* Mike Turner, speech to the Economic Club of Washington, May 10, 2006.

209 *Begun in 2002, the dialogue aims* From the Shangri-La Dialogue website, www.iiss.org/conferences/the-shangri-la-dialogue.

210 *170,000 U.S. troops on the ground* David Cloud, "Number of Soldiers to Be Left in Iraq Remains Unclear," *New York Times*, September 14, 2007.

210 *there are another 125,000 trained contractors* James Risen, "Contractors Back from Iraq Suffer Trauma from Battle," *New York Times*, July 5, 2007.

210 *has won diplomatic security contracts* Jeremy Scahill, "America's Shadow Army in Iraq," *Salon*, May 1, 2007.

210 *Blackwater has personnel* Ibid.

210 *P. W. Singer describes the rise of PMFs* P. W. Singer, *Corporate Warriors: The Rise of the Privatized Military Industry* (Ithaca: Cornell University Press, 2003), 18.

211 *the infamous Blackwater* The contractor received extensive (and largely negative) publicity following the involvement of Blackwater guards in the killing of seventeen Iraqis in September 2007. Sabrina Tavernise, "Iraqi Report Says Blackwater Guards Fired First," *New York Times*, September 19, 2007.

211 *over just the past few years* Chalmers Johnson, *The Sorrows of Empire: Militarism, Secrecy, and the End of the Republic* (New York: Metropolitan Books, 2004), 135.

211 *"the new business face of warfare"* Singer, *Corporate Warriors*, 18.

211 *beyond the reach of the law* P.W. Singer, "War, Profits, and the Vacuum of Law," *Columbia Journal of Transnational Law*, vol. 42, no. 2, spring 2004.

211 *"short-circuit democracy"* Ibid.

211 *Or, as one journalist describes it* Mark Thompson, "Generals for Hire," *Time*, January 15, 1996.

212 *"Richer is a former head"* Ken Silverstein, "Revolving Door to Blackwater Causes Alarm at CIA," *Harper's*, September 12, 2006.

213 *Ren Zhengfei, now president of Huawei Technologies* Mure Dickie, "Low-Profile Huawei Technologies Has Already Outgrown Its Roots in the People's Liberation Army," *Financial Times*, January 3, 2007.

213 *Other PLA holdings in the 1990s* Dexter Roberts and Mark Clifford, "China's Army Under Fire: Can Jiang Push the PLA to Give Up Its Complex Web of Businesses?" *BusinessWeek*, August 10, 1998.

213 *Late in 2006, the Chinese government took this trend* Mure Dickie, "Chinese Army Opens Door to Private Weapons Suppliers," *Financial Times*, February 2, 2007.

213 *China is announcing record military spending* Jim Yardley and David Lague, "Beijing Accelerates Its Military Spending," *New York Times*, March 5, 2007.

214 *According to the highly respected* Stockholm International Peace Research Institute *SIPRI Yearbook 2007*, yearbook2007.sipri.org/.

214 *the* Defense News *top 100 ranking* "Defense News Top 100," www .defensenews.com.

214 *SIPRI also has an Arms Transfers Project* "The Arms Transfers Project," www.sipri.org/contents/armstrad/.

216 *William Langewiesche's* The Atomic Bazaar William Langewiesche, *The Atomic Bazaar: The Rise of the Nuclear Poor* (New York: Farrar, Straus and Giroux, 2007).

216 *Bill Clinton once characterized nuclear weapons* William Clinton, "Remarks at the ECHOSTAR Team Summit 2003," speech given in Atlanta, Georgia, May 3, 2003.

216 *forging his identity as "father of the Islamic bomb"* Johanna McGeary, "Inside the A-Bomb Bazaar," *Time*, January 12, 2004.

217 *President Bush's 2004 assertion* George W. Bush, "Remarks by the President on the War on Terror," July 12, 2004, www.whitehouse.gov.

217 *"the entrepreneurial engineers"* Steve Coll, "The Atomic Emporium," *New Yorker*, August 7, 2006.

217 *one senior U.S. official* Moisés Naím, *Illicit: How Smugglers, Traffickers and Copycats are Hijacking the Global Economy* (New York: Doubleday, 2005), 40.

218 Foreign Policy *editor Moisés Naím* Ibid., 42.

218 *Naím cites Viktor Bout* Ibid., 49.

219 *From bases in "permissive jurisdictions"* Ibid., 48.

219 *Monzer al-Kassar, a Syrian arms dealer* Aram Roston, "Meet the 'Prince of Marbella'—Is He Really Supporting Iraq's Insurgency?" *Guardian*, October 1, 2006.

219 *The* Small Arms Survey 2006 *Small Arms Survey 2006*, www.smallarms survey.org.

220 *these weapons, which account for only one-fifth* "Small Arms: The Real Weapons of Mass Destruction," UN Office for the Coordination of Humanitarian Affairs, May 2006.

220 *Every year approximately sixty thousand to ninety thousand people* Ibid.

CHAPTER 7: THE INFORMATION SUPERCLASS

222 *"the Internet has helped fragmented networks"* Rita Katz and Josh Devon, "Web of Terror," *Forbes*, May 7, 2007.

222 *a British citizen named Younis Tsouli* Ibid. See also Rita Katz and Michael Kern, "Terrorist 007, Exposed," *Washington Post*, March 26, 2006.

223 *a grainy video called "Evolution of Dance"* Bob Garfield, "YouTube vs. Boob Tube," *Wired*, Issue 14.12, December 2006.

223 *According to Alexa.com* Alexa.com, available at www.alexa.com.

223 *they also regularly appear among the top ten* Alan Deutschman et al., "Vanity Fair 100: The New Establishment," *Vanity Fair*, October 2006.

223 *she witnessed one such revolution* Elly Page, interview with the author, March 2007.

225 *As of 2007, Facebook had more than fifty million* Brad Stone, "Investment by Microsoft Values Facebook at $15 Billion," *International Herald Tribune*, October 25, 2007.

226 *the rise and fall of Takafumi Horie* Norimitsu Onishi, "A Renegade's Tale of His Scorn for Japan's 'Club of Old Men,'" *New York Times*, January 6, 2007.

227 *"The people who found me the most offensive"* Ibid.

228 *When speaking about new media, though* Bob Wright, interview with the author, 2006.

229 *Pamela Thomas-Graham, a Harvard-educated* Pamela Thomas-Graham, interview with the author, 2006.

231 *Following the ministry's abolition* "Interview with Sheikh Hamad bin Thamer al-Thani," *TBS Journal*, Fall 2001, www.tbsjournal.com/Archives/Fall01/Jazeera_chairman.html.

231 *Qatar's emir saw the station as a chance* Amani Soliman and Peter Feuilherade, "Al-Jazeera's Popularity and Impact," BBC, November 1, 2006.

231 *as Hugh Miles put it in* Foreign Policy Hugh Miles, "Think Again: Al Jazeera," *Foreign Policy*, July/August 2006.

231 *led President Bush to contemplate bombing* David Leigh and Richard Norton-Taylor, "MPs Leaked Bush Plan to Hit Al-Jazeera," *Guardian*, January 9, 2006.

231 *many news agencies around the world depended* Peter Johnson, "Al-Jazeera's Stature Is Rising," *USA Today*, October 9, 2001.

232 *It has also sparked the establishment* Peter Feuilherade, "Profile: Al-Arabiya TV," BBC News, November 25, 2003.

232 *As chairman and chief executive of News Corporation* "News Corp. Shareholders Accept Liberty Deal," *New York Times*, April 4, 2007.

232 *The voting structure results in News Corp.* Eric Pooley, "Exclusive Report: Rupert Murdoch Speaks," *Time*, June 28, 2007.

233 *News Corp. has major stakes in satellite television* "Who Owns What," *Columbia Journalism Review*, 2007, www.cjr.org.

233 *Murdoch aligned himself with Ahmet Ertegun* "News Corp. Finds Partner in Turkish Broadcaster," *South China Morning Post*, July 25, 2006.

233 *"Fox taught TV news"* James Poniewozik, "What Hath Fox Wrought?" *Time*, October 6, 2006.

233 *according to* The Guardian Roy Greenslade, "Their Master's Voice," *Guardian*, February 2003.

233 *Other reports suggest that when attempting to take over* "Post editor Assisted Murdoch," *New York Times*, January 28, 1984. Jack Shafer, "Murdoch: The Filth and the Fury," *Slate*, June 22, 2007.

234 *Reed Hundt noted* John Cassidy, "Murdoch's Game," *New Yorker*, October 16, 2006.

234 *The former New York City mayor Ed Koch recalled* Ibid.

234 *his close friend Irwin Stelzer* Ibid.

234 *more Americans in the eighteen-to-twenty-five age bracket* Gail Shister, "Young Adults Eschew Traditional Nightly News for 'The Daily Show,'" *Philadelphia Inquirer*, May 13, 2007.

235 *they can also be found behind the scenes* Josh Tyrangiel, "The Constant Charmer," *Time*, December 18, 2005.

235 *Jolie has gotten credit for her energy* For example, "Angelina Jolie UNHCR Goodwill Ambassador Fact Sheet," www.unhcr.org.

236 *Mark Malloch Brown was in 2006 asked by* Time Mark Malloch Brown, interview with the author, 2006. Also Mark Malloch Brown, "Angelina Jolie," *Time*, May 8, 2006.

237 *When Shakira tells Chilean president Michelle Bachelet* "Shakira Highlights Youth Poverty," ITVNews, November 23, 2006, www.itv.com.

238 *There, he characteristically underscored* M. J. Molina and F. S. Rowland, "Stratospheric Sink for Chlorofluoromethanes: Chlorine Atom-Catalysed Destruction of Ozone," *Nature*, vol. 249, June 28, 1974.

238 *Mexico's president, Felipe Calderón* World Economic Forum, "The Future Is Now for Mexico's President," press release, www.weforum.org, January 26, 2007.

238 *Molina has said that growing up* Elizabeth Thompson, "Molina Wins Nobel Prize for Ozone Work," press release, October 18, 2005, www.web.mit.edu.

238 *But, as noted in Molina's Nobel citation* Ibid.

239 *Recent scientific data has demonstrated* David Perlman, "Ozone Hole's Growth Rate Slows Down," *San Francisco Chronicle*, July 30, 2003.

239 *In the mid-1980s, as the debate* Jeffrey P. Cohn, "Chlorofluorocarbons and the Ozone Layer," *Bioscience*, vol. 37, no. 9, October 1987.

240 *Molina remains an activist* Mario Molina, "The Ozone Treaty Can Do Much More for the Planet," *Financial Times*, August 24, 2007.

241 *President Kennedy was elected after proclaiming his belief* John F. Kennedy, "Address to Southern Baptist Leaders," 1960.

241 *The Harvard theologian Harvey Cox* Harvey Cox, *The Secular City: Secularization and Urbanization in Theological Perspective* (New York: Macmillan, 1965), 244.

241 *The following year,* Time *ran* "Toward a Hidden God," *Time*, April 8, 1966.

242 *The chief rabbi of Great Britain argued* Jonathan Sacks, *The Dignity of Difference: How to Avoid the Clash of Civilizations* (New York: Continuum Books, 2002).

242 *A number of polls reveal this rise* Timothy Shah and Monica Duffy Toft, "Why God Is Winning," *Foreign Policy*, July/August 2006, 39–43.

242 *84 percent of all people consider themselves* Numbers from Adherents.com, a religious statistics organization, www.adherents.com.

242 *Europe, notably, remains decidedly secular* Peter Ford, "What Place for God in Europe?" *Christian Science Monitor*, February 25, 2005. A similar survey by the Pew Forum on Religion and Public Life found that, in contrast, 59 percent of Americans called faith "very important." Cited in Ford. Across Europe, 15 percent of the population attends a place of worship at least once

a week (with variation by country), while 44 percent do so in the United States.

243 *"Consider what went on last Sunday"* Mark Noll, "The Global Rise of Christianity," remark made at event held by Pew Forum on Religion and Public Life, March 2, 2005, www.pewforum.org.

243 *Yoido Full Gospel Church in South Korea* Reena Advani, "Church in Seoul Full of Korea's Faithful," NPR, *All Things Considered*, August 25, 2005.

243 *According to the Megachurch Research Center* Jonathan Mahler, "The Soul of the New Exurb," *New York Times Magazine*, March 27, 2006. The "generally agreed-upon threshold" for megachurch status is an attending audience of two thousand.

243 *Rick Warren, author of* The Purpose-Driven Life Ibid.

244 *a stopover in Seoul* Lillian Kwon, "100,000 South Korean Christians Attend Rick Warren Stadium Gathering," *Christian Post*, July 14, 2006.

244 *Warren has identified the megachurch* "Profile: Rick and Kay Warren," PBS, Religion and Ethics, September 1, 2006, www.pbs.org.

244 *according to* The New York Times Mahler, "Soul of the New Exurb."

245 *Luis Palau has made a number of names for himself* Titles used variously by, for example, ABC News, the *Washington Post*, *St. Petersburg Times*, and others.

245 *"stealth evangelism"* Caryle Murphy, "Playing Up Party Instead of Pulpit," *Washington Post*, September 29, 2005.

245 *Palau even put on a spring break festival* Todd Hertz, "Beach Blanket Rebirth," *Christianity Today*, January 16, 2003.

245 *He has taken his ministry to seventy countries* From the Luis Palau Association website, www.palau.org.

246 *$3.5 million, paid in large part by corporate funders* "Is Luis Palau the Next Billy Graham?" ABC News, October 8, 2005.

246 *Bush included Palau in a meeting of "faith leaders"* Tony Carnes, "Bush's Defining Moment," *Christianity Today*, November 2, 2001.

246 *an event with a star-studded cast* "George W. Bush: Remarks at a Reception Honoring Hispanic Heritage Month," American Presidency Project, October 12, 2001.

247 *Based on audience numbers and website hits* David Hardaker, "Islam's Billy Graham," *Independent*, January 4, 2006.

247 *boasts "the kind of following"* Tarek Atia, "Amr Khaled: A Preacher's Puzzle," *Al-Ahram Weekly*, October 20, 2005.

247 *Khaled made his first religious speech* Ibid.

247 *Sales exploded* Samantha Shapiro, "Ministering to the Upwardly Mobile Muslim," *New York Times Magazine*, April 30, 2006.

247 *"He is so tender and most adorable"* Ibid.

248 *"In the best traditions"* Hardaker, "Islam's Billy Graham."

248 *On Khaled's website, which received twenty-six million hits* Shapiro, "Ministering to the Upwardly Mobile Muslim."

248 *It is the third-most-popular Arabic site* Ibid.; Atia, "Amr Khaled."

248 *A* New York Times *reporter recalls* Shapiro, "Ministering to the Upwardly Mobile Muslim."

248 *Rick Little, an American adviser to the UN* Hardaker, "Islam's Billy Graham."

249 *He has told audiences that to remove the headscarf* Ibid.

249 *"I believe that every one hundred years"* Atia, "Amr Khaled."

249 *He believes that aliens live* "Who Is Li Hongzhi?" BBC, May 8, 2001.

250 *In 2000, Amnesty International reported* "Falun Gong Deaths in Custody Continue to Rise as Crackdown Worsens," Amnesty International, 2000, www.amnesty.org.

250 *External sources, including* Time "Li Hongzhi: Messenger to Millions," *Asiaweek*, June 1, 2001.

250 *Protesters, though peaceful* Pui-Wing Tam et al., "China's Diplomats in U.S. Act to Foil Falun Gong Protesters," *Wall Street Journal*, November 24, 2004.

250 *"entirely unexpected" by government officials* Ibid.

250 *"Falun Gong had lots of ways"* Ibid.

250 *"It spooked the leadership"* Richard Baum, quoted in "Li Hongzhi: Messenger to Millions."

251 *His place in the Iranian power structure was well represented* Michael Slackman, "A Cleric Steeped in the Ways of Power," *New York Times*, September 9, 2006.

251 *winning the 1981 election with a 95 percent vote* "Governing Iran: Ayatollah Ali Khamenei," *Online NewsHour*, PBS, 2006, www.pbs.org.

251 *and has publicly condemned* Slackman, "Cleric Steeped in the Ways of Power."

252 *President Ahmadinejad himself has acknowledged* Azadeh Moaveni, "Power in the Shadows," *Time*, June 25, 2006.

252 *According to* Time *magazine, Ahmadinejad and Khamenei* Ibid.

Chapter 8: How to Become a Member of the Superclass

254 *In an article on the proliferation of 9/11-related* Lev Grossman, "Why the 9/11 Conspiracy Theories Won't Go Away," *Time*, September 3, 2006.

254 *"psychologically reassuring"* Quoted in Carol Morello, "Conspiracy Theories Flourish on the Internet," *Washington Post*, October 7, 2004.

255 *In the wake of the death of Princess Diana* Charlotte Parsons, "Why We Need Conspiracy Theories," BBC News, September 24, 2001.

255 *in 2004, a man from a small town* Morello, "Conspiracy Theories Flourish on the Internet."

255 *Barkun writes about the integration* Michael Barkun, *A Culture of Conspiracy: Apocalyptic Visions in Contemporary America* (Berkeley: University of California Press, 2003), 83.

255 *In 431 BCE* Benjamin Jowett, *Thucydides* (Oxford: Clarendon Press, 1900), Book 3.

255 *In AD 962, in Metz, France, hundreds of cats* Elizabeth A. Lawrence, "Feline Fortunes: Contrasting Views of Cats in Popular Culture," *Journal of Popular Culture*, vol. 36, no. 3, 623–35.

256 *The Romans destroyed Jerusalem and killed as many as one million Jews* "Anti-Judaism: 70 to 1200 CE," ReligiousTolerance.org, www.religioustolerance.org/jud_pers1.htm.

256 *In 1321, when it was asserted that local Jews* "Jewish Persecution from 1200 to 1800 CE," ReligiousTolerance.org, www.religioustolerance.org/jud_pers3.htm.

256 *many historians trace the first real "grand conspiracy"* Lynn Hunt, *Politics, Culture and Class in the French Revolution* (Berkeley: University of California Press, 1984), 39–44.

256 *As a result of their warning* Timothy Tackett, "Conspiracy Obsession in a Time of Revolution: French Elites and the Origins of the Terror, 1789–1792," *American Historical Review*, 105, no. 3 (June 2000): 691–713.

256 *According to one historian* Hunt, *Politics, Culture and Class*, 39.

257 *Brown's next focus was a novel* David Shugarts, "After *The Da Vinci Code:* Some Very Educated Guesses About the Masonic Content of Dan Brown's New Novel," *U.S. News & World Report*, August 28, 2005.

258 *Though not a religion, Freemasonry requires* H. Paul Jeffers, *Freemasons* (New York: Kensington, 2005), 4.

258 *Fraternal members have a system* From the "About" portion of the Masons of California website, www.freemason.org.

258 *The society revolves around four* James Barron, "A Secret Society, Spilling a Few Secrets," *New York Times*, October 4, 2006.

258 *Some claim that the one-dollar bill* Jeffers, *Freemasons*, 165.

258 *During the postwar Nuremburg trials* Ibid., 84–91.

259 *Freemasons have historically had a number* Ibid., 170.

259 *Franklin, a member of the Masons* Jay Tolson, "Inside the Masons," *U.S. News & World Report*, August 28, 2005.

259 *Today the society's aging membership* Mark Hazlin, "Dwindling Freemasons Hope to Attract New Blood," *USA Today*, October 30, 2004.

259 *They focus on the charitable component* "New Masons Drawn by Brotherhood, Not Myths," NPR, May 5, 2007.

259 *American Masons contribute around $750 million* Hazlin, "Dwindling Freemasons."

260 *"an incubator and meeting point"* Alexandra Robbins, "George W., Knight of Eulogia," *Atlantic*, May 2000.

260 *George W. is in fact* Ibid.

260 *It began admitting women in 1992* Andrew Cedotal, "Rattling Those Dry Bones," *Yale Daily News*, April 18, 2006.

261 *when George W. Bush was presented* Alexandra Robbins, *Secrets of the Tomb: Skull and Bones, the Ivy League, and the Hidden Paths of Power* (Boston: Little, Brown, 2002), 126.

261 *"Skull and Bones is not some ordinary"* Ron Rosenbaum, "Skull and Bones, Denying Its Rite, Suckers AOL-TW," *New York Observer*, July 14, 2002.

261 *David Brooks, a conservative columnist* "Skull and Bones: Secret Yale Society Includes America's Power Elite," *60 Minutes*, June 13, 2004.

261 *the Carlyle group, which manages more than $56 billion* Company profile, www.carlyle.com.

262 *its roster of prominent employees* Melanie Warner, "Down the Rabbit Hole," *Fortune*, March 18, 2002.

262 *Even the younger Bush had a stint* Jamie Doward, "Ex-Presidents Club Gets Fat on Conflict," *Guardian*, March 23, 2003.

262 *"Conspiracy theorists that obsess"* Dan Briody, *The Iron Triangle: Inside the Secret World of the Carlyle Group* (Hoboken: John Wiley, 2003), 158.

263 *newspaper articles and business magazine cover stories* For example, a Carlyle feature by Emily Thornton et al., "Carlyle Changes Its Stripes," made the cover of *BusinessWeek*, February 12, 2007.

263 *in 1990 Carlyle started buying up defense-related assets* Doward, "Ex-Presidents' Club."

263 *took the company public* Mark Fineman, "Arms Buildup Is a Boon to Firm Run by Big Guns," *Los Angeles Times*, January 10, 2002.

263 *Its $73 million purchase* Terence O'Hara, "Carlyle Shows It's Still Tops in Defense," *Washington Post*, February 13, 2006.

263 *He purportedly made a phone call* Warner, "Down the Rabbit Hole."

263 *"The problem comes when"* Oliver Burkeman and Julian Borger, "The Ex-Presidents' Club," *Guardian*, October 13, 2001.

263 *One of Carlyle's cofounders told* The Nation Tim Shorrock, "Crony Capitalism Goes Global," *Nation*, April 1, 2002.

263 *"Since 9/11, USIS's acquisition"* Briody, *Iron Triangle*, 152.

264 *Shafig bin Laden, one of Osama's numerous brothers* Warner, "Down the Rabbit Hole."

264 *As one top-level Carlyle employee* Ibid.

266 *One antiglobalist website, NewsWithViews* Available at www.newswithviews.com.

266 *"Business leaders go to Davos"* Available at www.foe.co.uk.

266 *"Davos is . . . the most visible symbol"* Jeff Faux, "The Party of Davos," *Nation*, February 13, 2006.

266 *now generating more than $85 million a year* World Economic Forum, "Annual Report 2005/06," www.weforum.org.

267 *The facts about the meeting are well known* "About Us," WEF website, www.weforum.org.

267 *As Henri Schwamm, former vice president* Jean-Christophe Graz, "How Powerful Are Transnational Elite Clubs? The Social Myth of the World Economic Forum," *New Political Economy* 8, no. 3 (November 2003): 330.

267 *As David E. Hoffman describes* David E. Hoffman, *The Oligarchs: Wealth & Power in the New Russia* (New York: Basic Books, 2002), 325.

268 *The American billionaire George Soros* John Lloyd, "The Russian Devolution," *New York Times Magazine*, August 15, 1999.

268 *"Boys, your time is over"* Quoted in Hoffman, *The Oligarchs*, 334.

268 *The oligarchs set aside differences* Gusinsky and Berezovsky, who had split in the past, met privately at Davos, as did Berezovsky and Chubais. Ibid., 328.

268 *The subsequent months saw a massive* Lloyd, "Russian Devolution."

268 *On a single night at the 2006 convention* Bruce Nussbaum, "Party Time at Davos," *BusinessWeek*, January 27, 2006.

269 *At a* Forbes *party* Dennis Kneale, "Gunning for Google," *Forbes,* February 3, 2006.

269 *"You always feel like"* Steve Case, interview with the author, 2007.

270 *When asked how the forum has changed* Klaus Schwab, interview with the author, 2007.

270 *that is why Bono comes to be* Tim Weber, "Bono Bets on Red to Battle AIDS," BBC News, January 26, 2006.

273 *Philippe Bourguignon, a former co-CEO* Philippe Bourguignon, interview with the author, 2006.

275 *Bob Kimmitt, currently deputy secretary of the U.S. treasury* Bob Kimmitt, interview with the author, 2006.

275 *Sometimes it takes on a lighter context* Tim Weber, "In Search of Davos Man," BBC News, January 23, 2004.

276 *An excerpt from the promotional materials* Andreas von Rétyi, *Bilderberger: The Timetable of the New World Order* (2006). Cited by Bilderberg.org, www.bilderberg.org/2006.htm.

277 *The annual meeting of the Bilderberg Group* Stephen Gill, *American Hegemony and the Trilateral Commission.* (New York: Cambridge University Press, 1990), 128–29.

277 *the BBC reported in 2004 that a phone call* Jonathan Duffy, "Bilderberg: The Ultimate Conspiracy Theory," BBC News, June 3, 2004.

277 *In 2006, the venue* Holly Lake, "Today Kanata . . . Tomorrow the World," *Ottawa Sun,* June 12, 2006.

277 *Local police told an Ottawa reporter* "Bilderbergers Meet Secretly Today in Ottawa," *World Net Daily,* June 10, 2006.

278 *Speculations about the group's agenda* Tom Spears, "Secretive Group's Departure as Low-Key as Arrival," *Ottawa Citizen,* June 12, 2006.

278 *"Crap!" pronounced Lord Denis Healey* Duffy, "Bilderberg."

279 *"I find the world government accusations"* Victor Halberstadt, interview with the author, 2006.

279 *It was founded in 1973* "Frequently Asked Questions," Trilateral Commission website, www.trilateral.org.

280 *It is a project of the William J. Clinton Foundation* From the CGI website, www.clintonglobalinitiative.org.

280 *Illustrating the power of the idea* Andrew Jack, "Clinton Initiative Wins $7.3bn Pledges," *Financial Times,* September 22, 2006.

281 *The CGI is tapping into a particular gestalt* For example, Maria DiMento, "Record-Breaking Giving," *Chronicle of Philanthropy,* February 22, 2007.

283 *G. William Domhoff, a professor of sociology* G. William Domhoff, "Social Cohesion & the Bohemian Grove," 2005, sociology.ucsc.edu/whorulesamerica/index.html.

283 *According to a recently revealed audio recording* Adair Lara, "Members Only: SF's Exclusive Clubs Carry on Traditions of Fellowship, Culture—and Discrimination," *San Francisco Chronicle,* July 18, 2004.

283 *For two weeks in late July* Peter Phillips, "San Francisco Bohemian Club: Power, Prestige, and Globalism," *Sonoma County Free Press,* June 8, 2001.

283 *Because of its high-powered membership* Nick Schou, "Bohemian Grove Exposes Itself!" *Orange County Weekly*, August 31, 2006.

284 *This ceremony contained a twist in 1996* Domhoff, "Social Cohesion."

284 *"In the summer of 1950"* Richard Nixon, *RN: The Memoirs of Richard Nixon* (New York: Grosset & Dunlap, 1978), 80–81. Cited in Domhoff.

284 *Nixon later claims that a speech he gave* Nixon, *RN*, 284.

285 *The Grove boasts a telling blend* All statistics on corporate representation at the Grove from Domhoff, "Social Cohesion."

286 *The Boao Forum for Asia* "Boao Forum for Asia," Xinhua News Agency, April 24, 2005.

286 *by many accounts the BFA has yet to achieve* Jamil Anderlini, "Amid Light-weight Attendance, Boao Struggles with Crisis of Relevance," *South China Morning Post*, April 24, 2007.

286 *high-profile delegates were forced to take a bus* Tom Mitchell, "Even Big Shots Can't Get into Hot Water at Boao Forum," *South China Morning Post*, December 17, 2002.

286 *an impressive roster of participants* "Boao Forum for Asia Annual Conference 2007," *China People's Daily Online*, April 23, 2007.

286 *The origins of BFA illustrate* Tom Mitchell, "One Forum, Four Agencies at Boao," *South China Morning Post*, April 14, 2002.

287 *After a few trips by Jiang to Beijing* Charles Hutzler, "China Exerts Too Much Control at Forum Created to Mimic Davos," *Wall Street Journal*, April 11, 2002.

287 *Slim is by far the dominant force* Michael Smith, "One of the World's Richest Men Turns to Mexico's Future," *New York Times*, May 4, 2006.

288 *its currently estimated value well in excess of $50 billion* "Mexican 'World's Richest Person,'" BBC News, July 3, 2007.

288 *He has been criticized for his near monopoly control* Tim Padgett, "Carlos Slim's Embarrassment of Riches," *Time*, July 11, 2007.

288 *According to a preliminary program* Kerry Dolan, "Secret Meeting of Latin American Billionaires," *Forbes*, May 23, 2003.

292 *"self-reliant and conscientious"* Michael Maccoby, "Narcissistic Leaders: The Incredible Pros, the Inevitable Cons," *Harvard Business Review* 78, no. 1 (2000): 68–77.

293 *"Throughout history, narcissists have always emerged"* Ibid.

293 *Northwestern University's Adam Galinsky* For example, Adam Galinsky, "Power and Perspectives Not Taken," *Psychological Science* 17 (2006): 1068–74.

CHAPTER 9: THE FUTURE OF THE SUPERCLASS

296 *U.S. investigations into* U.S. Senate Subcommittee on Investigations, "Money Laundering and Foreign Corruption: Case Study Involving Riggs Bank," July 15, 2004. See also Stephane Mayoux, "E Guinea Warning After Bank Probe," BBC, July 21, 2004. Riggs, you'll recall, was also the alleged repository for bribes paid to Prince Bandar by a major defense contractor in the 1980s, as well as an asset holder for former Chilean dictator Augusto

Pinochet in the 1990s. Riggs is a long-established Washington institution that is well plugged in to Washington elites, including Jonathan Bush, George W. Bush's uncle, who served as a senior executive at the bank.

297 *most of whom scrape by* "The Dictator Next Door?" editorial, *Los Angeles Times*, November 19, 2006.

297 *playing "Those Were the Days"* Alexander Smoltczyk, "Torture and Poverty in Equatorial Guinea," *Der Spiegel*, August 28, 2006.

297 *The country is sitting on an ocean* "Republic of Equatorial Guinea Article IV Consultation," International Monetary Fund, June 2006.

297 *Equatorial Guinea is the third-largest producer* U.S. State Department, Bureau of African Affairs, "Background Note: Equatorial Guinea," June 2007, www.state.gov/r/pa/ei/bgn/7221.htm.

298 *He had massive political* Peter Maass, "A Touch of Crude," *Mother Jones*, January/February 2005.

299 *one U.S. ambassador was tossed out of the country* Larry Luxner, "Equatorial Guinea Goes from Rags to Riches with Oil Boom," *Washington Diplomat*, August 2001.

299 *yet as recently as 2007 the United States found itself* Department of State, "Background Note: Equatorial Guinea."

300 *the number of people in the world living in extreme poverty* "Poverty Drops Below 1 Billion, Says World Bank," World Bank press release, April 15, 2007, www.worldbank.org.

301 *The richest 10 percent of the population* James Davies et al., "The World Distribution of Household Wealth," UNU-WIDER, December 5, 2006.

301 *The world's billionaires, less than 0.000015 percent* Luisa Kroll and Allison Fass, "The World's Billionaires," *Forbes*, March 8, 2007.

301 *The top 100 financial institutions* Scott DeCarlo, "The World's 2,000 Largest Public Companies," *Forbes*, March 29, 2007.

301 *Of ten thousand hedge funds worldwide* James Mackintosh, "Biggest Hedge Funds Tighten Grip," *Financial Times*, May 24, 2007.

301 *One investor, Fidelity, with nearly $2 trillion* "Fidelity Brokerage Assets Increase to Record $1.96T," *Boston Globe*, November 13, 2007.

301 *The world's 250 biggest companies* DeCarlo, "World's 2,000 Largest Public Companies."

301 *Out of roughly four thousand religions worldwide* "Major Religions of the World Ranked by Number of Adherents," Adherents.com, April 17, 2007.

301 *The United States and its allies in NATO* Population data from the CIA, "The World Factbook," June 2007, www.cia.gov/library/publications/the-world-factbook/index.html.

301 *control more than 90 percent of all operational nuclear weapons* Stockholm International Peace Research Institute, *SIPRI Yearbook 2007*, June 2007, yearbook2007.sipri.org.

301 *In a world of almost two hundred* For example, see distribution of voting powers in the World Bank, www.worldbank.org, and the International Monetary Fund, www.imf.org.

307 *when Hebe de Bonafini* Tom Gibb, "Internet Insults Traded Globally," BBC, January 29, 2001.

307 *attended by as many as one hundred thousand participants* "Background of the WSF Process," Fórum Social Mundial, www.forumsocialmundial.org.

308 *only thirteen women* Jenny Mero, "Women CEOs for *Fortune* 500 Companies," *Fortune*, April 2007.

308 *Around the world, women held on average* Inter-Parliamentary Union, "Women in Parliament in 2006: The Year in Perspective," www.ipu.org.

308 *Geeta Rao Gupta, the president of the International Center* Geeta Rao Gupta, interview with the author, 2007.

309 *If 90 percent of the members of the superclass* Data from "Superclass Census" conducted by author's research team.

309 *only 0.06 percent of Ethiopians* Task Force on Higher Education and Society, "Higher Education in Developing Countries: Peril and Promise," March 1, 2000, UNESCO and the World Bank, www.tfhe.net.

309 *"The biggest issue in the Middle East"* Ibrahim Dabdoub, interview with the author, 2007.

310 *Just as C. Wright Mills observed that the U.S. power elite* Mills, *Power Elite*, 274.

311 *His firm also owns forty-seven companies* Nelson Schwartz, "Wall Street's Man of the Moment," *Fortune*, February 2007.

311 *Li Ka-shing, the chairman* Kroll and Fass, "The World's Billionaires."

311 *Richard Li ranked 754th* Ibid.

312 *almost half of the twenty-five richest people in China* Ibid.

312 *millionaires in China increased by 6.8 percent* Merrill Lynch and Capgemini, "World Wealth Report," June 2006.

312 *the number of billionaires vaulted* Robin Kwong, "China's Billionaires Begin to Add Up," *Financial Times*, October 22, 2007.

312 *Chinese were among the largest sources* Kroll and Fass, "The World's Billionaires."

316 *In ICANN, the Internet pioneer Vint Cerf* Vint Cerf, interview with the author, 2006.

317 *It is linked to views such as those* Anne-Marie Slaughter, *A New World Order* (Princeton: Princeton University Press, 2004).

ACKNOWLEDGMENTS

Hundreds of people gave generously of their time to make this book possible. Their intelligence, energy, help, and kindness have made the process of writing it a continuous pleasure for me. And whatever insight or perspective you may have gleaned from this book is directly traceable to them, a superclass unto themselves.

I must start with enormous thanks to Eric Chinski, my editor at Farrar, Straus and Giroux, who is as smart, insightful, disciplined, creative, and entertaining as you could want an editor to be. He has been a great partner in this effort at every stage, although paradoxically some of the most compelling evidence of this are many, many pages you the reader shall never see. The entire FSG team, led by the wise Jonathan Galassi and including the fabulous Gena Hamshaw, who was a joy to work with throughout, have been a nonstop lesson in publishing done right. Special thanks must also go to those who have played important roles on that team and made considerable contributions to this gratifying collaboration: Laurel Cook, Marion Duvert, Michael Hathaway, Henry Kaufman, Cynthia Merman, Kendra Poster, and Jeff Seroy.

Of course, I would probably not have found FSG or begun writing books like this in the first place if it were not for the encouragement, support, and sound guidance of my agent, Esmond Harmsworth, and his team at Zachary Shuster Harmsworth. I am grateful to them all and especially to Esmond, who is absolutely terrific at what he does.

The Carnegie Endowment for International Peace has continued throughout the process of writing this book to offer an excellent environment in which to write and do research. Jessica Mathews, Carnegie's president, not only is a great leader who has reinvented the institution for the twenty-first century, but also has become a valued friend. The entire team, including especially Paul Balaran, George Perkovich, John Judis, Peter Reid, and Trent Perotto, have once again been helpful on this project, and I need to offer special thanks to Sherm Katz, who is not just a leading trade expert but who, while at Carnegie, was always willing to discuss baseball and tennis when musing about big ideas became headache-inducing. The guy who introduced me to Carnegie, who has been a great adviser throughout this book process and in much that I do, and who remains a great friend, is *Foreign Policy* editor Moisés Naím. He is funnier than he is smart, and that is saying something.

Carnegie has over the years also provided me with the opportunity to recruit and work with excellent research assistants. None have surpassed Elly Page, the lead researcher on this project. Remember the name. You will be hearing great things about her for years to come. She is exceptionally intelligent, tireless, and has brought terrific energy and industry to this effort. She has contributed immeasurably to this book, more than any other single individual by a wide margin, and she has managed to do so for long hours, on tough deadlines, and with great skill . . . and nonetheless has still found time to compete successfully in some of Washington's most prestigious ultimate Frisbee competitions. She has been assisted by a number of other researchers along the life of the project, including most notably Mathew Ferraro, Mark Partridge, Jonathan Bromma, and Christopher Burdett. Others who assisted from time to time with research and fact-checking include Bill Adams, Luci Canet, Nicholas Foster, Jeffrey Love, Lyubov Mullen, Heather Rosen, and Felipe Zuluaga. I'd also like to offer a word of thanks to my chief researcher on my last book, Geoff Taubman, who also took the time to read this one and offer a host of constructive comments. He is almost certainly the smartest Philadelphia Eagles fan on the planet.

Many of the book's interviews and its logistics were made possible through the support of my intrepid and indispensable assistants, first Leslie Fromm, and after Leslie went off to graduate school, Rachel Stegall. Both have helped not only with the book but made it possible for me to write it, run our rapidly growing company, Garten Rothkopf, do my other work at Carnegie, teach, and actually spend time with my family every so often. My other colleagues at Garten Rothkopf, notably the intrepid and smart Claire Casey, have also been great cheerleaders and sounding boards throughout the project and are, on a daily basis, a real privilege to work with.

There are a number of other people who have offered special advice and counsel throughout the process of writing *Superclass*, sharing ideas, offering encouragement and constructive advice, and, beyond even these contributions, providing reliable and sustaining friendship. Jeffrey Garten, who is truly one of the great mensches of the world, a wonderful business partner, teacher, and example, is very high on this list. So too is Tom Friedman, with whom I have had countless conversations that have taken us to every corner of the world and each of which has always left me full of new ideas and enthusiasm for the work. Also offering great guidance have been my good and valued friends (in alphabetical order): Lisa Anderson of Columbia's School of International and Public Affairs; Don Baer, most recently of Discovery Communications; Nancy Birdsall of the Center for Global Development; Jane Bussey of *The Miami Herald*; Sue Esserman of Steptoe and Johnson; Bob Hormats of Goldman Sachs; Susan Levine of Watershed Asset Management; Luis Alberto Moreno of the Inter-American Development Bank; Hilda Ochoa Brillembourg of Strategic Investment Group; Jorge Rosenblut of Terragroup; David Sanger of *The New York Times*; Julia Sweig of the Council on Foreign Relations; Antoine van Agtmael of Emerging Markets Investors; and Daniel Yergin of Cambridge Energy Research Associates. I also would be remiss if I did not cite the ongoing support and perspective offered by great lifelong friends such as Mark and Beth Holechek, and Richard and Abby Burns. Jane Prelinger and Mike Stadter, two of Washington's most distinguished psychotherapists, not only provided many excellent ideas reflected in the "Psychopathology of Success" section in Chapter Eight, but also happen to be the great mother and stepfather of my daughters. (More about the daughters later.) Dr. Susana Naím, Moisés's wife and a renowned psychiatrist, was also very helpful with the psychology section, inspiring it with a comment long ago.

Many of the people who made contributions to this book did so through interviews and conversations I have conducted with them over the past couple of years. Some who sought to protect their privacy cannot be acknowledged here, but I do want each of them to know how grateful I am to them for taking the time to share their candid views and insights into different aspects of the superclass, globalization, and the challenges and opportunities we are facing. Their assistance has been vital indeed. The book literally would not exist without it. Of course, many others allowed me to cite our conversations, for which I am also grateful. The discussions were fascinating and I only wish that I had the space to have included more of each. Meeting with such an extraordinary group as I did could fill volumes. It would literally be impossible to thank all of them here. Some of those deserving of special thanks in this regard and who I am able to thank here include: Prince Turki al Faisal, Charlene Barshefsky, Senator Evan Bayh, Sandy Berger, Nancy Birdsall, Admiral Dennis Blair, Philippe Bourguignon, Lael Brainard, Hilda Ochoa Brillembourg, Leon Brittan, Steve Chase, Kurt Campbell, Vint Cerf, Heng Chee Chan, Juan Claro, Riccardo Claro, David Cole, Ibrahim Dabdoub, Richard Darman, Anita Dunn, Alejandro Foxley, Arminio Fraga, Thomas Friedman, Al From, Timothy Geithner, Jorge Gerdau Johanpeter, Louis Gerstner, Hank Greenberg, Francisco Gros, Rajat Gupta, Richard Haass, Peter Hakim, Victor Halberstadt, William Haseltine, Richard Holbrooke, Robert Hormats, General James Jones, General George Joulwan, John Judis, General John Jumper, Susan Kaufman Purcell, Robert Kimmitt, Jim Kimsey, Henry Kissinger, Anthony Lake, Jennifer Linker, Haakon Lorentzen, Edward Ludwig, Andronico Luksic, Kishore Mahbubani, Thierry Malleret, Mark Malloch Brown, Jorge Marshall, Jessica Mathews, William McDonough, Thomas F. McLarty, Branko Milanovic, Bryan Moss, Moisés Naím, Indra Nooyi, Jeff Pack, Juan Carlos Pérez Dávila, Luis Felipe Pérez Dávila, Peter Peterson, Thomas Pickering, Karen Poniachik, General Colin Powell, Geeta Rao Gupta, Philippe Reichstuhl, Susan Rice, Stephen Roach, Jorge Rosenblut, Dennis Ross, Robert Rubin, Alvaro Saieh, David Sanger, Alejandro Santo Domingo, Klaus Schwab, Bernard Schwartz, Stephen Schwarzman, General Brent Scowcroft, Walter Slocombe, Gayle Smith, Admiral Stephen Smith, Stephen Solarz, Alfred Sommer, Rob Stein, Joseph Stiglitz, Lawrence Summers, Pamela Thomas Graham, Andres Velasco, James Wolfensohn, Bob Wright, Daniel Yergin, and James Woolsey. What I could not reflect in direct quotations is nonetheless visible throughout the book in terms of context, texture, support for key ideas, and in countless other ways that helped shape and enrich the end product.

Year in and year out, my greatest inspiration and support comes from my family. I have tried to reflect my deep and surpassing gratitude to my parents in the dedication of this book, but, I am sure, despite my best efforts, I haven't the skill or the words to convey the totality of my gratitude. The families of my brother, Paul, and sister, Marissa, have also been unceasingly adorable throughout this process, especially the smaller ones, of course—but we know that all that adorableness was taught to them by the larger and older ones whom I remember as once being pretty adorable themselves.

There are times when I am stalking through the house, a blanket draped over my head, mumbling incoherently to myself, that I imagine that living with a guy writing a book could get quite tiresome . . . and possibly even a little scary. (I look a bit like one of the sandpeople with a blanket over my head, or some cross between a monk and the Abominable Snowman.) But my beautiful, kind, and brilliant wife, Adrean, is always there, always supportive, always the best of best friends and the wisest and warmest of advisers. She is no less than a constant wonder and I am hugely grateful to her for everything she does and is. She is a treasure. She assisted in reminding me of my great good fortune in life by the wondrous presence of my two little girls, neither of whom is, to my considerable surprise, a little girl anymore. Joanna and Laura have at every turn proven that evolution is a more powerful force than heredity, and have demonstrated it by blossoming into the sort of graceful, gifted young ladies who would have petrified me when I was their age. Now, of course, as the father of two beautiful young women, I am petrified for entirely different reasons . . . and yet they fill me with such a constant supply of love and pride that I feel only joy at having the privilege to know them and spend time with them. If this book or anything I write ever makes my family proud or even just a little pleased, I will feel I have achieved my primary objective. (Of course, if it just helps a little to pay for the girls' tuitions, I won't be entirely disappointed.) In short, everything I do I do for Adrean and the girls.

What you may find that is good or worthwhile in *Superclass* is due to the collective contributions of all those listed here and those whom I have been unable to mention. For everything else, I am entirely responsible.

INDEX